Other Books

Days of Our Years
Afraid of Victory
The Time Is Now
That Day Alone
The Forgotten Ally
Earth Could Be Fair
Why Jesus Died
Palestine, Land of the Jews
The Tower of Terzel
Jerusalem Calling
Visions Rise and Change
A Pilgrim's Vow
A Crown of Fire

To Number Our Days

To Number Our Days

PIERRE VAN PAASSEN

So teach us to number our days,
that we may apply our hearts unto wisdom.
Psalm 90:12

Charles Scribner's Sons

NEW YORK

Contents

List of Illustrations

To Number Our Days

The Ashes of Klaas

AND IT CAME to pass in the tenth year of the reign of King Philip that a new wave of persecution broke over the Netherlands. In every town and village the clouds of smoke of the *autos-da-fé* hung over the market places like a pall of doom. On a mere whispered word of denunciation, men and women were dragged from their houses in the dead of night and led before the infamous Blood Tribunal. If a burgher was found guilty of heresy, all his goods, movable and immovable, were confiscated and he himself sentenced to be burnt at the stake.

And the informers received one third of the victim's property, and the King, though far away in his palace of the Escurial, inherited the rest.

Now it so happened that among the thousands of Hollanders and Flemings caught in the Blood Tribunal's dragnet was a humble charcoal burner by the name of Klaas who lived with his wife Soetkin and their twelve year old son Tyl, in a back street of the town of Damme in West Flanders. He was a man of open countenance and blue eyes wearing a trim pointed beard, ash-blond in color. Of frank speech and the jovial disposition of character often portrayed in the pictures of Jan Steen, Klaas talked a good deal, but he laughed still more. Once a day he drank beer in a tavern on the Grand' Place where he astonished bystanders with a display of inordinate physical strength by lifting a full barrel above his head. But he was not a heretic. His misadventures stemmed from the circumstance that he had lately come into some money through a legacy from an uncle who died in a faraway country.

An envious neighbor carried word to Johannes Titelman, the Grand Inquisitor, that the said Klaas kept a roll of gold ducats concealed in or about his cottage. Also that he had uttered blasphemy concerning the sacred oils employed by the Church in the administration of extreme unction.

Thereupon the civic guards came to Klaas' dwelling, clamped irons around the charcoal burner's legs and led him before the Blood Tribunal. Then said the Grand Inquisitor with a disarming smile: "I pray thee, Klaas, tell me what may be thine opinion of oil!" And Klaas, unsuspecting the trap, smiled back and replied: "Of oil, Most Reverend Father, I would say that it is a necessary, if not indispensable ingredient in the preparation of salad. . . . But it's also useful in another way in that one may conveniently grease one's boots therewith. . . ." And he laughed out loud.

Upon hearing these words the Grand Inquisitor rose and, turning to his clerks and assistants, exclaimed: "What further need is there to question this man? He has freely confessed his blasphemies. . . . Ye have heard how he cast vile aspersions on our sacred religion. . . . Methinks, he deserves the death penalty. Accordingly, I turn him over to the secular arm for further questioning and punishment. . . ."

Then the bailiffs seized Klaas and bound him to the rack or pain bench, the *pynbank*, as they say in the Flemish tongue. And they tortured him by holding burning candles to the soles of his feet and under his armpits. Yet, however fierce the torment, the man made no outcry, not even when red-hot pincers were applied to his flesh and his tongue was pierced for uttering ungodliness.

But he did not disclose the hiding place of the gold coins.

And for once the King did not inherit.

And Klaas was burnt by slow fire in the square of Damme before the portals of Our Lady's church in the presence of a vast throng while the bells pealed a salute to the incoming month of May, the month of Mary, full of grace.

And when darkness descended, Soetkin took her son Tyl by the hand and walked to the place of execution. She spoke to the sentinel who was posted where still hung the charred corpse of her husband: "Messire Sergeant, as a son of Flanders, have compassion on this man's widow and orphan, and suffer us to pray for the repose of his dear soul."

And the sergeant replied: "Pray if you will, but make sure to depart before dawn lest I be found transgressing the law which forbids granting favors to the relatives of a heretic."

And Soetkin thanked the guard and knelt down and wept bitterly. After a time she rose to her feet and approached the body and touched it. And with a knife she scraped some ashes from the region of her dead man's heart. And she caught the ashes in her hands and carried them home.

Then she made a sachet of two pieces of silk of equal size, one piece scarlet in color, the other black. And she sewed them together with needle and thread, and, after placing the ashes inside, hung the sachet by a cord around her son's neck.

Then said Soetkin to Tyl: "My son, the red is for the innocent blood shed in our land, and the black is the token of our mourning.... I place these ashes on your heart and the hearts of all those who come after you in these Netherlands as long as our race endures. And whenever an injustice is committed in any place whatsoever in the whole wide world, these ashes will warn you and your sons by stirring and beating upon your breasts. And upon feeling the ashes knock, you will open your hearts and go to the aid of those who are oppressed. And you will stand by those who are reviled and persecuted for conscience's sake. And you will fight their battle for those who cannot defend themselves because of their chains or dungeons. Nor will you count the cost to yourselves even if your life be imperiled...

"Will you, Tyl my son," asked she, "answer the call of the ashes of Klaas, your father?"

And the son answered his mother and said: "I will it!"

And the widow embraced the orphan and the sun rose.

CHAPTER I

In Holland Stands a House

IF I BEGIN by delving a little in the past, it is because like Baudelaire I can truthfully say that I carry more memories in my head than if my youth had lasted a thousand years. And their number and variety are still growing. In a quiet hour of reflection they rush to the surface from a seemingly inexhaustible wellspring deep down. On the other hand, concerning the immediate past the power of memory is unquestionably less vivid. Nowadays I need to read a book twice or three times before inwardly digesting its meaning and contents whereas formerly its significance and even its physical arrangement in chapters, pages and paragraphs remained fixed with almost photographic accuracy in my mind after one reading. I do not mean that emotions cannot still be stirred by what I read in books, or that I remain uninfluenced by events transpiring in my immediate surroundings or in the world at large. At the same time I readily grant that thinking of the unfrightening past is often preferable to inquiring into our awful human condition in the present.

Sitting on the rock of St. Helena, Napoleon sighed: "*Quel roman que ma vie!*" In comparison mine is but a slender tale that is told before flying away. For the greater part of my life I have lived in a world that was a house of mourning. I have lived in two generations, perhaps three, which were nourished by the thought of revenge: Get ready for the next round, next time we shall conquer! But if I have learned anything from life it is this, that the promise of victory constitutes a false value. Force is no argument for the spirit and the externals of success are no criterion of value for the soul.

In the course of a life which begins to be somewhat long, there has been much weaving of destiny, many strange encounters, some shaking ordeals and grave disillusionments and also some serious mistakes. Still I have no regrets. Physically I have always liked to live by the waterside, in places from which ships may be seen to sail away. I still like stormy weather and, if possible at all, I prefer to stand on the bridge with the captain. But wherever I lingered, this also must be said, I have never felt myself a stranger anywhere on earth. I have always felt myself surrounded by friendly voices rising from all the centuries and all the races and all the camps. Like Jean Christophe, I have tried to know man and still love him and this not by reason of any authoritarian religious command, but because I recognized myself in all of them, sometimes almost pathetically comical, sometimes downright stupid, but also great as a god on the mountaintops of thought. All my experiences are begot in the ventricule of memory, "nourished in the womb of *pia mater* and delivered upon the mellowing of occasion. . . . "

Why should recollections of the past take precedence in volume and vividness in most of us? This is so, I think, because in a child's mind, unruffled and placid as it may appear on the surface, there is nevertheless present the turmoil of a race. An infant's mind is a world in gestation. All the passions, instincts, fixations, yes, even the hopes and aspirations of former generations, lie in mazy motion intermingled. Carl Gustav Jung speaks of the archetypes amongst the brain cells. These, I take it, are the master cells, who, by their primacy, give direction to and stimulate the evolution of the mind. They are our oldest impressions hidden beneath the dark waters of our consciousness, the roots, as it were, of the mental flowers. They, or their content, control the transmission of hereditary characteristics and set the tone for whatever is to follow.

My feeling is that when we, as the saying goes, speak our mind, we do not speak alone. The archetypes also have their word to say. Our fathers speak with us and through us. Our mind is a composite entity, a collection of impressions in which ancestral elements and our own are blended and merged beyond the possibility of disentanglement.

In the course of his famous and only journey to Italy, Goethe remarked that the sight of the monuments of antiquity was as familiar to him as if he had seen them a thousand times before. He astonished his secretary Eckermann and other travel companions with his intimate knowledge of the architectural details of the ruined temples he explored. He told his friends, as if it was the most natural thing in the world, that he expected to see the sights of Italy a thousand times again. Can it be said that the great German saw things in Italy which his fathers had seen, objects and vistas whose shape and outline were transmitted through the master cells into his own brain and there by some unexplained process re-activated?

I have often wondered how it was that on my first visit to London I walked the immense distance from the Custom House at Victoria Docks to Threadneedle Street in the heart of the City, and, with unerring accuracy and without once asking directions, steered a party of Dutch immigrants into the Church of the Austin Friars where a religious service in their language was in progress.

"Here it is," I told the travelers, pointing to a narrow archway leading into a court. "At the end of this court you will find the church you are looking for!"

I had never been in London, nor had I ever seen a street map or plan of the city. But it is only in London's oldest quarters, I must specify, that I can find my way undirected. In neighborhoods built up in the last hundred years or so, I am as helpless as the next stranger. My father was never in London, nor my grandfather, but my great-grandfather was. Relatives have told me that old family portraits reveal, not merely a few superficial facial similarities between my great-grandfather and myself, but that we resemble each other like two drops of water.

I discovered early enough in life that in addition to this alleged outer resemblance, we shared at least one queer inner twist. Like my great-grandfather Amos I cannot suffer fools gladly or carry on a debate with specimen of their ilk without being seized by a fit of unreasonable fury which when it has passed brings the tears of contrition to my eyes. Though easygoing and cordial in ordinary ways of life, old Amos more than once resorted to regrettable acts of physical violence. Once, so the story ran in the family, he got into a dispute with a brother clergyman on some theological question or other. His visitor was heard to say: "If I was forced to make a choice I would rather be Judas than Cain."

"You hypocrite," Amos called back, choking with indignation, "you are both Cain *and* Judas Iscariot!" With this he seized his visitor by the scruff of the neck and pitched him into the street. . . .

I saw my great-grandfather Amos but once in my life. This happened when my parents took me and the whole family on a three-hour train journey to the province of Zealand where he resided. The occasion was the one hundredth anniversary of his birth. What we saw was a tall rather thin man, very straight, a full six feet in height. He wore a white ring beard but no mustache, an arrangement then considered somewhat of a mark of evangelical piety. He greeted us in the doorway of his house, fixed everyone in turn with an intent stare of his small blue eyes and then walked back into the dining room thumping a hawthorn stick on the floor.

While his housekeeper, a woman in her fifties, who still dressed in the old-fashioned Zealand regional costume, lace cap, voluminous skirts, a bodice of rose-colored linen and a large silver brooch, set about laying the table for us, the old man excused himself by saying that our arrival had interrupted his own noonday meal and that he wished to continue in order to keep to schedule.

He sat at a small table close by the chimney. In view of all of us he ate two slices of black bread, heavily buttered and laid with fat Gouda cheese, and drank a glass of whey. The whey he topped off with a jigger of Geneva. When he reached for the decanter to refill his glass, the housekeeper snatched the bottle from his hand: "You have had your ration for this noon!"

"Not so, not so," he retorted a little testily. "Ah, yes, it's true," he relented an instant later, "I remember now, I did have two gins, but the last glass I didn't taste. My mind wasn't on it!"

"Have it your own way," she said, handing him back the decanter, "after all this is *your* birthday. But please, bear in mind that it isn't water you're drinking."

He chuckled and helped himself to another slice of cheese. Evidently, they hadn't heard of blood cholesterol in those days. Then he bravely emptied the small tumbler and lit his long-stemmed clay pipe.

"Doesn't it burn?" we asked.

"Doesn't what burn?" he came back.

"This combination of gin, tobacco and cheese."

"Yes," he replied, "it does a little, but it should burn, you know!"

While puffing away and sending up blue rings of smoke, he began to talk of family affairs and gradually switched to financial matters: taxes, stocks and bonds and the like. In the end he was prevailed upon to tell something of his experiences as an importer-exporter.

Originally, Amos began, he served as a minister of religion in the village of Rilland-Bath situated on the north bank of the Scheldt at a point where that river leaves Belgium and enters the Netherlands. In Rilland he fell in love with and married one Christina Jacoba Laurusse, the only child of a well-to-do shipowner. Christina bore him seven daughters and five sons. The daughters were given Old Testament names: Sarah, Miriam,

Deborah, Rebecca, Rachel, Leah and Hannah, while the boys were called after personages figuring in the New Testament, my grandfather Pieter being the youngest.

When Christina's father died, the Reverend Amos gave up theology and devoted himself to administering the shipping business. He or rather his wife owned a fleet of tugboats plying between Antwerp and the mouth of the Scheldt pushing, pulling and piloting ocean liners in and out.

"That was the time," Amos explained, "now fifty-five years ago, when I changed from dominé* to commodore."

The bulk of the old man's considerable fortune, however, did not derive exclusively from the tugboats. It had in fact quite another source. When those girls with the lovely biblical names grew into their teens, they accompanied their father once a month on a trip to Antwerp. On such occasions they traveled on one of the tugs with the commodore himself on the bridge. As soon as the boat was moored at the Schippers Quay in Antwerp, Amos pulled the signal cord and set off a series of frantic whistle blasts.

Then father and daughters went ashore, strolled around for a while in the city of Rubens, sometimes went to market and sometimes visited a museum, and then took a room in a small hotel by the riverside. Pretty soon there would be a knock on the door and two nuns carried in a large bundle of Flemish lace. The nuns, of course, had been apprised of Amos' presence in Antwerp by the whistle blasts. The Misses Sarah, Miriam, Deborah, et cetera, undressed, wrapped the lace in long strips around their bodies, and then dressed again. The two sisters from the Ursulines' convent received payment for the lace, and the biblical procession with Amos in the lead wended its way back to the tugboat where all had dinner in the galley before starting the homeward journey to Rilland.

"Just before casting off," said Amos with a twinkle in his eye, "I blew seven long blasts on the whistle to notify the Mother Superior of the convent that everything had passed off well as usual."

"Why seven?" someone wanted to know.

"One for each of the seven deadly sins! ... I kept up the lace trade for seventeen years, though with diminishing returns, as one after the other of my daughters got married."

"How much did you make on the deal? ... "

*Dominé is the title carried by ministers of the Protestant religion in the Netherlands.

"I sold the Belgian lace in the Dutch market at 200 per cent profit, and in the English market at 300 per cent. . . . "

"How did you get the stuff across to England?"

"By tugboat of course!"

"By tugboat across the North Sea?"

"Why not? I made the trip twice a year. . . . "

"Were you never caught?"

"Caught by whom?"

"The customs officers!"

"Oh, those people? I simply kept out of their way, that's all! . . . "

When he finished speaking, the hundred year old Amos tried to refill his pipe, but did not succeed. His eyelids fluttered, his head fell gently on his breast, he slumped in his armchair, and in a few moments was fast asleep.

Though my childhood was one of radiant happiness, I must say that there was one incident of a less pleasant nature which left a deep impression and even caused for some years an impairment of speech. It happened when I cannot have been older than four, for my youngest brother wasn't born yet. One evening I was awakened by a fearsome noise, terrifying shrieks and howls, loud banging on the door and tapping on the street windows. There was nobody home save my brother Thomas who slept in the same bed with me. The maid's room was so far away from the street front that she probably heard nothing of the disturbance. At any rate, she didn't put in an appearance. When the noise became unbearable Thomas and I got up and went downstairs. What we saw and heard nailed us to the floor with fright.

There, right before our eyes, on the stoop of the house, was a whole crowd of boys and girls, dressed up in masquerade costumes. They wore masks and headgear of a weird and horrifying aspect. Two or three had on the lugubrious robes and the enormous black hats with which hearse drivers and funeral mutes adorned themselves while on duty. Some masks showed a human skull. One person wearing a tall cardboard hat had stuffed his clothes with pillows so that he resembled a gnome with a colossal hunchback. Still another individual was made up to look like the devil. His false hooked nose and protruding chin seemed to form a beak like that of some evil bird of prey. He had horns on his head and a wicked, blood-red, two-pronged tongue which he moved slowly up and down against the windowpanes as if he were licking them.

Even so, the devil did not scare me half as much as the boy or girl—you couldn't tell them apart because of their disguise—who carried and played the *rommelpot*. The word says what it is: a rumbling pot, a large empty round tin can over the top of which a pig's bladder is stretched tight. By inserting a stick in the middle of the securely fastened bladder and moving the stick up and down, an indescribably sinister noise is produced. The shapes in front of the window howled, stamped and yelled:

> We are the mummers from mummerland,
> Ho, hè, hi,
> Hand us a stiver and we'll pass you by.

This happened late in the evening of Shrove Tuesday, or *Mardi gras,* which is generally celebrated with carnivals, feasting and merrymaking in preparation for the great Lenten fast. Thomas and I stared the mummers right in the face and did not budge an inch. I need hardly say that this was not by reason of any superior courage on our part. We were virtually paralyzed by fear.

Nothing extraordinary occurred till two or three days later when I ran up such a fever that the family doctor was summoned. Dr. Mendoza diagnosed the case correctly: the fever was brought on by shock, and the shock was caused by fear. I readily admitted that I had been frightened out of my wits by the procession of mummers a few days earlier.

"In view of the fact," the physician remarked, "that the boy has never seen such a masquerade before, there must have been something else, some prior incident to cause so much of a shock. Who frightened him?"

It was then revealed that the maid sometimes scared us if we didn't go to sleep fast enough to suit her by saying: "If you won't go to sleep the spooks and ghosts will get you!" Once or twice she had gone to the extent of draping a white sheet over her head and stealing on tiptoe into the room where we slept. She moved one finger up and down under the sheet in a sort of warning gesture. It was enough to scare you stiff.

Psychologists know all about fear that produces fear, but the psychologist is an ultramodern phenomenon; there weren't many of them around half a century ago. Dr. Mendoza told my mother about St. Francis of Sales who said that all fears shake each others' hands. Fear sets up a chain reaction and ends up with a sickening, deadly fear to be afraid. I had been made afraid of ghosts and spooks.

The fever left me with a slight defect in speech, my lips trembled when I tried to speak rapidly, and I stuttered. Not till the age of twelve or thirteen was I cured of the stutter and at the same time of my fear of ghosts by a do or die remedy proposed by my uncle Kees, the landscape painter and church organist.

"I'll give you ten guilders," he said, "if you will go alone to the cemetery tonight, walk right to the spot where the graves of suicides and unidentified drowned persons are located, and place a piece of bread on a tombstone."

"But that cemetery is full of dread," I objected. "Everybody says so. Besides, it's a quarter hour's walk outside the town walls. It's raining cats and dogs. It is the most eerie place on earth."

"So you are still afraid of ghosts!"

"I am not afraid of ghosts. I am afraid of the big grisly cross that stands in the middle of the Catholic cemetery, the cross with the bleeding Christ on it!"

"Will you take the ten guilders or not?"

"I will!"

"Then walk right up to the cross, look up at the face and slowly and distinctly without stuttering recite the twenty-third Psalm: 'The Lord is my shepherd.... Even when I pass through the valley of the shadow of death ... I shall not fear ....'"

I did it. But the perspiration streamed down my face. The only "ghost" I saw was a white goat which somebody had put out to graze among the tombstones. The effort to pronounce the words of the psalm was a test of will power. I never stuttered again, though the vision of the mummers on that night in Lent returned for many years to come whenever I had a fever....

Thus I got rid of my fear of ghosts and spooks. But by the act of exorcism in the graveyard I was not liberated from the worst fear of all, the fear of the devil. Yet, if you came to think of it, it was the devil who stood as the prime source and mover at the head of all that long chain of fears that shake each others' hands.

I could now laugh at stories about witches and werewolves and hands popping out of a grave to wag a bony finger at passers-by. But the devil was a different cup of tea entirely. He couldn't be banished by the mere recitation of a psalm or a verse from Holy Writ. Everybody believed in the devil's existence. Grown-up men, very grave and learned men, men

dressed in black robes, standing in the pulpits of the churches, spoke
of the devil as a real person. In support of the devil's existence they cited
the testimony of the Bible. You couldn't doubt the Bible for to doubt
the Bible, any single word of it, was the worst sin of all. It was the sin
against the light, the sin against the Holy Ghost, the only sin together
with suicide for which there was no forgiveness.

Again and again you were told during the period of religious instruction in the parochial school that the devil went around like a roaring
lion seeking whom he might devour. In the Dutch version of the Lord's
Prayer, God is not asked to "deliver us from evil," but to deliver us from
"the evil *one*." The devil was evil personified, the embodiment of evil.

"What does he do then? In which way does the devil seek to get us
into his clutches?" I used to ask my mother.

"He is always very near," she said. "He stands behind us or whispers
into our ears when he wants us to commit some wicked deed or nourish
some evil thought.

"The great trouble is," she went on, "that we seldom recognize the devil
for what he is. He comes to us in all sorts of shapes and forms. He puts
on disguises and sometimes even tries to make us believe that he is God. . . .
He imitates, he mimics God. That is why the Bible calls the devil 'a liar
from the beginning.'"

And then I asked the question which Robinson Crusoe's servant, black
man Friday, asked his master: "Why does God permit the devil to tempt
us and lead us astray? Isn't that cruel? Doesn't God care? Doesn't God
love us? Isn't He almighty? Could He put an end to the devil's wicked
game if He wanted to? Why doesn't God kill the devil?"

To these questions my mother had no answer but to say that men in
general are so wicked as to require terrors to keep them in awe. She added
that it was all a very deep mystery, and that trying to delve into the
mystery might itself be sinful. "From one sin you fall into another," she
said. "If you begin to doubt the existence of the devil, you may well
end up by doubting the existence of God. . . ."

When I take into consideration that for ages and ages the most learned
theologians have sought in vain to excuse God for the existence of evil,
I cannot blame my mother for not having the answer. It took me many
years to realize that she came near hitting the nail on the head when she
linked belief in the devil with belief in God. The problem of evil continues to haunt all those who will not put up with going to sleep on the

soft pillow of mystery. The mystery persists as long as there are secrets which man has not been able to wrest from nature, from society or himself. . . .

Hubert van Gogh, my native town's historian and cousin to the painter Vincent, affirmed that Gorcum was besieged at least a dozen times in the course of history. But neither van Gogh, nor anyone else, knew of any approaching enemy who was ever kept out by those fortifications bristling with old muzzle-loaders. Spaniards, Burgundians, French, Prussians, even the Cossacks in pursuit of the beaten Napoleon, each in turn had a try at breaching the walls. . . and each succeeded. Round cannon balls still embedded in the façades of old houses testified to the fury of the struggles for the possession of the town.

There was one individual in my youth who remembered or claimed to have witnessed both the entry of the Russian cavalry and the passage of Napoleon. The witness was a very old man of tender almost angelic countenance, Murk Mick by name. He once owned or commanded a fishing trawler. From this occupation he inherited the title of captain.

In spite of the fact that he was tortured by arthritis, perhaps because of it, he walked as stiff and erect as a moving plank. Only his fingers were so atrociously knotted and twisted that he could not button his clothes. Many a time he stopped me in the street on a wintry day: "*Jonkske*, young one, will you do me a favor and fasten the buttons of my breeches?"

In addition Mick was stone-deaf. On his daily outings he carried on a running monologue to which nobody paid any attention. The only way to make him talk of the sights he had seen was to stop him in his tracks by holding out one's right hand. He immediately grasped it: "Now you can say that you have shaken the hand that shook the hand of the great Napoleon. Isn't that something?"

It wasn't only something, it was true. Napoleon frequently passed through our town which lies on the strategic highway which the Emperor constructed from Paris via Brussels to Amsterdam. What he was doing on those visits to our country concerned the affairs, both military and marital, of his brother Louis whom he had made King of Holland. Strange to say, Louis generally sided with the Dutch against his imperial brother in their quarrels over the number of Hollanders to be conscripted.

"I need 50,000 of your subjects for my next campaign," the Emperor would demand.

"I will send you 10,000," his brother replied, "and not one more."

In the thirty odd volumes of Napoleon's correspondence occur several letters of the Emperor to his brother Louis. One of these letters complains: "What's coming over you, Louis? You are getting more Calvinistic than your Dutch subjects.... I learn that you never give a ball at the royal palace, that you frown on light music and eschew the company of beautiful women. You make Hortense live the life of a nun.... Your conversation, too, is contaminated with religious drivel.... Let there be an end to this disgusting, unroyal conduct...."

The Dutch rather liked Louis for his independent attitude in military affairs. But Napoleon quickly put a stop to his brother's obstructionism. He deposed Louis and annexed Holland to the French empire calling it *le Département des Bouches du Rhin*. Holland was French land anyway, the Emperor argued with that fine logic that comes so natural to emperors. Hadn't its soil been formed by the alluvial deposits of two French rivers, the Rhine and the Meuse?

"First annex the country," he ordered. "If anyone protests I can always get some damn fool philosopher to justify my action."

To make things worse Louis was continually at odds with his wife, Hortense de Beauharnais, a daughter of Josephine by her first marriage. Napoleon made several trips to Holland ostensibly to make peace between Louis and Hortense. But he also loved the woman who was both his sister-in-law and his stepdaughter. Was there a child? Yes, there was: Napoleon III, who seized the throne of France in 1851 by a *coup d'état* and abdicated after the debacle at Sedan in 1870, was the made-in-Holland product of that strange liaison.

When Captain Mick saw the Emperor of the French it was winter. A storm was raging on the Merwe. Huge pillars of ice shot up from the water, wheeled around with dizzying speed and then crashed into the dykes, breaking into millions of splinters. The dyke guards, reinforced by hundreds of townspeople, anxiously watched the awesome spectacle. But they were impotent to intervene. Can a moving tower of ice, four, five stories high be stopped by human hands? The dykes were in utmost danger.

At this moment Napoleon's coach appeared on the scene. The Emperor got out and watched the agony of the dykes.

"What are you standing around for?" he shouted angrily at the citizens. "Why don't you stop the icebergs?"

"How, Sire? How?"

"Par l'artillerie, nom de Dieu! The artillery! Get the cannons from the walls and fire into the river!"

It took an hour or so to alert the garrison and bring up the guns. Three salvos sufficed to avert a breach in the dykes.

"I was right there when it happened," old Captain Mick would add. "Napoleon shook hands with me and pulled my hair. Isn't that something?"

When the time drew near for me to enter school, the question arose as to whether I should be enrolled in the public or *neutral* school, or in a parochial institution run on Calvinist lines and principles. The matter gave rise to a dispute in the family. With my parents, my aunts and uncles and several ministers of religion taking part in the discussion, the arguments pro and con often degenerated into wrangling. There even were high words now and then.

From the peculiar circumstance that in the end it was not my father but an uncle who took me by the hand one morning to lead me to "The School with the Bible," I knew that my mother's point of view had prevailed, as was, I may well add, invariably the case.

"Neutral school, to be sure," I heard her protest from the bedroom where I was supposed to be asleep. "What you mean is a school without God and His word!"

Be that as it may, the family quarrel delayed my entrance considerably. The school year had opened a month earlier so that my classmates had that much of a start on me. They showed the extent of their advance the moment I entered by singing as a sort of welcome to the belated newcomer one of the hymns they had learned by heart. The young teacher, Alida Nieuwenhuis, a creature endowed with a crown of golden hair, led the singing with one finger playing a small harmonium.

Forgive me for quoting three lines from my classmates' hymn in their native tongue:

> *De Heer' zal U steeds gadeslaan,*
> *En waar g'U ook heen moogt spoeden,*
> *Voor eeuwig U behoeden.*

> The Lord will never take His eyes off thee.
> And wheresoever thou mayest wander,
> Will watch and shepherd thee,
> In all eternity.

Overcome with emotion on hearing all those voices in unison, I burst into tears. This caused the teacher to stop the singing and dry my face with her handkerchief. She kissed me and gave me a seat on a front bench. Nonetheless, during that entire first morning I felt ill at ease. The other children laughed a good deal as they learned to read and pronounce the word *koek** from the blackboard, but I could not join in their merriment; I had a lump in my throat.

When I returned home for the noon recess, I cried again. To my mother's anxious inquiries, I could only shake my head and feel the tears starting to flow again. I could not explain. The words of the hymn about God's eyes being constantly upon me ran in my mind like a searing ripsaw, and not only then but for long years to follow. The views full of terror and despair with their cold vision of vengeance and condemnation which I heard expressed all around me in the Calvinist milieu where I grew up had made me, young as I was, terribly afraid of the super-policeman people called God.

To my mother I could speak least of all, for she said to me one day: "I know all your thoughts. . . . I can look right into your soul. . . . " These words brought on a sort of mental paralysis or an incipient revolt, I do not know which. They made me shun her presence. My tears that morning were drawn by a fear to show emotion. The attempt to repress emotion was my secret. I felt that my mother wanted me to divulge my secret, and also that she didn't really know what went on deep inside of me. I would have been hard put to it to explain in intelligent words to any living person what really troubled me. Of one thing I was certain, I felt that I had a right to have secrets. I realize now that in denying me this right, my mother, without the slightest tinge of malice on her part, denied me the right to freedom and self-determination.

I would not for the world have anyone believe that we were enemies, even secret ones. She had many fine qualities. Secretly, perhaps unconsciously, she entertained a profound aversion to Calvinism's cold and rigid beliefs, so foreign to her nature. She was a born teacher, and a wonderful storyteller. When she told us stories from the Bible, for instance about Jesus walking on the waters of Lake Galilee or about the Saviour hanging on the cruel cross, my father, who did not share her evangelical zeal, often interrupted her: "You talk as if you were present and saw these things with your own eyes!"

*Pronounce: cook-cake.

One particular view of hers on contemporary Christianity and the Church has never faded from my mind. She believed in the sects, all the sects: Quakers, Darbists, Mennonites, Plymouth Brethren, the Salvation Army, and later in life also the Swedenborgians. She held that God called these sects into being to act as correctives on the Church which, in her opinion, showed an almost ineradicable tendency to stray from the pure gospel of Christ. Historically I will say that she was quite right about the sects, for the sects reared in Holland made that country the freest and most tolerant in the world. This does not mean that she neglected the Church. She loved the Church with all her heart, and not only the Reformed Church, but the old unreformed Church as well.

"We must never forget," she used to say, "that however far she has strayed from the truth, the Catholic Church is our mother, and we must never cease to pray for her repentance and welfare. . . . "

"Even," I asked, "when Catholic boys tell us that some day they are going to wash their hands in the blood of us *ketters*?"*

"Exactly then," she would say, "exactly when they speak evil of us or treat us as though we were heathens!"

At school classes opened with a prayer by Miss Alida followed by one stanza of a hymn, preferably a psalm of David, and the reading of a short portion from Holy Writ. Before the noon meal my mother also read from the Bible, and once more, in the evening, after supper. At Sunday school one was required to recite by heart one verse from either the Old or the New Testament. If one verse was said correctly, a tiny silver star was attached to a sort of report card. A gold star was the reward for repeating without fault two verses from the sacred texts.

From the age of six I was permitted to attend the Sunday morning service in the "great church," so called in contradistinction to the "small church" of the dissenters, which will no doubt be recognized as the equivalent of the *wee free kirk* of the Scottish Puritans. At the age of ten I entered a catechism class held in the consistory hall on Mondays after school. This automatically stopped me from going to Sunday school, but it meant attendance at one additional church service on Sunday afternoon when the ministers did not preach from the Bible, but discoursed on a portion of the *Heidelberg Catechism.*

Ketter is Dutch for heretic. The word is derived from Cathar, the name of a sect in the south of France, whose members were exterminated in the crusade preached against them by Pope Innocent III in the 13th century.

In midweek on Thursday evening, the whole family, except my father, went to a so-called Bible reading given in the dissenters' chapel by a doctor of divinity, Jan van Andel, a very learned man, the author of many books on chiliasm and the millennium, the teachings concerning the second coming of Christ.

There was also a prayer meeting on Saturday evening to ask blessings upon the Lord's day to dawn in a few hours. From attendance at this conclave my brothers and I were excused, or rather, let me confess the truth: we were ignominiously expelled. There were no ministers present at the prayer meetings. The Elders ran the show. It was an interminable business of telling God, as if He did not know, who He was and what He had done in the past in delivering us, His "own Israel," from the Egyptian house of bondage and leading us into the Promised Land.

One Elder, Willem Swaan, a wealthy retired grocer, seventy-nine years of age, could easily have won first prize if length of words had been the goal towards which the brethren pressed. There was, moreover, one particular phrase which Elder Swaan, to our infinite amusement, never failed to insert in his supplications. Somewhere along the line, we knew by experience, the bearded and tottering grocer would make bold to inform the Almighty that he, Willem Swaan, was an orphan from birth. In tense anticipation of hearing this item of vital statistics restated in his querulous, whining voice, my brothers and I stuffed our handkerchiefs in our mouths and waited. No sooner had Mr. Swaan finished saying: "And I, great, merciful and dear God, *who am an orphan*," than we would chime in with unrecognizable muffled voices: "About time he's an orphan!"

It never failed; the interruption stopped him dead. He did indeed try to pick up where he broke off. It was all in vain. He floundered and floundered to the perplexity of everyone present, but could not resume the thread of his thoughts. In his bewilderment and confusion he finally sat down sighing and shaking his head disconsolately.

However, one day the foxy old boy caught us. There is no doubt in my mind but that he was tipped off. Swaan stopped praying just before reaching the key words, opened wide his eyes and looked around. Noticing our handkerchiefs, he signaled the beadle, a jackass of uncommon rudeness, who promptly seized us by the ears and expelled us—forever, as it turned out—from the prayer service.

What we lost in formal piety at the prayer meeting, we gained in simple joy in the street. Saturday night was the jolliest, merriest, most convivial time of the week. It was as if a good fairy queen had waved her magic wand over our town and loosened all the bonds and restrictions which conventional propriety and respectability ordinarily imposed. All dreariness, long-facedness and monotony vanished; good cheer, contentment and laughter reigned supreme. Everybody able to walk was out in the streets, everybody was in good humor and everybody was dressed in his or her Sunday best. People who scarcely noticed each other on ordinary days because of class, cast or religious differences, all at once recognized each other, fraternized and behaved in a civilized manner. Fundamentally, you could see it, differences were but a superficial veneer; under the skin we were all one people, whether under God or not. Boys and girls linked arms and walked up and down, down and up the principal narrow main streets, chatting, laughing and romping, youths and maidens, soldiers and civilians, rich and poor, Catholics, Jews and Protestants. Even the knights of the mournful countenance relaxed their sour mien for a few hours and actually seemed to enjoy life. Joy is more contagious than gloom, and shared joy is double joy. There was many a smile on faces that were usually as cold and tight-lipped as those in the pictures of the witch-hunters of old. . . .

What miracle brought on the change in the general mood? Answer: Saturday was payday. And besides there was the light. The newly installed gas street lamps burnt at double strength that evening. All the shop windows were brilliantly illuminated and the stores remained open till shortly before midnight. You moved from one display window to the next, gazing, admiring and sometimes gasping at the prices. Here a jewelry shop with gold and silver trinkets, brooches, bracelets and necklaces. There a pastry baker's *étalage*, many of the wares indicated by their names in the French language, *éclairs, réligieuses, tompouces,* and one particular delicacy of unsurpassed delight known as *gâteau de Moscovie.*

All the neat and pretty servant girls with freshly laundered and ironed white caps on their blonde hair, and wicker baskets on their arms, were going about from shop to shop, laying in supplies of meat, groceries and provisions for the Lord's day and the following week. The young lieutenants of the garrison strutted proudly as befitted defenders of the realm while holding their dames by the arm. Whenever a tavern door opened you heard the roar of an organ of Barbary or the wheeze of a mechanical piano, loud voices, singing and the musical tinkle of bottles and glasses.

In one short street, running off the main stem, stood a few stalls lit up by flaming ruddy torches. Here books, pamphlets and newspapers of a radical nature were on sale. I could never quite figure out why a policeman was posted at this spot. A policeman was appropriately stationed at the entrance to a certain other street where he tactfully questioned passers-by if they were aware of the nature of the amusements on tap in that particular neighborhood. This you could understand; it was a paternalistic civic government's measure to safeguard public morality. But why have a helmeted policeman armed with a broadsword stand watch over the hawkers of *Voorwaarts*, the journal of the socialists, and *Opwaarts*, the periodical of the Christian socialists?

That spot in the glare of the red torchlights was our little town's Hyde Park corner. Anyone who felt like it could step up on a small platform and shoot off his mouth on any conceivable subject under the sun. Workers were the usual speakers, but occasionally an out-of-town lawyer or minister of religion would hold forth and collect a vast crowd of listeners. It was there that I heard for the first time from the lips of Barthélemy de Ligt, the renowned international scholar, that the Karl Marx phrase about religion being the opium of the people was not the social philosopher's own. Long before Marx, Frederick Denison Maurice, professor of theology at Oxford, and Charles Kingsley, he of *Westward Ho* and *Hypatia*, the two founders of the Christian socialist movement in Britain, had designated a certain kind of religion which preaches resignation with one's lot in this earthly vale of tears with reward abundant held out for the sweet by-and-by: "a horrible narcotic poisoning the souls of men."

It happened, though not often on Saturday night, that the spirit of good cheer caught even the usually crotchety old carillonneur and warmed him to a point where he felt constrained to climb the two hundred steps to the belfry of Sint Jan's tower and ring out the most popular old and new songs. Several times my brothers and I accompanied the carillonneur to his perch in the bat-infested bell loft and saw him pounding away with leather gloves on the metal keyboard.

Our town had one of the finest singing towers in the Netherlands, on a par with those of Malines, Bruges and Antwerp. She still has the carillon, though the Nazis once took out the bells for the purpose of melting them down for cannon. The bells were discovered standing on the deck of a flat-bottomed Rhine barge lying moored at the quay in Coblenz by an American army officer in 1945. When he had identified them, this unknown

benefactor of humanity ordered the bells shipped back to their rightful
owners. Talk about *a* bell for Adano! Here were 47 bells all in one
shipment!

On Sunday night the town was plunged in darkness in accordance with
the dictates of the old-time religion, which may have been "good enough
for Paul and Silas," but certainly not good enough for me. Nine o'clock
was curfew hour for us on Sundays. Just when things got most interesting in the half-darkened streets and in the rural lanes we had to go
home.

Of Doctor van Andel, the minister of the dissenters, I must say something more, not only because he was a friend of the family, but by reason
of the fact that he was more than once extraordinarily kind to me in a
difficult situation.

A venerable patriarchal figure with a snow-white beard falling down
his waist, dressed in black cloth, he kept his right hand clamped tightly
to his body in the region of the liver. He was said to be in such pain that
he could not stand up for long in the pulpit. He served as a curator or
supervisor at the local gymnasium or Latin school. Knowing of my
nervousness on days of examination, he never failed to come into the room
where I was undergoing some test or other. Before seating himself on a
chair nearby, he placed his hand on my head for an instant and whispered
in my ear: "You do not mind if I rest a little, do you?" He then sat silently
till the test was over.

Upon hearing his whispered words the burden of my anxiety, which
amounted to an almost morbid sensitivity, rolled off my shoulders. It
seemed as if a calming, almost magic healing force emanated from the
touch of his hand. All at once my mind cleared, my thoughts ranged
themselves in proper order like soldiers on parade, and I wrote my paper
without hesitation or interruption.

One matter in connection with Doctor van Andel's preaching I mention
here because it has a pertinent bearing on events transpiring in another
part of the world right now. When I was still a very small boy the Boer
War raged in South Africa. No other historical event had so tremendously
telling an effect on my mind as the Anglo-Boer War. The Boers were our
kinsmen, our blood brothers. They spoke our language. They professed
the Calvinist doctrine. Every day, in church and school, I heard prayers
offered up in their behalf. The Boers had not started the quarrel with

Britain. In order to avoid strife they had made enormous sacrifices. When the region of the Cape, first settled by the Dutch, filled up with British immigrants and fortune hunters, the Boers, fearing to be outnumbered and with a resulting dissolution of their Calvinist way of life, trekked in a thousand oxen wagons across the Dragon Mountains and established two republics, Orange Free State and Transvaal, in the virgin and virtually uninhabited regions north of the Orange and Vaal rivers.

Again the British followed in steadily increasing numbers. With the discovery of gold and diamonds in the territory of the Transvaal republic, the influx became a wild stampede. The Boers sought to prevent the immigrants from gaining a preponderance by instituting a law requiring five years' residence before full citizenship could be conferred on *uitlanders*. But now the British government intervened, and it came to war. A first British expeditionary force was decisively defeated at Majuba Hill in 1881. A provisional peace was patched up and a period of relative calm ensued. Then the second Boer War broke out. A new British army was dispatched with the avowed intention of annexing the two Dutch republics.

This was the war of 1899–1902. At first the Boers, riding in hastily assembled burgher commandos, inflicted serious losses on the British regulars. A highland division, known as the Black Watch, was shatteringly defeated at the Modder River. In fact, the Boer victories were so spectacular that the German Kaiser, Wilhelm II, gave the British lion's tail a dirty twist by sending a telegram of congratulations to his "good friend" President Paul Kruger of the Transvaal.

Wilhelm, however, soon betrayed his good friend in the most despicable way imaginable. In order to regain his grandmother Queen Victoria's good graces, he drew up a plan of campaign for the British army in South Africa and dispatched it secretly to the General Staff in London. The plan envisaged a roundup of all the Boer women and children and their confinement in . . . concentration camps. The farmhouses were to be burnt, the cattle and crops destroyed and the land laid waste. This measure was intended to sever the Boer men in the field from their families, and deprive them of victuals and munitions, for their bullets were mostly cast at home.

Thirty-seven thousand Dutch women and children, among them the grandmothers, mothers and sisters of men still living, perished in the British camps!

There are other things to weep over in Alan Paton's "beloved country" besides the nationalist party's *apartheid* policy!

When Jan Smuts carried word to the British commander in chief, Lord Roberts, that the Boers, seeing the futility of further resistance, had decided to surrender, and the Peace of Vereeniging was concluded, Doctor van Andel preached a sermon on the burning of the thousands of Boer farmhouses and estates. For his text he used the words from the Book of Genesis describing Abraham's view of the burning cities of the plain, Sodom and Gomorrah: "And, lo, the smoke of the country went up as the smoke of a furnace."

He spoke of the Peace of Vereeniging and told the congregation: "Do not think that the last battle has been fought.... This war will go on for the better part of this century. Our South African brothers will never submit, for they are of the same indomitable mettle as our fathers who did not quail before the dreaded Spanish infantry and the Inquisition in a war of eighty years' duration.... There are some here, in this congregation," he went on to predict, "who will yet see the Republic of South Africa restored and the flag of our fathers again floating over the veld down there...."

That sermon was preached on Sunday, June 1, 1902.

The Republic of South Africa became a reality on May 31, 1961.

In Gorcum the petty bourgeoisie, the middle class, was Calvinist of various shades. In line with the Calvinist way of life, we children and youths were not allowed to attend the theatrical performances given occasionally by actors from nearby Rotterdam or Amsterdam. We were forbidden to pass through streets or go into areas where stood the carousels, the cakewalk, the waffle booths and the circus during the annual fortnight of *kermess*. People had to shift for themselves if they wanted diversion. Accordingly, the "godless" (thus the liberals were called), the proletariat and the common soldiers, of whom there were generally from two to three thousand in the barracks, found their way, like water seeking its lowest level, to the myriad of taverns, saloons and beer cellars.

In one street where there was a primitive dance hall, one official brothel and several free-lance institutions of that kind, my mother opened a small meetinghouse where she went on Sunday nights to preach the gospel to harlots, vagabonds, drunken fishers, soldiers and nondescript little old women. For years she had prodded the churches to take an interest in these people who were usually referred to as the unchurched. When no support from the churches was forthcoming, she went it alone in desperation.

As a rule she had a policeman at the door of the hall to keep order. Once I saw the policeman on the floor getting a pummeling from a band of young hoodlums. On the backdrop of the platform in the hall appeared a painting of the Crucified holding out His pierced hands, and the words: "This I did for you! What will you do for Me?"

My mother preached and another lady played the harmonium, mostly songs by Moody and Sanky. She kept up this rescue work till she collapsed from fatigue, but not before the Salvation Army set up a post and took over from her. I don't know where so frail a person as my mother got the strength to stand up under all this hectic, nerve-wracking labor. The work was entirely voluntary; nobody paid her. Her only reward was the thought that she might have been instrumental in directing some boy or girl into the narrow path that leadeth unto life.

My father would have nothing to do with "these antics of Christian endeavor." His aversion to the Christian doctrine rested upon what he called his "inability to swallow the story of salvation." As he did not want to spend his whole life in controversy, nor offend the sensibilities of others, he seldom spoke of the matter. Time and the advance of modern science, he felt, would in the end catch up with and dispel the New Testament's "childish oriental myths" which, as he saw the situation, were invented and handed down to us by the famous tentmaker of Tarsus, known as St. Paul.

"Rationally," he once told me, "we are too far advanced to take the Christian doctrine seriously when it teaches that the Creator of millions of suns and stars selected our little world, a second- or third-rate planet, as the scene for staging the drama for which the New Testament writers furnished the script.

"How can modern man accept as truth, as divinely revealed truth at that, the story that God caused a little child to be born unnaturally or supernaturally in a forlorn village in Asia Minor, and that this child—which was God Himself in disguise—had to be bloodily done to death in order to appease God's anger, and at the same time save the human race?"

I had an awful time of it as a boy trying to disentangle the story of divine love from the vengeful character attributed to God by my orthodox teachers. My father and mother pulled in opposite directions. Successive teachers did the same and the process hasn't ended yet. That wonderful equilibrium, to which some believers refer as the peace which passeth understanding, was never quite mine. It had too tame and saccharine a flavor. Religion was something more serious to me than going to sleep with a lollypop.

Though my father strictly forbade us children to accompany my mother to her gospel hall, one creature which never failed to follow her at a discreet distance and wait for her outside was our affectionate and intelligent Sultan, a shaggy black-and-brown-haired mongrel. Sultan came to us a starving, whining puppy, picked up by my youngest brother Jozinus from a rain-soaked straw hut standing in a freshly plowed field a mile from town. He grew up with my brother, was his constant companion in daytime as well as at nights when he slept across the foot of his bed. In the end that dog chose not to be separated from his young master in death.

Sultan had many friends and no personal enemies except two, the one human and the second canine like himself. Against both he nourished an enduring animosity. For his human foe he had selected the *tambour-maître*, as we called the drum major who strutted in front of the military band when it headed the parade of the local garrison through the streets. The sight of this individual, a giant of a man, made to look still taller by the bearskin busby on his head, sent Sultan into tantrums of fury. Strange to say, he left the man strictly alone when he walked by himself. It seems to have been the multicolored and gilt-knobbed stick or staff the drum major carried aloft and swung around in rhythmic accompaniment of the drums' beat which aroused Sultan's resentment. He went for the man as soon as he caught sight of him. Though not, I should add, in one or two wild leaps; he crouched up to him in the manner of a panther stalking its prey.

When the *tambour-maître* saw Sultan coming he immediately lowered his staff, an act which the drummers mistook for a signal to stop drumming, so that the whole parade was often thrown into confusion.

The situation with his fellow dog, another mongrel, Bello by name, was quite different, more deadly and vicious, I would say. Their feud originated inside the house of Bello's owner where Jozinus took Sultan one day. Bello's owner, a baker by trade, whose son was my brother's schoolmate, left the dogs in the hall where they duly made acquaintance and got on very well. . . for a time. All at once there was a fantastic racket, growling and howling and yelping. What had happened? Sultan, sniffing the odor of a nice fresh-roasted pork roll, got up on his hind legs and found what he looked for in a niche in the wall. Such niches in the thick stone walls of old houses were used as cooling-off places before the invention of the icebox and the electric refrigerator. Sultan could reach the niche without difficulty; Bello, who was somewhat shorter in the legs, had never been able to manage.

The two dogs fought like tigers. The baker, his wife and their children rushed into the hall and went after the battling champions with broomsticks and anything else they could lay hands on. They belabored the dogs unmercifully. However, the baker made one mistake; he opened the door leading into the street. Sultan raced off as fast as his legs could carry him. But he brought the pork roast with him and ate it at leisure and with great gusto on my brother's bed.

Just before reaching the street from the baker's house, Sultan, who was holding the roast clamped tightly between his teeth, and thus temporarily defenseless, had received such a nasty cut in his tail from Bello's fangs that he bore the mark of it for the rest of his life. This injury Sultan never forgave nor forgot. Whenever the two met, Sultan attacked Bello just as the most civilized nations do without any such formality as an ultimatum.

When my youngest brother fell ill as the result of walking through a November evening haze and slipping into a cesspool on a farm where he visited, Sultan refused to eat and started to waste away. Before he was rescued Jozinus lay at the bottom of that hole for ten hours, his head scarcely raised above the level of cattle urine and soft lime. When brought home he vomited for a week and then lay still. He could not bear any food in his stomach. Our family physician summoned a specialist from the University of Leiden for a consultation. The professor examined the boy thoroughly, but left the house shaking his head.

On the day following the funeral, Sultan was missing. In the midst of our grief nobody paid much attention to the dog's absence. A week later the gravedigger called at the house and I opened the door. "Sultan is dead," he said, taking off his cap. "He fell asleep in the cemetery on your brother's grave!"

"Father," Martin Luther's boy once asked the reformer, "father, are there any little dogs in heaven?"

"*Gewiss*, most certainly," replied Luther. "Little dogs and big dogs and lambs and lions and deer, and they play together in meadows of gold."

Sultan is there, I am sure of it.

I also owe something to Sultan, and maybe I don't. One night, returning from a late errand, I took a short cut through a narrow unlighted street, a mere alley, where a popular hostel was located. The hostel, really a dive of the lowest sort, faced a high wall behind which rose the dark hulk of the gas reservoir. There were no pedestrians for the alley was a dead-end passage, which I had entered by climbing over the town ramparts at the end of it.

As I passed the house I happened to glance in the direction of a lighted window. What I saw there made the goose flesh creep down my back: a soldier was holding a woman on his lap, and the woman was stark naked. Another soldier stood by the table helping himself from a crock of Bols' gin. All three were laughing at the top of their voices. When the woman rose, one of the soldiers danced playfully around the room with her. Suddenly she caught sight of me standing in the middle of the alley in the full glare of the light coming from the window. She picked up a glass from the table and waved it at me in a gesture of invitation. The soldiers, too, made beckoning motions. When I started to leave, the door of the hostelry opened and the two men stepped outside.

"Come inside, *kameraad*," said one of the soldiers. "There are some damn fine girls here, and it won't cost you a cent!"

One of the men put his hands on my shoulders and the other seized my wrist. "Come along," they urged, "you might as well start now. . . . You'll never regret it!"

The two began to drag me towards the door, but we never reached it. Suddenly, a lumbering black shape leaped from the semi-obscurity of the alley, and bit the soldier's hand. Though an artillerist, the man swore like a trooper. He reeled under the impact of the dog's assault. Both men ran back into the house and slammed the door.

Sultan had appeared just in time. As I ran home, he raced ahead of me and stood on the doorstep barking joyfully and wagging his tail. No doubt he expected to get a pat on the head from my father for saving me from dire peril. But I did not say a word about my adventure in the alley, though I shivered as with the ague in my excitement. I had seen a nude woman and this had something to do with sex. Sex was never mentioned in our home.

Why was sex never mentioned? Sex belonged to the realm of the night, and the night was the devil's part. In order to save us from the devil, we were to remain as long as possible in total ignorance of everything pertaining to the sexual act. The almost universal fairy tale which has the stork pick up babies somewhere and deposit them in their cribs did not work out very well with us, even when we were mere kindergarten mites. The reason was that we knew the stork and his ways too well. His nest was built on top of the tallest chimney in the community, that of the home for the aged. In summertime we saw the stork and his wife busy all day carrying frogs and eels to their nest to feed their young. But they never carried a baby. On moonlit nights you could see the male stork stand guard on one leg watching over the sleeping town. In November the storks left us and flew to Egypt to hibernate. Still, babies were born in wintertime, too. Who brought the babies during the cold months?

When we grew old enough to ask questions, which was pretty early, my mother solved the problem for a time by hanging up two large colored lithographs on the wall opposite our beds. The lithographs represented angels carrying children in their arms. One angel with a very Dutch face, lovely blonde hair and the rosy cheeks of a milkmaid, smiled happily as she flew a blue-eyed boy down to earth. She was called the Angel of Life! The other, a rather foreign-looking mama, whose wings were not of such brightly polished silver as the first, carried another child. The second angel and child were going upward, to heaven. She was called the Angel of Death! New puzzle: how did my mother know that the second child wasn't being flown down to hell? She knew: "Of course, that child is going to heaven! It has been baptized!"

I had to wait till I entered catechism class before I became vaguely aware of the ins and outs of the sexual situation. The second lesson of the *Heidelberg Catechism* informed me that my parents conceived me in sin; in other words, that they had engaged in that detestable filthiness which, according to St. Paul, was not to see the light of day. Nobody seems to have realized that this very thought produced a psychological upheaval almost too great for small boys to bear, that it poisoned many a life from the roots upward. For one thing, it led one to despise and be utterly ashamed of one's own father and mother, not to speak of the slimy thickness of unnatural vice into which our sexual ignorance plunged us. It multiplied our impure visions and nurtured the very depravity from which it was supposed to save us. . . .

Till this day in certain communities of the Netherlands the adherents of different denominations wear clothes of a particular cut and color to indicate their specific religious affiliation. For example, in the famous seaside resort of Scheveningen, a suburb of The Hague, which has nowadays as many cabarets, night clubs and things of that kind as Ostende, Deauville or Cannes, the Catholic women still wear capes of light blue, the Reformed black, the Christian Reformed dark blue, and so on and so forth. In Amsterdam you once could tell that an orphan boy was of the Protestant faith by the red color of one sleeve of his black jacket and one leg of his trousers. These vogues are fast going out, but some instances remain, though even in the case of the last bitter-enders, I notice that the skirts are getting shorter and shorter.

My brothers and I wore black; black blouses when still very young, later black suits with high vests buttoned right up to the chin. To our infinite disgust this somber puritanical apparel made us marked men, odd fish, peculiar people like the Amish in Pennsylvania or the Quakers before their liberalization. My mother's purpose in dressing us up that way, I imagine, was to convince the world that our hearts were empty of vain thoughts and mean desires.

The late Thomas Sugrue once wrote a book or an article entitled: "It's Hell To Be a Catholic!" I don't know what it's like to be a Catholic, but I know only too well that it's triple hell for boys to be exhibited as samples of pure, innocent Calvinist sainthood. Still, I do not complain or plead for commiseration. We were not in the least unhappy; we learned to adapt ourselves to the color situation and we had fun like all other boys. In some ways it was perhaps an advantage to be dressed in the hue of night.

Nobody in authority ever found out or suspected that my brother Thomas was easily the most accurate slingshot operator in the community. Proportionately speaking, he could and sometimes did demolish more street lights in one evening than the so-called youthful delinquents of modern times in a whole year. But it wasn't hooliganism or vandalism which drove him into these sudden fits of destructiveness. He put the street lamps out of commission by request of young lovers who wanted to be undisturbed in the out-of-the-way nooks and corners which they selected for their trysts.

In wintertime when he fired from ambush after having concealed a small piece of stone or rock inside the snowballs, his favorite targets were the high silk hats of the Protestant ministers and the stocking-clad calves below the knee breeches of the Roman priests. When no clergymen were about he tried his skill on the policemen's helmets. He liked to hear the sharp ping-pong-like click his loaded snowballs made on the coppers' metal headgear. I can say this now without endangering his security or giving him over to the belated vengeance of burgomasters or cops. The burgomasters and cops of those far-off days have all crossed to the further shore, and so, alas, has Thomas.

Soon after Jozinus' death, his menagerie also vanished. It was almost like a miniature zoo. In the rear of the house, bordering on the living room, the kitchen and a stream of water, was an open space, a courtyard one might call it, where Jozinus kept his collection of animals, two of each species, like the beasts in Noah's ark. There were two goats in a small stable, something like a lean-to, two guinea pigs, a pair of rabbits, a rooster with seven hens, frogs without number and, with the frogs, salamanders and lizards kept in tanks, several cats, finches and two canaries who, for some mysterious reason, sang only when my brother draped a scarlet piece of cloth over the side of their cage. The finches drew their water up to the cage in tiny buckets. Presiding, or rather hovering, over this motley assortment in uncertain short flights was a large crow who answered to the name of Black Pete. He had only one leg and one of his wings also was injured. Pete flew around loose and often came into the house. On Sunday mornings he pecked on the windowpanes of the living room to notify us, just a few minutes before the bells started to ring, that it was time to go to church. How he knew that it was Sunday and the hour to make ready for services, neither I nor anyone else ever found out. In summertime he flew in through the open window and sat on my brother's head during dinner. However, when my mother began reading from the Bible, he screamed the three or four dirty words which, we suspected, his former owners had taught him and departed with a *caw* of disgust.

One extremely wealthy citizen supported my mother in defraying the expenses involved in running her Sunday school and gospel hall. He paid for the furniture, for the light and heating and the rent. On St. Nicholas' day, which falls on December 6th, he provided the wherewithal for the distribution of gifts amongst the poorest children. Armand de Chaupertuis was this benefactor's name. A bachelor, he descended from a family of

Huguenots which settled in Holland following the revocation of the Edict of Nantes by Louis XIV in 1685. Denied freedom of worship by their sovereign—a sentence of death was imposed on being caught listening to a Calvinist sermon in the woods or in some old ruined house—two hundred thousand or more Huguenots left France to take up residence in the Netherlands. They never returned to their homeland.

Chaupertuis' ancestors built the French church in our town. Though the building was seldom used as a church in my day, it was still known as *La Chapelle*. It had a fine slender tower with a clock just below the spire.

For a number of years Armand de Chaupertuis served in the royal artillery attaining the rank of major when an incident occurred which changed him from a genial, affable gentleman-about-town into a somber recluse and eccentric.

Major Chaupertuis had one hobby: he painted, and he painted very well. He lived in one of the finest mansions in the community. Here he entertained lavishly the ladies and gentlemen of his own military upper class, and frequently received visitors from abroad. Of his compositions two at least, to my knowledge, were purchased by Her Majesty. Others hung in the various museums in Holland's major cities.

After he resigned from the army at the age of forty or so, he stopped painting, he stopped entertaining, and he stopped talking. It was as if the man had been struck dumb. Even with his servants, a woman and her husband who had been the major's orderly while in the service, he scarcely exchanged a word. He used to pass his best friends in the streets without noticing them.

What made Major Chaupertuis change his way of life is one of the strangest stories I ever heard. It seems that Major Chaupertuis was heckled one day on the parade ground by a young recruit. The major had reprimanded the man on several occasions previously for talking in the ranks. It did no good.

"This is a free country, isn't it?" the recruit asked insolently. "So let's have a little freedom of speech!"

"Everything in its place, my boy," Chaupertuis replied. "But here you must keep silent. You're in the army now. It is I who give the word of command in this battalion."

After several exchanges of this kind, the major became aware that the soldier was deliberately taunting him and trying to make him lose his temper. He avoided the man as much as possible. He should have left him entirely to the tender mercies of the drill sergeants. Chaupertuis noticed, however, that other soldiers were catching the recruit's disciplinary indifference and insolence. There was a lot of mumbling and snickering in the ranks as the major passed by. Even so, nothing special or startling would perhaps have happened were it not that the recruit one day gauded the major beyond the limits of human forbearance.

"Here he comes, boys, the phony Rembrandt, the botcher and bungler," the recruit said loud enough for the major to hear as he passed in front of the ranks on a morning of inspection.

"Silence in the ranks!" the major called out.

"Christ," spoke up the recruit, ignoring Chaupertuis' admonition, "this guy thinks he can paint, but the women's faces in his pictures look like a pig's a——!"

"Sergeant," said the major, turning to the N.C.O. walking behind, "take that man's name! Have him report to the orderly room. . . . "

"You know my name a damn sight better than you know how to paint!" the recruit interjected disrespectfully.

"What do you know about painting?" the major shot back in a sudden fit of anger.

"I know enough to say that your paintings are the shoddiest, shabbiest things I've ever seen. You call yourself a naturalist, well, it's true, you are a naturalist, you paint with the natural color of s——!"

"Shut up, you Jew!"

"You dirty anti-Semite," called back the recruit, "I'll report you to the colonel!"

For answering Major Chaupertuis walked up to the Jewish boy and struck him a blow in the face. But almost at the same time he said: "Oh, I am so sorry. . . . Will you forgive me? I lost my temper. Will you forgive me?" He addressed the whole company. There was no answer.

The major immediately left the parade ground, walked home and took off his uniform. He wrote a letter to the Minister of War resigning his commission: "I am not worthy to wear Her Majesty's uniform any longer," and he gave the details of the incident on the barrack square.

There seem to have been some attempts to patch up the quarrel. It was suggested that both men apologize and that the major be transferred to another garrison. But Chaupertuis would not hear of any such arrangement. The only thing he volunteered after resigning his rank was to reenlist as a private soldier. For this, however, he had passed the age limit, and his offer was refused.

From that day onward Major Chaupertuis watched the bridge across the canal leading to the barracks and the parade ground. When the soldiers walked out in the afternoon after the day's exercises, the major was on the lookout. One day he caught sight of the recruit whom he had struck, and followed him. The man strolled along the main street, passed through the towngate and took the road to the village of Dalem. Near the church in Dalem, the major caught up with him. The soldier, fearing an act of revenge, was frightened. But Chaupertuis calmed his fears. They walked into the graveyard behind the church and sat down on a tombstone. The major took the Jewish boy's hand and asked forgiveness.

"I could not have done a greater wrong than by insulting one of your race in this land which gave my ancestors asylum when they were persecuted. I've not only hurt you to the quick, I have broken Holland's tradition of tolerance."

The two men sat in the graveyard till long after dark. Then, the hour drawing near when taps is sounded, they walked together arm in arm through the gate and along the main street. They parted near the barracks.

From that day the major's life changed. He seldom appeared in public. All the joy of life had gone out of him. He never wore the uniform again. He told uncle Kees that nothing in the whole world could atone for his act of violence. All his wealth he expended in good deeds of charity and philanthropy. This is how my mother happened to come in for a share of his bounty.

Chaupertuis wouldn't leave town and take up residence elsewhere. "It is here in this place that I fell," he would say, "it is here that I must pay the price and show repentance."

When I knew Major Chaupertuis he attended the service in the great church every Sunday morning. But he would never take a seat. He stood still and erect, a lone figure in the left transept away from the congregation. This was the form of penance he imposed upon himself.

Idleness, says an old proverb, is Satan's pillow, a hearth, a breeding ground for evil thoughts and actions. In order to wean me from hankering to join the devil on his pillow, my mother set me to work on the only afternoon when I was free from school. The task she thought up for me was the distribution of a journal of about six or eight pages that went by the name of *Peniel*. The Hebrew word *Peniel* meaning literally "Face of God" occurs in that mysterious story in the Book of Genesis about the patriarch Jacob's struggle with a "man" by the side of the brook of Jabbok till the break of day. "And Jacob," says the Bible, "called the place *Peniel*, for, he said, I have seen God *panim el panim*, face to face."

The periodical was published in the ancient university city of Utrecht situated about twenty-five miles to the north of Gorcum. Its editor, Dr. J. H. Gunning, a theologian of the evangelical school, devoted several pages a week to the Jewish question under the heading: "An attempt to fill the urgent need of spreading enlightenment amongst the unenlightened Jews." This high-faluting language was a mere cover up: *Peniel* was a missionary propaganda sheet pure and simple, though it also enjoyed a rather wide vogue amongst evangelically minded readers in our community.

Although there was no salary attached to the distribution of this journal, my mother was convinced that if I undertook the work as a labor of love, God would most certainly reward me in his own good time for taking an interest in the fate and destiny of "his own people." This is the phrase "the ancient people of God" with which she and many others in Holland referred to the children of Israel. My father, of course, held a contrary opinion; he didn't think the Jews were any more God's own people, or a chosen race, than the Dutch or the French, not to speak of the British. He conceded that there was an aura of wonder about the Jews because they alone of all the peoples of antiquity had come through the thunderstorms of time. But this was not, he believed, the result of some divine predilection or favor. It was the Jewish people's sense of destiny and their own strong will to live which had preserved them. Like many Hollanders he was proud that a large number of Jews had found refuge in the Netherlands following their expulsion from Spain by the Inquisition in the year 1492. He was still more grateful to the sixteenth and seventeenth century Jews for having given our capital city of Amsterdam the byname of *Eleutheropolis*, the "city of freedom of conscience." He often pointed out to us that the dawn of the "Golden Age" in Dutch history, what Lord Acton calls "the later renaissance," when art, literature, industry and commerce placed the Netherlands in the forefront of civilization, coincided with the settlement of thousands of Spanish Jews in our midst. Many of these were scholars, physicians, mathematicians, architects, goldsmiths and pottery makers. The famous Delft faience, for instance, with its amazingly soft and delicate blue color, was the invention of Jewish refugees from Spain.

Gorcum had about 300 Jews; half the local physicians were Jews, further many schoolteachers and lawyers, but also shopkeepers and paper and rag collectors, all humble people, hard-working, but full-fledged citizens and solid supporters of the public school system. At the head of the Jewish community stood a *Jodenmeester*, a Jews' master, who, I suppose, was a rabbi. His name was Isak Cappadoce; he taught Hebrew at the gymnasium and also ran an elementary Hebrew school, a *cheder*, for the Jewish children after school hours in *het Joodse leerhuis*, the Jewish house of learning, the synagogue. All the Gorcum Jews were orthodox and strict observers of the sabbath. On that day they dressed in black and the men wore high silk hats. As is well known the Dutch people are a little off the beam in the matter of cleanliness; they even wash the façades of their houses, though one would think the frequent rains a sufficient cleanser. But some Christian houses standing on the way to the synagogue, on the route which the Jews had to take to their house of prayer, were not washed on the sabbath in deference to the sensibilities of Jewish passers-by.

To the homes of these people I had to carry old *Peniel* in spite of my father's objections that the paper was an insult to the Jews. "Enlighten the unenlightened Jews," he'd snort. "What does Dr. Gunning think the Jews are; cannibals or Papuan head-hunters? . . . No self-respecting Jew will read this *Peniel* trash and if you should get a knock on the head one of these days, please don't come to me for redress. . . . "

"But we must tell them about the Lord Jesus," my mother would argue back. "This is our duty. The Lord commands us to preach the gospel to all creatures. . . . In Christ has come a deeper, a fuller revelation of God. The Jews must share in this revelation. The Church can never be full, complete and healed from its divisions as the Body of Christ till the Jews come in." She also figured that the second coming of Christ would be preceded by a return of the Jews to the land of their fathers; hence she sympathized with the Zionist idea.

The bundle of *Peniels* from Utrecht arrived at the railway express office on Saturday morning. I had to wait till sundown before I could ring Jewish doorbells to present my wares. To my surprise I was not turned away anywhere. Every Jewish family bought a copy. In certain houses

I was kindly invited inside and given a cup of coffee and honey cake or some other delicacy. Such was the case especially at the home of my classmate David Dalmaden whose father was an umbrella merchant and who had more books than any other man in the community save our family physician, Dr. Baruch Mendoza and my uncle Kees.

Though the price of a copy of *Peniel* was only ten cents, many Jews handed me a quarter or even a whole florin, bidding me to keep the change. I don't know whether any Jew actually read *Peniel*. One thing is certain: no Jew was ever converted to Christianity as a result of *Peniel's* proselytizing pap, certainly not in our community.

However, the distribution of *Peniel* was not wholly a case of love's labor lost. It put some money in my pocket for the first time in my life. With the extras received from Jewish readers I bought and proudly paid for a set of dictionaries, rather heavy tomes, all in a similar binding and virtually indestructible. I still have those books in my possession.

After successfully peddling *Peniel* for one year, the publisher sent me as a premium a fine gilded clock. At the close of the second year I received a set of books, 25 blue paperbacks by Luise Muehlbach, dealing with the private history of the members of the Hohenzollern family: the Grand Elector, Frederick the Great, Queen Luise of Prussia whom Napoleon sought to seduce, Kaiser Wilhelm I and his Iron Chancellor Bismarck, in short the whole Prussian gang of world disturbers. Frederick the Great was the *pièce de résistance* in Madame Muehlbach's collection. I learned a good deal about him which the school history books glossed over or omitted altogether: the concerts he gave at Sans Souci with himself playing the flute; his correspondence and friendship with Voltaire; his philosophical writings; his homosexualism; his father's tobacco college where the generals were compelled to smoke pipes while discussing plans of conquest and other military imbecilities.

At the end of two years I quit my job as *Peniel's* distributor. My conversations with our family doctor were the direct cause of my resignation. Doctor Mendoza was the last customer to be served on Saturday night. His house bordered ours in the rear. The two gardens were separated by a narrow stream over which ran a small bridge connecting the two properties. In that stream I learned to swim and on its ice wore out my first set of skates.

The doctor was the only Jew to discuss the contents of *Peniel* with me. To my utter bewilderment he told me one night that Jesus of Nazareth presented no problem to the Jewish people. The Jews neither hated nor liked Him; they were absolutely indifferent to Him. The doctor did believe that the Nazarene was a historical person, but the stories in the New Testament about great multitudes following him, he called "obvious fabrications." Jesus passed almost unnoticed through the Palestine of His time. There is no mention of Him in any contemporary source. The miracles, said the doctor, attributed to Him are without exception childish fairy tales. When you read the New Testament attentively and see that there was a whole crop of resurrections at the time when Jesus expired on the cross—"the graves were opened; and many of the bodies of the saints which slept arose... and appeared unto many"—the story of His being seen alive after His death by a half-demented woman is without the least historical value.

Dr. Mendoza did by no means blame Jesus for these extravagancies. "Had Jesus ever learned of the fantastic claims made on His behalf, He certainly would have been the first to repudiate them.

"Your paper [meaning *Peniel*] may talk all it likes about the Jewishness of Jesus," said Dr. Mendoza. "The editor knows nothing at all on the subject. It's all wishful thinking and catechism and theology.... It is *not* history. The man who invented Jesus as the Christ, who raised Him to Christhood, was St. Paul, an apostate Jew, who was brought up in a city where a pagan mystery cult was in vogue. That cult of a dying and rising god he transferred to the person of Jesus of Nazareth about whom he knew absolutely nothing and had never seen.

"As to the missionary endeavors with which you are associated, let me tell you frankly: I admire your zeal and believe in your integrity, but you are wasting your time. No Jew, let alone the Jewish people as a whole, is ever going to come into the Christian Church, at least not voluntarily or because they are convinced of the superiority of the Christian religion...."

And then he told me a story which made so shattering an impression on me that all thoughts of Christian missionary endeavor amongst the Jews were for all time eradicated from my mind. He cited Shlomo Virga, a Jewish historian of the sixteenth century: "I have heard from old people who had themselves been amongst the Jews who were driven out of Spain, how on one of the exodus ships the pestilence known as the black death broke out. The ship's captain immediately put all the refugees ashore in an uninhabited place. Most of the wanderers died of starvation, some decided to march on and seek a place to settle. Amongst these was a Jew, his wife and two sons. The woman succumbed to the hardships of the trek. The father carried his two boys in his arms till overcome with exhaustion he sank unconscious to the ground. When he regained consciousness it was full daylight, but his two sons had also died in the night. Turning to the East the bereaved father began his morning prayer with the words: 'Master of the Universe, You don't make it very easy for me to praise You. You almost make me lose my faith. Yet, so that everything be in the clear between us You should know one thing: I am a Jew and will remain a Jew. None of my afflictions, past, present or future, can turn me from You.'"

"How dare Jews speak that way to God or about God?" I asked. "I don't remember any Christian saint or father of the Church talking to God in so familiar a tone.

"The Jews dare talk that way to God because He is *their* God," said Dr. Mendoza. "They know Him through and through, for they made Him what He is as much as He made them what they are. Their relationship is a covenant. God dwells on the prayers of the righteous. That is, He exists by virtue of the faith men have in Him. If man loses faith—that is, if men act unjustly and only pay lip service—God goes out of existence and dies of inanition."

Sometimes, even today, the sense of what it was like to live within a world so narrow and confined returns to me with a shock of recognition. In addition to the town's isolation, chiefly for lack of modern transportation facilities, we, the pupils of a parochial school, were doubly barred against intruders by our esoteric religion.

To start with, the profound differences of opinion on religious matters between my parents made our home a house divided against itself. That my parents never separated I attribute to the fact that, in spite of all their squabbles, they were never bored with each other. My mother, moreover, I suspect, nourished a secret hope that my father would return to the light and pick up where he had left off in his theological studies. Yet, though there was no real estrangement between them, the situation could hardly be said to have been conducive to the children's harmonious development. In my case the gymnasium made it worse. But the gymnasium was not to blame. The stifling parochial atmosphere of the School with the Bible was the cause of the near-schizophrenic split that resulted.

When I entered the gymnasium it was as if I had suddenly been released from prison and thrown, quite unprepared, into a world as unfamiliar as the Arabian desert. At the gymnasium, a secular institution run on humanistic principles, nobody paid any particular attention to the Bible or things of a religious nature in general. During the first months I felt like a fish out of water and was very unhappy. The change had been too abrupt.

All at once I was confronted with wholly dissimilar, not to say contradictory standards of education. Ideals other than those held before me by my earlier teachers were not only alien to my spirit, but had, more or less subtly, sometimes forcibly, been impressed upon me as evil and dangerous.

At the gymnasium, where the emphasis lay on the Latin and Greek languages and the study of the civilizations of Hellas and Rome, their culture, literature, their mythology and systems of administration, the orthodox Christian faith was not considered of much consequence. For the greatest part the instructors adhered to the liberal party; that is to say, they were, as liberals go generally in Europe, sceptics, agnostics, humanists. Their company included men of great learning and tolerance. If it came very early to a clash with one of them, a certain Dr. Conrad Curtius, it was wholly my fault; I spoke out of turn.

One day Curtius, in commenting on the death of Socrates, called attention to the fearless, stoical manner in which the Greek philosopher met his end by calmly drinking the cup of hemlock. The instructor compared Socrates' attitude in the presence of death with the flight of the founder of Christianity and His hiding in the woods on Mount Olive. Curtius called Christ's "whining, blood-sweating, blubbering" attitude when confronted with the troop sent to arrest him in the Garden of Gethsemane "a contemptible exhibition of cowardice."

I felt as if I had been slapped in the face. I blushed to the roots of my hair and bit my fingernails. No doubt I ought to have kept silent, but the words that rose to my lips slipped out before I could press them back: "I beg your pardon," I said, "but the Lord Jesus was not a coward. He was the central figure in God's plan of redemption . . . . He went to His death voluntarily in order to conform to the will of God . . . . His blood was shed as a ransom for many . . . ." I could have continued in this vein, for there was no lack of sacred texts and verses that came to mind. I was stopped short by Curtius: "Please, bear in mind that you are not in a Sunday school here . . . . The Christian mythology does not figure in our curriculum."

The other boys roared with laughter and I felt deeply humiliated. But I was determined to have the last word. "If," I said, "you call our religion a mere mythology, why did you treat your comparison of the attitudes of Socrates and Jesus as historical fact?"

"Leave the room," ordered the instructor. "What do you think you are anyway, a missionary?"

For much less of an affront to the Christian faith, my mother, had she learned of it, would have withdrawn me from the Latin school. This was the last thing I wanted. I, therefore, made no mention at home of the clash with Curtius. I discussed it only with my mother's brother, uncle Kees. He and I thrashed out everything that came up, from religion to politics and war and peace and whatnot. Though not an orthodox believer himself, he respected the views and opinions of others and liked to listen to them.

"Those remarks by Curtius," said Kees, "struck you like a bolt from the blue. And no wonder; you lived far too long under the tyranny of that parochial school. You have yet to learn that there exist different interpretations of the origins of Christianity than those given by the traditionalists. It is time you began reading Renan's *Life of Jesus*. Renan is very respectful of the Christian religion, but he looks for the kernel of historical truth under the layers of legend, myth, fairy tale, propaganda and apologetics with which successive generations of theologians have covered the man of Nazareth."

And so I read Renan, and I was enchanted with him. But the novelty has so completely worn off that I cannot with the best will in the world summon up either the energy or a desire to disinter Maître Renan. Kees called Renan's famous book "one of the lamps that never goes out." I soon tired of Renan and his "sweet little Jesus meek and mild" with "the eyes of a gazelle" and "blond locks" of a woman. How did he know what Jesus looked like when nobody else knew? . . .

Fortunately, there was no lack of other subjects to discuss and argue over with Kees and my schoolmates who often gathered after the day's classes in his studio to smoke a pipe and drink a glass of beer.

The names of my classmates who most frequently met in Kees' studio were Ary Brandt, David Dalmaden, Alfons Boogaert and Yetze Sissingha. Brandt was the son of a rural burgomaster, an attractive boy, loved to a

frenzy by all the girls in the community and feared by all the instructors
at the gymnasium because of his unexpected questions and his still more
startling responses. He might look as though he were merely showing off,
yet behind that sparkling wit in him there was a genuine humility and a
warm heart. He talked with enthusiasm and fire on almost any subject
that came up, but his favorite topic was poetry. He knew whole stretches
of Shakespeare, Milton and Victor Hugo by heart, not to mention the
Dutch poets. He was the youngest and one of the most valued members
of the *rederykerskamer*, the guild of rhetoric, over which my father presided at its weekly session on Wednesday evening.

Ary Brandt planned to become an actor, and called the theater the
church of the future. He had not been brought up in the Christian way;
his father, the village burgomaster, served as president of a society of free-
thinkers, known as "The Dawn"; his mother died at his birth. Yet one day
he discovered the Church as a spiritual treasure house and a source of the
truth which he had previously ignored or denied. He studied theology in
Leiden and became a minister of the Reformed Church. In his sermons he
took so provocative and fearlessly critical a line on the infamous Nuremberg laws which the Nazis introduced in Holland that he gained a reputation as a dangerous enemy of the Third Reich. His championship of the
Jews made him a mouthpiece of the living Church, but it cost him his life.

He was one of the Reformed pastors arrested as hostages by order of
Arthur Seyss-Inquart, the Nazi governor general of the Netherlands in
1943, and one of the last to be executed on the very eve of South Holland's
liberation by the Canadian army.

Dalmaden, the son of poor Jewish parents, became a physician. Our
family doctor, Dr. Mendoza, paid for his tuition at the local gymnasium
and later at the Amsterdam medical faculty. With his wife, children, father,
mother and all his brothers and sisters, David Dalmaden was shipped to
Poland in a cattle truck and there done to death by the brown marauders
of humanity.

The most pathetic victim of the Second World War, Alfons Boogaert,
the most brilliant member of our class, became a Roman Catholic priest
and missionary in the Solomon Islands. His father ran a butcher shop
and had his clientele in the slummiest part of our town. The son never
took part in any of our athletic games or sports for fear of ripping his
trousers or wearing down his shoes in the rough and tumble of the play.

The Boogaert family belonged to "the decent poor" in the community; the shabby genteel, the most miserable class in society.

After Alfons left the gymnasium he studied at a seminary in Roeselare near Bruges in Flanders. According to a dispatch in *Time* magazine, he died a martyr's death when the Japanese invaded the island where he was stationed. For his own diversion, a Japanese colonel ordered Boogaert crucified, nailed to the door of the little mission church he had built.

Thus they all perished, though Yetze Sissingha went down illumined with courage as the commander of a Dutch submarine which lay ready for launching in May, 1940, when the German army invaded Holland. Ordered to take the submarine on a trial run, he invited a party of German naval officers on board. Before starting on the trip, he informed his wife that he wouldn't be back. A few miles out in the North Sea, he scuttled the sub, and thus like Samson at Gaza took the Philistines into death with him.

Are those boys worth remembering? I think they are! They are always with me, anyway. They all liked Kees and Kees was a generous host. In his studio we could say what we liked, and said it. The only persons on whose account my uncle permitted no banter or lighthearted chatter were the members of the royal family. To him the House of Orange was above the law, almost sacrosanct. However, he didn't mince words when it came to criticizing the government, either national or local. Yet, he was not one of those mirror-image patriots for whom their own nation is always peculiarly in the wrong. In France, on the other hand, he saw something like a prototype of the undying fatherland which was above and beyond the land of his birth. Britain, on account of the Anglo-Boer War, was just about at the bottom of the ladder. He would get terribly excited about the oppression—that's the word he used—of the Irish people by successive British governments. The British record in Ireland was as barbarous in his opinion as that of the Russians in Poland.

His cast of mind and temper, the values he held and lived by, were those of a cosmopolitan, but a fighting cosmopolitan. Some of the ministers of religion in our town put him down as an anarchist because of his veneration for Tolstoy, though not so much for Tolstoy the novelist as for Tolstoy the writer of "The Kingdom of God Is Within You" and "What Is Religion?" He thought and said it often enough that Tolstoy's religion, in contrast with the religion of our "petty churches, those ice-cold churches with their frozen dogmas, spiritual torpor and smug self-satisfaction," was "as high as a palace, solemn as the starry night, wide and immense as the universe."

When we asked him after one of his turns of duty as organist at the great church what kind of sermon he had heard, he would say: "Words and words again, empty phrases, double-talk, platitudes and sweet pious lullabies to rock human misery to sleep. . . . "

Kees had remained unmarried; he never got over the death of his childhood sweetheart who succumbed at the age of eighteen to the ravages of tuberculosis. The girl's portrait hung in the unused living room in his house above the mantelpiece beneath a sort of votive lamp in the shape of a small ornamental lantern. As the blinds were always drawn, and the slip covers on the chairs and sofa, as well as the wallpaper, were of a dark green pattern, the room seemed pervaded with the drearisome atmosphere of an undertaker's chapel.

A man of middle height, Kees' soft dark eyes darted flashes of lightning when he grew angry or indignant. With his brown mustache and goatee and somewhat swarthy complexion, he could have been, and sometimes was, taken for a foreigner in that country by the dykes where fair skins predominate. His and my mother's family had settled in Gorcum about a hundred years before. They were Waldensian refugees form Torre Pellice in the Italo-French border region who got tired of the persecutions to which they and their Church were subjected for seven long centuries.

An outlandish style in clothes further heightened my uncle's unconventional, not to say alien, appearance. His buttonless black cloak, really an immense flowing cape, reached nearly to his knees. He wore it like a Roman toga, the top fold covering his mouth and half his face to protect himself, as he said, and as all superstition-ridden Southerners say, against the cold moist air, especially at eventide. Like his *flambard*, a soft flapping black hat, the cloak was a Paris importation. This unusual sartorial accouterment served him as a reminder of the happiest years of his life which he spent in the city on the Seine.

With bated breath we listened to my uncle's descriptions or watched his mimicking of the mannerisms and eccentricities of the masters, mistresses and lesser gods of the French stage and letters. "I was a neophyte," said Kees, "watching the great and near-great come and go.

Henri de Toulouse Lautrec, who quaffed absinthe till he went insane, habitually boasted, not as you might expect, of his famous lithographs, but that he was the best swimmer in France . . . . One of my companions was Joris Karel Huysmans, the writer, whose family hailed from the Dutch city of Breda. Huysmans was a versatile fellow who worked in some government department. After years of struggle he reaped an immense success with his book on the miraculous cures at Lourdes . . . . Twice a year he walked on a pilgrimage from Paris to the Cathedral of Chartres. Each time he came back, his mind had taken on a more mystical and magical turn. He began to see visions and hear voices. Towards the end he joined the Catholic Church because an angel, he claimed to have met in the crypt of Chartres' Cathedral, advised conversion as a cure for cancer of the mouth . . . ."

From Kees we learned of Emile Zola's inability to pronounce the letter "r," a speech defect in so voluble a talker that threw the company at the Café Montmartre into uncontrollable fits of hilarity. Auguste Rodin accused Zola of obscenity and pornography. "Some day," Rodin warned the author, "you will be taken off the pot and have your nose rubbed into what you deposit there." Who'd have thought that Alphonse Daudet was so much of a prude that he refused to discuss Victor Hugo because he suspected the Olympian of sleeping with his servant girls while in exile on the isle of Guernsey.

"Did you ever see Renan?" we asked.

"Just once, but I wish I hadn't . . . . The moment he walked into the café everybody rose. He had been to the theater, perhaps for the last time in his life. I was aghast at his appearance . . . . The mark of death was upon him . . . . His breath came in quick, painful gasps. He walked with difficulty, leaning heavily on a stick. His body and legs were swollen out of all proportion by the dropsy. His face was disfigured by a hideous rash. He wasn't a pretty sight . . . ."

"And Sarah Bernhardt, did you see her?"

"From a great distance, yes, from the last seat in the topmost gallery of the Porte Saint-Martin theater. She was playing *Cleopatra* the night I saw her. Her voice, *la voix d'or de Sarah*, and her emotional acting, held that large audience spellbound. There was such fire and passion in that woman that she seemed almost superhuman, divine or demonic, I do not know which. She seemed to me the incarnation of the Orient, a magnificent odalisque from *The Thousand and One Nights* . . . ."

"A Greek goddess!" Yetze suggested eagerly.

"No, not Greek. Everything about that woman was Jewish, her eyes, her undulating gait, her drawl over the syllables; a woman of languor and sensuousness, of fierce passions and the tenderest smile . . . . With hundreds of others I waited at the stage door to see her at close range. She was smoking a cigarette when she came out and I noticed she was loaded with jewels, rings with precious stones on all her fingers . . . . It was the smoking habit which killed her in the end. She smoked one cigarette after the other, all day long . . . ."

Of one of Kees' Parisian demigods, I myself retain a vivid personal impression: I mean of Georges Clemenceau, the "Tiger of France." During the most agonizing months of the First World War when France, with two million killed, was bleeding to death, and Clemenceau, as prime minister, just in the nick of time, snatched victory from defeat by his ruthless iron will power, I often thought back to what Kees told us of the role the Tiger played in Parisian society two decades before.

Clemenceau then had a reputation as one of the biggest lady-killers. "He was easily the best-dressed man in the capital," said Kees, "an elegant dandy with dark wavy hair. All the women were in love with this Casanova with the Mongolian slit eyes and jutting cheekbones. Whenever he visited the Comédie Française or the Odéon, and ostentatiously took his seat in a box near the stage, the women in the audience would leap to their feet in one spontaneous gesture of admiration and give him a standing ovation.

"Still, I don't think it was pure admiration they felt for the little radical politician he was then," Kees would add. "The women were actuated by a peculiarly feminine trait of bloodthirstiness and sadism. For when he appeared at the theater, Clemenceau, as like as not, had just come back from fighting a duel in the Parc des Princes. The boulevard press kept the Parisians closely informed about his love affairs. When he took his seat in the theater it was taken as a signal that he had once more successfully disposed of a rival in love. . . . "

Though still walking around and barking out his sarcastic bitter comments on men and events, Clemenceau was a dying man when I saw him on April 16, 1926, at number 8 Rue Franklin where he had his town residence. Nobody, it was said in newspaper circles, ever got an interview from the Tiger. But when Louis Weitzenkorn, the feature editor of the New York *World*'s Sunday edition, insisted, in view of Clemenceau's declining health, that I get an article from him by hook or by crook on the saddest episode of his life, his defeat for the presidency of France, I took a desperate chance. . . .

"I'm sick," he growled and snapped at me as I was ushered into his study by the famous Albert Brabant, his chauffeur and butler. "I just recovered from an attack of uremia. . . . The next attack will finish me. . . . Are you glad? Some people are! . . . Have you ever been to Stamford, Connecticut? I was a teacher at Miss Aitkin's girls' school there. . . . The best three years of my life. . . . First I tried to practice medicine in New York, but couldn't make a go of it. . . . The medical board insisted that I start my studies from scratch. . . . I would willingly go back to America if they would have me. But they won't. . . . "

"Why wouldn't they, Monsieur le Président?* I'm sure you'd get a marvelous reception. . . . "

"Young man, I'm an atheist. Isn't that enough reason in America? . . . By the way, let me tell you once and for all: I give no interviews. . . . Never did in my life. . . . If there is one creature I detest it is what you call the feature writer, the man who writes no matter what, no matter how . . . for money. When I was a journalist I wrote my own opinions on men and events. I didn't go around fraudulently picking other people's brains. . . . I was a damn fool in many respects, I know, but a garbage collector, that: *jamais!* . . . "

"That's just it, Monsieur le Président, our opinions don't matter very much. It's your opinion that counts. . . . I'm sure all the world would still like to hear your view on the present situation with Germany falling down on her reparation payments. . . . Why weren't there some clauses with teeth inserted in the peace treaty?"

"Why not? You ask me: why not? *Sacrebleu!* What a question! Figure it out for yourself. . . . What could I do? At the Versailles peace conference I sat between Jesus Christ and Napoleon Bonaparte.** I couldn't get a word in edgeways . . . . Lloyd George, the imbecile, thought the Boche a decent fellow. . . . Your Woodrow Wilson imagined he was doing God a favor in dealing gently with a defeated enemy. . . . What kind of a God is it anyway who needs the help of a man like Woodrow Wilson? . . . For my part I held and still hold that there are forty million Germans too many in this world. . . . They should be disposed of quietly. . . . It still could be

*President, that is, of the Council of Ministers.
**Thomas Woodrow Wilson and David Lloyd George.

done and the quicker the better. . . . The Boche is born standing to attention. . . . I am absolutely certain that he'll march again the moment he
hears the whip crack. . . ."

"A second world war?"

A second war, that's certain! And a third, too, if we let them! They
think of nothing but revenge. . . . That's the essence of their mentality:
revanchisme. . . . But I shouldn't talk so much. I just came back from the
grave. . . . I still feel like a ghost. . . .

"The papers say that it is a miracle that I came through. As usual, the
papers don't know what they are talking about. . . . The truth is that I was
as good as dead. In fact I *was* dead. . . . I was in coma for twelve days.
When I came out of coma the other day, I remembered that I had been
right up to the gate of heaven. The reason you see me here tonight is that
I couldn't get into the place. . . . I asked a little angel at the entrance to
let me in. . . . She was a pretty appetizing dish, *midinette* type, you know
the kind. . . .

" '*Citoyen*,' she objected in shocked embarrassment, 'you can't get into
heaven unless you first confess your sins. . . . ' So I said: 'Do me a favor,
mignonne, go in there and find me a priest. For the pleasure of being in
your company I'll do anything that's reasonable and even unreasonable.'

"*Ma foi*, she stayed away a hell of a long time and came back all
abashed. . . . She hadn't been able to find a single priest. . . . There you
have the explanation of my resurrection: No priests in heaven. . . . Are you
surprised? . . . I'm not! . . . "

Almost as far back as I can remember Kees took me along on his painting and sketching trips during the summer vacation. At first we merely
wandered about in the immediate vicinity of Gorcum; later we went
further south crossing the great rivers Rhine, Meuse and Scheldt and the
borders into Belgium. On two or three occasions, my schoolmates,
Dalmaden, Brandt and Sissingha accompanied us and then our joy was
complete. Then we lived those heavenly days that can never die because
they awakened our sense of wonder and the feeling that all things belong
together, man and sky, land and sea.

Those Flanders' fields soon to be drenched in blood were then still
full of charm, a lovely country, growing lovelier the deeper we penetrated;

in the cities stately old mansions and guild halls, museums and cathedrals, outside the most wonderful gardens in the world and those "meadows of astounding green" so frequently mentioned by Maurice Maeterlinck, one of that country's greatest sons. We spent the nights at rural hostelries, in rooms so clean, adorned with curtains so dainty and smelling so fresh as if the beekeepers had perfumed them with the aroma of honey. We were up with the break of day and, looking out, saw how beautiful were the surroundings of our inns: hedges of elms and wild roses, noble limes and groves of chestnuts, fields full of clover with the wine-colored poppies running like a ribbon along the edge of ripening wheat fields.

When I think back of those visits to Flanders, I know what Gogol meant when he wrote about his village in the Ukraine: "What rapture, what intoxication, what splendor can be found on one single summer day in Dikanka!" Dreamy, languid was the atmosphere, scented with the sweet smell of honeysuckle and new-mown hay. At noon the sun covered the world with a quivering gloss of gold and emerald. The warmth was of that beneficent brooding quality which one suspects to have been the essence of the creative spirit moving upon the face of the waters in the beginning of time. Above our heads, the immeasurable ocean of blue, blown up into a voluptuous cupola, looked down on the earth with passionate friendliness. Towards twilight a scarcely perceptible breeze tempted the leaves and flowers to whisper of the mysterious nostalgia in their hearts. Sometimes when the moon rode high, Kees awakened us to come to the window and look into an orchard and see the rain-freshened cherries like a mass of blood-red rubies glistening amongst the dark foliage.

Many times, just before sunset, the birds gave us a concert, a riot of song and melody, yet infinitely harmonious. So forceful and agitated and full of trills were their voices that it seemed inconceivable for such small lungs to produce so great a volume of sound. In a flash the music stopped and the silence of night descended. Then one nightingale, taking advantage of the stillness, stole a march on his feathered friends by giving us a solo so rich and pure as to make us stand in hushed wonder.

Every man, woman or child we met, as if incapable of holding down the elation and wonder in their hearts, had something to tell us. I recall one red-haired country priest calling out from a distance as we approached: "*On dirait que la terre palpite d'un amour béat!*" He swept off his shovel hat to the strangers, wiped his face and then shook hands all around. "One would say that the earth throbs with blessed love. . . .Growing weather, messires and friends, growing weather! D'you feel it? How rich will be the harvest in Flanders' land! O! . . . "

In ancient Palestine, we are told, the Galileans were the most loquacious of the Jews. In the Netherlands it's the Flemings who carry off the palm in this respect. Whether they know you or not, they shake hands and seem to feel under obligation to pour out a flood of information on their personal affairs, taking it for granted that, as a newly discovered member of the family, you will be interested to hear what aunts and uncles and nieces and nephews have lately been up to. When we entered some country tavern or other for a glass of beer in the afternoon, a sudden silence would fall upon the assembled patrons. Surprise and shyness lasted but a minute. Soon there would be friendly nods in our direction. The least gesture of acknowledgment on our part brought three, four, five men to our table. When they discovered that we spoke their language, their satisfaction knew no bounds. We had to tell them everything, for the curiosity of these external chatterboxes is as inexhaustible as their joy of life.

On Sundays after Mass, we discovered, the Flemings go traveling, preferably by train. The Yperites go to Langemarck and those of Langemarck go to Ypres, and so on all over the country the excursions get under way. What makes a train ride on a hot Sunday afternoon so enjoyable? To see the sights? To sit packed tight like herrings on the hard seats in a third-class train compartment? All this discomfort was merely preludial. What they looked forward to was the moment when the train from Ypres would pass the train from Langemarck and the two would halt for a few moments at opposite platforms at some jerkwater station en route. Everybody hung from the compartment windows calling greetings, waving hats and handkerchiefs. If there was a short wait, the two trains discharged their passengers in a minute and an impromptu mass meeting got under way on the crowded platform. Whether anybody knew anybody else did not matter at all; it was so good to shake hands, to say a few words or laugh at each others' jokes, most of which, I am afraid, would not bear repetition in milady's drawing room. For the Flemings are people of frank speech; they never put a fig leaf before their mouths. . . .

We were fortunate enough to strike Bruges one evening when a religious procession was passing through the Grand' Place. The gas light in the street lamps was dimmed and the square plunged into darkness. A huge crowd had assembled, but not a sound was heard save for the silvery tinkle of the carillon playing an old Netherlands hymn dating from the sixteenth century war with Spain. Following the priests in full canonicals, and a bishop under a golden baldaquin, came the young women and girls of Bruges, walking with utmost reverence and piety. All wore a dress of peculiar cut and dark shade made rather low at the neck where the somberness was relieved by a touch of color given by the gold and coral necklaces. Each person in the procession carried a taper protected by a thin glass cover in the shape of a bowl to shield the flame against the breeze that blows from the North Sea at eventide.

Because of the prevailing darkness and the somber hue of the girls' clothing, one saw virtually nothing of the processionists but their heads. Each head was covered with a cap of sheerest white lace; five hundred madonnas walking by silently. The scene was so breathtaking in its ethereal purity that it might have served Dante for a description of a street in Paradise. Suddenly all the people in the square, accompanied or led by the carillon, burst into song, the bystanders as well as the priests and the women in the procession: "Dear Lady Maria, dear Mother of Flanders!"

When the procession had passed the street lights came back. Then the booths became visible where the white-aproned bakers baked waffles, crullers and *beignets.* Through the square was wafted the savory smell of the dishes carried by the waiters and waitresses to the tables of the sidewalk restaurants.

"Here you'll find steaks and roasts, not too rare, not too fat, but tender as rose petals," an advertisement announced with the added information by the proprietor: "My name is Jerome, my wife's name Greta!" The poultry to which Kees treated us that evening, it was either chicken or duck, swam in wine sauce. The sauce was mixed with spices, cloves and nutmeg, tiny fresh carrots, tender June peas, strips of ham and calf's liver, roosters' combs, sweetbreads, and other heavenly delicacies.

While were were eating we scarcely noticed that another procession got under way in the Grand' Place though there was nothing official about this one. It was made up of a long chain of tightly interlaced pairs of lovers wending its way to *'t Minnewater,* the Lake of Love, those still waters where the swans glide under the bridges between the ivy-covered walls of medieval towers.

By September we started on the homeward journey, sometimes passing through Ghent and Antwerp, sometimes through Brussels. In the town of Oude God, we witnessed an archery contest and in St. Niklaas a ham-eating contest between two opposing teams who had both brought their brass band along. These contests were the preliminaries to the annual *Kermesse Flamande* than which there is nothing more gaily hilarious. Unfortunately, we could not stay to watch one of these *kermesses* since they commence in the latter part of September when school was waiting.

The weather, too, became chilly and the morning mists hid the world behind a luminous white veil. With the first rays of daylight we heard the thrushes, hummingbirds and finches sing their magnificats as they flew from the fog banks above the ditches by the roadside. Straight into the sky "the bravely singing larks" winged their way to the golden door of the many mansions. . . .

One year we walked the last part of the homeward journey in the company of a group of Flemish peasants going to Holland to seek work on some dyke-building project. One of the peasants, a strong, yellow-haired customer, was so sad at the prospect of leaving Flanders that he was crying.

"You love your native land that much?" Kees asked him.

"Yes," replied the man, "the thought of leaving Flanders breaks my heart. . . . But I give myself courage by pinching my own behind now and then and saying: 'Dear behind of mine, you may be glad that you belong to a man who will some day carry you back to Flanders again!'"

2. Father Adriaan

1. Grandfather, the Reverend
Pieter van Paassen

3. Mother Antonia

4. The author as a soldier in the Canadian Army, World War I

5. Pierre van Paassen in the garden in St.-Germain-en-Laye, outside of Paris, 1929

CHAPTER II

Frisian Interlude

IN THE SUMMER of 1911 I was suddenly withdrawn from Gorcum's Latin school and taken to Franeker, a town located in Frisia or Friesland, the kingdom's northernmost province. The reason for my departure was my father's financial situation. It had never been very flourishing, but about that time it took such a disastrous dip that he doubted his ability to continue paying my tuition fees. When notified of the sorry turn of events, my grandfather, who was a pastor in Franeker, took the first train he could catch. He refused to entertain the idea of my giving up the study of the classical languages since this would mean an interruption in my initial preparations for the ministry. After a day or so of discussion and argument he took me with him on the understanding that he would personally tutor me during the ensuing year.

For once I traveled in grand style through the whole length of the country in a first-class railway compartment with red plush cushions. In the steamer on the Zuyder Sea we had a private cabin. The two hours it took for the crossing I spent on deck. There I saw the first American I ever laid eyes on. The man was pointed out to me by a deck steward: "Look sharp now, there is a fellow with a gold tooth in his mouth. . . . He comes from America!"

I looked in amazement at the transatlantic phenomenon, though in truth I must say that there wasn't much to look at. The man hung over the railing in the throes of a violent attack of seasickness. I went to notify my grandfather of my discovery and he immediately left the cabin to accompany me on deck. After he looked over the green-faced stranger with his eyes rolling in his head, he called on the steward to bring the sick American a cup of hot bouillon. "First thing to do," he told the waiter, "is to weigh down this gentleman's stomach." The Yankee gratefully accepted the proferred mug of beef extract and soon recovered sufficiently to inform us that during his entire voyage on the broad Atlantic in a raging storm, he had not experienced the slightest discomfort, while on this small inland sea he thought that his last hour had struck. "How come?" he asked my grandfather. "How come?"

The *dominé* explained that the shallowness of the Zuyder Sea in comparison with the ocean's depth, and the choppiness of the weather, which caused the steamer to dip and plunge by fits and starts, lay perhaps at the bottom of the stranger's physical distress. "Perhaps," he answered. "Perhaps!"

I listened avidly to their conversation, for it was the first time I heard English spoken outside a classroom. As was almost inevitable, the two men's talk before long turned to the subject of religion. I don't remember what particular phrase brought it on, but all at once the stranger and my grandfather were shaking hands and nodding their heads and calling each other "brother." I also learned that in his younger years my grandfather had received a call to a newly founded pulpit in the city of Pella in the state of Iowa. Had he accepted, I dare not speculate as to where I would have come in. . . .

Franeker, the town where I took up residence, once boasted a university. René Descartes, the philosopher, who coined the phrase *cogito ergo sum*, "I think, therefore I exist," was one of its professors. In Franeker were also several renowned publishing houses where many of the most radical pamphlets and tracts, which prepared the way for the French Revolution, were printed and then smuggled into France. Franeker's collegians held so many demonstrations against the French usurpation of the Netherlands, that "the tyrant," as they called Napoleon, ordered them drafted into the imperial army and closed the university.

At the parsonage I lodged in the *dominé's* study, a long low-ceilinged, rather narrow room in the rear on the first floor with one window at the end looking down into a small square or court with lime trees planted *en carré*. On the opposite side of the walled-in square stood the church where my grandfather ministered. It was through this court that he walked on Sunday mornings garbed in his black gown, preceded by six frock-coated Elders who all bore typical Frisian names: Bergema, Popta, Botha, Pettinga, Jellema and Havinga.

The solemn procession entered the church through "the narrow gate," which was actually so called. The main entrance lay on another street.

But you could also see a part of the church's interior through an oblong window, a mere slit in the wall, located on the second floor of the parsonage. Though he seldom climbed the stairs to his study on the first floor, the *dominé* went up and down the two staircases to his lookout post at least half a dozen times each Sunday morning before the service. He was nervous, he said. He counted the number of worshipers and five minutes later returned to verify his earlier calculations.

I slept in the study, though not in an ordinary bed. At the other end of the room, opposite the window, was a built-in closet, known as a *bedstede*. You opened the two small doors at about the height of a man's shoulders, took out a small ladder of the kind one uses to climb into the upper berth of a Pullman sleeping car, and dived in. I say "dive," for there was no mattress, only an enormous soft feather tick. Above your head, at the end of a cord fastened to the *bedstede*'s ceiling, hung a horseshoe-shaped contraption of mahogany. By seizing hold of this thing you could pull yourself up from the depths of the feather bed into a sitting position. On the farther side of the deep closet ran a shelf with a place for a candlestick, an alarm clock and a certain household utensil known in French as *un pot de chambre*.

The *dominé* drew up a schedule of studies for the entire year and then left me strictly to my own devices. "If you really have a passion for study," he remarked, "you'll do it without prompting. If you have not, even the best teacher cannot be of much avail."

He did his own writing and reading at a roll-top desk in the living room downstairs where a stove burnt virtually the whole year around. But the good man never sat really comfortable on his swivel chair. He merely managed to hang on, perilously perched on its uttermost edge. The largest part of the seat was taken up by Castor, an ancient, toothless fox terrier, who growled every time my grandfather stirred.

When not lying in the back of the *dominé's* chair, Castor busied himself rubbing his body against the rungs, for he suffered from a perpetual "dry itch." This infirmity involved me in a great deal of extra work. My grandfather sent me to the local homeophatic pharmacy to fetch a bottle of tincture of arnica, a greenish liquid which, under his direction, I poured into a saucer. By dipping my fingertips into the tincture and rubbing it on Castor's back twice a day, a new coat of hair was supposed to sprout from the old dog's back. The result was the very opposite. He lost more and more hair till the veterinarian one day, to my infinite relief, pronounced him incurable.

In my grandparents' bedroom, also located on the ground floor, stood two enormous fourposters with green curtains hanging from the canopies. Towards evening, my grandmother Adriana (Yana for short), with the assistance of a Frisian girl, Frouke, laid a wood fire in the bedroom in order, as she never failed to explain, to draw the moisture out. In my room was neither stove nor fireplace. I sought to make up for this deficiency by wrapping myself in a voluminous velvet pulpit gown, which I found hanging in a closet, the abandoned property of one of my grandfather's predecessors. My overcoat lay on my lap and I covered my head with a blanket. This left my feet and nose still freezing on days and nights when the wind stood from the north and shook the house to its very foundations.

The other two members of the household, both females, were Lena and the aforementioned Frouke. Lena spoke only Frisian, no Dutch. She was a dour-faced, powerful, broad-hipped though good-natured woman with a lace cap on her head. Widowed within a year after her marriage, she had come to the parsonage at the age of twenty-five and had remained ever since, forty odd years in all. She referred to my father, his brothers and sisters as "our children," but made no bones about it that my father was the most troublesome from a kitchen superintendant's point of view. Her own son, an only child, served as a cashier at the local postal savings bank. Without fail he and his wife and children visited Lena on Sundays to partake of the noon hour dinner and stayed till evening when they, like all of us, drank hot chocolate with wafers of Lena's own confection.

Lena commanded universal respect as a cook. In France she would easily have been a *cordon bleu*, though she had never followed any classes in cooking. Her pears braised in red currant juice with some sugar and a dash of cinnamon which she served with the roast or beefsteak were literally out of this world. On Sundays she often made chocolate soufflé with a vanilla sauce for dessert. I think she put a few drops of liqueur, *kirsch* or *cointreau*, in the sauce to give it a special flavor.

When my grandfather finished dinner prepared by Lena he used to say: "I don't expect to eat a better meal in heaven . . . . God bless the cook!"

And then the bread she baked! Its golden brown crust you could hear crickle and crackle as the Emperor Marcus Aurelius says he liked to hear it sixteen hundred years before. The first loaf of the weekly batch came to the breakfast table on Saturday mornings when Lena rose at an ungodly hour to bake.

I often watched her knead on Friday night and place the huge bowl containing the dough behind the cookstove, which burnt all night on that occasion. Not the slightest draft of air was permitted to blow into the kitchen lest the dough catch cold and fail to rise. There was something of a ritualistic flavor about Lena's preparations. Bread was something sacred to her; not a single crust was ever to be wasted or thrown away. She performed the task of kneading with reverence, solemnly and deliberately. While slapping and rolling the dough with her bare arms she muttered all sorts of incantations, both pagan and Christian.... "Do good to them that eat thee," she would address the dough. "Make them strong, wise, *uprjucht* [Frisian for upright]. Do what thou art expected to do .... In the name of the Father and of the Son and of the Holy Ghost. . . ."

"And no 'amen,' Lena?"

"Oh, no, you will say 'amen' if you are a good boy, please!"

Frouke was of a different nature. She was an outright pagan, but a lovely one. On the day when I arrived at the parsonage, it was she who opened the door. She threw her arms around my grandfather's neck and kissed him as if she hadn't seen him for ages. Divining the girl's intention, my grandmother quickly stepped between us, so that Frouke could not reach me and I missed the best part of her welcome.

For the occasion of our reception she had woven a blue ribbon through her long tresses and on her head wore a crown of flowers from the fields. In fact she had placed fresh-cut flowers all through the house, on the tables, on the window sills, in the hallway, everywhere. Even old Lena had some corn flowers and poppies stuck in her lace cap.

Frouke's big blue eyes flew with wonderment from my collar to my shoes and back again and then laughed so wholeheartedly that everyone was carried away by her merriment.

She was just eighteen years of age when I arrived. She was not in the least prudish and knew everything. We understood each other at once. Very tall, she had orange-colored hair, perfect even teeth, and a skin glowing with health and beauty. She had duly followed the courses in my grandfather's catechism class, but the *dominé* confirmed her as a member of the Church without bothering to give her the usual examination.

"There is no use plaguing this dear child with these intricate theological questions," he said. "She doesn't understand them, and never will! . . . In that girl is the joy of life which is the possession of the pure in heart . . . . Nothing should be added!"

Frouke was not really a servant girl. The Frisian people do not like the expression and its connotations. She was an equal among equals, what they call a *Haustochter* in Switzerland, a daughter of the house. Her parents were burghers than which there is no higher title amongst a people who call themselves "the Free Frisians." She was in the parsonage as an apprentice to Lena; in other words, she was learning to cook.

Once a week, on Saturday night, I had a bath, though not in a bathroom. I don't think there was at that time a bathroom in any of the private houses. There was a public bathhouse and there may have been a bathroom in the hospital, but in that institution a bath was still referred to as hydro-therapy.

In preparation for my bath, a large wooden tub, which hung suspended close to the ceiling when not in use, was lowered by a pulley to the kitchen floor and filled with hot water by Lena.

"Get undressed and get in, the water is right," she would order me as once she ordered my father and his brothers and sisters.

The soft soap I used, green in color and lye its chief ingredient, was a gluey paste. If one particle of it got into your eyes, it stung and smarted as if someone had dropped in a cup of vitriol.

Lena scrubbed my back with a brush so hard that it would probably kill today's perfumed poodles if ever these beasties were subjected to such inhuman treatment. I howled like a soul in distress. "Shut up! Do you want to waken the whole neighborhood?" Lena rebuked me. At the same time, without any warning, she would smack me on the head with the wooden side of the brush.

The soap may have been green, but your body was not after a scrubbing of that kind. Nor were you that delicate roseate pink which Zola so tantalizingly describes in *Nanette*. You were red, violently red, as if a layer of skin had been peeled off.

"Give it to him, Lena! Scrub him till he yells!" Frouke would call from

the passage which ran from the kitchen to the rooms where the two women were lodged. "Do you need any help?"

"You stay out of here," Lena returned, "at least till he gets his shirt on!"

"But I want to see him without his shirt," Frouke called back.

"I can tell you what he looks like," Lena shouted. "He looks like a
skinned pig. But clean, my dear, oh, he is as clean as a whistle!" With that
Lena heaved me bodily from the tub, and I weighed 170 pounds, just as
I do today.

At the approach of winter my grandmother reinforced the covers on my
feather bed with a remarkable invention of her own. She stuffed a worn-
out floor rug into a red-flowered linen sack and called it the eiderdown.
With the aid of Frouke and myself, she hoisted this monstrosity into the
bedstede and placed it on top of the covers. It was absolutely useless; no
warmth whatever, just dead weight!

Passive support of this smothering quilt would have been about the only
physical exercise I engaged in were it not for the rubbing of Castor's back
and a daily promenade with the *dominé* on the town's old defense works.
Once upon a time, I presume, these *bolwerken** as they were called kept
out Scots, Picts, Vikings and other such bandit races. Now they were
transformed into a sort of elevated tree-lined parkway. When you walked
on the *bolwerken*, you looked down on one side into the town of Franeker.
On the other side ran a ship canal that circled the entire community.
Everyone of consequence in Franeker strolled on the *bolwerken* in the
afternoon. What happened there at nights I can only imagine, for I was
not permitted to leave the house after dark.

I soon became aware that the Frisian young ladies, after nodding their
heads in greeting to the *dominé*, did a lot of giggling behind our backs.

"Why do they snicker so much?" I asked my grandfather.

"They notice that you are a stranger," he replied. "But we'll fix this
quickly; you must learn the Frisian language."

"Don't they understand Dutch?"

"Of course they do. That's the language they learn at school. It's the
language of instruction here as everywhere else in the Netherlands. But
among themselves the Frisian people prefer to speak their own language.
As soon as you have acquired a few expressions, you may as well go out
and walk by yourself. You won't need me. You'll soon be talking with the

*The English word is bulwark. Unable to pronounce the word bulwark, the French,
as is their wont, gave it an exotic allure by calling it *boulevard*.

girls and you'll find that they are better teachers than any book or any amount of lessons in Frisian grammar that I can give. . . . By the way," he added, "you can start learning Frisian right away by attending church on Sunday evenings when I preach in Frisian. . . . "

Thus another subject was added to my already overloaded curriculum. But I have no regrets. It was fully worth the trouble.

On both sides of the *dominé's* study behind thick red baize curtains ran long rows of bookshelves. On the bottom shelves, like so many rocks of Gibraltar, stood the ponderous tomes of the no less ponderous Fathers of the Church, Calvin's *Institutes,* Luther's *Sermons* and *Table Talk,* Augustine's *City of God* and his *Confessions,* diverse encyclopedias, dictionaries and theological works, and one biblical *Concordance* of such enormous size and weight as would have taxed the strength of a Samson to shift it.

St. Augustine's *Confessions* is unquestionably one of the greatest books of all times; everything is in it, though the author, I found, is rather hard to follow at certain points as, for instance, where he debates the question whether women retain their sex after the resurrection. In another interesting passage the learned and sainted Bishop of Hippo tells of having seen—seen, with his own eyes, he says—certain living creatures who resembled man in every respect but one. These freaks, which, I trust, have happily become extinct, had only one eye, and this one eye was not Cyclopslike fixed in the middle of their foreheads, but in the middle of their breasts.

Other books followed from the opposite side of the room: Victor Hugo's novels, poems and speeches; Brantôme's volumes of court gossip; Jean Jacques Rousseau's works; Chateaubriand's *Memoirs from Beyond the Grave.* There was a whole section devoted to books dealing with the Oxford movement in which John Henry Newman, Keble and Pusey were the animating spirits. I must have read Newman's story of his conversion to the Catholic Church a dozen times, and still read it occasionally as one of the most moving and noble battles of conscience ever waged.

By contrast I read Carlyle who contemptuously dismissed Newman's philosophy as "the product of the brains of a rabbit." Carlyle's *French Revolution* can never be praised enough. With his seven volumes on Frederick the Great it's a different matter; I found them a monstrous monument of boredom and triviality, a sorry attempt to curry favor with Goethe, a bootlicking job if ever there was one. But then when Carlyle wrote his

Frederick, the old "moral desperado," for so Matthew Arnold called him, had grown bitter, reactionary, anti-Semitic and perhaps schizophrenic.

My favorite historian was Michelet. He was carried away to a point of exaltation by his love for France and his admiration of the French character. Michelet not merely wrote history; he plunged into it and fought its battles all over again. To Michelet the French people was the hero of world history. France's proclamation of freedom, equality and brotherhood was written and sealed with her own blood. . . .

Naturally, I read Tolstoy from the great novels *War and Peace* and *Anna Karenina* to the pamphlets with their serious call. Though the sage of Yasnaya Polyana had died the year before there was still a feeling current in Europe, even in an out-of-the-way small Frisian town like Franeker, that with Tolstoy's physical disappearance all mankind had suffered a grievous loss.

One of my most cherished memories is that afternoon, a week or ten days after Tolstoy's death, when the common people of my home town, the workers and clog-wearing proletariat, honored Tolstoy's memory with a procession and a mass meeting on the football field. Though we knew that we would be heavily punished for staying away from school and walking behind the trade-union band with anarchists, socialists, avant-gardists, proletarian poets and other social raggamuffins, the poorest of the poor, my schoolmate Ary Brandt and I followed the procession with the band playing: "The Flowers of the Forest," and, on the rain-soaked field (every church and hall having been refused), *Dit is ons heilig ideaal,* "This then is our sacred ideal. . . ."

My grandfather said: "Tolstoy is the last of the prophets. If his fate is to be that of all the prophets before him, that is, if no heed is paid to his warnings, the human race will, perhaps in our time yet, stand face to face with the prospect of total destruction, self-inflicted destruction."

This was hard to understand for a seventeen year old boy, and I certainly do not pretend that I understood the meaning of Tolstoy's message at that time. I heard my grandfather and his colleagues and friends argue the point whether Tolstoy was a Christian at all and not merely, as the more orthodox called him, a "Jesuanist" for his rejection of Christ's divinity. To some the Russian author appeared an anarchist and an abominable heretic. Yet I could not, however much I searched, detect the least trace of antireligious or even anti-Christian sentiment in him. He thought more of the Sermon on the Mount, and especially the text about not resisting evil as the pith and marrow of Jesus' teaching, than all our divines put together.

We were on the whole but imperfectly informed about the circumstance which caused Tolstoy, at the height of his glory as the greatest novelist of the time, to throw away all he had gained by way of fame, reputation and wealth.

The sharpness of Tolstoy's powers of observation made this great religious socialist regard nothing as more damnable than the factual inequality in which men live. Because he recognized that it is, generally speaking, the riches of the few which empoverish and degrade the vast majority of men (and countries), the responsibility weighed so heavily on his conscience, as the owner of a landed estate, that his position became impossible and he fled from it.

Nowadays it is almost customary to say that Tolstoy has become antiquated, that his passion for nonviolence does not belong and does not fit in our time. Still it was through the power of nonresistance to evil that Gandhi changed the destiny of his people in India. It was in Gandhi that Tolstoy's heart triumphed over the world. And as to being antiquated, how is it that Tolstoy's books, also those on the Kingdom of God, are published and read in the millions in Russia?

Two of the books in the library dealt with conditions in the Congo when that country, before becoming a Belgian colony, was still the privately owned domain of King Leopold II. The stories about the Congo made my blood alternately boil with indignation and freeze with horror. First came Arthur Conan Doyle's *Atrocities in the Congo*, and then Mark Twain's satire entitled *King Leopold Talks with Himself*.

Conan Doyle wrote his Congo book immediately after exonerating the South African Boers of inhumanity in their treatment of British prisoners of war. What he said about the Congo stunned the civilized world into speechless horror. He wrote that he saw thousands of men and women with a hand or foot cut off in penalty for not bringing in enough rubber from the forests. Heaps of skulls and skeletons lay outside the deserted Congolese villages, the survivors having fled into the brush where they perished by the tens of thousands for lack of food.

He related how hard-drinking white soldiers, rubber dealers and slave drivers, just to pass the time of day, sat around on camp chairs watching and laughing as batches of black men were tied to the trees. Dynamite caps with fuses attached were inserted into their rectums and exploded. Black women had the dynamite sticks inserted elsewhere! . . . And this was going on day after day, month after month.

Here is one of Mark Twain's observations: "If the innocent Congo blood spilt by King Leopold was put in pails and the pails were placed side by side, there would be a row of blood-filled pails 2000 miles long. . . ."

In the light of that inhuman episode of colonial history, we may well marvel at the relative mildness of the upheaval which followed the double-cross of 1960 when, by a cynical flaunting of solemn covenants, the rich Katanga province with its rubber plantations, copper, uranium and diamond mines, was allowed, and most likely urged, to secede from the rest of the country shortly after the Congo gained its independence. The Union Minière, a Belgo-Franco-American holding company for a dozen big business enterprises became the real owner of Katanga. By taking Katanga out of the Congolese confederacy, the other provinces were reduced to stagnation and poverty. They revolted and threatened to destroy all the Union Minière's properties if Katanga wasn't brought back into the Congolese union.

Rather than looking for, and, of course, finding plenty of evidence of Russian interference, our correspondents and newscasters, who roamed the Congo in all directions, would have found it much easier to get the facts straight and in proportion had they taken the trouble to consult a few of the Congolese grandmothers.

In Franeker's parsonage nobody was permitted into the living room on Thursdays. On that day the *dominé* was not to be disturbed: he prepared his sermon or sermons for the following Sunday. In the morning he wrote them out by hand, in the afternoon he memorized them, and paced up and down, reciting out loud what he had written. Before he started his pacing exercise Yana entered the room to turn up the edges of her "good rug" lest my grandfather's marching feet wear out the carpet. This is known in German as *Teppich fressen*, chewing the carpet to pieces. Adolf Hitler was said to be a *Teppichfresser*. This doesn't mean that he lay on the floor biting and chewing the rug. The Fuehrer marched up and down the room just as my grandfather did, though meditating on quite different subjects, I dare say.

Driven to distraction by the sound of the monotonous rhythmic thump of her husband's shoes on the bare boards which could be heard all through that silent house, my grandmother went out on Thursday afternoons, thus affording Frouke and myself an opportunity to get a little better acquainted. One of my stratagems was to get her to pose for a drawing of the human form divine, on the false pretense that I knew how. . . .

I read by the light of a kerosene lamp. Does anyone today remember the kerosene lamp; how you had to trim the wick every few hours with a pair of scissors in order to prevent the lamp from smoking and the glass chimney turning as black as night?

When I came downstairs in the morning to wash my face and hands, I did so in the kitchen sink, the water in the earthenware jug in the dressing room upstairs having frozen to a solid block of ice.

"You've again read too long last night," my grandmother would say. How could she tell? My eyes and nostrils were filled with soot from the lamp's smoke.

One day I made a discovery in the library which gave me a first inkling of my grandfather's way of looking at life and society. Behind a row of books I found a certificate written on parchment stating that he had once been a member of a club or society known as "The Friends of the Human Race." When I showed him the document, he burst out laughing, but added quickly: "Put it back where you found it and don't let grandmother see it, for she doesn't trust the Friends of the Human Race."

"Then, who are they?"

"They are no more," he replied, "but once they were a fraternity at the university. . . . They called themselves after the Baron Anacharsis Cloots, who was known as *L'Orateur du Genre Humain,* 'The Orator [in defense] of the Human Race.' Although of Dutch origin, Cloots was a member of the French National Convention. He had made his way to France that he might live for freedom. In pursuit of freedom he lost his head under the guillotine. He was a martyr to idealism."

Far from being regarded as a youthful deviation, my grandfather's adherence to the Friends of the Human Race rendered him suspect of radicalism and republican ideas to the end of his life. The congregations thought it strange that he, like the Roman Catholic priests in Holland, though for a widely different reason, refused to have the national anthem sung in church. Nor would he recite the prescribed prayers for the members of the royal family, "although," as he often said, "they need them badly."

Anything with a nationalistic flavor did not belong in the service. The Church was universal, ecumenical; nationalism was a mangy beast that had no place in the house of God, the Father of all mankind. Republicanism, he held, with reference to Geneva and the United States of America, was the form of government best suited to a people professing the Protestant religion. He always spoke of America with pride, calling it "the empire of Calvin."

"If ever you were to visit America," I asked, "which site or locality would you most want to see? Would it be New York with its skyscrapers, its elevated and underground railways, its colossal bridges. . . or the Grand Canyon or Niagara Falls?"

"If I visited America," he replied, "I would most of all want to see the graves of the Pilgrims at Plymouth. I think that cemetery is one of the most sacred spots on earth. It should be a place of pilgrimage for Protestants from all over the world, just like Calvin's Geneva or Luther's Wittenberg. I think that in Plymouth I would perhaps feel something which the earliest settlers in the New World felt when they breathed their first breath of freedom; free at last from the yoke of the Old World and the old churches. . . . To live according to their own faith in freedom, what a glorious experience it must have been! . . . I am too old now, but if ever you cross the Atlantic," he continued, "always bear in mind that America's freedom and grandeur are the outcome of a great religious movement. . . . It is in America that the Reformation really came into its own. I have an almost religious veneration for America. . . ."

He was a man of the people, or, more exactly, he lived all his life amongst farmers, fishers and small-time merchants, but he was also a graduate of a renowned university.

"Once," he said, "in the first year of my ministry, I preached a sermon on the end of the world. The horrors of the Franco-Prussian War seemed to me an indication of the fulfillment of prophecy concerning earthquakes, upheavals, wars and rumors of war foreshadowing the end. . . . Do you know what happened?

"Some of the wealthiest members of my congregation, as a precautionary measure, withdrew their gold from the bank. The Elders were very angry with me. 'Say what you like in the pulpit,' they told me, 'but don't interfere with business.'"

"So you stopped talking of the wrath to come?"

"Yes, I apologized to the local consistory, but added that my mistake was pardonable inasmuch as the holy apostles themselves made precisely the same miscalculation in connection with the fall of Jerusalem in A.D. 70. They, too, predicted that the end of the world would come in their own time.... I never again tried to scare people with threats of doom or persuade them to live the good life by conditional promises of long life and material prosperity. That kind of preaching makes no sense, anyway. Experience proves that it is not the good who are rewarded. It's more often the other way around...."

His parishioners heaved a sigh of relief, he said, when he left off scaring them with the last judgment. They began to send him baskets of apples, pears, plums and other produce from their farms and orchards. In November, which is precisely called "Slaughter Month" in the Dutch language, he could count on at least half a dozen fine smoked hams safely hung in the attic, and sausages without end.

"Did you surrender your principles," I asked, "or change your opinions?"

"I did neither," he replied. "I discovered as you will discover some day that in these old Germanic countries, the people remain distant and aloof from the dogmas of Christianity. Oh, they are good people, no doubt! They are the best people on earth. They make virtually no profession of religious beliefs, but at heart they are deeply religious. They cannot tell you just what they believe, they cannot formulate their beliefs. But they do believe, for they have hope, faith and courage. There's an inner light in them. They look for a new day, and none of them doubts that a new man is coming on the scene, a loftier race.... The overwhelming majority of the Frisians vote socialist, like the Danes, their kinsmen a little further north.... There are also some intensely Calvinist congregations, though not many....

"There is a very low incidence of crime in Frisia," he went on. "Alcoholic consumption is lower per capita than anywhere else in the world. Their educational system is on par with that of the Scandinavian countries, that is to say, the best. But deep down in their hearts they don't know what to do with the Christian dogma. There is a secret, unavowed aloofness, aversion, I would almost say, to the mysticism and orientalism of Christianity...."

"Would they sooner have their old gods Hengist and Horsa back?" I asked him with a laugh.

"Of course not! But this is no laughing matter. Here in Frisia, more than anywhere else in the Germanic world, there is an awareness that the introduction of Christianity brought about a split, a fatal split in the European spirit. The imposition by the sword—wasn't Charlemagne who forced baptism on them called the Slaughterer of the Saxons?—the forcible imposition of a primitive, untenable system of metaphysics made a harmonious development of the Western spirit impossible. The imposition of an alien religion has prevented Europe from developing its own conscience. Europe is afflicted with a split conscience. It's an incurable wound. Christianity in its present form doesn't fit in here. . . . "

"Then what's the use of preaching the Christian doctrine?" I asked. "Why don't you close the church? What do you need Jesus for?"

"Don't talk so flippantly," he rebuked me as a note of sadness crept in his voice. "You mustn't say such things. Never must you say such things. Never forget what Jesus means to millions: hope of earth and joy of heaven. . . . There is no other figure in world history like the carpenter of Nazareth to have made men go out of themselves and beyond themselves. . . . I am aware, of course, that you are reading the books of historical criticism upstairs. I won't keep you away from them. After all, you must learn to make up your own mind. . . . It is quite well possible that as a result of the work of the historical critics Jesus will ultimately drop out of history altogether. . . . But the spirit of Christ will remain with us till the end of time even if it be under another name and other symbols. . . . As for me personally," he said with tears in his eyes, "if the Lord Jesus were to ask me what He once asked Peter: 'Lovest thou me?' I would answer like Peter: 'Lord, thou knowest all things. . . . Thou knowest that I love thee. . . . ' "

After a long pause he went on: "In my preaching I shun all dogmatic assertions. I merely try to penetrate the people's minds with ideas of justice, charity, freedom and beauty. This they understand. This appeals to their natural inclinations. Didn't I say that they are a good people? On the whole they are of a rectitude of mind and morals that should be an example to the rest of Europe. . . . " Some years ago, before World War II, I went over the yellowed, handwritten sermons by my grandfather, and found that he had indeed dwelt on those four points—justice, charity, freedom and beauty—with admirable clarity. His bundles of sermons were piously preserved in the family till the year 1944 when they were destroyed. One of the Germans' V-bombs misfired and exploded in the town of Zutphen above the parsonage of my uncle Cornelis who escaped as by miracle and is still living at this writing, though he lost his mind as a result of the tortures suffered during two years in the concentration camp of Dachau.

In the evening the *dominé* played checkers with Yana. She beat him without fail. He suspected her of cheating, and looked at her with a questioning sideway glance when she won. The game was played in their bedroom on a table standing right in front of the fireplace where the logs crackled and sent up bursts of ruddy flame. The room was as hot as an oven. It was the most comical scene in the world to see them deeply immersed in a game at the moment when a chance late caller rang the doorbell. They both jumped to their feet, and Castor barked for all he was worth in his croaking, worn-out voice.

"Frouke, oh, Frouke, help!" my grandmother would sing out into the hall. "Frouke, quick, remove the checkerboard, and put it under the bed!"

They didn't want the late caller, whoever he or she might be, to see them absorbed in so "worldly" an occupation as playing a game of checkers. Frouke, of course, did as she was asked, and left the room to open the front door. A moment later she re-entered announcing the visitor's name. "Shall I let him in here?" she would ask. "Yes, everything seems safe. . . . " my grandmother would say. She or her husband had quickly placed some edifying book on the table giving the impression that one of the two had been reading out loud to the other.

One evening there were three visitors, all three respectable citizens who stayed a long time. I came down to see if I could get a glass of hot milk for the temperature in the bookroom must have been near zero. Frouke was just carrying in a tray with a bottle of rum, sugar, glasses and a kettle of hot water. She was serving punch. The three gentlemen and my grandfather drank two large tumblers before saying a word. This was an almost ritualistic procedure: "No talk till the ship is loaded." Then after a lot of hemming and hawing, one of the visitors came to the point.

"Well," asked my grandfather, "what seems to be the trouble?"

"No trouble, no trouble at all, *dominé*," the man reassured. "But we thought we had better consult you on a matter of civic importance."

"Of civic importance? Good heavens, what can it be?"

"Well, some people in town are a little worried about the goings-on on the *bolwerken* at nights . . . the boys and girls, you understand. . . ."

"On a night like this? Who would venture out in ice-cold weather like this?"

"Oh, but they do, *dominé*, they do! The weather makes no difference to the young ones. . . ."

"Love is strong, isn't it?"

"It's stronger than death, *dominé!*"

"But why come to me? Hadn't you better see the burgomaster or the police?"

"Well, we thought we'd better see you first. The right-wing dissenters, you see, are talking of hiring a midnight missionary to keep an eye on the boys and girls."

"What do you say: a midnight missionary?"

"Yes, so they are called. They have midnight missionaries in the big cities."

"They get beaten up," said my grandfather. "I read of their exploits in the out-of-town papers. It's outright provocation to send a snooper like that into every little corner of the parks. Where is a poor boy going to take his girl for a little quiet *tête-à-tête*? Are we to banish love?"

"Pieter," interrupted my grandmother, utterly scandalized at her husband's words, "how can you talk that way? Is that an attitude to take for a minister of religion?"

"Yana," he came back, "I wish you would get me some more hot water and sugar. I like plenty of sugar in my rum toddy."

When Yana left the room, he told his visitors: "Gentlemen, I don't think it's as grave as you think. We all were young once. I know what goes on. You know what goes on. It has been going on since the year one, and even before. The boys are good practical Frisians, aren't they? Have you ever heard of a good Frisian buying a cat in the bag? . . ."

But there was my grandmother back already. And the glasses were filled once more. The visitors drank two more tumblers.

"It's a beastly cold night," said my grandfather, "people should keep warm as best they can. Shouldn't they?"

"We see what you mean, *dominé*," put in one of the visitors. "By the way, this is excellent rum."

"The very best," my grandfather agreed.

"So, no midnight missionaries, eh?" asked another man who had been silent till then.

"Only think what an evil reputation this town would get if it were to import one of those human bloodhounds. I shudder when I think of the violence that may result, not to speak of the broken hearts and the frustration. What a sad prospect! God forbid!"

The men nodded their heads, emptied their glasses and went their way rejoicing.

"Those old hypocrites came only to drink *domine's* rum," remarked Frouke to me after she let the visitors out. "What do they know what happens on the *bolwerken*, anyway?"

"Do you know what goes on, Frouke?"

"Sure, I do!"

"What then?"

"Nothing really, not on the *bolwerken* at least!"

"Where is the best place?"

"In the meadows beyond the canal. That's where the haystacks stand and the fairies dance, though not in wintertime. They dance in the moonlight on warm evenings. Wait till next summer and I'll take you there one night. . . ."

But that promise was never fulfilled. When the next summer came around I was far, far away. . . .

It must have been around that time of heavy frost that we had a burglar. Not in the house, but in the courtyard. I heard a noise just after I had crawled under the aforementioned rug sack. I got up and looked out of the window, but could see nothing. I knew that there was a heap of firewood piled against the church wall. I could hear the logs falling and rolling.

I went downstairs. My grandfather heard me coming down. "What's up?" he called out.

"I think someone is carrying off your firewood."

"Let's go and investigate. Hand me my overcoat. . . ."

He took a lantern from the kitchen cupboard and then walked into the court. A man was just crawling over the wall.

"Do you know him?" I asked.

"Sure, I know him," he came back. "I recognized him by his bulging posterior.

"Mynheer van Zandt," my grandfather called out, "please don't take all the wood! Leave some for me. If you will call in the morning, you can have all the wood you want. I'm having a fresh load delivered at nine o'clock."

We could hear some logs falling on the other side of the wall and then swift footsteps crunching in the snow.

"What about your Frisian rectitude now?" I asked.

"Van Zandt is not a Frisian," replied my grandfather. He's a Hollander like yourself! . . ."

For his preaching turns in other towns and communities, the *dominé* was allowed the use of a two-wheeled carriage known as a tilbury. I do not recall whether he owned this vehicle or not. It stood in a stable on a back street night and day at his disposal for instantaneous use. The tilbury carried a collapsible leather hood and a leather shield or curtain in front of the single seat to protect the travelers against the inclemencies of the weather. Koba, the dappled mare, also wore a blanket when it rained or snowed. In summer a pair of cotton covers went over her ears, in winter a set of woolen protectors. They were knitted by my grandmother in the shape of a pointed pair of socks with a red tassel at the top. As long as I lived in Franeker I acted as coachman. Rain or shine, off we were on those Sunday afternoons when he had to preach outside.

Thus we visited Leeuwarden, the Frisian capital, the port of Harlingen, the cities of Sneek and Bolsward and villages lying in a circumference of about fifteen miles. The first thing that struck me was the bodily height of the average Frisian who, as statistics show, is from two to three inches taller than the common run of Hollander or Fleming. Pliny, the historian, who visited the country before the dawn of the Christian era and shivered in the boreal blasts of a Frisian winter, found the inhabitants "a handsome and powerful race." He was particularly intrigued by the platinum color of their hair.

The Roman legions did not conquer the Frisians, nor, for that matter, the Batavians, as the inhabitants of Holland were then known. Julius Caesar, the "bald-headed adulterer," concluded a treaty of friendship with the clans inhabiting the Low Countries. The tribesmen were the most trusted of the Roman soldiers; they served in the imperial bodyguard.

Some historians have advanced the opinion—whether seriously or not, I do not know—that a legion drawn from the Low Countries was stationed in Palestine during the procuratorship of Pontius Pilate. If true, the question as to who really crucified Christ should be examined again. That none of our legionnaires ever wrote home about the harrowing event on Calvary's hill must be attributed, I think, rather to their general state of illiteracy than to lack of interest. . . .

Still, what a pity! If one of those boys had been able to write just one word to his sweetheart of what he had seen in Jerusalem, we might have at least one authentic reference to the drama on Golgotha. . . .

All around us in the Frisian rural regions we heard a language spoken which of all continental languages is nearest akin to English. An old Frisian saying:

> "Bread, butter, and green cheese
> Is good English and good Friese. . ."

gives a startling indication of the close kinship of Anglo-Saxon and the Nether-Saxon tongue spoken by the Frisians.

One item in Leeuwarden's art museum, which we visited several times, has become an object of dispute with Russia since the Kremlin museum began to exhibit an enormous wooden bowl of which it is claimed that Peter the Great filled it to the brim with vodka and emptied it in one gulp in the presence of his astonished ambassadors on New Year's day.

The Russians boast that Peter's bowl represents the biggest *Schlock* of strong drink ever taken by any human being. In challenging this claim the Frisians, without any intention to start a cold war, point to a silver cup in the Leeuwarden Museum which is nearly twice the size of Czar Peter's wooden bowl. The Frisian cup has a quaint *lingua franca* inscription dating from the fifteenth century on its side:

Ic, Yonker Sissingha	I, Baronet Sissingha
Dronk deze henza	Drank this cup
In eene stenza	In one gulp (stanza)
Door myn kraga	Through my collar (throat)
In myn maga.	Into my stomach.

Evidently, the next move is up to Nikita Khrushchev!

One Sunday we drove to the village of Wieuwerd which shares with the city of Bordeaux in France the distinction that the bodies of the dead do not moulder or disintegrate. The soil in the local cemetery, and under the church where a number of tombs are located, is intersected by veins of crude arsenic, a powerful preservative. Even the features of men and women laid to rest ages ago remain recognizable, though the parchmentlike skin stretches itself tightly around the bony structure of the cheeks and skull.

Wieuwerd, however, has a far more intimate claim on our interest. From this sleepy village went forth one of the parent streams of American civilization. The Lord Protector, Oliver Cromwell, visited here, but returned to England when the mission upon which he came failed to bring results. William Penn, the leader of the Quakers, had better luck. Penn came to Wieuwerd in the spring of 1667 accompanied by George Fox, Robert Barclay, John Robinson and George Keith. Their object was "to find tolerance, to nourish their faith, and to borrow some of the seed ideas which found congenial soil in America." They also, and this was their chief aim in visiting Wieuwerd, persuaded a colony of sectarians, known as Labadists, to emigrate to Pennsylvania.

Who were the Labadists? They were followers of a French divine, Jean de Labadie. Amongst them were the daughters of "the richest Frisian of the time," the Lord of Sommelsdyk. On the death of their father these girls donated their medieval castle, the Thetinga State at Wieuwerd, and its extensive farmholds and grazing grounds, to the sect for the purpose of establishing a religious settlement modeled on the life and primitive communistic practices of the earliest Christian church in Jerusalem.

One of the best known Labadists was Anna Maria van Schuurman, who is called "the wonder of the age." Besides being a woman of great beauty, she was also an astonishing linguist, speaking and writing fluently in Greek, Latin, Hebrew, Arabic, Syriac, Turkish, Coptic and Chaldean. Her writings have been carefully preserved including the manuscript of her famous Latin book *Eucleria*, meaning "The Choice of the Good Part." This book served the Labadists as a manual of devotion as long as they remained in Frisia and for a considerable time after their migration to America.

Two hundred of the Labadists accepted Penn's invitation and were settled by him on farms in and around Bohemia Manor which was later incorporated in part in the territory of the state of Delaware. Holding all property in common, the ideal of the Labadists was to make of the human race one united family striving for a devout and holy life. That they did not succeed we may easily verify by taking just half a glance around. In America they gradually merged with Quakers and Mennonites and other such pietistical bodies.

With their kinsmen and fellow Labadists remaining behind in Frisia the American sectarians communicated regularly. Even during the American Revolutionary War, couriers went to and fro between the colony of Bohemia Manor and the Frisian mother institution. The result was that our first Fourth of July, the day of the signing of the Declaration of Independence, was just as enthusiastically celebrated in Frisia as it was in Philadelphia, Boston or New York.

Two months before the event, word had come from America that the Founding Fathers were about to draw up and pass a resolution affirming the independence of the thirteen colonies. Without waiting for confirmation, the Frisians laid plans to mark the occasion with a "day of national rejoicing." When the Fourth of July dawned, the Stars and Stripes floated from the towers and city hall of the capital city of Leeuwarden. In Franeker, thirteen American flags waved from the university buildings. The students went around in procession to celebrate the American colonies' severance of the British connection. An enormous banner of black velvet moved at the head of the collegians' demonstration. On it with gold letters appeared the Latin inscription:

Plus valet una dies quae libera dicitur acta
Quae mali sub domini mille jugo!

One day spent in freedom is worth more
Than a thousand centuries under the yoke of a master!

The masonic lodges held solemn sessions to honor the new republic across the Atlantic. In the capital city the burghers' club, Liberty and Zeal, did more than indulge in the hilarity of a Fourth of July. They made the occasion permanent. They struck a gold medal commemorating the recognition of the independence of the American Republic by the Frisian commonwealth. In each of Frisia's eleven cities the civic guard paraded in gala uniform with white plumes on their black top hats. Fireworks were set off in the evening. The carillons pealed Crueger's great hymn: "Now thank we all our God. . . ."

"It was," says a contemporary writer, "as if the Frisian people celebrated their own independence. . . . "

Once again the Frisians struck a gold medal when John Adams, as the first American minister to the Netherlands, signed a treaty of commerce and navigation between the American and the Dutch republics on October 7, 1782. At that time, when Frisia still enjoyed self-government in the former Dutch republic, John Adams came to Franeker and Leeuwarden to express the gratitude of the American people and their government for the support Frisia gave the colonists in their struggle for freedom. While other far more powerful nations in deference to British sensibilities refrained from showing their sympathy for the American cause or had at best given it lip service, the Frisians never made a secret of their sentiments. They actually considered themselves in a state of war with George III and would not trade with Britain as long as the struggle for independence lasted in America.

The Frisians, I discovered, are not a very talkative people. I have never heard one of them or seen any of their history books boast of the fact that *their nation was the only one in the world which spontaneously collected funds and treasure and sent these across the ocean to George Washington in defiance of the British blockade.* Secretly, however, they still take great pride in that splendid show of solidarity and are overjoyed when you mention that you know about it.

One of the most curious spectacles I witnessed in Frisia was that of the entire population of a given village or a town's quarter on the march. We met such processions time and again while driving in the tilbury. Men, women, youths, girls, Protestant, Catholic, freethinker, socialist and conservative, all took part in these mass promenades where no mechanical devices of transportation such as bicycles or motorcars were tolerated.

"What's the idea of all these people on the go?" I asked my grandfather.

"It's part of the curriculum of the Folks-high-school," he said. "The Folks-high-school is an adult educational movement, an experiment in harmonious living. Teachers, farmers, laborers, clergymen, rich and poor, everybody sits on the school benches once more. One joins a 'High school for life' (such is its unofficial name) without being asked a certificate of previous schooling, and one leaves it without getting one.

"Discussion and debate evenings are arranged. The way of life of other peoples and nations is explained by means of lantern slides, motion pictures, travelogues and lectures. Singing, wood carving, folk dancing, listening to music and poetry are included with the intention to develop a feeling for style in one's own life. The most important subject in the curriculum is the art of living. When the inhabitants of a community go on the march they are learning literally to walk together."

Christmas week when nearly everybody in Franeker went skating or on vacation, my grandfather set aside for "repetition." That is, I had to undergo an oral examination. On the day when we dealt with the subject of history, the *dominé* asked me which countries, in my opinion, had been the most powerful agents of political progress in history.

"England, France and America," I answered.

"Correct," he nodded his head, "but you should add that the Dutch preceded all three of them. . . ."

"Impossible!" I said with an incredulous laugh. "Aren't you a little over-patriotic?"

"Impossible, you say? Just listen to this." He picked up a book from the table. "I read you a passage," he said, "from a lecture by an international authority, a famous Roman Catholic scholar and professor of history at Cambridge University:

" 'The Dutch,' says Lord Acton, 'made their universities the seat of original learning and original thinking, and their towns were the center of the European press. The later (Dutch) Renaissance, which achieved by monuments of solid work what dilettantism had begun and interrupted in the Medicean age, was due to them and to the refuge they provided for persecuted scholars.

" 'Their government, imperfect and awkward in its forms, became the most intelligent of the European governments. It gave the right of citizenship to revolutionary principles, and handed on the torch when the turn of England came. . . . It was by the Dutch that the great transition was made, that religious change became political change, that the Revolution evolved from the Reformation. . . .'

"What do you say to that? And this yet," he added: " 'The principle and practice of tolerance reached a height in Holland absolutely unknown anywhere else in the world.' "

"Obviously your professor goes too far," I observed. "How is it possible that the principle of tolerance stood so high in a country where the Calvinist religion predominates? Calvin certainly was not a tolerant person, nor, it seems, are his latter-day followers!"

"You are quite right," he replied. "Only our tradition of tolerance does not stem from Calvin or Calvinism. It comes from Erasmus.

"Erasmus is not only the educator of Holland, but of all Europe. I look upon the history of Europe," he went on, "as an ongoing struggle between the ideas and the school of Erasmus of Rotterdam and those of Machiavelli the Florentine. Fundamentally, the struggles of modern history are struggles between tolerance and fanaticism.

"Erasmus said: 'We should not merely pray as has been done throughout the ages: From pestilence, hunger and war, good Lord, deliver us, and at the same time do nothing to abolish the conditions from which pestilence, famine and war ineluctibly issue. We should reform personal and social life in such a manner that these evils through the power of the human will, disappear forever.

" 'Oh, God,' he exclaimed in 1524, 'oh, God, what a world! Christendom is torn in twain. The [German] Emperor and the King [of France] want to destroy each other. Immortal God, why doesn't the Pope forbid war and prevent his children from cutting each others' throats?' "

Wasn't he talking of conditions in 1963?

Tolerance versus fanaticism! I do not know if this view of history was in any way new or original. But I found it an almost perfect guide in disentangling the myriad currents and crosscurrents, political, social and ideological which tear modern society apart.

Tolerance! Not mere toleration!

In the word tolerance the emphasis lies on active, full-fledged consent, not a mere half-hearted permission or shoulder-shrugging resignation, or putting up temporarily with something which we only half like.

Tolerance is of the very essence of freedom!

Tolerance stands for complete equality and the citizen's absolute right, without experiencing intimidation or secret pressure, to give expression, orally and in writing, to his innermost convictions, however unorthodox they may be from an economic, religious or social point of view! . . .

Shortly after noon on a Saturday in mid-February, Frouke received a letter from the town of Dokkum where her family lived, informing her that her father lay seriously ill. The news threw our entire household into consternation, for the girl, as I mentioned, was like a member of the family. Frouke wept, Lena wept, my grandmother clutched her head in a gesture of despair as she paced up and down the living room.

"You must go at once," the *dominé* told Frouke. "There is no time to lose."

"Today's train has left," the girl replied, "there's no train on Sunday.... I better get my skates and start immediately."

To this mode of travel my grandfather would not agree. "There is too much snow on the ice," he shook his head. "But what about the tilbury? Do you think," he asked, turning in my direction, "that you could drive Frouke to Dokkum? I can't go myself, for I could not be back for the morrow's service.... Can you make it, d'you think?"

"I'll do my best," I assured him.

"Well, that's settled then," he said with finality. "You'll take my overcoat with the fur collar. Also take an extra blanket for Koba and a sack of oats.... You'll lodge the mare at Mr. Hobbema's livery stable in Dokkum."

"Yes," chimed in my grandmother, "and you'll take some fortifying food for Frouke's father."

All at once there was a scurrying to and fro in the kitchen, a bustle and animation as if a great emergency was upon us. My grandmother and Lena made up a hamper of sandwiches and a parcel containing a prodigious fine old ham, a cheese, sausages, and apples and pears from the bins in the attic. Grandfather went out to get the horse and tilbury and presently returned saying: "I put the harness with the bells on Koba. The snow is so dense that people might not see you. With the bells on, I'm sure, they'll hear you coming."

"Here," summoned my grandmother, "open your shirt! I want to sew this small sack of money on the inside of your underwear. There's ten guilders and seventy-five cents in it," she whispered. "Mind that you go sparingly with all that money!"

And then—by the Lord Harry!—she made me go upstairs and bring down the impossible quilt from my bed. "You'll put this on your laps," she said ever hopefully. "If anything will keep you warm, this is it!"

At the same time my grandfather wrote a note to his colleague in Dokkum, recommending the bearer, his grandson, for a night's hospitality at the parsonage.

"Frouke, come along!" everybody called out. "The tilbury is at the door."

And along she came. But it wasn't the same Frouke of half an hour before when she went to change her clothes. There wasn't a trace of tears left. She walked into the hall like a princess going to her coronation. Her gown was of a soft blue tint. She wore high-heeled shoes and over her shoulders an expensive strawberry-colored woolen shawl. On her head she carried the golden casque with the gold rosettes at the temples, and over it the transparent lace cap which is traditional with the Frisian women.

Suddenly there was a fascination about our Frouke as about a fairy maiden. Even my grandmother stepped back astonished. "My goodness, Frouke," she gasped, "my goodness!"

But my grandfather, in whose glance I thought I detected the merest flicker of suspicion, took me aside to whisper in my ear: "As man to man, let me warn you: be on your guard! There's more here than meets the eye...

Lena must have nourished similar apprehensions, but she, as usual, was rather more direct: "Drive straight on, you two! No nonsense now! And no picnics in the snow! D'you hear?"

After all this sage advice, we drove off, our heads just above the leather curtain in front of the tilbury seat. It snowed heavily and it was bitter cold. Soon the shawl was pulled over Frouke's head and she looked as bewitching as a nun in profound reflection. Her face was one to haunt a man's dreams. I have seen her portrait a hundred times in later years. That is, I have seen the paintings by Master Rubens of his wife, the lovely Helena Fourment, whom Frouke resembled like a twin sister.

For a time she was silent and grave. Then she grew so communicative that I rapidly revised my opinion about the taciturnity of the Frisians. Frouke talked my head off. She even sang the Frisian national anthem for me: *Frysk bloed, tjoch op, wil nou 'ris bruze en siede*, "Now, seethe, noble Frisian blood, and leap like a storm through our veins. . . ." She took off her gloves to clap her hands in applause when she had finished. Her laughter came in cascades of silver and crystal. But she displayed no other coquetry than the very innocent delight which nature itself would demand.

The only trouble we had on that journey—it was really no trouble to me—came when Frouke kicked off her shoes because her feet got so cold. She drew up her knees and placed her feet in my lap with the urgent request to rub them. How can one rub a girl's feet and simultaneously hold the horse's reins? I really can't tell; I never tried to do two things at the same time. . . .

I drove her back to the old parsonage in Franeker on the following

Monday. Her father's illness, as I suspected all along, did not amount to much. En route to Dokkum she hadn't been the least apprehensive about his condition. I saw the alleged sick man; he was sitting up and drinking black coffee with rum or perhaps just rum with a few drops of coffee to give the glass a deceptive coloring.

There was a young physician in the house who could not keep his eyes off his patient's daughter. For this I could hardly blame him, but when he volunteered to drive her back to Franeker, my heart shrank as if it had been pierced by a pin of ice. Imagine my elation when Frouke firmly replied: "No thank you, doctor, I have my own man!"

While waiting for her father to recover, I took the opportunity to look over Frouke's home town. Dokkum has an interesting history. In this town a crusade was preached in the thirteenth century and the men of Dokkum defeated an army of Saracens in the battle of Damietta in Egypt. Once upon a time it was also a Hanseatic city and still has a fine admiralty building, though the town is no longer situated on the sea. Where the great galleons lay moored along the quays in far-off days runs now a narrow canal navigable only by small craft. The North Sea is several miles distant.

On the Sunday morning I attended Mass at the Roman Catholic church of Saint Boniface and drank a beaker of water from the holy well which sprang up on the site where the Apostle of the Germans was slain in A.D. 754.

CHAPTER III

In the New World

IT MAY WELL BE that a flood of loving recollection has intensified my memories of Holland, but at the time of our departure, even the wonderful prospect of travel and adventure did not begin to compensate for the secret nostalgia gnawing at my heart. There's nothing so true as the saying: *Partir c'est mourir un peu.* I have felt the pangs of parting a dozen times in life, but in leaving the land of my birth it was as if I was being torn up by the roots; never a happy experience for any living creature. When I returned from my year in Franeker and my parents announced their decision to emigrate, I was so saddened by the thought never to see Frouke again that I fell into a state of mental depression where nothing seemed to matter any more. . . .

For weeks on end my father spoke in glowing terms about South Africa as our future home. The Boogaard, Jansen and Verwoerd families from the nearby village of Ouderkerk, with whom he was acquainted, had moved to that country and done well. One of the Verwoerd boys, Hendrik, did so well that eventually he became prime minister of the Union of South Africa. The date for our departure was practically set when my father relapsed into his old calamitous inability to make up his mind. He suddenly switched his attention and hopes to Canada where the great railway companies, the Canadian Pacific and Grand Trunk, were said to offer free land to any farmer willing to settle in the Dominion's far western provinces.

Everybody in the family sought to dissuade him. From far and wide came letters of protest. My uncle Kees was in despair, my grandfather furious, while my mother to whom South Africa, on account of the similarity in the spoken language had at first seemed less forbidding, now expressed extreme reluctance to leave the town where her youngest boy lay buried. It was all of no avail; every objection was brushed aside.

Canada, my father proclaimed, was a free and open country, and the sky the limit. While floating on that sea of optimism he overlooked one slight personal infelicity; he was so little of a farmer that he could scarcely distinguish plain grass from Brussels sprouts.

My brother Thomas and I were packed off on a steamer of the Batavier Line plying between the Hook of Holland and London. Our ultimate destination was Toronto. In that city we were to wait for our parents' arrival when we would go together in search of a suitable farm. We never found that "suitable farm," nor any other, nor did we look for one. The moment my father set foot ashore in Canada six months after his sons' landing in Montreal, the raw reality dispelled all his back-to-the-soil illusions; he wanted forthwith to return to Holland. However, for this there was no money, and he remained in Toronto, a relatively happy man till his death in 1950 at the age of 85. My mother, on the other hand, who did not know any English when she set out on the one great journey of her life, wasn't a year in Toronto before she had a circle of friends around her to whom, as of old, she taught her own particular version of the gospel truths, but now in a new language.

In Liverpool Thomas and I boarded the S.S. *Teutonic*, a White Star liner carrying some 2700 passengers, all British nationals save for a small party of Dutch immigrants, the last remaining inhabitants of a Brabant village who went to join their kinsmen already established in the new country. These immigrants were the men and women whom I directed to the Church of the Austin Friars on Threadneedle Street on our passage through and brief stay in London. The ocean voyage lasted thirteen days. We saw icebergs and whales and gathered in the salon with our British fellow passengers who taught us the (then) latest popular songs: "Oh, I do like to be beside the seaside"; "She's a lassie from Lancashire"; and "Has anybody here seen Kelly? Kay, ee, double el, why!"

The food on the *Teutonic* had a distinctly disagreeable taste. Breakfast, lunch or dinner, it was always the same melancholy mélange: tea with toast and fish, fish with tea and toast, and an occasional soft boiled egg, also of a sickening fishy flavor. The baked potatoes with the skin left on, we considered an insult to our national dignity, and did not touch at all. Fortunately, those Dutch farmers and their wives carried their own provisions. A very old lady called us to her cabin at nights and cut us a couple of slices from a round loaf of black bread as big as a millstone and laid a slice of cheese between. As she handed us one of her colossal sandwiches she would say: "May this help you on the way." To which we all returned a fervent: "Amen!"

As long as we were in the company of our countrymen, Thomas and I did not worry in the least as to what might lie in store for us in the Dominion, though we had only a hundred dollars or so in our pockets to defray expenses till... Till when? Till what? I simply did not know. My grandfather's last words to me on the steamship quay were: "Cast all your burdens upon Him, He cares for you!"

Thus it turned out, and not only on that occasion, but many times!

On board the *Teutonic* going around amongst the passengers was an immigration chaplain, a Church of England clergyman. One day he asked Thomas and myself where we were going.

"To Toronto," we replied.

"What will be your address in that city?"

"We have no address. We don't know a soul in the whole of Canada...."

"In that case," he said, "I will give you an address." He tore a slip of paper from a pad. On it was written: "The Reverend J. E. Gibson, Rector, The Church of the Ascension, 110 Beverly Street, Toronto.

It was to this address that we marched after getting off the train at Toronto's old Union Station. The door was opened by a young man who informed us that Mr. Gibson was away on a trip to Italy, but that he, Henri Roche, was taking care of the house in the rector's absence. He invited us inside and led us into the study. Pointing to his clerical collar, Mr. Roche explained he was preparing for the Anglican ministry at Wycliffe College.

"I'm doing my homework," he said. Amongst his books and papers on the table lay a Greek New Testament, open at the third chapter of St. John's gospel.

"Can you read this?" he asked with a smile.

"Maybe I can," I said, "let me try: *Hootōs gar ēgapēsen ho theos ton kosmon....* 'For God so loved the world that he gave his only begotten son,'" and so forth.

"Do you believe this?" asked Mr. Roche.

"With all my heart," I said.

He clapped his hands in delight. "You must come with me to Principal O'Meara of Wycliffe.... He is looking for young men willing to enter the ministry...."

I was not unwilling, but the more practical Thomas put on the brakes:

"The first thing for us is to get a job!"

"That also can be fixed," Mr. Roche assured us.

The next afternoon, a Sunday, he showed us around the city and drew our attention to various industrial plants where "Help Wanted" signs were posted. At the employment office of one of these factories, Christie, Brown & Company, biscuit manufacturers on Duke Street, we applied on the Monday morning, and were promptly hired as packers at a salary of $7 a week. The company's timekeeper, Charles Brett, took us upstairs in the first elevator I ever saw in my life and escorted us to the department where we were to work. One of the sleeves of his jacket was empty.

"See," said Mr. Brett, "that's what the dirty goddamned Dutch did to me. . . ."

He volunteered the information that he had served in the British army during the Anglo-Boer War. "But we beat them!" he shouted. "And how! God, how we beat them! We killed and killed Dutchmen till we nearly dropped with exhaustion."

"We're Dutch, too," Thomas interrupted, "and we're not goddamned and not dirty!"

"None of your lip now!" cautioned Mr. Brett. . . . "You needn't tell me that you're Dutch. I could tell the moment I saw your snoots. Better behave yourselves, else out you go! I can't stand the sight of a Dutchman. . . ."

"It is to be very much regretted," said Thomas slowly, searching for the right word in the new language, "that you have an arm lost. If otherwise, I would knock your block gladly off!"

Brett stopped in his tracks and looked around at my brother.

"Good boy!" he said. "You've got guts! . . . It's true, I have only one arm, but I will ask a friend of mine to put on the gloves with you. We'll soon see who is the better man, the English or the Dutch."

"Any time!" said Thomas.

That boxing bout, I am glad to say, never came off. Thomas and Charles became the best of friends. When the five o'clock whistle blew and we left the factory Henri Roche was waiting at the gate.

"I have an appointment for you with Principal O'Meara at six. Let's change clothes quickly, and be on our way to Wycliffe College."

Dr. O'Meara proved graciousness personified. He made me read some New Testament Greek and pushed a Latin book, the *Chronicles* by Cornelius Nepos, across the table for me to translate.

6. André Gide

7. Henri Barbusse

8. Romain Rolland

9. Hendrik van Loon

10. Clemenceau, the Tiger of France, in his home in La Vendée

11. Mussolini

"Show me your diploma or your credits," he said. "I think you'll soon be with us here at Wycliffe."

"I haven't the money for tuition," I objected.

"The Lord will provide!" replied Dr. O'Meara. "He has led you thus far, and He will take care of the rest. See to it, Roche," the principal said to Henri as we were about to leave, "that he improves his English. Here," he turned to me, "take this Bible, it's the Authorized Version, still the supreme example of the power and majesty of the English language."

"You'll soon change jobs," said Henri Roche when we came outside. "You'll join me at Eaton's department store and you'll learn to wait on table. It's hard work, but it's only four hours a day. That will leave you plenty of time to attend classes at Wycliffe.

Then I bought myself a dark blue suit of clothes, and on the Sunday following, I accompanied him to an Anglican church on Toronto Island where, as a graduate student, he conducted the service. A month later, dressed in cassock and surplice, I was reading the lesson in that church for Henri.

However, I did not enter Wycliffe. The Anglican service seemed too far removed from what I was used to at home. It appeared too liturgical, too ceremonial, too Romish. One day I had an interview with the chancellor of Victoria College, Dr. Edward W. Wallace, who informed me that the way into the Methodist ministry would be opened for me upon application and an examination as to my personal beliefs.

Henri Roche objected vehemently. "John Wesley was an Anglican minister," he declared. "You can follow the ways of the people called Methodists as well in the Anglican communion as in their own chapels. . . . The Church of England is all-inclusive, the freest church in the world; there is room in it for high and low, evangelical, latitudinarian, modernist, Calvinist, even for Anglo-Catholics. . . ."

"Still I don't think I belong in a church that can't make up its mind," I said, and Roche fell silent.

But he never failed to wait for us at the factory gate at closing time, and take us to his parents' home where the argument started all over again. Roche's parents were staunch Anglicans, of Huguenot descent, I think. They strongly supported their son's animadversions in favor of the Church of England. Papa Roche had a novel argument; he was a top-degree Orangeman. I, he reasoned, born and reared in the reign of Queen Wilhelmina, Princess of Orange, was an Orangeman by birth, while he

was one only by choice. I had never heard of the Orangemen.
"Who are they?" I asked. "What do they stand for?"

They were, I learned, worshipers (the word is not too strong) of the
"Glorious and Immortal Memory" of William of Orange, not the founder
of the Dutch Republic, but of his great-grandson, William III, King of
England, who went to the aid of English Protestantism when his father-
in-law, James II, brought back the Roman Mass to the great cathedrals
of London and Oxford.

Once a year, on the twelfth of July, Toronto's Orangemen held a
parade, tens of thousands strong. On that day they carried fancy swords
and were dressed in Swiss admirals' uniforms with plumed hats resembling
those of their bitterest opponents, the Knights of Columbus. At the head
of the procession walked a man carrying "The Open Bible." On their
banners appeared the words: "Remember the Deeds of our Forefathers."
This referred to the exploits of their ancestors or predecessors in the
Battle of the Boyne in Ireland on the twelfth of July, 1690, when William
III defeated the combined armies of Louis XIV and James II, and, by
his victory, finally made the exercise of the Protestant religion safe and
supreme in the realm of England.

Papa Roche claimed that William III became a member of the Church
of England immediately upon his arrival in Britain. I should do the same,
he insisted, now that I stood on British soil, and begin by joining the
lodge. Anybody amounting to anything in Toronto, the mayor, the alder-
men, Archdeacon Cody, later president of the University of Toronto,
the police chief, the heads of the municipal departments, all were "true
and faithful brother Orangemen." The Orange Order was then something
like a Tammany Hall in reverse, a Protestant wigwam let us say.

Horatio Hocken, one of Papa Roche's cronies and editor of *The Sentinel,*
the Orange Order's fiercely anti-Catholic journal, waived payment of the
initiation fee, and I was duly sworn in one night at one of the lodges.
After the ritual I was called upon by the Worshipful Master to say a few
words. It was the first speech I made in English. For half an hour I discoursed, very poorly, I am afraid, on the history of the House of Orange,
winding up with a panegyric on the Orangemen's own hero, "King Billy."
I told the story of William's coronation as sovereign of Scotland when
he refused to swear the oath "to extirpate heresy by the sword if needs
be." "My lords," William replied amidst the astonished silence of the
peers of the realm, "I will never lay myself under obligation to persecute
any man for his opinions. . . ."

At the close of my remarks, it was moved by Papa Roche and seconded by Horatio Hocken that I be elevated to the second degree. I received a sash, striped with blue, gold and orange colors. More secrets were imparted, plus a medal to be worn at the annual parade. That was the only Orange lodge meeting I ever attended in my life. As to the sash, I used it as a wall decoration in the room Thomas and I occupied on John Street for three dollars a week.

At Victoria College I was duly inscribed on the student role after Dr. Wallace certified that my credits obtained in Holland were the equivalent of matriculation. For English language and literature, I went twice a week to University College. By then I had also a new job; I became a streetcar conductor. I owed it to my pull with Papa Roche and the Loyal Order of Orangemen that my "run" fell from 5 in the morning till 9, and once again in the evening from 8 till 11.30, leaving me ample time to attend classes in the daytime. The morning run took care of a couple of loads of Bulgarian and Macedonian workers who reeked strongly of sweat and unwashed clothes. On the evening run we transported part of the theater crowd back and forth. By "we" I mean Padraic Flynn the motorman, and myself.

Flynn was an anarchist, an extremely well read fellow, who wore a heavy black mustache of the walrus type. He was as meek as a doe, but at the same time something of a premature beatnik; never polished the brass buttons on his uniform, nor his shoes. Most of the time he didn't shave either, his excuse being that he was too busy studying anarchism.

The first part of our late evening run terminated in a small park near Scarboro Beach in the east end of the city. In the park we waited for a quarter of an hour before starting on the return trip. Flynn took this opportunity to initiate me in the philosophy of the man whom he considered his "master and teacher," Elisée Reclus. He had learned most of that scholar's works by heart, and quoted him heatedly and voluminously. So much so in fact that one night we overstayed the allotted span of time at our resting place so that the downtown theater crowd was forced to seek other means of conveyance for its homeward journey. The penalty for this dereliction of duty was suspension for ten days. Flynn utilized his free time to go fishing and for memorizing more Reclus.

The end came a month or so later when the pole on the top of our streetcar jumped the wire at the intersection of Broadview and Queen Street. A street railway inspector, who was posted at this juncture where the poles habitually jumped the wire, ordered us to climb on the roof of the car to adjust the pole. Flynn refused, claiming that it was too dangerous: the top of the car was insufficiently insulated, one might be electrocuted. The inspector turned to me: "You get on there!"

"Comrade," Flynn warned, "if you climb on top of that car, you're liable to get such an electric shock that you'll be thrown to the ground and break your neck. Don't do it!"

I turned to the inspector: "I better not try, you heard how dangerous it is!"

"You're both fired," came back the inspector.

"Thank you, comrade, for your show of working-class solidarity," said Flynn as we parted.

It was only then that I joined Henri Roche in the dining room on the top floor of Eaton's department store where he officiated as host or usher. He was the only one to wear black; all the other waiters wore white linen jackets with black bow ties. The new position had one irresistible attraction: in addition to a wage of eight dollars a week, the waiters were entitled to a free meal before serving the luncheon customers.

The other dining room employees, most of them college students, may have been better waiters; they were certainly not better eaters. I was told that I could eat anything appearing on the menu, the management figuring, no doubt, that one or two selections would be ample to satisfy a normal person's appetite. However, I took them at their word; I ate through the whole menu from the proverbial soup to nuts and a double scoop of ice cream on top of the apple pie. In addition, I smuggled out enough biscuits in my coat pockets to keep me nibbling through the night while poring over my homiletics, patristics and dogmatics.

What I wondered at most in those days was how little my fellow students knew or cared about the ways of life, the customs, habits and the speech of peoples inhabiting other parts of the world. None of them spoke any language but English. For French they entertained a contempt amounting to hostility, a circumstance which I found hard to understand in a country where a recent prime minister, Sir Wilfrid Laurier, had been French and whose parliament was, and still is, bilingual. They shook their heads incredulously when I told them that in the high school entrance examination in the Netherlands, a child at the age of twelve or thirteen is expected to be proficient enough in French to speak and write a fairly advanced exercise in that tongue.

"Why French?" they shrugged in their provincial self-complacency. "What earthly use is French?"

I did not realize till later that the root of the Anglo-French animosity in Canada resides in the historical evolution of the country where English is the language of the Protestant conquerors, while French, to old-time Torontonians at least, was almost synonymous with Roman Catholicism.

On the other hand, I can scarcely find adequate words of appreciation for Canada's educational system which allowed a total stranger to enter college and work his way through without being held up or embarrassed by financial considerations or tests of class, caste, race or religious affiliation. Such a system was then unheard of in Holland. When a Dutch boy's father was a shoemaker, it seemed foreordained that he would be a shoemaker in turn, and so on, generation after generation. Higher education was out of the question once and for all for working-class children. Autodidacts, no matter how great their learning, seldom got anywhere. Without diplomas they were snootily treated and rejected as freaks and upstarts.

In Toronto the situation was exactly the reverse; everybody considered himself working class more or less. No shame, false or otherwise, attached to the performance of the most menial task. There existed no barriers which an intelligent boy or girl might not scale. In Canada I made acquaintance with an honest attempt to put democracy into practice. As a result of that first encounter my admiration and affection for the country and its people have never waned. Toronto was a good city to me: Never once did any man, high or low, throw it up to me that I was an alien. When I received the naturalization certificate, I read on it that "in all circumstances" I was "to be regarded and treated as a British subject *born*," a phrase conspicuously lacking from a later naturalization certificate which merely states I am allowed "to enter the United States for permanent residence." There is a big difference!

I studied hard and made good progress. When my parents arrived, Thomas and I had saved up enough money to rent a cottage on Eastern Avenue overlooking Toronto Bay. Fortunately they brought some of their furniture, rugs, paintings, tables, chairs and cupboards, old as the hills, no doubt, but serviceable though quaint, and, as I am told, worth their weight in devaluated dollars today.

Hardly were we installed in our new home when my turn came to run into a little trouble. Among the students in the English class at University College was a girl by the name of Margaret. Her surname I have forgotten. Maggie was the daughter of one of Toronto's district fire chiefs. I accompanied her home as far as the door two or three times, and once, just once, took her for a walk in High Park on a Saturday afternoon. On that occasion she informed me that her father, an Englishman by birth, forbade her to keep further company with a Dutchman. The poor man walked around with the absurd notion that Dutch and Germans are identical creatures.

After her father's warning the obedient Maggie refused to speak to me. When classes were over she walked off with the other young ladies and didn't even look around at her still fervent admirer. Fool that I was, I wrote her a letter and addressed it to her home. In the letter I asked her to intercede with her father and allow me to call and explain how honorable, noble, and so forth, were my intentions.

After a week or so when no reply had come, I decided to brave the lion in his own den, and one evening traveled to the western suburb where Maggie dwelt. I rang the bell and the chief himself opened. I didn't need to introduce myself. The fellow evidently knew me on sight.

"Will you stop pestering my daughter?" he snarled.

"I'm not pestering your daughter, sir! I just want to see you for a minute if I may. . . ."

"Alright, so you *have* seen me," he replied. "Now get the hell out!"

With this he gave me a push which made me almost tumble from the porch. But not quite! I gave him a push in return and he fell smack on the seat of his trousers, and I, having abandoned all hope anyway, made a resolute about-turn.

As if he had heard the alarm bell, the chief was in the street behind me in less than a minute. I walked faster and faster hoping to reach a streetcar stop before he would catch up with me. He caught up with a policeman instead, and the cop took over the pursuit. Foolishly, I broke into a run, but the bobby outran me, and grabbed my arm just as I swung aboard the rear platform of a streetcar. The next thing I knew I stood before the desk in the Dundas Avenue police station and saw and heard a sergeant book me on a charge of assault and battery. The constable who arrested me led me to a cell, opened the ironclad door and shoved me in. Then he opened the spyhole and stuck in his face: "In here you won't have a chance to molest Maggie, the fire chief's daughter. Ha, ha!"

A moment later the desk sergeant entered the cell and brought me "a nice cup of tea." "If you wish to make a statement," he said, "be advised that anything you say may be used in evidence against you!"

"I won't say a word," I replied, "but please telephone the Reverend Henri Roche...." I sat on the bunk in great trepidation and thought of all the jails, dungeons and bastilles I had ever read about. In the end I fell asleep, most convincing evidence, as I see it in retrospect, that I had no consciousness of guilt whatever. My incarceration lasted a little more than six hours.

In the middle of the night I heard Henri's voice and the voice of Papa Roche from the direction—what do they call it in a police station—of the common room? After I signed some papers, the sergeant released me on Papa Roche's assurance that he would produce me in police court at ten o'clock in the morning. This he did. And there I saw Maggie and the fire chief for the last time. Both glowered at me as if I were Jack the Ripper.

"Do you know this man?" the magistrate, Colonel George Denison, asked Maggie.

The faithless Delilah shook her head.

"Do *you* know him?" asked the colonel, turning to her father.

"No," replied perfidious Albion. "He came to the door last night and tried to beat me up! He was on the point of breaking in...."

"Why then isn't he charged with burglary?" asked the colonel, looking around the courtroom.

"He didn't break in," piped up the cop who arrested me. "He rang the doorbell! Then he pushed the plaintiff aside."

"Is this true?" the colonel-magistrate asked me sternly.

"It is not true, Your Worship," I said. "The chief pushed me first without the least provocation. And I, taken by surprise, pushed back. He had the misfortune to fall. That's the whole story...."

"You were thrown to the ground by this lad?" Colonel Denison asked the fire chief who was at least half a head taller than I.

Touched in his sense of honor and manliness the chief replied contemptuously: "Does Your Worship really think that I could be thrown to the ground by *that*? ... I stumbled over the doormat and slipped, that's what I did...."

"You slipped? Then why do you come here to waste the court's time with complaints about being beaten up? Get out of my sight, both of you. ..."

In the same moment Papa Roche walked up to the throne of judgment and whispered something in Colonel Denison's ear.

"Wait a minute!" the magistrate called me back. "Let me shake the hand of a brother Orangeman. . . ." He gave my hand the secret squeeze. "Take my advice," he whispered, "stay away from that Maggie. She's bad medicine. . . ."

That would have been the end of the affair Maggie, were it not that the desk man in the police station later served in the same unit with me in the First World War. Whenever he caught sight of me in the camp, he intoned a scandalous ditty giving me a wholly unmerited Don Juanesque reputation in the battalion:

> Oh, there was young Maggie, the fire chief's daughter,
> Who let this guy do to her what he shouldn't have oughter. . . .

Towards the close of the third semester, I was suddenly notified by the college chancellor, Dr. Wallace: "You are going into the mission field as a 'probationer'. . . . You'll continue your studies *extra muros,* outside the walls. Next year's examination papers will be sent to your superintendent and you'll write your paper in his parsonage. . . . You speak the Austrian language, don't you?"

"The Austrian language, sir? There is no such thing, sir!"

"The language spoken in Austria, don't you know it?"

"The language spoken in Austria, yes, sir. . . . But you're not sending me to Austria, I hope?"

"Oh, no! But I clearly see the hand of God here! We have 50,000 Austrians in the Province of Alberta. They have hardly any teachers or ministers or schools and only one small hospital. You are going to help extend our evangelistic work among them!"

Before starting for the mission field I was grilled for a whole day by a trio of theology professors as to my views on the doctrine of justification by faith through grace à la Martin Luther and John Wesley. There may be a slight difference in the conceptions of these two eminent theologians on that ominous subject over which men once tore each other limb from limb. If there is, it has, thank heaven, faded from my memory!

Then I journeyed to the Far West on a cut-rate harvesters' train, and had the biggest surprise of my life. My superintendent the Reverend John K. Smith, M.A., whom I met in an Albertan village called Andrew, asked me:

"Where did you learn Ruthenian?"

"Ruthenian? Is that a language? Is there a country called Ruthenia? I've heard of Ruritania, but never Ruthenia. . . . "

"Ruthenian is the language spoken in the Austrian province of Bukovina and it's the language of the settlers here in Alberta. Ruthenian is akin to Ukrainian. . . . "

"In that case," I said, "I'm afraid that I won't be of any use to you. I don't know a word of Ruthenian, Bukovinian or Ukrainian. . . . "

"But you can learn! And you're going to learn! Here is a Ruthenian grammar and New Testament. Please get busy. . . . "

I lodged with a family of Moravian Brethren, about fifty miles to the east of the city of Edmonton in the province of Alberta. The Moravians were the only people I could talk with; their language was German. They were pious, grave, hard-working farmers who wouldn't take any money for my board and lodging. It was ample compensation, they said, if I read them a chapter from their German Bible at eventide. Besides, they assured me, they owed Holland a debt of gratitude. Thousands of Moravians had found asylum in the Netherlands after their defeat in the Hussite wars. In remembrance of Holland's tolerance shown their ancestors, those Albertan farmers treated me as one of their own. The patriarch of the family, Stefan Hauser, wasn't sad at all when we parted a few months later. We'll surely meet again," he said, pointing upwards.

All around the Moravians, for some 50 miles in circumference, lived the Ruthenians in their *isbas*. The Reverend Mr. Wesley once spoke of the whole world as his parish; I certainly inherited a goodly chunk of it. However, my labors in the far western portion of the Lord's vineyard did not last very long. An epidemic of typhus broke out amongst the settlers who, as now became painfully evident, needed physicians and medication far more urgently than itinerant preachers on horseback—circuit riders we were called—who did not even speak their parishioners' language beyond the Lord's Prayer and a few sentences from the Sermon on the Mount. For a time a medical missionary came to my aid, or rather I became his helper in burning the vermin-swarming straw sacks on which the Ruthenians slept, and disinfecting and whitewashing the walls inside their cottages.

"I preach the gospel according to the holy syringe and needle," the medical man, Richard Costello, would announce as he shot an immunization serum into Ruthenian buttocks.

Not *dobré dĕn*, "good day" in Ruthenian, but *Slawa Isusu Christu!*, "Glory be to Jesus Christ!" was the set formula with which Ruthenian men, women and children joyfully greeted us when we reined in our horses and dismounted in front of their straw-roofed *isbas*. "*Slawa! Slawa!*" we replied. "*Slawa! Slawa!*" it was again when we got through with the last chore which consisted in cutting their hair, that of the women and girls too, incidentally. We could, unfortunately, not accept their hospitality or partake of the meals they generously offered. The bread or cold boiled potatoes which they laid out on the bare wooden tables were in the twinkling of an eye covered with swarms of green flies.

Although there was a number of fatalities, our missionary teams were well on the way, I believe, to conquer the typhus-carrying lice, when news came that Germany had violated the neutrality of Belgium. I read an account of the first battles in four or five successive issues of an eastern newspaper which a chance visitor left behind. "The river Meuse flows red with the blood of the Germans," colorfully announced one of the headlines. On another page the unsuspecting reader was informed that the Belgians were still "of all" the Gallic tribes "the bravest," as Caesar wrote of them two thousand years before.

On the other hand, the mighty forts of Liège had fallen after an heroic defense by General Léman. The Kaiser was decried as a bloodthirsty monster, an imp of Satan; Von Kluck, the German commander in chief, punningly dismissed as a frightened clucking hen; and Marshal von Hindenburg, who commanded on the Russian front, made ludicrous as a soft-brained senile who went to bed at nine and wrote his reports to the All-Highest Wilhelm on toilet paper.

All this was bad enough, but worse was still to come. In a few days we received news that a British expeditionary force of 10,000 men under Colonel Winston Churchill had fled across the border from Antwerp to Rilland-Bath, the town of my great-grandfather Amos, and was there disarmed. Churchill personally escaped internment by commandeering one of the family tugboats and transferring to a British fishing trawler outside Dutch territorial waters.

Louvain's university buildings and its precious library had gone up in flames. Wherever the Germans penetrated, it was reported, they covered their advance with a human shield of captive civilians, men, women and children. The inevitable atrocity stories were not long in making their appearance: German soldiers, it was said, cut off the breasts of Belgian nuns, and newborn infants were carried like Halloween pumpkins on the points of bayonets and Uhlan lances.

For us at the mission stations, the war in Europe presented a new and curious problem. Since very few if any of the Ruthenians had as yet been nationalized as British subjects they were still Austrian nationals, owing allegiance to the dual empire and its ruler Francis Joseph, Kaiser Wilhelm's partner in crime. All at once our parishioners became, technically at least, alien enemies. Dr. Costello packed up and left to join a medical unit in formation in Winnipeg, and I myself was summoned to the city of Medicine Hat to attend a general conference of church workers of all ranks called to deliberate on the empire's critical situation.

At the conference we heard a reverend superintendent of missions denounce the German soldiers as blasphemous Huns for carrying the motto *Gott mit Uns* on the brass buckles of their belts, and then lead us in prayer imploring the same God—at least, I assume it was the same God—to grant the victory to King George and the Asquith government which had so gallantly unsheathed the sword in Belgium's defense.

In the matter of the Ruthenians a motion was made, seconded and carried unanimously (with one abstention), inviting them to participate generously and to their fullest capacity in a fund-raising campaign for the construction of and the presentation to the British motherland of a battleship of the dreadnought type.

That let me out! As an alien, though not an enemy alien, I could not very well, I felt, urge other aliens to support a war against the land of their birth and political allegiance. I informed my superintendent that my usefulness had evidently come to an end, and had decided to return to college. "To preach the gospel is one thing," I said, "if only in a stammering way, but to raise money for battleships lies outside my province now and forever."

I ventured to ask for some money for train fare back to Toronto. I was supposed to draw a salary of $27 a month, but had never yet received a cent. If not for the good Moravian Brethren I would have starved to death. The superintendent replied that there were no funds available, but that the Lord would surely provide if he wanted me to depart.

"But the Lord is not supposed to provide," I dared object. "I thought it was understood that you were to pay my wages...."

"Don't be impatient, don't get rebellious," he cautioned. "Let us rather kneel down here quietly! . . ."

"I'll pray in Edmonton if you don't mind," I said angrily. "I have a return ticket to that city in my pocket."

In Edmonton they were excavating for the building of a prison. Seeing that forty odd years have elapsed, that jail must be up by now, though still uninhabited, I hope. On this project I got a job as a concrete mixer. It was tough going for the mixing was still done by hand. A circle of a dozen workmen standing on a wooden platform mixed gravel, sand, water and cement with the aid of shovels. After one day my hands were blistered beyond recognition. On the second day the blisters burst, I was in pain, and I slowed up. A Swedish foreman with blubber lips and the elastic voice of a crowing rooster screamed at me: "Wassa matter, you asleep? This is the way to do it." He grabbed the shovel from my hands and quickly turned over a little sand and gravel.

"Here, take my gloves!" said one of my fellow mixers. "With gloves on, the blisters won't hurt so much!"

"You're Dutch," I said. "What's your name?"

"Wybe Haringa," he replied.

"You're Frisian," I corrected myself quickly.

"Now y're talking!" he said with a broad grin. "Shake hands! We better stick together. That Swede bastard has it in for us!"

"You think so?"

"I know; all Swedes are bastards and footlickers. . . . But I never take sh—— from a Swede. I'm a free Frisian and an independent farmer. My farm is far away though, near Lethbridge. I got a house on it, but no windows in it yet. That's why I'm working at this job, you see, to earn money to put in the windows. Next year I'll be all set. . . . Where are you staying?"

"Nowhere yet! I've just come to town. Last night I stayed at a small hotel near the station."

"Crummy place, I bet! Why don't you come and live at the boarding house where I am staying?"

"I have no money yet."

"What? No money? When did you eat last?"

"I ate this morning!"

"What did you have?"

"A cup of coffee with a roll."

"That ain't enough eating for a job like this, kid.... You must be starving. . . . Come with me, we'll blow this job and get our time. We'll find other work tomorrow. There are buildings going up all over the place. . . . A good country, isn't it, this here Canada?"

"I will ask the foreman for my two days' wages at quitting time this evening."

"Don't do that! Never ask anything of a Swede. He'll make you crawl on your knees for it. . . . I'll tell you what we'll do; we'll quit right now and tell him: 'Fork over our money, Svenska, and kiss our you-know-what!' "

Just then the foreman walked up and sneered: "Hey, you two, can't yah talk civilized like white men?"

For answer Wybe picked up a crowbar and advanced on him, staring him right in the eyes with one of those steely, ice-cold Frisian looks I knew so well.

"Take that back, Svenska! Take it back or I'll brain you!"

"I take it back," quailed the foreman. "I didn't mean any harm! I take it back, don't hurt me! . . . You fellows want your time?"

At the end of six weeks I had saved up enough money to buy a railway ticket to Toronto, $51.80. Wybe helped me carry my trunk to the station. On a Saturday about noon I started crossing the continent for the second time in a little less than a year, but now in the opposite direction.

By eventide I felt the first pangs of hunger and I reproached myself, when too late, for not having kept up shoveling gravel for just another week to make enough for the purchase of victuals while en route. I had nothing to eat nor any money to buy food. The other passengers did nothing else but eat all night long, even when the lights burnt low. I sat gazing from the window into the semiobscurity of a moonlit night and saw the prairie roll by like a dark green sea. It was all very well, I thought, for Pottier, the composer of "The Internationale," to call upon the prisoners of starvation to arise, but what's the use of rising when there is nothing to rise for except a cold water tap at the rear-end of a railway coach.

At dawn a trainman came through the car. Seeing me awake he informed me that we were making good time. He pulled a plug of chewing tobacco from his pocket. "Piper-Heidsieck," he said, "champagne-flavored, bite off a chew." I thanked him, and sat chewing tobacco for an hour or so as if under contract. In the end I swallowed the wad as if it was one of old Lena's fruit tarts, but for a wonder experienced no evil aftereffects.

Shortly before pulling into the Winnipeg depot, the same man walked through the car shaking the shoulders of sleeping passengers: "All change! This is as far as the train goes!"

I showed him my foot-long ticket: "I'm going to Toronto!" I said, greatly upset.

"Don't get your bowels in an uproar," he admonished. "Don't you think I know that you're going to Toronto? . . . Your train leaves at eleven tonight from this same platform."

That meant seventeen hours of a layover; I tightened my belt another notch!

It was a splendid day in Winnipeg, dry, crisp and sunny. I walked the streets from 6 till 8 without meeting a soul save for the police constables going home from the night watch. At one point I noticed a man opening the doors of a large church and I entered.

"The prayer meeting is upstairs at nine o'clock," the door opener informed me.

"I just want to sit here a while," I said.

"Okay, but if you should want to go to the prayer meeting, the stairway is through that door to the left of the platform." He vanished in that direction himself.

I read a little in a hymnbook which I found in the pew, and then sauntered towards the indicated door, and through it, but did not go upstairs. After passing through the door I saw a room with a very large table in the center. On the white linen tablecloth lay twelve beautiful loaves of bread. Evidently the congregation was celebrating holy communion that morning.

I stared a long time at the bread and thought of the twelve show loaves, one for each of the tribes of Israel, which the Levites placed on the golden table in Yahweh's sanctuary. No one but the priests were supposed to touch the show breads. Still, one day, David, the son of Jesse, feeling very hungry and exhausted, with King Saul on his heels in hot pursuit, entered the sanctuary and took away five of the loaves reserved for the Lord's service.

Good old David! Surely, the king whom the Bible calls "the man after God's own heart" couldn't be a bad example to follow! Accordingly I took a similar course. After scribbling a note, offering my excuses and citing

King David's theft of the show loaves as recorded in the first Book of Samuel, I placed the piece of paper on the communion table. Then I hid one loaf under my coat and returned to the station waiting room for a royal Davidic repast.

It never occurred to me to ask one of the officers of that church for a handout or the loan of a dollar to keep me in food for the rest of the journey. In the end, though, I did pay for the stolen loaf, albeit many years later when I came to Winnipeg to deliver a lecture, and to my utter amazement found myself in the same church where I once sinned against the tenth commandment. The pastor's name was then Dr. William Laird Armstrong. He had been one of the professors who examined me at Victoria on Wesley's theology.

"Your note made us suspect that it was a very hungry brother who went so far as to take a communion loaf," said one of the older church officers who remembered the incident. "Why didn't you sign your name?"

"And have you send for the police?"

"Not the police," he answered in shocked surprise. "It's we who looked for you all day, all over the city."

In a burst of belated gratitude I waived my fee, greatly to the chagrin, I am sure, of the manager of the Colston Leigh lecture bureau in New York.

Toronto was a changed city. Recruiting rallies were being held every noon hour on the steps of the city hall. A band played: "O God, Our Help in Ages Past," and Archdeacon Cody and other clergymen orated in a similar vein. Troops filled the buildings at the exhibition grounds and trained in the parks. On Yonge and Bay streets one saw men and boys hobbling around on crutches, legless and armless fellows, the first fruit of the gory harvest in Flanders' fields. The newspapers published casualty lists, exercising great caution to give but a few names from day to day in order to camouflage the magnitude of the losses suffered in the first Battle of Ypres where the Princess Patricia Light Infantry and the Canadian First Division had been heavily engaged.

At first I took little interest in the military situation: I wasn't a British subject, nor was Holland involved in the war. What business was it of mine, I reasoned callously, that Germans were killing Britishers, Belgians and Russians, and vice-versa? Also, I must add, the official accounts of the origins and causes of the war were hedged about with many reservations in my mind.

Born in a small country lying in the shadow of the German empire, I entertained no illusions of the conquering ambitions of the Kaiser and the Prussian Junker class. But I also knew that for years Admiral Sir John Fisher had been calling for a preventive war against Germany, principally to destroy the Kaiser's high sea fleet which threatened Britannia's rule of the waves.

It is true that responsibility for the outbreak of war does not always devolve upon the power which strikes the first blow. To the power which makes war inevitable goes the greater part of the blame. What was incomprehensible to me was the affirmation, which I heard on all sides, that Britain and France, and the whole world in fact, had been completely taken by surprise by Germany's attack on Belgium and France. How this was possible I could not understand since as school children in Holland we already learned of Heinrich Heine's warning: "Everything in Germany stinks of blood!" And hadn't Nietzsche prophesied: "It's going to snow.... The crows will seek refuge in the cities.... Soon begins a period of wars and ever more ferocious wars . . . for Europe." The statesmen might not know, but we children knew that war was coming; the "glorious Kaiser" had rattled his saber and shaken his mailed fist a little too often. The First World War was the logical sequence of Germany's "will to power," a policy pursued with iron determination for nearly a century by the German militarist school.

After another year of study, an examination and a trial sermon between waiting on table, I was glad to go back into the mission field. This time my parish lay in North Ontario as assistant to the Reverend J. Oscar Johnston, who was stationed in the Porcupine gold mine area. My brother Thomas came with me and soon got himself a job running a Rand waterline drill five hundred feet underground in the Acme gold mine near Timmins.

I lived in Golden City and had three churches to attend to: Golden City, South Porcupine and Schumacher. My superintendent, Mr. Johnston, resided in and operated from Schumacher. We met twice a month on Sunday afternoon on the ice of Lake Porcupine, he on his way to hold service in Golden City, and I on my way to Schumacher for the same purpose.

It was also part of my duty to visit the mining camps and bunkhouses and arrange, if possible, for religious services amongst Polish and Italian mine workers. I had no luck with these men; the Catholic Church claimed their allegiance and saw to it that the sheep of its pasture remained unsullied by Protestant innovations.

On the other hand, I met with a hearty welcome in the village of Pottsville, situated in the woods on the east bank of Lake Porcupine. Pottsville's population of about five hundred souls was predominantly Scandinavian. Their houses were not the usual rough timber shacks one encountered almost everywhere else in the area, but log cabins, the neatest, cleanest, most picturesque structures in that sheer boundless wilderness of forest and rock.

The Scandinavians worked as timbermen in the mines throughout the region, but their homes, where they spent their week-ends and other leisure time, stood in Pottsville. They, and especially the Finlanders amongst them, were the only workers who had brought their wives and children to the new country. The Italians, Poles, Bulgarians and other Slavs, who were contemptuously referred to as *Dagos* and *Bohunks*, labored for periods of five or six years, saved a little money and then returned to their respective homelands.

In Pottsville the Scandinavians had built a large public hall with a seating capacity of 250, equipped with a stage for theatrical performances and a magnificent hand-carved speakers' rostrum. In this community center, known as the Finnish Socialist House, the whole population gathered on Sunday afternoons to hear a concert by a band of Jan Sibelius' countrymen. For its opening number the band was in the habit of playing "The Internationale" till the Royal Mounted Police objected and requested them to shift to "God Save the King." This they flatly refused. I was instrumental in bringing the disputants to a compromise: "If you want to play a revolutionary hymn, why not try the 'Marseillaise?'" I suggested. "The police will probably acquiesce in the belief that you are honoring France, Britain's ally."

Since the villagers showed no great enthusiasm for a religious service, I proposed a sort of Folks-high-school on the model of the "High school for life" such as I had seen in operation in Frisia. With this idea all and sundry fell in at once. I volunteered to give readings from the British poets, but they preferred Henrik Ibsen, Björnstjerne Björnson and Georg Brandes (in English translation, of course, else I wouldn't have been of much use).

But best of all, it almost goes without saying in the case of those dyed-in-the-wool socialists, they liked to discuss the writings of Marx, Engels and Kautsky, to whom I added Jean Jaurès, because I considered him the first great saint produced by modern socialism.

It was a curious and heart-warming experience to find a tiny island of culture in that vast frontier territory where the rough-and-tumble stage of a gold rush had just begun to taper off. Those Norsemen had a fine library. Both men and women read a good deal. They liked music and poetry. Thanks to the excellent educational system in their native countries, they talked quite intelligently about the issues of the day, more intelligently, I am almost ashamed to say, than some of the leading national newspapers who would repeatedly and in all seriousness advance such enormities as the proposition that the Flemish and Walloon populations of Belgium forget all about their ethnic and linguistic differences and both learn to speak English.

It should not be thought that we remained for long in the serious, solemn mood induced by our first reading from Marx' *Kapital*. As a matter of fact the hushed rather formal atmosphere of our first gathering soon gave way to a more convivial, intimate spirit. To all intents and purposes we became a fellowship; we discussed the weather, and some of the (to me) weirdest subjects under the sun, like the merits of different breeds of cattle, Jerseys, Holsteins, Aberdeens, bulls, bullocks and cows, or, a very favorite subject: the co-operative farming system in Denmark and Frisia. Another Sunday we took up the ways in which Christmas is celebrated in different countries. From this subject we shifted to Ibsen's *Doll's House* and Björnson's *Storm*.

"What are we going to talk about this afternoon?" I would ask the assembly.

"First come down from that pulpit and sit with us here for a cup of coffee," called back Haakon Lindquist, a Norwegian timberman, who was something like the president of the board of directors of Socialist House. When Lindquist said that my heart gave a leap, for it meant that all the barriers between us were down.

"Well, what's to be the topic?"

"Tell us a Sherlock Holmes' detective story or something about the dancing girls of Bali. . . . "

In this way I came to tell the story of Jean Valjean from Victor Hugo's *Les Misérables*, and that of Joan of Arc; Voltaire's history of Charles XII, the war of the Swedes against Peter the Great, and Multatuli's* poignant and world-famous account of Dutch colonialism's methods of operation in Java....

Hans Andersen's fairy tales, as can be imagined, were a perpetual joy, though my friends knew them all by heart, reason the more, I dare say, to hear them once again as told by a stranger. Once in a while we tackled one of Bernard Shaw's *Fabian Essays* or discussed Carlyle's *French Revolution.*

This famous work served us a pretext—the spearpoint of an Ariadne's thread to penetrate into the labyrinth of contemporary international and social issues. To the Finnish subjects of Czar Nicholas, events in Russia were naturally of paramount importance. They took it as an axiom that war is the portal to revolution. Even as the Russo-Japanese conflict had produced the 1905 revolution in St. Petersburg and Moscow, so the new war between Russia and Germany would lead to a much greater upheaval, terminating, as they confidently expected and correctly foresaw, in the final liquidation of the Czarist autocracy. All their hopes, therefore, were vested in a shattering Russian defeat. Only from a defeated Russia could the Finnish people hope to extract cultural and political autonomy and set Finland free to pursue a policy in harmony with its own spirit and national ethos.

A free discussion of Finnish national aspirations, however, was hampered by the circumstance that the Czar of all the Russias figured as George V's ally in the war; the British monarch was also sovereign lord of Canada. We had to go easy on the subject of imperial Russia, but got around it by proclaiming Tolstoy Russia's spokesman before the world....

Some of my comments in Pottsville's community center on the European war found their way into print in the old *Appeal to Reason,* the organ of the socialist party in the United States, and in *Cotton's Weekly,* a publication issued by a group of independent American socialists in support of the "One Big Union" as advocated by the I.W.W., the Industrial Workers of the World. Charles Barton was the name of the correspondent who, unbeknownst to me, put those rambling remarks of mine into deft literary shape and sent them to the newspapers.

*Multatuli, literally "I have suffered much," was the *nom de plume* of Eduard Douwes Dekker, a Dutch consular agent in Indonesia, who shocked Holland and the world with his book on life on the Javanese coffee and tea plantations. The book was published in the 1890s and translated into twenty different languages.

Never in my life did I come across another human being of such pure and childlike gentleness as this man Barton. Here was an angel in disguise! But what a disguise! His bodily frame was of elephantine proportions, and his features utterly repulsive. He was six feet seven inches tall and weighed well over 400 pounds. He had originally come into the area as a "walking delegate" or organizer on behalf of the United Mineworkers of America. Because the U.M.A. stood high on the mining companies' black list as "criminally syndicalist" (whatever that may mean), Barton had a hard time trying to unionize the miners. His face had been kicked out of all human semblance by the hobnailed boots of the mine guards. His eyes looked like two windows located on different stories of a house. All his fingers had been smashed with hammers wielded by Pinkerton detectives who swarmed over the mining properties and often far beyond, like so many private armies. Following that mutilation by the henchmen of law and order, Barton had taken to the woods, and lived in a log cabin located on Moose Creek, one of the many streams flowing into the Frederick House River.

Though I had as little money as formerly in the far west, I was able to travel as far north as Cochrane and as far south as the Cobalt silver mining district on a courtesy pass provided by the management of the Temiskaming and Northern Ontario railway. With the help of this pass I visited Barton's cabin. He met me at Frederick House flag station and we proceeded to his dwelling place in a large canoe.

Barton's only companion was MacDougal, an enormous black cat. This animal raced up to him the moment we debarked from the canoe in front of the cabin and in one jump poised itself on his broad shoulders. Wherever Barton went or whatever he did, light the fire, cook the beans or dip water from the creek, the cat accompanied him staring with a peculiar curiosity from its perch on his shoulders at its master's doings. During the meals the cat sat on the bench by the table between the two of us. I am afraid that I did not quite come up to MacDougal's expectations. Whenever I looked sideways at him, I found his green eyes boring into mine with unconcealed resentment. In the darkness of night, I saw the cat's eyes like two coals of fire follow every move I made. He was better than a watchdog; I never saw another cat quite like him.

In and around Barton's cabin the solitude was so immense as to be almost tangible. His nearest neighbor, another "independent" by the name of Herbert Mabee, lived four miles away. Like Barton, Mabee was of

Scottish extraction and resolutely refused to discuss anything pertaining to the war or the international situation. "The sage," he said, "has no time for such *absurrdities*." Mabee had married an Indian girl, a soft-spoken, patient person with big black eyes to whom he read poetry sitting in the doorway of their cabin while she kept the mosquitoes away by burning pots of smudge fire all around him. "The ainly thing I lack is ma haggis," Mabee told me. "For the rest this is heaven on earth."

Through Barton, I received friendly messages from Morris Hilquit of New York and Victor Berger, the socialist congressman from Milwaukee. Mr. Hilquit, whom I never saw in my life, wrote that he shared my veneration for Jean Jaurès the murdered French socialist leader. By way of encouragement, he sent me a red morocco-bound set of books: Jaurès' *Socialist History of the French Revolution* which still stands in my library, a silent reminder of the days before the storms of this century.

To Mr. Hilquit's written question how I could possibly bring myself to preach the Christian gospel and hold to the socialist doctrine at the same time, I replied: "To me socialism represents the vehicle on which the Kingdom of God advances in history and will ultimately lead mankind to the realization of the prophetic vision of justice and universal peace. . . . I am an Isaiah socialist. . . . "

"Good enough, comrade," replied Morris Hilquit, "I hope your ticket wins!"

The three pulpits I served lay a long way apart. The distance from Golden City to Schumacher, for instance, was a full nine miles. I covered it in two hours, once in the afternoon and once again on the homeward journey after the service. Mr. Johnston, of course, had to make the same trip for the gospel's sake, though in the opposite direction. But he enjoyed one advantage: at nine on Sunday evening the weekly train came through. He, champion varsity sprinter that he was, made it by running cross-country and catching the train at a flag station which for some unfathomable reason was called Rosedale. There was no train going my way at that hour, so I walked.

Probably nobody seeing me today would believe me if I said that I covered those nine miles in the middle of the night on the run, all the way! Was I scared? Frankly, yes, a little! People warned me that hungry wolf packs roamed the forest, and also that the lynxes had a habit of dropping down in the dark from their perch in the trees on a passing wayfarer's shoulders and tearing him to pieces. I heard the wolves howl more than once, but never saw any, nor any lynx. What I did see one evening at twilight was a brown bear with two cubs.

I had left the corduroy road to pick some blueberries in a patch of shrubbery with an azure sheen over it caused by the thick clusters of the wild fruit. Suddenly the bear, who was also feasting on the berries, stood in front of me on her hind legs, a cub on either side. . . .

When Tolstoy got to preaching nonviolence and kindness to animals in his old age, his moujik visitors would pester him with the question: "Lev Nikolaevich, please tell us, what would you do if you met a tiger?"

"There are no tigers in Russia!" he would angrily dismiss his questioners. But bears there were, and one huge bear once mauled the young Tolstoy to within an inch of his life. The remembrance of reading about that incident flashed through my mind as I stood face to face with not one but three bears. I thought: If I turn and make a dash for it, the mamma bear will jump me from behind and I'll be a goner. But nothing so drastic or dramatic happened. As the bear and I stood staring at each other, she growled as if she had a rattle in her throat. This went on till one of the cubs suddenly bolted and ran back into the wood. Mamma and the other cub followed in short order.

More perilous than the bear episode was the time when I got lost in a snowstorm. On the outward journey to Schumacher some flurries flew across my path, but I did not judge them serious enough to take precautions. And, come to think of it, what precautions could I have taken?

I had a sledge with three dogs, two huskies and one, the leader, a Newfoundland dog, Paddy by name. At the rear-end of the sledge stood a pole in a vertical position. You held on to this pole while running behind the sleigh and from time to time jumped on for a short ride, an on-and-off process which pleasantly shortened the distance. As I ran I prepronounced the sermon I was to deliver in the evening. It was good exercise; shouting against the wind strengthened my voice so much that I never needed a loud-speaker in later years.

On the way back through the forest after the service in Schumacher all went tolerably well, but on Lake Porcupine I could not see a foot ahead of me. A blinding tempest lashed into my face; I had to brace myself against the storm to keep on my feet. Paddy slowed up and presently turned and stood by my side pressing his big muzzle in my hand. By his whining I could tell that he had thrown in the sponge.

The time was shortly after midnight, the lake was two miles wide, and I had just entered upon its frozen surface. I decided to turn back and make for the shore I had just left behind. Perhaps I could locate a prospector's or a trapper's cabin, build a fire and spend the night. There were quite a few such cabins about, and, though abandoned, they were generally stocked with canned food and plenty of kindling and firewood ready to light the stove. Here is one of the finer traditions of the high north: no door was ever locked. It was an unwritten law that you could enter at will, brew coffee and eat pork and beans. Before leaving you were honor bound to chop enough wood to replace what you had used.

We didn't make the shore that night. Paddy couldn't pick up the scent. The two huskies were absolutely useless. I found huskies the nastiest, most vicious canine breed I know of. In fact, I don't believe they are dogs at all. The dog is man's best friend. A dog will never abandon his master, but a husky will, and he will devour him too, if the man should grow so weak as to collapse.

From midnight till eleven in the morning when the sick dawn finally broke through the white shroud lying over the world, we literally fought our way inch by inch through the blizzard. Since I had no snow shoes, I sank nearly out of sight. Paddy followed. I could not see him, but whenever I slowed up he poked me in the back with his snout.... We could not afford to rest or stand or sit still, for immobility meant certain death, the temperature having sunk to some 50 degrees below zero. When I could finally identify the spot where I stood, I discovered that we had been walking in circles for nearly twelve hours.

What kind of sermons did I preach? I would be able to give a more precise answer to this question had not the French government in the fall of 1939, ordered me expelled from my house in Maisons-Laffitte near Paris with special instructions to the police to allow no papers or books to be taken out. The old sermon notes from the Porcupine period were in the library which remained behind when I walked (part of the way) from Havre to Le Verdon in the Department of the Gironde, and there caught a ship which carried me back to America. The result is that I can speak only about the general tenor of those old sermons. One thing is certain: they were short and to the point. In accordance with John Wesley's advice to his preachers that no soul is ever saved after the first quarter hour, I never spoke longer than fifteen or twenty minutes. My grandfather invoked another equally wise and homely consideration to spare his hearers' sensibilities. He used to say: the human brain cannot stand more than the human posterior.

Having committed my sermon to memory in the course of the week, I spoke without looking at my notes. I had no inhibitions, nor did I suffer from stage fright. This is a plague which descended on me in later years. Nowadays I am as nervous as a schoolgirl when I see an audience in front of me. I promptly forget everything I had planned to say. Not till I hear the sound of my own voice do I regain confidence and overcome these awkward hesitations. In the far north I felt ill at ease only when I noticed the presence of certain members of the intelligentsia in the congregation, mining engineers, county officials or medical doctors. I was particularly upset when I spotted the face of Mr. "Happy" Langmuir among my hearers. Mr. Langmuir was the chief engineer at the Hollinger mine. In private conversation his superior learning and wisdom frightened me. But he never failed to attend, and when I left he did me the great kindness of saying that he had learned a good deal from my homilies. It is just possible that he pulled my leg a little! I rather think he did.

It should not be thought that I disliked my work or performed my task merely by rote. I can honestly say that I preached with gladness and that I firmly believed myself called to be a *verbi divini minister*. The desire to make money by getting a job in the mines or go prospecting for gold far, far away, as my brother Thomas did, never stirred me, though I was so poor that I not only had to wash and repair my own clothes and cut my own hair, but seldom ate anything but bread and fish. Rabbits or deer I couldn't bring myself to kill. I caught fish by hacking a hole in the ice and simply scooping up the specimen that came up to breathe. When a fish fell on the ice, it was instantly frozen stiff and I figured that it did not suffer. It was a godsend to be invited for a meal, be it ever so far away or deep in the woods. On those Sundays when my preaching turn in Schumacher came around, I ate dinner at the local parsonage where my superintendent's wife, dear Mrs. Florence Johnston, received me with winning affability. At her table I ate so much that I still wonder sometimes if she didn't think me a terrible hog.

For every sermon I prepared as for a battle—with far more joy in my heart, I must say, than for the military battles in which I was called upon to participate later. Perhaps I was a little brash, but I believed firmly that I spoke in the name of God, in the name of the highest justice. "Whom shall I send?" the voice of Yahweh asked Isaiah. "Then Isaiah said: 'Here I am; send me!'" Such was also my own prayer in those days. Something which I would not dare do now, I imagine, occurred when a strike was threatening and the U.M.A. called out the workers; I announced as the title of my next talk: "God's Program and the U.M.A."

"Two great currents of new life are coursing through our world today: the religious and the social. Like two parallel streams of water running to the same sea, these two seek each other. In the hearts of those who are seized with the religious ideal, a certitude is growing that God has sent them to build a bridge towards those brothers who, while perhaps denying God's existence, are, nevertheless, athirst for justice and righteousness. Our hope and desire is to walk and to work together with them.

"As long as the churches try to kill socialism by silence—socialism which is the only reminder in the world today of the original impulses of Jesus— so long is the anger of socialist atheism, which prefers no God at all to the kind of God who is bound up with the capitalist system of production and war, absolutely justifiable and justified.... What the Church should do, the socialists do. Where God should live, there He stays away from. And where He is not acknowledged, there precisely He takes up His abode.

"Jesus walks amongst us right here in the Porcupine area announcing the Kingdom of God, the era of co-operation and comradeship when cut-throat competition and poverty and hunger and war shall be no more.... We do not see Him as one enveloped in the mystery of the Holy Trinity.... We see Him as a helper, as a brother, as a fellow worker, as the banner bearer in the workers' cause.... If it comes to a strike, we shall walk together behind His banner, the scarlet banner of the cross...."

The reason I remember that particular sermon is because someone took it down stenographically and sent it to the general superintendent of the church in Toronto. The purpose was to denounce me as an agitator and, if possible, have me expelled from the district as *persona non grata* with the mining companies. From Toronto came a telegram in reply: "Say it again and again and again! You're on the right track!"

Barton and my Scandinavian friends, fearing that I might meet with some bodily harm, sent two husky young fellows to accompany me on the long night walks. One of these, Olav Ingeson, played a harmonica while on the march. He brought forth such a dismal, nerve-jangling screech as might well have stopped any eventual prowling wolf or Pinkerton in their tracks.... Though we expected riots and fights, not much harm was done save in one case. Some mine guards sneaked up to Barton's cabin in his absence and riddled MacDougal with buckshot. They hanged the cat's dead body in front of the door....

Back in Golden City where I had plenty of time to study, I discovered Martineau, Emerson, Matthew Arnold, Parker, Troeltsch and Rauschenbusch. The thoughts of these men led me gradually to reject the peculiar interpretation given in orthodox seminaries to the opening chapters of the Bible, notably the doctrine of the utter sinfulness of all human creatures born into the world and the necessity of the sacrifice of the Son of God for the redemption of the race. I could no longer believe that this Saviour had come into the world for the removal of original sin and the attainment of salvation. Each creature must be his own saviour; no miraculous intervention removed sin. The divinely implanted power in the human breast alone was capable of triumph over evil and wrong.

It goes without saying that I held out no hope of a better, fuller life in the hereafter. "The proper study of man," said Martineau, "is not how to die, but how to live." The prime object of religion was to live this life nobly and well. Only people who have no life, whose conditions of life are subhuman or inhuman, are apt to dream of a life in the hereafter as compensation for the ills and injustices suffered in this "terrestrial vale of tears." The myth of celestial compensation seemed to me a most convenient doctrine imposed upon the so-called underprivileged by the reactionary classes in society as a police measure to block the rising tide of discontent and revolutionary sentiment. In short, the hope of paradise was a device to divert the people's attention from the evils of the system under which they lived. The ruling powers, ably assisted by the ecclesiastics, encouraged the myth in order to remain undisturbed in the possession of their property and privileges.

To be sure, I did believe in heaven, but not in a heaven somewhere beyond the clouds. I believed in a much more realistic heaven, one that was still to be made, a paradise that was constantly under construction, so to speak; in this world, by man himself. . . . As the highest goal of man's striving I held out the vision of the Kingdom of God, though not as a mystical and misty pipe dream, but as the dynamite which is to blow the status quo asunder and replace it with "new heavens and a *new earth* wherein dwelleth righteousness.

What I upheld in my stumbling way was an application of religion to the social relations between man and man. It was a repudiation of orthodoxy's stress on individual salvation. Orthodox Christianity, I felt, taught a negation of life. I did not deny life. I accepted life and accepted this world and I loved it. I love it still more today in the measure that my course through it draws towards a close.... I believed and still believe that the earth is the Lord's, a garden for all of God's children to walk in: Chinese, Russians, Germans, Americans, all. Yes, and Bantus and Angolese, too!

> Hark the rolling of the thunder!
> Lo, the sun, and lo, thereunder
> Riseth wrath and hope and wonder,
> As the host comes marching on! ...

From South Porcupine, the amusement and relaxation center of the gold fields, the power and the glory had already departed. But evidence of stormier and more hectic times in the recent past still lay plentifully about. In South Porcupine, where I conducted the service in the Presbyterian church on Sunday mornings, you could still see the prospectors and trappers come in from a year's search for gold and fox skins. Some of these men, quite a cosmopolitan lot they were, had been to other gold countries, the Klondike, Mexico or South Africa. They had married squaws or taken half-breed women as concubines. They sat on the porches of the dilapidated, though once gaudy hotels and saloon bars, rocking their chairs and aiming squirts of tobacco juice at brightly polished brass spittoons and, to my never-ending amazement, hitting the objective with unfailing precision. As a rule their conversation was a little monotonous: gold and women, women and booze, and back again to women and gold.

One famous prospector, the redoubtable Ben Hollinger, who had sold his first discovery for, 't was said, a million dollars, came to town carrying a sack of gold nuggets on his shoulder. Once more Ben had struck it rich and once more the whole town celebrated. The money he received for his first claim had vanished to the last cent. On his former property stood the largest stampmill in the world which still bears his name, as do the company's quotations on the Stock Exchange. The way he went about disposing of the money he received for his new discovery, a mere pittance of $100,000 in cash, was a repetition of his first jollification, though necessarily on a somewhat less extravagant scale.

A man of enormous size, broad shoulders, and an Assyrian bowman's raven-black beard, Hollinger bought himself a dress suit and silk hat. He chartered a train made up of three Pullman cars, a diner and a locomotive, and invited some twenty slightly damaged female saints to accompany him either to Ottawa or Montreal, I forget which. They all accepted and were off in a haze of whisky and furs. The delightful company was absent for a month. Then, one day, half the girls slunk back; the other half hadn't been able to raise the train fare. Ben Hollinger returned a few days later in the caboose at the end of a freight. He had lost everything *including* his shirt. But he still wore his silk hat and the frock coat, though in its crumpled and disheveled state it more than anything else resembled a burlesque comedian's get-up.

Once more somebody grubstaked Ben Hollinger, and he tramped off on the lonesome trails toting a rifle and a huge packsack containing blankets and provisions.

Some years later his skeleton was discovered in an abandoned cabin in the Kapuskasing area. The onetime millionaire had died of starvation.

The solution of certain problems of a personal nature lay far beyond my competence, and understandably so; I was far too young and inexperienced to function as a referee or arbiter, for instance, in cases of marital discord or conflict. Yet I was more than once drawn into such unhappy family affairs, or called upon for advice or counsel. When such incidents occurred I grew aware how hopelessly inadequate and even irrelevant was most of the instruction given at seminaries and theological schools. It wasn't life these institutions of higher learning dealt with. They dealt only with a part of life, that part namely in which the average man or woman takes least interest. It may be vastly edifying and instructive to meditate upon the secrets of salvation and the immortality of the soul, or to dwell in the company of the great fathers of the Church. But it isn't enough! At any rate, what I felt I needed most of all "in the field," were some sound and solid courses in psychology, or at least some books on the subject. I received plenty of other books and read them too, but most of them were mere variations on the same old theme of the alleged *regina scientiarum*, the queen of sciences, theology. What a future minister should learn most and first of all is how to talk as a man to men. And not only when they come to him with questions of religious doubt, which they seldom do, but when they confront him with actual problems of life:

sickness, unemployment, wages, vice, crime, drink, the fear of death....

On these subjects one received no advice at all, or at best a pass-the-buck, don't-bother-me directive: "Take it to the Lord in prayer!" Psychology, moreover, was in those days still widely regarded in orthodox Christian circles as something filthy, and Freud with his teaching of the libido but a *piscator sordium*, a fisher of dirty things.

Calvin, who was a great exegete, told his students that they were not priests and must never take upon themselves the role of priests. They were to be "shepherds and teachers." That's the whole sum and substance of the Protestant ministry. But how would Calvin have acted, I often wondered, if he had met up with some of the experiences that came my way? One day a man called on me: "I want you to go and talk to my wife.... She has been playing the whore with a hoist operator of the P— mine. She lives with that s.o.b. in his cabin.... If you don't do something about it, I'll have to go out there and kill both of them."

Most likely Calvin would have clapped the wife-snatcher in jail.... and the faithless wife as well, plus, as like as not, the plaintiff. For such drastic action, however, which would have been no remedy anyway, I lacked the authority. Nor could I think of interesting the Royal Mounted Police in the case. The sergeant, Philip Thompson, a good friend of mine, would most likely have said something like this: "We can't prevent him from going out and shooting the guilty couple, but if you'll do me a favor, just remind him beforehand that we'll hang him as sure as God made little apples."

I didn't want anybody hanged, so I said to the plaintiff: "Do you want your wife back?"

"Sure I do, we have two kids."

"Will you take her back and forgive her and never mention her lapse again as long as ye both shall live?"

"Sure," he said. "I won't throw it up to her. I ain't been so perfect myself!"

"In that case I'll go and ask her to come back to you."

But the hoistman proved no easy customer to deal with. For a start he cursed me to high heaven. Then he took his rifle down from the wall and loaded it. "I give you till I count ten to get out of the house," he said.

"Thank you, I appreciate your hospitality. I am a little tired, I have come a long way. I'll sit here in this chair till you cool off. But don't forget that if you shoot, you'll dangle by the end of a rope. Phil Thompson always gets his man."

So we sat down and waited, the three of us.

I said to the woman: "Ma'am, your children are expecting you. . . . Come with me; I have a sleigh outside. . . . Your husband will be glad to see you. He told me so. . . ."

When she broke into tears, the hoistman walked up to me with fists clenched: "If you don't get out, I'll break every goddamn bone in your body."

I didn't wait for that calamity, but administered a tap on the jaw which sent him sprawling. While he sat on the floor a little dazed, I took his rifle, a .42 Winchester, emptied the chamber and smashed the gun to pieces on the cabin's threshold.

After I took the woman home, I went to Sergeant Thompson.

"Hello, Phil!"

"Hello, clergy!"

"Phil, I have a confession to make!"

"Fire away!"

"I took Mrs. R—— back to her husband. . . ."

"You did? That's fine, you took a big load off my mind!"

"But I had to beat up the hoistman before I could get her away from him. . . ."

"Good boy, clergy! Good for you!"

"He'll probably be in tomorrow to lay a complaint for breaking his rifle."

"It'll be a pleasure!"

"What'll be a pleasure?"

"What do you think? To get in a few licks myself, of course."

Since the *Discipline* of the Methodist Church forbade unordained probationers to administer holy communion, I naturally obeyed this rule. Mr. Johnston was there to perform this rite. He was my superior, but he was far away, sometimes snowed in, or otherwise inaccessible. . . . What to do in the event of an emergency call? The Scandinavians were all nominally Lutherans and though little concerned with religious matters, it was a different story when the hour of death struck. To a Lutheran, it seems that partaking of holy communion is endowed with certain magical qualities. Its administration in the hour of death is like a seal on or guarantee of forgiveness of sins . . . by the administrator taking the place of God. I didn't believe in these things. Still, I dared not give offense to one of "these little ones," and stay away when summoned. On three or four occasions I performed the rite and pronounced absolution in a priestly fashion according to the formularies of the Anglican Church. When a man was gasping for breath and his body was rent by unendurable pain as in the case of a serious heart attack, and the doctor could do no more than administer a little opium, communion had a beneficient effect. It assuaged anguish, brought alleviation, calm and resignation to the sufferer. It was all a little dishonest on my part, I know, but then, I am sure, God will forgive me. After all, that's His business!

I did not hesitate to hear an Italian worker's confession—no priest being available—when the man was caught in a cave-in on the sixth level of the Dome mine. He could not possibly be extricated without the use of dynamite. Tons and tons of loose sliding rock were slowly squeezing him to death. There was no time for long discussions, for no discussion at all as a matter of fact. When I was called and climbed up in the stope where the man lay trapped and dozens of carbide lamps of his would-be rescuers illuminated the spot, I knelt down, listened to his words of repentance and gave him absolution, promising him with the words of Jesus to the thief on the cross: *Amen dico tibi hodie mecum eris in paradiso.* "Surely, I tell you, this very day, you shall be with me in paradise. . . ." The man held my hand to the end. Before dying he gave me a message to his wife far away in San Daniele del Friuli, near the Austrian border.

If the Roman priests ever get wind of this, I thought, they will be furious with me, but there I was mistaken. One of them, a certain Father Jean Marteau, who was the dead man's parish priest, came to thank me.

"So I did no wrong from your point of view?" I asked.

"No," replied Monsieur Marteau, "in exceptional circumstances God allows unworthy persons to do His work for Him. . . . It's the act of administration that is sacred, not the man who performs the act. . . ."

Jack Kerry came to see me one evening. Kerry was an American, a veteran of the Spanish-American War. He drew a pension of one dollar a day for life, and was thus, by my standards at least, a rich man. I often visited him in the woods, staying overnight, talking, playing checkers and drinking black coffee. With Jack Kerry lived his partner, Jimmy McCarthy, a thin, pigeon-breasted man, who went around mumbling:

"A hundred thousand dollars or nothing! A hundred thousand or nothing!" This figure referred to the price he was willing to accept for the claim which the two men worked and owned.

When Kerry came to the parsonage, he said to me: "Jim is dead. I killed him. . . . We had a fight. He fell and struck his head against the stove. . . . What d'you think I ought to do?"

"What did you fight about?"

"Oh, we had an offer. A mining syndicate offered us $75,000 for our claim. We struck a vein of gold on a quartz and schist contact fifty feet down after fourteen years of labor. . . . Jimmy wouldn't sell. You know his argument: 'A hundred thousand or nothing.' I was more than willing. I have my fill of living in the woods, never seeing a soul, eating rabbit meat and fish till you. . . . That kind of life drives you nuts. Jimmy, as you know, was completely nuts. So we quarreled . . . and you know the rest. He was my best friend, really I don't know what to do. . . . Should I go to Phil Thompson and give myself up?"

"I'll go and see the sergeant. . . . "

"Phil, if I knew a man to be a murderer and kept silent about it, what would you say?"

"I'd say nothing, but I would hold you as an accessory the moment I discovered the truth. . . . "

"Would you really?"

"No doubt in the world. I couldn't do anything else, clergy. That's the law. . . . "

"Well, I know a man who killed his partner. . . . "

"Is that what Jack Kerry came to tell you? . . . He was in town the day before yesterday. I saw him in Bob Polluck's saloon. He was drinking far more than was good for him. When he left the saloon, he turned in the direction of your cabin. . . . Did he tell you he killed Jimmy?"

"He did. He says 't was accidental. . . . What'll you do, arrest him?"

"No, I won't. You bring him in. It'll go easier with him if you bring him in. . . . "

We had a trial; a judge came up all the way from Haileybury. I testified and told the jury that the Kerry-McCarthy claim had been sold and that 75 per cent of the money received was being sent to the dead man's relatives in the United States.

Kerry was found guilty, but Sergeant Thompson said that my testimony indicated extenuating circumstances. The jury made a strong recommendation for mercy. Kerry received an indeterminate sentence from one to five years.

"May I ask a question?" Kerry asked the judge after being sentenced. "Certainly!"

"Can I go and dig up the body and give it a decent Christian burial? He lies out there in the woods . . . so alone!"

"Will you undertake to perform the burial ceremony?" the judge asked me.

"I will, Your Honor!"

"Alright, this will make Kerry eligible for parole in a year's time," said the judge.

But though I helped to disinter the body, I did not bury Jimmy. Jimmy had been a Catholic, so I asked Father Marteau to officiate. James McCarthy was buried from the Catholic Church in Golden City. Phil Thompson and I . . . and Kerry were pallbearers at the service of requiem. . . .

One more memory before leaving my parish under the northern lights never to return. Just beyond the South Porcupine boundary by the side of the road to Schumacher, somewhat hidden in the woods, stood an enormous log house, two stories high and about a hundred feet long. I do not recall whether there hung a sign outside giving the establishment's name. Everybody referred to it as The White Rat. In that place rip-roaring, tumultuous celebrations went on night after night; a player piano rattled; drunken men staggered in and out; shouts and curses in all languages rent the air; there were fights and brawls; poker and crap games were in progress at all hours of the night and day.

There were plenty of other brothels in the area, but The White Rat took the cake, so to speak. It was the classiest, the most distinguished of all the houses of ill fame. The downstairs part served as a gaming room. Against a background of mirrors and shelves loaded with bottles ran a bar as long as the one at the old League of Nations' building in Geneva.

Upstairs were the cubicles where *mesdames les pensionnaires*, some twenty odd in number, exercised their profession. I would gladly have taken a look inside, but this was clearly out of the question: I had to think of the dignity of the cloth, threadbare and scanty though it was. In passing I merely glanced at the lighted windows. When payday at the mines came around, business at The White Rat was phenomenal. The following day the girls lined up at the teller's window in the timber shack which served as a bank, to deposit their earnings. One morning, the bank manager, Bill Todhunter, told me: "More than two thousand dollars were deposited by The White Rat's ladies this week."

"Which makes it exactly two thousand more than was taken up in the collection plates last Sunday in church," I commented sadly.

How this remark of mine got out, I cannot imagine. One of The White Rat's girls with a strong mother instinct and a compassionate heart was reported to have asked if I really got enough to eat. She told a friend of mine: "I would like to call him inside when he passes and give him a good square meal. He needs it!" Thereafter several of The White Rat's inmates came to church and contributed handsomely to our budget. They also wafted a heavenly odor of perfume through the house of God. . . .

As is customary all over the American continent, though not in Europe, the officiating minister stands at the church door to shake hands with the departing members of the congregation. This is how I came to know the names of a good many of the local daughters of Rachab.

"I'm Elly," one of them would smile kindly as she passed out of church, "please pardon my glove!"

"I'm Fanny. . . . I'm Gertie. . . . I'm Jean," and so on.

"And I'm Flo Fabri, they call me Big Flo," said a deep-bosomed and expensively garbed brunette, who wore a black seal coat, a muff of the same material, and what was known in those days as a picture hat. "I'm the madam at The White Rat. Thank you very much for your sermon!"

"Glad to see you, sister Flo! Come again!"

"I sure will, big boy! Here," she said, "take this." She tried to slip a twenty dollar bill into my hand.

"Flo, that's very kind of you, but I can't take the money." I noticed that all eyes were on me. "Give it to Mr. Vance over there! He's the treasurer!"

"Him?" she drew up her nose, "no sir, never! Not to that tightwad!"

Miss Fabri seldom failed to show up, though she was often late. Saturday night, as a rule, was a big night at The White Rat. She always cried a little during the sermon, sniffing and daubing her large black eyes with a lace handkerchief. My mother would have taken this as a good omen, tears being the first sign of "a broken and contrite heart. . . ." But I can't for the life of me think what made that girl cry so bitterly at times. It may be that in her case we were in the presence of a remnant of those collective weeping bouts which are mentioned by Coulton, Huizinga, Levy-Bruehl and other celebrated medievalists. Bauman calls the mass-weeping in the Middle Ages a phase of "the divine madness."

When the preaching friars came to a town, say in France, Italy or Germany, to call for penitence, which usually meant scaring the people with hell-fire, men, women and children not only cried, they sobbed, they howled, they wailed, they threw themselves on the floor, and writhed as if in the throes of an epileptic fit. The churches were turned into bedlam. The history of the Middle Ages is filled with the sound of weeping and gnashing of teeth. The Florentine Savonarola's sermons very often had this maddening effect upon a crowd. Sometimes he had twelve, fifteen thousand "weepers" in the Duomo of Florence! That's where his followers got their nickname: *piagnoni*, crybabies, snivelers.

Was Flo Fabri a latter-day *piagnona*? Maybe! I have no other explanation for her tears. They cannot possibly have been caused by anything I said to her. For I liked her very much. . . .

In the spring of 1916 occurred a crisis of conscience which shook me to the depths of my being and radically changed my course through life: I abandoned all thoughts of the ministry. Although it is true, *que l'on revient toujours à ses premières amours,* and that some years later I resumed my studies in the theological school of the Reformed Church of France, I then left dogmatics severely alone. Having reached the conclusion—not without a deep sense of loss and disillusionment—that centuries of theology have brought us not one step nearer to the solution of the mystery of our existence, I took up the study of the history of religion with special emphasis on the origins of Christianity. . . .

As I see it now my mistake in 1916 was that I took the Christian gospel too seriously. When I returned to Toronto from the north, I was invited to follow a course that would lead in quick order to a commission as a military chaplain. I declined on the grounds that in spite of my sympathy for Britain's stand, her cause did not seem to warrant desertion from the Militia Christi. I decided to take the side of the conscientious objectors. It was by no means an easy decision to make, but a truth remains only half a truth so long as it exists merely in verbal formulation. It is in action that a thought becomes genuinely alive.

The thought to be made alive was that of nonviolent but nevertheless active resistance to war and all its works, though not as a phase of the class struggle, but as an attempt reverently to follow in the footsteps of

Jesus. At the seminary it was objected that there exists no direct evidence of the Nazarene having pointed to nonviolent action as the road to peace. I argued back that the early Christians were still so close to Jesus in history that their attitude in this matter must have refleced some important aspect of His teachings. It was their understanding of His mind which they applied when they refused to take service in Caesar's armies. They felt confident that in this manner Jesus had shown them the way to overcome the world. And so immense was their hope and so powerful a spiritual weapon their nonviolent action that they, a handful of despised sectarians, actually overcame the decadence of the Roman world.

After some correspondence with the Reverend Dick Sheppard, the Vicar of London's St. Martin in the Fields and head of the Peace Pledge Union, I joined that body of pacifists, antimilitarists and conscientious objectors who subscribed to Einstein's declaration that war is a crime against humanity.

I must say that on the whole the churchmen and the civil authorities showed great tolerance and forbearance when I began to debate the question publicly. True, the Sunday evening meetings in Toronto's Labor Temple under the chairmanship of the president of the typographical union, James Simpson, a later socialist mayor of the city, were more than once disrupted by invading bands of war veterans and super patriots who indiscriminately and howlingly decried all present as slackers, cowards, defeatists, paid agents of the Kaiser, and so on.

Those ruffians, finding it easier to beat an opponent into unconsciousness than reason with him, got into the habit of reinforcing their catcalls and epithets with rubber truncheons and chunks of lead pipe. As long as we stayed inside the hall we had police protection. No sooner did we come outside than we, not the rowdies, were deemed to have disturbed the peace. We got it in the neck from both sides, the veterans *and* the cops.

As a result of these scuffles my personal situation became doubly awkward; for while the nonreligious antimilitarists did not need to take things lying down, and indeed, whenever attacked, promptly and effectively retaliated, I was talking about nonviolence, reverence for life, love of neighbor, the fatherhood of God and the brotherhoood of all men, including the Germans, as my motives in opposing war.

Although it was a hard road to travel for one not altogether bereft of physical strength, I thought it my duty to bear up silently under revilement and opprobrium—and knocks on the head—without in turn having recourse to the methods of those whom I qualified as barbarians and un- converted pagans.

In the end, it was before the argument that the war was "a righteous war" that I capitulated. Two serious-minded elderly citizens, Newton W. Rowell, the leader of the Liberal opposition in the Ontario parliament, and Justice John J. Maclaren of the provincial supreme court, persuaded me to look upon the struggle with Germany as the war to end all wars.

The two men sat with me in a small room in the back of the Metropolitan Church in Toronto from nine in the evening till far into the night trying to show me the error of my ways. They readily granted that war was evil, that it was Christianity's most grievous sin. But the war was on. It could not be stopped till a decision had fallen one way or another. "If evil is to be done, however much we detest it, let it be done quickly! . . . Help us to put an end to war for all time to come! . . . This war is waged for liberty, in the defense of weak nations, and to set the whole world free. . . . "

I was no match for two such dedicated and learned Christian gentlemen. I had also grown thoroughly disgusted, I must say, with being stopped in the streets by women who insisted on pinning a white feather, the badge of craven cowardice, on my clothes. I stood six feet two in my stockings at the time, and looked most fit for the service to these militant females. I could not begin an argument each time a woman halted me to ask: "Why aren't you in uniform?"

CHAPTER IV

Soldier of the King

I WAS PROMISED that I would be given a noncombatant position as interpreter. As soon as I had sworn allegiance to His Britannic Majesty, and thus became his subject, I signed my name to a declaration that I would willingly go wherever the King deemed it necessary to send me. In the same instant all was forgotten about the interpreter's job. I was shipped off to Camp Borden and given a rifle like any other recruit. The unit in which I enlisted was known as the Corps of Guides, though what we were to do by way of guiding, I never discovered.

I practiced on the rifle range and went route marching. The exercise I liked best fell shortly after reveille at six in the morning when there was a wild scramble for the ice-cold water taps by hundreds of recruits stripped to the waist, and right after the ablutions a two mile run on the double. Four sergeant instructors clad in white sweaters ran in front to set the pace. Twenty others ran alongside the ranks bellowing and yapping: "Up those knees! Chests out! Swing those arms! One-two, one-two, one-two!"

The first morning I thought I'd never make it. The fellow running by my side, Bill Vaughan, who easily weighed 250 pounds, collapsed with a groan of anguish. But I was not permitted to go to his aid . . . and, incidentally, steal a little breather myself. One white sweater spotted me: "Keep going, that man! What do you think this is, a damn nursery? Keep going! One-two, one-two, one-two! Don't drag those feet like a bloody elephant! Up those knees! Up, up, up!"

After the run the battalion sergeant major, a gentleman of British extraction, known in the ranks as Peppy, who sported a pug nose and a red mustache, the ends waxed to needle-point sharpness, asked the still puffing Vaughan: "How the hell did you get in the family way, me lad? What d'you do in civil life?"

125

"I'm a bartender, sir!"

"A bartender? Blimy! Well, you won't tend any bar 'ere, me lad, at least not till you get rid of that beer barrel up in front!"

"I'll never get rid of it," Vaughan confided to me disconsolately. "If I have to run like that again, I'll have a heart attack!"

But wonders never cease; after a month the beer barrel had vanished. Vaughan had reduced 40 pounds and ran with the best of us. That morning promenade on the double was a real boon. During the first week we shivered in the draughty and leaky tents. There was dew on the ground and streaks of hoarfrost on the blankets. After a couple of weeks of ice-cold washing at dawn and a run around with "knees-up," we didn't know what it was to be cold. You glowed with sheer animal fire from top to bottom.

I thought I knew how to walk. The army did not think so, and the army was right. It is the army's general opinion that the elements in which physical endurance is most usefully manifested are the capacity of bearing a weight for long, and marching long and far, "between a sleep and a sleep." We were allowed to fill our water bottles before a route march, but at the same time advised not to drink from them or at most take a swig now and then to rinse the mouth and spit it out quickly.

During the first weeks this procedure amounted to torture. Many a soldier could not resist the temptation to quench his raging thirst after a few hours' walking and sweating. I was one of the first to succumb in spite of Peppy's solemn warning that I would get as sick as a cat. I promptly confirmed his prognostication and had to fall out and be sick by the roadside. After that first fall from grace I never drank water again, not in Canada, nor in Britain, nor in France. The abstinence from water dried me out till I became as thin as a lath, but easily twice as strong. There wasn't a dram of superfluous fluid in my body. Not even under the strongest sun did I perspire.

During the second week of training we had a sad accident. Six men were struck by a bolt of lightning. They walked in the front ranks of the column while on a route march through the sand hills in Camp Borden's extensive wastelands. For some unexplained reason the first two ranks carried their bayonets at the fix. Six of those eight men never knew what struck them. A unit of field artillery buried our first casualties on the outskirts of the camp, six coffins draped with the Union Jack.

We were apparently considered presentable enough to appear in public after eight weeks of flexing and limbering up, and entrained for Brockville, a quiet, lovely town situated on the north bank of the St. Lawrence River opposite Morristown in the state of New York. We were quartered in the buildings on the fair grounds and slept in wooden bunks four stories high. Shortly after establishing ourselves our manpower was increased by two companies who had been recruited in British Columbia and by one company of Acadians from Nova Scotia. The British Columbians enriched us with a brass band, while the Nova Scotians, the New Scotlanders, appropriately, brought a band of bagpipes and drums. The pipers wore kilts and multicolored tartans. Like the Orangemen on "the glorious twelfth" (of July), the drummers swung their drumsticks from leather straps around their wrists. When in top form and high battle spirit, they freely, savagely and proudly bespattered the drums with drops of their Highland blood. For our regimental tune we had the "Colonel Bogey March," while the pibroch players' favorite was:

> There our foes that burned and slew—
> Bonnie laddie, Highland laddie!
> There at last, they got their due,
> Bonnie laddie, Highland laddie!

In Brockville the training became more intense. We had mock battles; maneuvers they were called. We dug trenches in the daytime outside in the farmlands, and at nights occupied them waiting for an enemy who, fortunately, never came. As far as I can remember, those exercises under actual battle conditions were always held at nights in the pouring rain. The rain was to accustom us to the climatic conditions said to prevail on the real battlefields overseas. We fired blank cartridges and occasionally fixed bayonets and sloughed and slithered through the mud for an attack on an invisible foe. Those night maneuvers would have been a huge farce except for our getting soaked to the skin and marching back to barracks at the peep of dawn looking like so many cats fished up from the river.

To make things more realistic, each company was equipped with two machine guns. Two, I said. There may have been but few of those Maxims, they were nevertheless formidable. They were as awkward to transport as the iron rocking horses you see in a merry-go-round, and heavy as lead. One man carried the barrel, another the tripod on which the barrel had to be screwed down before it could be fired. It fell to my lot to be a tripod bearer. In moments of not so pious retrospect I can still feel that instrument of dull torture boring into my neck and shoulders. My inseparable companion, the gunner, was Arnold Tremblay, a French-Canadian. It was no trick to discover whence he hailed, for he had one song, and one song only which he sang bilingually come hell or high water:

> *A Montréal, à Montréal!*
> That's the place I like to be
> With all the girls so dear to me
> *A Montréal, à Montréal!*

One night, in the course of a raging mock battle, blunderbusses and firecrackers going off, red and green flares shooting up and sizzling out, N.C.O.'s blowing whistles, and a general racket fit to raise the dead, Arnold and I, not quite unintentionally, became separated from the company's main body just as we had planted the machine gun by the side of a ditch for a little rest. We didn't know whether we belonged to the defending or to the attacking force, the "blues" or the "reds." Nobody came to enlighten us. One officer in passing switched a flashlight in our direction and called out: "You fellows reds or blues?"

"We don't know!"

"Then you're green, damn you!" he shouted, laughing at his own joke.

It was pitch-dark and, as I mentioned, it rained. No! A storm, a tornado, a cloudburst was upon us. The Maxim slipped off the mudbank into the ditch. Try as we may, we couldn't lift it back on more or less solid ground for the whole terrain was by then a pool of mud and slime. We stayed faithfully by the sunken Maxim till the first rays of daylight when we heard the bugles far away blow the retreat.

The British infantry manual says that in exceptional circumstances, such as when you are confronted with a *force majeure*, you are allowed to withdraw. Wasn't that Noah's flood a *force majeure*? I thought so. Accordingly I gave Arnold and myself the order to retreat. We straggled into the barracks by ourselves, two wet and weary soldiers of the King. The others were already drying themselves out.

"Where's the Maxim?" demanded Peppy as we walked past the guardroom.

"Gone down the drain!" said Arnold with a shrug of the shoulders.

"Go back and get h'it! H'it's the King's property. If you ain't back by noon, h'I'll prefer charges against you!"

"What charges?"

"Sequestering 'is Majesty's property. Go get, on the double!"

"We can't do it alone," I said. "We've been trying our best since three o'clock this morning. It can't be budged!"

"H'alright then, h'I'll find a detail to go with you! But get the gun! That's stryte from the flag. . . . H'it'll go tough with you blokes if you fyle. . . ."

After a cup of tea and some biscuits as hard and gritty as concrete smeared with the eternal plum and apple jam, we set out to look for the Maxim. Six men came along to assist us in our search. The long and short of it is we didn't find it, either then or afterwards. The gun had "sunk without a trace" as the German communiqués used to say of our torpedoed convoy ships. But this meant that Arnold and I were "up for orderly room" the next evening.

"Mark my word, you two'll be shot at sunrise as you damn well deserve!" remarked the amiable Peppy as he "paraded" us into the colonel's presence.

There he was, Colonel Ross MacDonald, the man upon whom in time I came to look as a friend and big brother, and who unquestionably saved my life at a later stage in the war by digging me out of a bombed tunnel with his bare hands in three days and nights of unimaginable bone-wracking labor.

Very tall, a clipped pepper and salt mustache, deep brown eyes, a strong chin and a prominent Celtic-type nose, there was a touch of frost at the colonel's temples announcing the proximity of middle age. When he looked up casually from where he sat behind a plain wooden table as the sergeant major paraded us into the orderly room, I noticed that his mouth was firm, though marked by patience and kindness. In front of him stood a water carafe and a glass. On the table lay some papers which he was reading and turning over rapidly, frowning and intent.

"What's the charge, sergeant major?"

"H'I beg to report, sir, these two men lost a Maxim gun. . . ."

"Lost a machine gun? Where?"

"Answer the colonel," ordered Peppy. " 'E's h'askin' you a question, stupid!"

"Sir," I said, "the gun sank in the mud the other night. We can't even locate the spot where it disappeared. . . ."

"Stolen, you think?"

"No, sir, I don't think so. Nobody could carry it off. It's too heavy."

"They probably sold it to a junk dealer across the river in Morristown," suggested Peppy, ever eager to speed our doom.

"In the middle of the night?" I asked him. "Floated it across, no doubt! ..."

"'Old yer tongue! And stand to h'attention when you speak to the colonel...."

"That's alright, sergeant major," hushed the colonel. "We'll have to make another search, I guess. You had better take charge yourself...."

"Very well, sir!"

"By the way, what do the accused do in civil life?"

"H'it's all in front of you, sir, in those files. This 'ere one is a pipe fitter. 'E comes from Montreal. The h'other one is a bee hay...."

"A *bee hay*? What's that?"

"Them's the funny letters behind 'is name, sir. D'you see, sir? Them's put in to 'igh 'at us regular army men, sir, if you'll pardon me saying so."

"Very well, sergeant major, you may go. Take Tremblay with you. I want to keep the other man here for a minute...."

"Shall h'I 'ave 'im locked up, sir, this 'ere Private Tremblay?"

"Lock him up? What for? We need him for the search tomorrow, don't we?

"How is it," asked Colonel MacDonald, after the others left, that you are marked down here as Holland born? Is that true?"

"Of course it's true, sir."

"And you a volunteer in a British army?"

"Yes, sir."

"Well, that's fine! I can't tell you how much I appreciate that, my boy. You must be the only Hollander in this man's army."

"Not the only one, sir, but one of very few, I dare say!"

"Presbyterian, too?"

"Dutch Reformed!"

"*Guid, guid*! That's the same thing, isn't it? John Knox and John Calvin! I needn't tell you. By the way, why weren't you ordained?" He looked in the files again, and then stared me straight in the face.

"The time hadn't come, sir!"

"I see, but you can help me a lot, anyway. I want to start a Bible class in this battalion, you see."

"A Bible class, sir? Isn't that forbidden?" I shuddered at the prospect.

I thought I was through with Bible classes for ever and ever.

"It's forbidden to discuss religion in the ranks, if that is what you mean," said MacDonald. "But it's not forbidden to teach God's word, I trust. . . . Now look, let's be realistic. We are going to war, aren't we? All these fine lads will be thrown into battle. How many will come through? Nobody knows. But we can't let them go unprepared. They must stand before the judgment seat. It's up to you and me to tell them about Jesus, the mighty, to save! . . . We will start a Bible class next Sunday afternoon. Of course, attendance will be on a voluntary basis. We won't force anybody. But we may not withhold the saving word of grace from any man, high or low! You agree?"

"Sir," I said, trying desperately to get away from this frying-pan-into-the-fire project, "most of the French Acadians are Roman Catholics. What about them? You don't expect them to come to your Bible class, do you?"

" 'S long as the light holds out to burn, the vilest sinner may return. . . . The Acadians are my own boys. I come from their district. I know their parents, brothers and sisters. . . . Did you know that many of them are illiterate? That I write their letters for them and read the letters that come from their homes? There you can help, too. . . . Some painful letters will have to be written when we get to France. . . . "

"Sir, isn't that the chaplain's work? We have a chaplain, haven't we?"

"Indeed we do. But the less said about him the better. The fellow isn't a believer in our sense of the word. . . . "

In *our* sense of the word!

I felt the beads of perspiration run down my forehead as I realized that I was back where I started; in the old-time religion of Holland's deepest fundamentalism. But there was no escape.

"I'll give you a couple of stripes now," resumed Colonel MacDonald. "When we move overseas I'll promote you to sergeant. I need you by my side. Can you use a typewriter? You can? I'm so glad to have found a man that I can depend on in matters of faith. . . . "

It may come as a surprise at this late hour to learn that the war of 1914–18 was a religious war. Still, that's the way Colonel Ross MacDonald looked upon the struggle with the "Hun." In his book the British Empire represented the greatest power for good in a world of wickedness and sin. The Kaiser—"oh, that cursed fiend!"—was antichrist in person. Sir Douglas Haig, our commander in chief, was referred to as "Jehovah's terrible swift sword." And wasn't the Prince of Wales providentially called after that David who shed Philistine blood by the bucketful?

After my first interview with Colonel MacDonald I lay on the top bunk in the barrack room staring at an electric light bulb on the ceiling, and fell asleep dreaming of the Prussian Guard, the Amalekite and Jebusite guard, and all the other guards on record as enemies of the faith. . . .

From the 'Cadians I learned that Colonel MacDonald was the owner and operator of vast timberlands in New Brunswick and a paper mill in Iroquois Falls. In his younger days he worked as foreman in one of his own lumber camps. From that time dated the nickname "Foghorn," given him by the lumberjacks whom he awakened with the thundering shout: "Daylight in the swamp!" Old Mac was above the military age when he enlisted, but, in collusion with the Right Honorable Sam Hughes, the Minister of War, he wormed himself into the army by keeping his age a secret. In his own bailiwick, a village near Sydney, Nova Scotia, he functioned as a banker. On Sundays he taught an adult Bible class in the Presbyterian church. He owned a bank, the general store, fishing boats, apple orchards and extensive pieces of real estate in different cities.

All this wealth, I gladly testify, stood the battalion in good stead, especially when we reached France. The colonel received so many food packages and extras that he could not have possibly disposed of them by himself. We were the envy of the brigade, of the whole division, in fact, for having such a generous commander. The band's new instruments he paid for with his own money. As for the bagpipers, they were the apple of his eye. When these dudelsackers started their katzenjammer, Ross MacDonald whispered in ecstasy: "Ah, *mon*, what heavenly music! It is as if we were entering the pearly gates, don't you think?" Nobody thought so, but everybody agreed. For it is not wise to disagree with colonels. I say this for the benefit of the young who are still to face that ordeal.

At Christmas he distributed thick woolen khaki-colored scarves among his fourteen hundred odd followers. What this meant once we crossed the ocean could perhaps be best ascertained by inquiring—some are still living today—amongst the girls, or rather the grandmothers, of Picardy and French Flanders. For we were irresistibly contaminated by the colonel's generosity. The *demoiselles* and their *mamans* shivering in the coldest winters of the war were indirectly the beneficiaries of Old Mac's bounty. With the same impartiality, I should add, the girls also disposed of our surplus jam, cheese, white bread, bacon and... underwear!

I don't know how many letters I wrote, hundreds at least, maybe a thousand. When the men of the Acadian company learned that they needn't importune the colonel any longer, but could confidently address themselves to me for their correspondence, they weren't slow to take advantage. Most of their missives dealt with family affairs or financial matters. Our battalion baker, Sergeant Jean Baptiste Pinay, had nine children and he wanted each of them mentioned by name in his weekly letter home.

I didn't mind, for when I wrote letters I didn't have to take part in other more onerous "fatigues." Before long I came to like Pinay's children so well by long distance communication that I signed myself *Oncle Pierre*. Moreover, Pinay was a good friend to have around. Everybody admired him because, short, multiple-chinned, and ruddy-complexioned, he was well over the military age and still determined to do his bit. His head was as bald as a billiard ball, but he had one qualification which gave him a fine reputation and brought in some extra cash for our pockets. He could lift a chair with his teeth with a man sitting on it. He didn't perform till all the bets were placed, generally with visitors from other units. It goes without saying that we always won. When the battalion went to Britain and was inspected by the King in Windsor Great Park, Sergeant Pinay was pointed out to His Majesty. "Glad to see you!" said George V. "The same here," replied Shorty who couldn't say more because he was out of breath with the exertion of holding in his potbelly in the King's presence.

In France Pinay became more useful from a general point of view. He never went up the line with us, but stayed behind in the various billets behind the front. He not only baked bread, he could also make a fine loaf cake. The French people ate bad bread and no cake at all during the war. Pinay made money on the side baking cakes for his friends at five francs apiece. Soldiers and officers carried the cakes away as presents for their girl friends and other acquaintances.... I didn't have to pay for my cakes. The letters to Madame Pinay and the children did the trick....

In the case of other clients for whom I wrote letters, it was I who usually put in a few words of endearment or a love paragraph at the end.

"Don't you want to tell her that you still love her?" I would ask one of those 'Cadians far away from home.

"Sure I do! What'll I say? Don't forget," the man would caution me, "that Annemarie (or Susanne or Solange or whatever her name) can't read, and that she will have to get *monsieur le curé* to read my letter for her!"

In this way a rather interesting contest as *postillons d'amour* developed between various anonymous French Canadian parish priests and myself. Before long we were vying with each other in the fine points of love's terminology. Some of those clerics, to my surprise, put in a good deal more than one would expect from men who had made a vow of chastity.

I could not very well stay away from Bible class. The colonel counted on me. Captain the Reverend Cyril Jones, M.A., also attended. He felt it his duty to sit in, and occasionally venture an opinion. Though twenty-six years old, Cyril Jones still looked very much like a boy. A shock of soft blond hair gave him a somewhat feminine allure. He was unassuming and shy of manner and about six feet tall. The only son of an Anglican vicar stationed in some rural community in Ontario, he was British born and a graduate of Gonville and Caius College, Cambridge. He held two degrees and called himself a neoplatonist. For diversion he played the mandolin, singing Neapolitan songs, his supreme hope being a trip to Italy after the war. I never met another man so magnificently unprepared for the bitterness of life; absolutely without guile, almost a saint. Sometimes he seemed to be sojourning in another world as he sat meditating on what he had just read in some book on mysticism or prayer, his favorite subjects also in his sermons. It was Jones' firm conviction that the British people were the chosen race and the English gentleman type the nearest possible approach to human perfection.

"Let me tell you one thing," he said one day as we sat drinking tea on the floor of a ruined farmhouse in the neighborhood of Bethune, "with all its faults and defects Western civilization has produced few things more admirable than the English gentleman. . . ."

"You mean strong, courageous fellows, knights in shining armor, hearts of oak and all that sort of thing? But such people you find everywhere," I objected.

"The character of the English gentleman is not based only on force and courage, but on truth, on public spiritedness, on a due sense of proportion and a sober enthusiasm for justice. . . ."

"Is the English gentleman type found anywhere else on earth?"

"Obviously not!"

"Aren't the Americans and Canadians of British stock? Couldn't some gentlemen have slipped in amongst them?"

"Well, I don't want to appear uncharitable, we may perhaps go as far as to say that they are apprentice gentlemen.... There is indeed some hope for them...."

"Is there any hope for creatures like myself?"

"Decidedly! The more English you become, the broader will be your sympathy for others, the more Christian you will be...."

"Jonesy, do you consider yourself a gentleman?"

"I am trying, though I still apprehend the idea very imperfectly and realize it more imperfectly still.... Even so, I thank God every day that I was born an Englishman."

"I'm glad Old Mac isn't hearing you. He doesn't think much of you Sassenaghs."

"Oh, he knows my sentiments.... There's definitely something fine in the man though he is but poorly equipped with knowledge. I think he's sincerely striving to be civilized. Did you know that we both smoke the same brand of tobacco?"

"I didn't know.... But could I have some more tea?"

"Definitely! I notice that you too are making progress!"

"I like coffee better."

"You can't help that! It's one of the faults of the Americans and the Dutch.... Poor people! They're rather to be pitied than blamed for it."

"Yes, we must have broad sympathies with others even though they are only coffee drinkers."

"Quite right; I see that you are getting the point!"

The sessions of the colonel's Bible class were held in the messroom. Twenty, perhaps thirty men turned out, never more. We sat along the sides of a dining table, Colonel Mac presiding and Cyril Jones at the opposite end. Jones always began by offending our teacher by taking out his underslung pipe and filling it.

"No smoking, please, Captain Jones!" warned Mac.

"I'm not smoking, sir, I'm just holding my pipe in my mouth. I feel more comfortable that way."

"Now," said Old Mac one afternoon as he told us the story of the miraculous fish catch on Lake Galilee, "now you see, fellows, all those great men

in the Bible, the apostles and the prophets, all of them had a trade or profession quite apart from their position in the Church. . . . For instance,
Peter and James, as we saw this afternoon, were fishermen. . . . Paul was
a tentmaker . . . Luke was an M.D., and Mark an author. . . ."

"Were there any bankers in those days, sir?" one boy asked not so
naïvely.

For a moment the colonel seemed nettled by the question. He puckered
his brow, sure sign of an approaching storm, for he understood perfectly
well that it was a loaded question aimed at his own profession. Soon, however, he bethought himself: "Sure," he replied kindly, "sure, there was
Matthew. . . . Matthew was a banker; he was a publican, a tax collector—
in other words, a financial expert. As I said, every great figure in the Bible
had a trade or profession. We are told that Joseph was a carpenter, David
a musician, Amos a plowman. Stephen, who was stoned to death, ran the
charity distribution department in Jerusalem. . . ."

"Sure, sure," spoke up Cyril Jones, "and Jehovah himself ran the barbershop."

Dumfounded, the colonel's jaw dropped. He stared at the chaplain
as if he had seen a ghost.

"None of your smart-alecky tricks now, Mr. Jones! We're here to study
the word of God. Do I understand you to say, sir, that God ran a barbershop? Aren't you ashamed of yourself, sir?"

"Sir, it says so in the Bible!" came back Cyril.

"What does it say, sir?"

"It says: 'And God himself will shave the beards of those of Babylon!'
Look it up yourself. You've got a Bible there! Look it up, sir! The passage
occurs in the seventh chapter of Isaiah, the twentieth verse." With these
words the chaplain got up and walked out.

The colonel located the passage, read it and passed the book to me:
"What does it mean?" he asked. "Isn't this a heluva puzzler?"

"The passage must be understood allegorically," I said, taking a desperate chance at interpretation. "The Assyrians and the Babylonians in
their brazen arrogance were inordinately proud of their beards. They
wore their beards defiantly, challengingly, you might say, for they considered themselves the masters of the world. If Isaiah says that God will
shave off their beards, he means, no doubt, that they will be punished for
their ungodly arrogance. Their magnificent beards will be snipped off and
swept up with the dust. . . ."

"I see, so that's what it means! . . . But did Jones have to say this in front of all those boys? Isn't he the craziest chaplain you ever heard of? Isn't he coming very near to atheism?"

In the course of our stay quite a few of our men were united in holy matrimony to Brockville girls. I served as witness at no less than four weddings. The possession of a marriage certificate entitled the women to a separation allowance and a monthly gratuity from the Patriotic Fund. But those weddings also brought a lot of trouble, for the newlyweds preferred being together at nights in the rooms they rented on the streets leading to the fair grounds where we were quartered, and Peppy wasn't very generous in doling out night passes.

But as always, love found a way; the married men went over the fence at nights after the last roll call. The bunk next to mine belonging to Corporal Charles Pearce was usually empty, as were a dozen others. If the absentees returned before dawn they had little difficulty. The sentries posted around the grounds usually closed one eye or in comradely solidarity pretended to be totally eyeless when they noticed a belated prodigal rejoining the home base. Occasionally, however, the Benedicts weren't back for morning roll call, and then there was the devil to pay. When they finally showed up, Peppy had no mercy and locked them up in the guardroom. At one time the clink was filled to the bursting point with unhappy married men. Old Mac then took a hand himself; he delivered a lecture to the battalion threatening to send repeaters to the military prison in nearby Kingston, Ontario.

Nineteen men, three N.C.O.'s amongst them, wouldn't put up with Mac's no-sleeping-out decree. One night they hired a boat a few miles down the river and deserted to the American side taking their wives with them.

"You only have yourselves to blame," the colonel quite illogically told the remaining 1400 loyal ones, "if after this wholesale desertion, we move overseas much earlier than first anticipated."

This, however, was no threat; we wanted to go overseas! At that time most of us were still anxious to have it over with. Had we known what was in store for us, we might well have tried to dally as long as possible in the peaceful Laurentian environment.

On the evening of February 1, 1917, the battalion suddenly received orders to entrain for Halifax. The entire population of Brockville, its streets and civic buildings festively illuminated, was out to bid us adieu. Thousands of people walked with us to the station. Many girls linked arms with the troops. Everything was permitted. One young lady, a radiant beauty with hair the color of a freshly minted gold coin, who said her name was Dorothy, suggested that she carry my rifle for me.

"Why didn't I meet you before?" I asked.

"It's your own fault," she said. "I saw you a dozen times on the streets at nights, but you never looked at me."

After two minutes the rifle proved too heavy for her. So she put on my cap and held on to my arm as if starting on the honeymoon.

The band stood playing at the end of the railway platform: "If her eyes are blue as skies, that's Peggy O'Neil" and "Oh, don't deceive me, Oh, never leave me! How could you use a poor maiden so?"

Women and girls, members of the local ladies' aid societies of all denominations, loaded us with boxes and packages of cake and pie, chocolates and candy. Girls you had never seen before walked up, threw their arms around you and kissed you till they took your breath away.

It was a gay scene, but also a sad one; mothers and fathers, sisters and sweethearts clung to their departing boys as if they would never let go. Peppy's wife, leaning on her husband's shoulders, sobbed her heart out. The colonel's wife, smiling bravely through her tears, clutched her man's arm. Nor could Cyril Jones control his emotions as he embraced his father and mother. . .for the last time!

Old Mac himself had to wipe his eyes time and again. Then suddenly he straightened out and signaled to the bandmaster. A whistle blew and for an instant no sound was heard save for the puffing of the locomotive far up in front.

A cold chill ran down my spine. Was it the angel of death passing by, serving notice that all the fun was over and the real business of war about to commence?

Again Peppy's whistle shrieked! The color guard stepped forward. We presented arms as the band struck up; first the national anthem:

O Canada, terre de nos aïeux. . . .

then Old Mac's favorite:

God be with you till we meet again!
When life's perils thick confound you,
Put His loving arms around you. . . .

We slept on the floor of a huge armory building in Halifax where we arrived late at night. Early the next morning we went on board the S.S. *Metagama*, a medium-sized C.P.R. passenger liner. We were scarcely installed in our cabins when the ship raised anchor and we moved out to sea. There were seven or eight ships in the convoy; one boat was loaded with New Zealand troops who had traveled across the Pacific to Vancouver and from that city by rail to Halifax. Another ship carried Manchurian labor units, for China was in the war too—on our side, that is. The other ships were freighters carrying guns and munitions.

"We'll be safe," Peppy said as we stood leaning over the railing watching the convoy ships taking up their positions. "I mean the Jerry subs won't attack us."

"Why not?"

"They say Prime Minister Borden is on board with us here. The Jerries never fire at prime ministers. . . . "

They might not have fired at the prime minister; we had a good scare nevertheless. A little more than halfway across, a whole flock of British destroyers hove in sight. They dashed to and fro, circled the convoy, then moved off again into the fog. Suddenly in the middle of the night the alarm signals screamed. The *Metagama*'s engines stopped and we were all ordered to the top deck where we stood in three rows with life belts around our necks. We all thought that a submarine had been sighted, but how anyone could see anything in that pitch-black night was inconceivable.

Pretty soon a destroyer hove to, lowered a boat and a party of British naval officers clambered up our bridge ladder on the starboard. The naval officers talked with the *Metagama*'s captain who summoned Old Mac, who in turn summoned Peppy. All went below deck and stopped before the door of a cabin on E deck. The Britishers got from Peppy the names of the men quartered in that particular cabin, but who were for the time being on deck standing by during the alert. When the boarding party returned, revolvers were drawn and a naval lieutenant seized hold of one of our men. They took him off in their boat and at the same time the *Metagama*'s engines started up again.

We all knew the fellow who was removed. He had told us that he was a naturalized Swiss. "He's more likely a German," explained Old Mac. "He has been signaling the subs with a flashlight from the porthole of his cabin. He attracted a destroyer's attention. Maybe the sub's attention as well. We'll have to stay on deck till we get word from the destroyers that the coast is clear."

Three hours we stood waiting. At the peep of dawn there was a burst of gunfire from two of the destroyers and from the naval gun mounted on the aftdeck of the New Zealand troopship. Whether a German submarine got near our convoy, I don't know. We only saw the flashes of the guns.... When daylight came all the ships were seen steaming in proper order. We never saw our "Swiss" fellow soldier again.

In Liverpool's harbor the New Zealanders went ashore first. We followed soon after. First a roll call on deck under the critical gaze of British officers who scanned every man's face, asked his name and regimental number and checked these off on their lists. Another roll call followed on the quay with more questions and a third time on the railway platform by intelligence police.

Our first stop was the railway station at Oxford where we got off the train and had tea with crackers handed out by a detachment of WAACs.* The sun was sinking fast, but in the distance we could still see the towers of the famous colleges and Christ Church Cathedral outlined against the day's afterglow.... It was night when we reached our destination.

"Is this Purfleet?" I asked Peppy.

"H'I don't know where we are, but it ain't Purfleet, that much h'I know."

After one more roll call we marched off in the stygian dark, the pibrochs skirling to drown out the curses of the men stumbling and bumping into each other on a poor narrow country road or, as the British call it: a lane. By three in the morning we reached our camp and were quartered in wooden huts after getting another cup of tea from another squad of WAACs.

These young ladies informed us that we were in the middle of Windsor Great Park and that the royal castle was about two miles off. With that it started to rain and it rained for a solid month.

Though we were in quarantine for a fortnight, this did not mean that we could rest on our laurels. In the first place, there were no laurels to rest on. We dug trenches, we marched miles and miles over the endless roads through Windsor Great Park, we put up some huts, we had special instructors sent over from Aldershot to improve our manners in the gentle art of bayonet fighting and we were taught boxing and wrestling. I made

*Women's Auxiliary Army Corps.

but one appearance in the ring against a certain Sergeant Phillips, who flattened me with one terrific blow on the chin which made me feel groggy for a week. Two weeks later I took revenge on him in a place where no gloves were available and the Marquis of Queensberry rules did not count; in a pub at Sunningdale.

It rained so heavily during those first weeks that the colonel grew worried. He remembered the experience of the First Division which lost nearly half its man power in an epidemic of spinal meningitis in the rain-soaked huts of flooded Salisbury Plains in the course of the winter 1914–15. The troops were coughing and sneezing and developing respiratory ailments. Several cases of pneumonia were diagnosed. The entire band was on its back with influenza. The general feeling was that if we could only get a little more wood for the tiny stoves standing in the middle of the huts, we would soon be ourselves again. For this a remedy lay close at hand; Windsor Great Park grows plenty of trees. Put two and two together, that is: trees and a gang of bushwackers from New Brunswick, and you have the solution. A tremendous sensation was the upshot. One of the trees chopped down dated from the tenth or eleventh century. It was so worm-eaten and decrepit that its ancient branches had to be supported with poles. It had a fence around it and a sign on the fence saying that in this hollow oak the Black Prince or Richard or some other King hid for a few hours during some battle in the long-ago. The tree was so dry and dead that, when cut up, it burnt like pitch.

A whole troop of Coldstream Guards from Windsor Castle called at our camp to raise hell for the burning of the King's tree. We had destroyed "a national monument." We were guilty of an act of vandalism, disrespect, *lèse-majesté*, I don't know what else. The gold-braided, beribboned Guards' captain spoke to our colonel within hearing of a score of men. Old Mac's temper rose to one of his rare Highland furies when he heard the word vandalism applied to his lambkins. Who chopped down the tree, the beautiful captain wanted to know.

"I chopped down your bloody tree," Old Mac replied in his best fog-horn style. "The health of my men, sir, is worth more than all the damned trees in England, Wales and Scotland put together...."

"Don't your men realize, sir, that there's a war on, that we must conserve fuel?"

"A war on? You don't say? Who the hell are we fighting now, sir, the bloody Afghans again?"

When the colonel occasionally reversed the sequence of the companies on the march, I found myself in the first rank of the fifth company right behind the band, which meant that in front of me moved the bass tuba, the oompah. This was played by one Michael Brophy, a North of Ireland man who had transferred from the Mounted Rifles so as to change his spurs from his heels to his elbows in order, as he said, to be able to scratch his back properly.

Brophy hailed from the town of Ballyshannon. He was a perpetual joy with his gift of the gab and his uninterrupted stream of Irish brogue. Sergeant Major Peppy might scream for silence in the ranks till his face was as red as his hair, the irrepressible Mike paid not the least attention.

"That limey can't put me in the clink," he commented. "There's only one oompah in this outfit. . . . They can't do without me."

In a stentorian voice and an accent reminiscent of the Emerald Isle, he kept up a running comment on whatever or whomever we passed in the streets. When on the march in Windsor Park, he entertained all within hearing with a rollicking description of the members of the British upper-classes.

"Did you blokes ever notice how closely the dukes resemble their butlers? D'you know how that is? Without the endeavors of the gentlemen butlers all the earls and baronets would be pure nitwits and Mongolian idiots. Butlers and chorus girls are the saviors of the British aristocracy. . . .

"When I see all those harmless does and deer lying about and grazing, I lose all the respect I ever had for the king. . . . Isn't the man a little bit ashamed of himself now? Is this what he hunts and boasts about when he has his picture taken for the newspapers with the cadavers of gazelles at his feet? . . . And all those gamekeepers standing about; ach, they are the most disgusting, degenerated, detestable duds I ever clapped me eyes on. I would gladly crush them like bedbugs if I didn't know that dead they stink still more!

"Alright, Chester," he'd shout to the sergeant major bandmaster over the heads of the other bandmen. "Chester, I have a dirty taste inside me mouth. Let's have a tune that's fresh and clean! Wadda yah say, Chester? 'Eyes right, a—— tight, foreskins to the front. . . .' Let's go!"

Thus I remembered Corporal Brophy, D.S.M., * young, carefree, tall and lithe, the joy of the battalion . . . till exactly forty years later when I

*Distinguished Service Medal.

came to Ottawa (one day in 1957) and stayed at the hotel Château Laurier. In the evening I went down to the basement cafeteria and was pushing a metal tray along when the food dispenser behind the counter called out: "Hey, Brophy, some more plates here!" At first the name didn't ring a bell. But when the employee carrying a stack of plates passed right in front of me, my heart sank in my shoes. There was Mike Brophy! He had shrunk and walked with a stoop. He shuffled his slippered feet, his hair was white as snow, his mouth had fallen in for lack of teeth. . . . Was it possible?

"Hi there, Corporal Brophy!"

He looked at me for a moment after he put down the plates: "Oh, it's you, Peerie?" Then he came from behind the counter and walked up to me. We shook hands and he muttered something incomprehensible.

"Anything wrong, Mike?" I asked.

"You knew Mary, didn't you? And Jimmy, me boy? Well, she's gone, Peerie, and Jimmy's gone, too! Ah, you'll never fathom the pains she suffered. She died of cancer, Peerie. . . . Jim was taken prisoner by the Japs in Hong Kong. . . . He died in one of their bloody camps. . . ."

When the quarantine was over, we received permission to walk out or catch a bus at nights and on Sundays to Maidenhead, Virginia Water, Windsor, Eton, Richmond and other towns in the vicinity. They tell me that sailors have a girl in every port. I can well believe it. It's one of the risks of their job. But the Corps of Guides easily went the navy one better. In those English towns, as William Langland found long ago, "all was buxomness . . . and great love and liking; for each loveth other." In no time every guy was in love or at least thought he was. No doubt, 't is bliss to be in England, but it's got to be spring to be very heaven. During our sojourn it was winter; the grass was much too wet. Every night the stoves in the huts had to be fired up: the ceiling was draped with tunics, great-coats and especially breeches hanging up to dry. . . .

Two weeks before crossing over to France, Old Mac assembled his followers to tell them that they were to have ten days' leave of absence and could go wherever they liked, rail transportation being free throughout the British Isles. I found my way to London town. Since the passengers from the leave boats from France had just come in, there was no room at the Canadian Maple Leaf Club on the Strand, so that I was assigned to a large wooden shed built up against the walls of the then half-finished

Westminster Cathedral. The "hut" or hostel was run by the Catholic Women's League. There was a huge sitting room and WAACs behind a counter serving tea. The price per night for a cubicle with two beds was one shilling. I was alone for an hour when Cyril Jones walked in with his mandolin under one arm and some books in his other hand. . . .

"Can I sleep here?"

"Of course! What books have you got there? All Italian, I see!"

"Yes, we're going to do a little studying."

"You won't have a chance, there's too much to see in this town."

"In Soho there are Italian clubs and restaurants; I'd like to try my luck there. I must get into practice. After the war I'm going to Italy, you know. . . ."

It was Friday night, March 16, 1917; we had till Saturday, March 24, at eleven o'clock in the evening before we were expected back in Windsor Park. We spent the next day looking at Madame Tussaud's waxworks, the Tower of London, the British Museum and in the evening went to a vaudeville theater accompanied by two WAACs from the Catholic Women League's hostel who had free tickets for "lonesome soldiers." On Sunday Jones was off at daybreak to attend an early service at Westminster Abbey. I went to St. Paul's Cathedral and had the immense pleasure of hearing the famous Dean, the Very Reverend William Ralph Inge, preach a magnificent sermon from the text: "Be of good cheer, I have overcome the world. . . ." In the evening I paid a visit to the Church of the Austin Friars on Threadneedle Street and heard a sermon in Dutch, far too long, far too tedious and far too sanctimonious. . . .

Next to me in the pew sat a man with a blond beard in a black suit. He looked sideways at me to see if the fellow in the British uniform could follow the words in the Dutch psalmbook. When the service was over we walked out together. In ten minutes I knew his whole life story. He was a sea captain, had been torpedoed twice, but, instead of blaming the Germans for his misadventures, he charged them up to the British.

"I tell you what we'll do. You'll come aboard my ship. I'm moored near London Bridge. Till I'm cleared by the customs, I'll hide you in the hold. In three days you'll be back in Holland where you belong. . . ."

"No thanks!"

"You won't come along?"

"No!"

"Why not? You'll be rid of the red necks!"

"I won't, I tell you. I don't belong in Holland any longer."

"Go to hell!" He turned away. "You *landverrader*, traitor!"

That visit to London, short though it was, and my purse dwindling with every passing day, has remained a treasured memory throughout the long succession of years. None other of the many visits I paid to London in afteryears was so memorable. The town was full of soldiers, most of them on leave from the front in France and Belgium or the various training camps in Britain itself. When Jones left to visit his old college in Cambridge, a Cameron highlander became my neighbor in the cubicle. Next door stayed two Anzacs, members of the Australian and New Zealand army corps, and on the other side two men belonging to the South African Springbok Division who told me in their quaint Cape Dutch that they were as good as excommunicated by their Calvinist parents for serving in the army of "the enemy."

Strange to say, it seemed almost a rule of Medes and Persians for all these "colonials" to go and see the changing of the guard in front of Buckingham Palace at eleven in the morning. I stood with the two Springboks in a dense mob of soldiers watching the Grenadier Guards do the honors in front of the royal residence one morning. "Imperial"* military police went around amongst the spectators demanding that a coat button be fastened here or a cap set straight there; suggestions which were not universally accepted with good grace. All went well, however, till the M.P.'s started their sartorial hectoring on some Australians. They did not get very far.

"Who the hell are you?" demanded one Aussie of the M.P.'s who accosted him. "Will you bastards bloody well keep your hands off my hat or must I teach you a bloody lesson?"

The M.P.'s, who probably had previous experience with antipodeans, blew whistles and other M.P.'s came to their aid. I fear that a detailed report of the ensuing conversation would not make for interempire or commonwealth unity even at this late hour of the common market, and hence omit it. The officers amongst the Australians were already removing their badges of rank from their shoulder straps in anticipation of fighting it out, when an elderly gray-haired inspector of the Metropolitan Police interposed himself between the contending parties. To the M.P.'s he said: "You're not the only pebble on the beach, you know! The diggers have as

*All troops from the British Isles proper were called "imperials" by us.

much right to stand here as you. . . even if they wanted to stand stark-naked."

"You just came in time, Mac," the Aussies told the inspector, "for that's just what we planned to do. . . . We were going to strip the pants off every bloody M.P. in London. . . ."

Could they have done it?

They did it, once in Le Havre, France, and once before in Cairo, Egypt, where in addition they burnt down 24 blocks in the red-light district near the Fish Market. . . .

With Jones when he returned from Cambridge, I went to Canterbury by train. Except for lunch and tea in an establishment on High Street, we spent the entire day in the cathedral. Jones knew the place like a book. I visited Canterbury several times in later years to see my friend the Dean, Dr. Hewlett Johnson, but I never again had a guide so perfect and omniscient as Cyril Jones. He showed me the hall where Archbishop Becket ate in public of pheasant and roast beef and nineteen other courses, washing it all down with goblets of red wine from Poissy with which the King of France supplied him. Of course, we looked at the flagstones where Becket's blood was shed on December 29, 1170, and sat in front of St. Augustine's Abbey which is second in seniority only to Monte Cassino in the Benedictine Order.

As we sat on a stone bench in a brief spell of sunshine, a venerable clergyman with long white hair and a marvelous fine face who looked, I thought, very much like "The Warden" as pictured in Anthony Trollope's novel of that name, greeted us: "Where may you be from?"

"From Canada," replied Cyril.

"Good heavens," the cleric exclaimed, "you have come a long way! Many thanks for coming!"

"May I ask what is your position in the cathedral, reverend father?" queried Cyril.

"I'm only a pop gun. . . . "

"What's that?"

"A Minor Canon!"

It was like living for a day in the Middle Ages except for the fact that in that distant time the cathedral was a much livelier place than now. Not only because of the pilgrims from all over the world seeking healing and miracles near the tomb of St. Thomas à Becket, but because mystery plays and communal dinners were given in the cathedral with the people sitting on straw on the floor. The cathedral was their theater, their symphony orchestra, the lovers' trysting place and club as well as their house of prayer. Becket was as magnificent, if not more so, than King Henry. The churches were not then as they stand today, to use Richard Church's somber definition: "quiet solitudes of ghostly masonry."

We crossed the Channel on April 8, 1917, and heard a loud-speaker on the steamship quay at Boulogne blare out the news that America had declared war.

"What does it mean, Pierre?" asked Ross MacDonald.

"It means that we are going to win," I said.

"That was never in doubt," he came back. "I only hope that the Kaiser will not try to knock us out before the Yanks get here. . . . "

Just then a Frenchman in civilian clothes with a lady on his arm walked to the edge of the quay and, quite unconcerned by the stares of 1500 men, stood urinating into the harbor. The battalion shook with laughter, and of comment on this touchingly pastoral scene there was no end that afternoon.

It's eighteen miles as the crow flies from Boulogne to Etaples. It took us a full twelve hours to cover the distance. The colonel drove off in a staff car. And then there were so many alluring pubs near the waterside that the troops could not withstand the temptation to taste what was on tap in those dives and taverns. It took nearly two hours to round them up for the fall-in to Etaples where we were immediately swallowed up in the melting pot of a hundred thousand men from the four corners of the earth and learned the eternal lesson that we too weren't the only pebbles on the beach.

If the Corps of Guides didn't do any guiding when it got to France, what other function, it may well be asked, did it perform in the general scheme of things? Well, sometimes we were pressed into service as plain infantry. Other times we were set to digging tunnels underneath the German trenches for the purpose of blowing their occupants to hell. This work fell literally in the category of a rat race since Jerry was a swift and thoroughgoing digger himself. The listening devices being seldom of much use on account of the steady roar and rumble of the artillery, the German sappers as well as we had to guess as to the moment of truth when to set off the charges of dynamite which would produce an artificial volcano and a landslide engulfing, burying and obliterating in one fell swoop as many of the opposing team as was humanly possible. It was a nerve-wracking business, enough to drive you insane, if you let yourself go and think about its hazards. But then, luckily, we didn't do much thinking! In this respect we were perfect soldiers.

The next item on our program turned us into a common ordinary gang of "navvies." This happened when the Guides were ordered to sew small square patches of red cloth in the middle of the back of their uniforms between the shoulder blades, and were rebaptized "a battalion of royal engineers on a temporary basis." The reason was that the railway line Abbeville-Hazebrouck, along which moved the supply trains for our hard-pressed infantry divisions in the Franco-Belgian border region, had come under a withering artillery attack.

The bottleneck between the enemy's advance position to the east of us and the North Sea to the west was no more than fifteen kilometers wide.... The coastal dirt road from Dieppe to the Belgian frontier and German-occupied Dunkirk, which ran to the west of the railway line, was choked with guns, troops, transport and an endless stream of ambulances going to or returning from the forward dressing stations. One needn't be a Moltke or Treitzke to figure out that if that rail line had been permanently cut, our forces up north, British, Belgian and Portuguese deprived of munitions and supplies, would have been annihilated or forced to surrender.

It was our job to keep the trains moving by repairing the tracks which were damaged almost uninterruptedly. The area under fire extended for some twenty-five kilometers to the north where French railway troops were employed on the same task of keeping the tracks clear. On both sides of the line, as far as the eye could reach, lay a jumbled mass of smashed-up freight cars, tenders and locomotives. The German barrage came from the direction of Amiens. On rare clear days we could see the towers of the cathedral, a perfect target for the German artillery, and the white and black puffs of smoke of their exploding shells.... Twice the Fritzes aimed their poison gas cylinders at us, both times the northwest wind kept the vapors from coming near.

We were two long months on the railway line, divided in day and night shifts, sleeping in ruined farmhouses and barns, eating hard tack with canned meat called Mackonachie. We lost more men in that period than during the whole rest of the war. We weren't exactly sitting ducks, but came very near it. The infantry had it soft compared with us; they at least had their trenches and dugouts.

The night shift was the worst. There we were in parties of twenty, soaked to the skin, lifting a piece of railway track by means of gigantic pincers, slipping and sliding in the mud up and down the embankment, and then a parachute flare suddenly opening up above our heads revealing every moving object as far as the eye could reach. In such moments the "royal engineers on a temporary basis" dropped the rail line like a hot potato and plopped headlong in the mud and lay there most unroyally till the light burnt out.... Old Mac was the hardest worker of all, for he alone knew the secret of the emergency. His face was haggard and tense with exhaustion and worry. I never learned till after the war that while we were busy on the railway line, General Gough's Fifth Army was annihilated and we lost 149,000 men in prisoners in ten days.

When the danger of a German break-through had passed by the reduction of the salient, Sir Arthur Currie, C.O.C., Canadian Expeditionary Force, rewarded us with a well deserved period of rest in the base camp of Etaples. We were issued new clothes and made a festive bonfire of our old uniforms and greatcoats which had been ripped to shreds on the railway line. There being a shortage of Canadian greatcoats, I was given a brand-new British specimen which was better tailored, double-breasted and far more glamorous....

Colonel MacDonald fell in with the idea to give the troops a little more lively diversion than was occasionally provided by entertainers sent over by the Y.M.C.A. and the Women's Christian Temperance Union. Cyril Jones, myself, and three or four others were commissioned to arrange for a theatrical performance by scaring up some local talent from St. Omer, Le Touquet, Le Tréport, St. Valéry, and other towns in the vicinity. The colonel gave us a thousand francs to start with, a fortune in those days, and the advice to do our best.

While Raoul Desormeaux a newcomer, Jones the neoplatonist, and I scouted for talent, the band, whose members served as stretcher-bearers during our periods in the line, got its instruments back and learned to play appropriate light music such as "Keep your eye on the girl that you love," and "Oh, Johnny, oh, Johnny, heavens above...."

We recruited thirty young ladies for a revue which was provisionally known as *The Boulogne Scandals,* so called in honor of Boulogne-sur-Mer, about which there is really nothing scandalous to report except perhaps that the town at that time had an unusually large number of clip and gyp joints.

A certain captain, who claimed to be a theatrical agent in civil life, trained the girls in the ballroom of the Hotel Lion d'Argent in Etaples, where the *artistes* were also lodged, at Old Mac's expense it goes without saying. While watching the rehearsals, I gained the impression that strip-teasing *en masse* doesn't really require much training. At any rate, disrobing seemed to come perfectly natural with those girls. I had never been in a theater in my life and thought the performance "exquisite, explosive, an erotic riot." Such at least were the adjectives which I, as the publicity man for the show, used to describe the attraction on the announcement posters in camp.

One day we had a visit at the Lion d'Argent from Lady Diana Duff Cooper who ran the canteen for the high brass on the hill in Camp Etaples. Lady Diana was accompanied by General Gerald F. Trotter, V.C., and H.R.H. the Prince of Wales. Each spoke a word of encouragement to the trainees after our girls gave an exhibition of their high-kicking art. After that everybody wanted to see the show in the making. The entire general staff moved up so that it became a little crowded at the Lion d'Argent.

The *répétition générale* came off very well. But on the night when the *Boulogne Scandals* were to appear for their premiere at the big dreary hall near the Bull Ring, thousands of would-be spectators were forced to wait in vain.

A division of Australians had moved into camp on the very morning when we were to stage the grand opening. These antipodeans were also in from the line for a period of rest. By eventide their officers crossed the dividing line between the camp and the town of Etaples and, as fate would have it, found the Lion d'Argent. They took our only too willing *artistes* in to dinner and by eight o'clock, when we sent out six staff cars to pick up the *mademoiselles,* they and the Aussies had vanished in the night. . . .

The whole camp was in an uproar. Thousands of men went in search of the vanished *Scandals.* Not one was found. In the street in front of the hotel such a riot took place that the Provost Marshal had the alarm sounded and police troops came running on the double, and. . .drove us back like sheep to our tents. . . .

The British poet Robert Graves mentions in "Goodbye to All That" that the unit in which he served, a battalion of Welsh Fusiliers, suffered heavy casualties as a result of German sniping activities. He adds that the Canadians finally put an end to this deadly game. What he does not say is that the stunt of silencing the snipers was pulled off, not by Canadians, but by a crew of Red Indians from the Six Nations' reservation near Brantford, Ontario. These Indians were our men, and they alone were responsible for getting our honored name of "Guides" restored to us.

There's no denying that the German snipers for a time played havoc with our troops. They were nearly all head wounds which they inflicted, in other words, the most dangerous and deadly. How to overcome this insidious evil had long occupied the so-called best brains of our high command. No solution was found till our Ruby the Indian chief and his friends took a hand, and in their own way brought the enemy sniping to an end for good.

The Indians used specially fabricated Ross rifles of extraordinary precision. Before using these guns, they carefully explored the terrain to familiarize themselves with the German snipers' positions and the enemy's methods of operation. It was a battle of wits and agility, for it involved crawling into no man's land in the middle of the night and making their way like snakes between the thousands of wooden stakes and posts on which the barbed wire was strung. In many a spot the Fritzes, also by the crawling method, had stuck tin cans or even pots and pans on top of the stakes. In daylight the Germans trained their seven-foot-long barreled sniping rifles on these tins and pots so that when darkness came and one of our patrols or wire-repairing parties accidentally touched the posts and set the cans a-rattling, all the Germans had to do was fire in the direction of the sound and were almost bound to hit somebody.

As a sample of their marksmanship I might cite the occasion when I walked through a front line trench in the middle of the night. A man carrying his rifle with bayonet fixed immediately ahead happened to stumble over the duckboards. Somebody turned on a flashlight for an instant and...ping! a sniper's bullet struck the bayonet. A shot fired from 600 yards' distance broke off the tip of the bayonet. The splinter embedded itself in my left leg just below the knee. I poured some iodine on the gash and carried on till, two days later, I developed a stiff ankle and then a stiff knee: septic poisoning had set in....

After cutting holes in the barbed wire, Ruby and his men tied strings to all these German tin cans and contraptions, a highly hazardous undertaking, for the least jingle or rattle brought on an immediate riposte from the German rifles which were trained on these objects. When they had tied on the strings, the Indians crawled back to our trenches and waited. Then they pulled the strings and the cans moved. The Fritzes fired, hitting nobody of course, and the Indians fired back aiming at the spurt of flame from the German rifles. In this way they silenced one sniper after the other.

Another stratagem employed by Ruby was to crawl out into no man's land and paint a tiny streak of luminous paint on the wire posts and props on the side facing the German line. When back in our trench, the Indians would toss a sack of straw or a bundle of old clothes across the barbed wire. Then very slowly they pulled the sack towards them. When the sack moved past the painted stakes, the Germans invariably mistook the moving object for the body of one of our men on crawling patrol. The German snipers fired immediately and thus disclosed their own position. This is what Ruby was waiting for. Again he and his men fired back, knocking out the snipers by a lightninglike crack at the tongue of fire leaping from their long-barreled guns.

On our section of the front the snipers were demolished in a month's time whereupon Ruby and his men moved to other sections of the line. Everywhere they were highly successful.

Although many of our fellows were killed in action or permanently disabled, such was not the case with Raoul Desormeaux, the newcomer, who became the best friend I had in the army. It was fickle Eros who brought him to a fall. Raoul's mind went to pieces on a double-barreled love affair. The young lady to whom he was engaged to be married lived in the Lachine suburb of Montreal. The other damsel was a French countess, the granddaughter of a retired French army general in the resort town of Paris-Plage just south of Boulogne-sur-Mer ten miles from Etaples, whose dinner guest I was once, but Raoul half a dozen times.

We met the countess through her grandfather whom we encountered one afternoon strolling near the seashore of Paris-Plage. The general, François de St. Gervais, looked as old as Methuselah. His white mustaches streamed like two wayward banners in the sea breeze. He had more decorations than I had ever seen before. He wore a red and gold kepi, and a uniform featuring a pair of violently red trousers which may have been regulation in the third Napoleon's time, but now looked as if they had been retrieved from some scarecrow in the fields.

When we saluted, the general stopped, and mistaking us for Russians (not an unusual occurrence) complimented us on a victory lately won by the man to whom he referred as "your noble commander in chief, His Imperial Highness, the Grand Duke Nikolas Nikolaevich." We hadn't heard of that victory, nor did we receive confirmation of it ever after. Raoul and I became aware that the old boy was pretty well *gaga* when he started to tell us that the Franco-Prussian War of 1871 was by no means the harrowing debacle "the dirty pig" Emile Zola makes it out to have been in his book on the battle of Sedan. General de St. Gervais commanded an infantry brigade in that war and, if you could believe him, won it hands down all by himself.

He invited us into his house, and showed us an immense map of France spread out on a specially constructed table of the kind the general staffs have at their disposal in the *châteaux* where they think up the next offensive. On the map stood whole forests of tiny pin flags, red, blue, green and yellow in color. Red flags indicated the spots where "our noble British allies" held the line. The blue flags represented General Foch's divisions, while the green and yellow symbols stood for the Belgians and Portuguese, whom the general, *en passant*, also raised to nobility.

Red Pants walked up and down the room, his hands clasped behind his back, discoursing on the battles of the Marne, Verdun, the Chemin des Dames and the Somme front. Suddenly he pounced on the map and with his ebony walking stick pointed to a cluster of blue flags.

"*Ici*," he said, "stands General Pétain! . . . If that nincompoop would not always allow the enemy to make up his mind for him, we would already be in Berlin. . . . Look, if you please, if Pétain would pay heed to the many letters I wrote him on the subject, he would attack *là*, over there, *oui*, right there. . . . Without the slightest difficulty he could roll Hindenburg back on the Meuse, while Giraud and Magnin, standing here, *ici*, at this point, would catch the Boche on the rebound. . . . The war," he snapped his fingers, "would be over in one stroke just like that. . . ."

"*Moi, je suis Liliane*, I am Liliane," announced a black-velvet-gowned madonna who was adjusting a cross set with tiny diamonds around her neck as she entered the maproom in the moment of near-victory. "How would you like to catch me on the rebound?" she laughed.

Liliane's grandpa sank down in an armchair. With his knees wide apart, his hands leaning on the knob of his walking stick, he looked like one of those military commanders you see in the old battle pictures, surveying a cavalry attack from a very, very great distance. "*Mon Dieu*, Liliane," he sighed, "I wish you wouldn't always upset my campaigns. . . ."

Liliane paid no notice; she just laughed. She may have been twenty-five years of age, though she looked more mature. Her eyes were of a peculiar liquid gray with long black lashes. Her voice was of a deep and passionate timbre. You felt at once that all the secrets of night, of jeweled light, of whispering, laughing voices and red carnations, were hers. . . . Her body swayed softly in its tight-fitting revealing gown with a split skirt, a very daring fashion at that time. Raoul swallowed hard and stuttered. I saw right then and there that he was a lost man.

"*Mademoiselle*," he blurted in an awe-struck whisper, "*mes compliments, mes compliments!*"

"But I am not a *demoiselle*," she replied. "I am a *madame*, and a widow to boot. My husband, the Count de Jouvenceau, is one of those silly casualties of whom *pépère* never wants to speak. He was lost on the Salonika front. . . ."

"*Comtesse*, I am so sorry!"

"No sentimentalities, please. Have a dry sherry and stay for dinner. I dare say *pépère* hasn't even invited you. He's so forgetful!"

We had several sherries, but when, because of the absence of any other table or sideboard in the room, we placed our empty glasses on the map of France, the general, who had dozed off in the meantime, woke up and jumped like a watchdog from his armchair: "For God's sake, *messieurs*, don't put your glasses there, I beg of you, not right on the Argonne front! . . ."

We hastily removed our glasses and carried them into the dining room with us. . . .

"I'll be right in," the general called after us as he fumbled with his trouser buttons. "I have to make *pipi* first. . . ."

Before leaving, Liliane presented Raoul with the cross which she took from her own bosom and sewed on the inside of his tunic. It was so clearly a case of love at first sight for both that I felt it a pity to have to sound the retreat. The lady gave me also something, a protective amulet: a silver medallion of the Sacred Heart, but she didn't sew it on, though I wouldn't have minded in the least to play second fiddle.

On the way back to our hole in the chalk hills, Raoul talked of nothing else but Liliane. Had I ever seen a woman so gracious, so witty, so charming, so divine? He talked till his vocabulary ran out of superlatives.

It was a long stiff walk along a narrow road in the sand dunes. We would certainly not have made it before reveille had we not come upon two Algerian *sous-officiers* fast asleep on that balmy summer night in a bush of shrubbery. Apparently the two had been celebrating heavily; a half a dozen empty wine bottles lay around. Against a nearby tree stump stood their bicycles. We stealthily approached the machines, jumped on and peddled off as fast as we could.

Looking back over my time of service, I must say that being part of a sapper's detail was the most agonizing experience of my life. Not that I thought much of death or of the thin strand of luck by which hung my life and the lives of my companions. Not then at any rate! It's now, nearly half a century later, that in thinking of the episode, I undergo the full measure of claustrophobia's dread and anguish over which I skipped so lightly and casually in the long-ago.

It was May, 1918, when the accident occurred. We were digging a tunnel in a chalk hill in a spot where the authorities planned to install an underground surgical hospital. The tunnel was half finished and partly shored up with pit props when a Messerschmitt dropped a high explosive on top of the hill under which we were at work. The tunnel caved in and I was trapped with seven other men in the forward part near the face of the cut. I owe my life to the fact that I fell with my head near the end of a pipe leading to a hydraulic drill. The drill was demolished but the water kept running. Still, if my entombment had lasted twenty-four hours longer, I think I would most likely have suffocated like the others.

On my left arm lay a piece of rock the size of a table. There was little pain, though the arm was fractured in three places and the bare bones were sticking through the skin. After two days and three nights I was brought out on a stretcher and felt myself being heaved up. In the light of day I saw Ross MacDonald and looked at the sleeve of my tunic which had turned black. In the hospital my arm lay next to me like something that didn't belong to me. I had no feeling in it.

The colonel said: "Blessed be God! So now, what? Do you want me to recommend you for a decoration? Or maybe you want to go home to Canada and be a recruiting officer? What shall it be? Just tell me!"

"I had a lot of time to think things over down in that hole," I said. "I have vowed to go to the Holy Land, after the war of course, and walk on my bare feet in every spot where Jesus once walked, in gratitude for having been plucked like a firebrand from the fire...."

"That's a capital idea," nodded the colonel. "And I'll come with you, and you'll be my guest! Agreed?"

"Agreed, of course!"

"Let's hope that we both get through this war more or less intact!"

I was up and around and in less than three months' time went with the battalion to Albert and Bapaume and to Cambrai when the Germans began to fall back at last. On November 11, 1918, we were in the vicinity of Mons, the spot which the British "Contemptibles" had abandoned in the month of August four years previously. There, on the morning of the Armistice, Ross MacDonald was killed, shot through the heart by a retreating German patrol. He lies buried in the British cemetery at Etaples behind the huge granite cross with its single line from John Keble's hymn: IT IS NOT NIGHT IF THOU ART NEAR.

CHAPTER V

The First Time I Saw Paris

No GREATER CONTRAST can be imagined than that between the joyful celebrations of the Armistice of November, 1918, in the great cities of the allied world, and the sullen, brooding silence of the soldiers still in the field. We heard of rejoicings and boisterous revels, music and dancing in the streets of Paris, London, New York and a hundred smaller centers of population. With us the same old grind and addleheaded military fuss went on day after day as if nothing had happened.

No doubt, every man heaved a sigh of relief that the end was in sight, but the hastily arranged festivities here and there on our march to the German border were so pitifully forced and artificial as to be almost farcical. Not even the two or three extra rations of rum which the King sent over with his compliments could break or dispel the general feeling of disillusion in the ranks.

It was as if something had gone out of our lives, something to which we had grown deeply attached. We had a vague feeling that we were on our own again, or soon would be. Instead of buoying us up, this impression left us with an inexplicable sense of insecurity and helplessness. The men became irritable and short-spoken, they sulked like children who have been deprived of a toy. The ranks were riven by all sorts of little tensions, unuttered resentments, suspicions and jealousies. For my own part, I felt like a derelict in a vast empty space; nothing to look forward to, nothing to go back to, anchorless, up in the air. In one word: absurd.

For months, in many cases for years, the men had supported the privations and sufferings with relative good cheer and resignation. They had looked forward to the end of the war with high expectation as if it would produce some miraculous flash event like the return of Christ on the clouds of heaven. Now there was neither token nor portent nor sign of fulfillment.

The sense of frustration was heightened by the burden of sorrow lying on the land of France. It was as if all the tears since 1914 were incarnated in one mass of woe. You felt like crying out, a wordless, desperate cry of anguish over the abysmal horror of it all and the senselessness of human existence. Cannon fodder! Two million French dead! A million British dead! Eight million Russian, Austrian, Italian and Belgian dead! Does anyone imagine that the two million German dead did not count in the scales of the Great Weigher? God has no favorites!

Had it been feasible to transfer us on some gigantic magic carpet in one swift dash to our homes across the Atlantic, the spirit of the troops might have been lifted up with anticipation of reunion with dear ones and the familiar scenes of home and childhood. Nothing could be more depressing than the spectacle of our environment. On every hand in the liberated areas you saw shell-torn woods, bomb-pitted meadows, trench-scarred greenswards, ruined buildings, orchards, schools, churches. And on top of it all, the squalor, the hunger and the mute despair of the French population.

Politicians, statesmen and prelates, accompanied by newspaper correspondents and certain creatures designated on the bulletin boards as "diplomatic observers," who came to take stock of the war damage, swarmed all over the newly liberated areas of northern France and Belgium. In spots where large numbers of troops were concentrated, some of these announcers of the shape of things to come took occasion to fire off a speech. The orators thanked us on behalf of George V and Christian civilization and promised that, once back home, we would all get a pension, and nothing would be too good for us.

Five of the most eminent speakers whom I went to hear—Lloyd George, Jan Christiaan Smuts, Sir Philip Gibbs, Colonel Repington and the Bishop of Sodor and Man—hammered away at one and the same subject: "Germany will be made to pay for everything, and the Kaiser will hang as high as Haman." All that was required of us was just one more little effort: Ludendorff and Hindenburg and their "Hunnish hordes" were to be pushed across the borders, and a watch placed on the Rhine to see that they stayed in their own bailiwick forever and ever....

These harangues left the men as unresponsive as fish. A growing resentment against further service in the armies slated to occupy the trans-Rhenan bridgeheads was spreading in all directions. At times this spluttering discontent assumed a bitter, ugly tone, though it never showed mutinous tendencies, which is something that cannot be said for the French. Our fellows had but one thought in mind: "The war is over.... The Kaiser has scrammed.... Let's go home!"

Near the huge encampment at Huy in Belgium, halfway on the road to Germany, where Lloyd George mounted a specially constructed open-air platform to address a mass meeting of Australian and Canadian "colonials," the Prime Minister, after platitudinizing and wisecracking for a quarter hour through a screeching megaphone, was unceremoniously howled down. One giant Australian with the voice of a hungry lion interrupted the speaker: "I'll tell you what we'll do. We'll carry out the bargain we myde. ... We'll march as far as the border and see to it that Jerry gets across.... Then we'll all piss in the bloody Rhine and we'll go back to Lee 'Avre.... And better see to it, Mister Lloyd George, that you 'ave enough boats on 'and to tyke us back 'ome."

The Prime Minister, who was surrounded by a bevy of general staff officers, backed away as if he had been pulled by his coattails. He and his glittering retinue motioned for silence. But fifty thousand men laughed in his face and the Welsh Wizard walked off very unwizardly, to say the least.

There was no breakdown in discipline, no revolt or refusal to obey. The men felt themselves liberated from the draperies of convention and red tape. Saluting stopped as by preconcerted design. Nothing, neither promises, nor threats, could stir the troops to hate the enemy enough to continue the campaign. The war was *napoo,* * *fini,* and the Rhine the end of the journey.

I do not believe that there had been the least feeling of hatred for the Germans in the first place. The British soldier seems once and for all incapable of hatred and lacks every sentiment of revenge. He looked upon the whole business of war as a competitive sports event, very inconvenient, no doubt, and uncomfortable at certain moments, but nonetheless a game to be played according to the Marquis of Queensberry's or somebody else's rules. The British are the last survivors of the age when chivalry was in flower. After a bloody fight they shake hands with the foe as if to say: "Well done, good and faithful servant. . . ." Can anyone imagine a German commanding officer, in the midst of a murderous campaign, admiring his chief adversary to the extent of pinning the man's picture above his desk,

**Napoo: cockney for *n'y a plus* — is no more.*

as Montgomery did in the case of Erwin Rommel? As they sank the Kaiser's high-sea fleet at Skagerrak, Beatty and Jellicoe ordered a flag salute for the enemy's drowning battle cruisers. Hadn't Von Tirpitz fought like a gentleman? That was the sole criterion!

According to the terms of the Armistice there was to remain a space of twenty-four hours' walking distance between the advancing allied armies and the retreating Germans. After ten days we had fallen some 72 hours behind, if not more. The reason for this delay was the vicious, swift-killing epidemic of Spanish influenza which raged through the length and breadth of Europe for the second time that year. It struck down thousands of our men, and, of course, did not spare the Germans either. As soon as we left the mining town of Lens behind, we found that every available bed or shelter in the succeeding towns and villages was taken by sick Germans. Some of their hospital units and medical orderlies remained behind to look after the afflicted and bury the dead.

Our delays caused whole batches of German prisoners of war to catch up with us. The French simply emptied their prison camps and turned the men loose to let them find their way home as best they could. The whole system of prisoner evacuation had broken down chiefly through the flu epidemic.

Near Seneffe in the province of Hainaut, a group of German officers going in the same direction passed by just as we were loading our own sick in ambulances and sending them off to the various hospitals. The Germans asked if they could be of service. We had seen many prisoners before, but never any like these. They were mere walking skeletons. Their clothing hung in tatters, their unshaven faces were haggard with hunger and privation. Some of them were so weak they could hardly stand on their feet. All were more or less afflicted with the flu.

One *Oberleutnant*, the youngest of the lot—his companions were nearly all elderly *Landwehr* officers—said to me that they preferred not to go to the hospital because of the rain. The unheated tent hospitals, he claimed, theirs as well as ours, were deathtraps. "No man who goes to the hospital with the flu comes out alive. . . . It's a headache one day, the second day it's double pneumonia, on the third day comes the funeral! . . . On the road we have a chance . . . in the hospital, none!"

"How long have you been a prisoner?" I asked.

"Two years and a half," he said.

"Where were you?"

"At Dunkirk working on the sea defenses."

"For the British?"

"No, if that were only true; we were prisoners of the French."

"Didn't the French treat you well?"

"Please look," he said, as he unbuttoned his ragged uniform. "See, I have had no underwear for two years. This tunic is crawling with lice. . . ." His neck and chest were indeed scratched to the raw. "The French refused to let us fumigate our clothes. . . . They fed us twice a day, soup they called it. None of us has eaten a mouthful since we were turned loose. . . ."

"How long ago is that?"

"Three days, this is the fourth day. . . ."

"Christ!" exclaimed our Captain Farquharson, "that's tough! Come to the rolling kitchen. We'll get you something to eat. Our bakers just baked bread last night. . . . No, just sit down here by the roadside, we'll bring it to you."

Our men were as good as their word; everybody brought something. Hot tea was always on tap. With it the ex-prisoners had bread and jam and cans of Machonochie and boiled potatoes, using our spoons and forks and dixies. . . .

Pretty soon they were showing us family photographs and our men showed theirs.

"You married, Fritz?"

"*Ja*, married *und drei Kinder!*"

"Are these yours? Fine looking kids, Fritz! How long since you last saw them?"

"Three years!"

"Well, you'll soon be home, quicker than we, I'm thinking."

We made the Germans stuff their knapsacks with all the food they could carry, cartons of jam, bully beef, tinned vegetables, loaves of bread. We even supplied them with can openers, blankets and tobacco. . . .

Then the Germans conferred amongst themselves and suddenly rose to their feet as one man. They clicked their heels and the *Oberleutnant* made a speech. He took a ring from his finger and presented it to me. Captain Taylor got a cigarette lighter, Desormeaux a leather billfold. They insisted on giving us their home addresses, and before we fell in to continue our march to the Rhine we all promised to write. . . .

If any animosity remained it seemed directed, not against the Kaiser or any other German, but against the Flemish people who, if rumors could be believed, had shown themselves very unco-operative when our troops had been fighting—and dying in their tens of thousands—in defense of their country. I came too late in the war to take part in the struggle on the Yser, but every veteran of that early campaign had a story of personal resentment against the Flemings. Handles had been removed from the pumps in farmyards, it was said, and village squares at the approach of our men. Food was refused even when exorbitant sums of money were offered. Shops and *estaminets* were shut in the faces of friends and allies, while Flemish girls—this was perhaps the offense that rankled most—had gone so far as to express preference for the "good Fritzi *Kameraden*." According to reports, obstructionism, sabotage, and even betrayal and treachery had been common occurrences in Flanders.

I wanted to find out what lay behind those stories of anti-British feeling in Flanders and thought I had a chance when, in passing through the southern suburbs of Brussels, I had the unexpected good fortune to develop a loose kneecap. Raoul got the flu and several of the Guides were down with the scourge. Sergeant Pinay, our regimental baker and famous father of nine children, was one of them.

As luck would have it all the hospital beds in Camp Huy were occupied so that we were assigned to one of the small huts made of rough lumber slabs which stood in long rows on the camp's outskirts. Bearing in mind the German officer's warning about the danger of the unheated hospitals, I managed to sequester a pile of blankets from the quartermaster's store, and put my two companions to bed. With the wood I gathered in the forest and the aid of a German saw-bayonet to split the tree branches, I kept the little cookstove in the hut burning night and day. My patients got no other nourishment but hot tea and toast, and twice a day a rubbing of their chests with turpentine. The rubbing was intended to make them sweat—and sweat they did under that load of Hudson Bay blankets. In fact they sweated till they squealed. When they squealed, I figured that they were on the way to recovery, and I wasn't wrong. I got the idea from Dr. Hahnemann's book on homeopathic medicine which, now in tatters, has accompanied me for half a century all over the world. The turpentine was my own invention. Hahnemann doesn't mention it. He prescribes a certain kind of liniment which proved unobtainable at Huy.

In the meantime I went before a medical board with my loose kneecap. The three medics behind the table were in exceptional good humor. They asked me whether my sore knee derived from collegiate or varsity football. One of them was trying to suck beer from a bottle through a stethoscope. Their compassionate verdict was that I needn't and couldn't possibly accompany the Guides to the Rhine. I was assigned for a month's rest to one of the resort hotels or villas in the neighborhood of Ostende which the British had commandeered for those recovering from the flu.

However, when I asked the transport officer for a railway ticket to the seashore, he referred me to the intelligence service.

"Do you speak Flemish?" asked the officer.

When I replied in the affirmative, he said: "In that case you're not going to Flanders.... Don't argue." He put up his hand as I began to remonstrate. "Flanders is out, definitely and irrevocably!"

"For what reason?"

"Political and diplomatic reasons! Just be a good fellow and put Flanders out of your mind!"

Raoul, who was standing by, pulled me away. "Don't irritate him," he cautioned. "If you keep on shooting off your mouth, he might cancel our month's leave, and we'll have to go and piss in the Rhine after all! ..."

"Our leave?" I asked. "Are you coming?"

"Yes, *vieux*," he said. "How d'you like that? The medical board found a spot on my lungs.... You and I are to proceed to the base hospital in Rouen for an X-ray checkup. Isn't that a pip? Pinay is coming too. He has a pain in the chest, probably from all the rubbing you gave him...."

"Strange," I said, "my knee feels better already."

"I thought so," nodded Raoul, "Liliane's scapulars sure work wonders.... I haven't coughed once since I learned that we are going on a vacation...."

When we boarded the train at Brussels-South, we found Shorty Pinay already installed in the compartment. With him was Gordon Gilchrist, a lieutenant in the 72nd Battalion, Seaforth Highlanders, gloriously accoutered in kilt, sporran and tam-o'-shanter. They had swiped two bottles of cognac each from a display stand in the buffet of the waiting room and were busy hiding the flasks under the seat cushions.

"Nobody speaks a word of French," the French-Canadian baker warned. "That's our surest line of defense. When the customs officers come in, or the police, or the conductor, mum is the word...."

As he spoke, the conductor did indeed make his entrée. "Tickets, please!" The man looked at our transportation slips: "You are on the wrong train," he said. "This train goes to Paris.... You are going to Rouen. ... For Rouen you take the train at platform 3. The carriages are marked Lille-Amiens. ..."

"We can't quit this compartment now and leave the cognac behind," remarked Gilchrist under his breath.

"Give him a bottle and make him shut up!" I suggested.

"Are you nuts? Not a whole bottle," objected Shorty. "If the worst comes to the worst, he can have a swig. ..."

With the customary *tra-là-là* of French railway employees, customs officers and sundry other state functionaries, the conductor, who had disappeared for a moment, returned presently, bringing a whole squad of railway police in his wake. Our visitors twirled their mustaches to show their superiority and shifted their revolvers back and forth in their belts. After ten minutes of gesticulating and palavering in the sign language, we parted with one bottle of cognac.

"D'you know what's happening?" I asked. "We're going to Paris! We're going to the forbidden city! Let's celebrate!"

"I won't believe it till the train starts rolling," mumbled the cautious Scot. "There's many a slip, yeh ken, and this slip may be marked by an imperial transport officer's veto. I think I see one of them beasties walking up and down the platform now.... For the love of God, keep your heads down!"

A few minutes later, the train set in motion. But we were too overcome with surprise at our phenomenal luck to do any celebrating just then. After ten hours of travel plus four of shunting on and off sidings on the Ceinture line, the old strategic railway circling Paris and linking all its suburbs, we debarked at the St. Lazare station at ten in the morning. According to our cognac-mellowed conductor, the main line was out of order, else we would have come in at the Nord station.

Our unforeseen visit to Paris started with a fight right outside the railway station in front of the Hotel Terminus.

"Where shall we go first?" I asked.

"I'm going to the Place d'Iéna," said Raoul. "I'm meeting Liliane. Her grandpa has a town house on the Place d'Iéna. There's a hotel on the Avenue d'Iéna, just around the corner. Why don't you fellows take a room in that hotel so that we'll be close together? ..."

"I think I'll have a little session with that dame over there!" spoke up the sergeant-baker.

"What dame?"

"The one coming up, can't you see? Isn't she a doll? Look how she wiggles. . . ."

"For God's sake, Shorty, be sensible! Let the bitch wiggle! That girl has just been talking to a guy on the corner. He's her pimp. He sent her over! Look, he's watching us now!"

"I'm old enough to be your grandfather," snorted the baker. "I can take care of myself. I like that dame! She's my type! Nobody's going to stop me. . . ."

"Before you go, let me have some of your money for safekeeping," suggested Gilchrist. "In case they rob you, you won't lose all you have!"

"What d'you think I am, a boob? I won't be robbed. I'll see you at the Hotel d'Iéna. Here, hold my pack a while. . . ."

We watched poor Jean Baptiste Pinay walk away on the arm of the mopsy. The two were talking and laughing as if they were old acquaintances. Her pimp sauntered up as we stood on an island in the middle of the street waiting for a streetcar going in the direction of the Place d'Iéna.

"Want to change some money?" he asked.

"*Fous-moi l'camp!* Buzz off! said Raoul.

"What d'you have to interfere in my business for?" asked the pander. "You tried to keep my woman from earning some money. I saw you!"

"You saw right, you bastard! . . . If anything happens to our friend, I'll cut off your damn gee-gee with my own hands," said Raoul.

Hearing this threat, the pimp whipped out a knife and slashed the sleeve of Raoul's greatcoat from shoulder to cuff. As he backed away, he bumped into me, and I, weighed down under the heavy pack on my back, and Shorty's in my hand, lost my balance and fell to the ground. I struck my nose against a lamp post and bear the faint mark of that encounter till this day. However, I managed to grab the mackerel's leg, and he fell too. Gordon Gilchrist was on top of him in a flash, and reduced his face to a bloody jelly. . . .

But there stood Gilchrist with the pimp's wicked-looking blade in his hand. A whistle blew! Two whistles blew! French cops who, like other cops in certain other cities we know, can never be found when you need them sprouted from the asphalt like so many toadstools after a night's rain in the forest. They came running from all directions. . . .

Naturally we had to go along to the police *poste*. Even in Paris you can't disturb the peace and get away with it. However, the interrogation ended on a happy note. When Raoul gave the *commissaire* or station chief the name and address of General de St. Gervais, it made a tremendous impression on the assembled cops high and low. A telephone call to the house on the Place d'Iéna to verify our statements changed the situation completely. An inspector was ordered to drive us in a rattling old jalopy to Liliane's home. Arrived there, we shook the man's hand and, in gratitude for his promise to look for our wayward baker, donated a bottle of cognac to the cause of freedom and justice.

After Raoul vanished into Liliane's boudoir, Lieutenant Gilchrist and I went around the corner to the hotel which turned out to be a recreation center for American doughboys. We duly registered at the reception counter presided over by a man carrying the red triangled Y.M.C.A. badge on his collar.

They actually had a clothes-pressing department and a barbershop on the premises. We paid for our pressing and coiffeuring with our last bottle but one, and came out smelling like the dames of the old White Rat in Porcupine. After that we were shown to our room and had a bath. While Gordon lay in the tub, a waiter brought in a bottle of Scotch, some soda water, and six tumblers. Gordon lined up the six glasses on the rim of the tub and drank them down in swift rotation. . . .

After he got out of the bath, he marched up and down the room imitating a high-stepping drum majorette:

> Scots wha ha'e wi' Wallace bled,
> Will henceforth bleed nae mair. . . .

"What'll they do instead?"

"They'll love a lassie, a bonnie, bonnie lassie, as soon as they can find one. . . ."

"Take it easy! . . . Wait and see how Pinay makes out! . . ."

Our first walk through Paris took us along the Seine quays, past the Chancellery of the Legion of Honor, the Foreign Office and the Chamber of Deputies at which point we turned left, crossed the bridge and arrived in the Place de la Concorde. The immense square, dismal and dreary under a lowering December sky, was filled with captured German tanks, cannon, rolling kitchens, transport trucks, searchlights and other heavy materiel.

In the open spaces between this green-gray mass of war trophies lay incomprehensible rolls of barbed wire. A mountain of red roses almost hid from view the statue of the Maid of Strasbourg, the monument which had been draped in black mourning for forty-seven years. Now, with the Alsatian capital liberated at last, the monument had been restored to the light of day and the company of the other Maid statues representing the other cities of France.

On the terraces of the Tuileries Gardens, overlooking the Place de la Concorde, a regiment of Senegalese infantry was bivouacked. Steel-helmeted sentries with fixed bayonets walked up and down. The presence of all these troops in the heart of Paris gave the city an eerie, almost sinister air of malaise. This certainly wasn't gay Paree, *la Ville Lumière*, of which I had dreamt all my life. We tried to mount the steps leading to the gardens, but a Negro sentry stopped us.

"*On ne passe pas!* No thoroughfare!" he said.

"Isn't this a public garden? What's the trouble?"

"No trouble yet," the infantrist grinned back. "But you never can tell. Things might liven up any moment!"

A white officer belonging to a colonial regiment, judging by his shoulder straps, stepped nearer. "What business are you on?" he asked.

"No business at all, *mon capitaine.* Just sight-seeing. This is our first visit to Paris. . . . "

"You've picked a bad day. *Ça va barder!* It's going to boil over! Keep moving, please! These are my orders, I'm sorry. . . . "

A little further, on the Rue Royale facing the Madeleine church, more colonial troops were standing and sitting about. Barbed wire was strung on posts in the shape of sawhorses. The men had their rifles stacked on the sidewalks and the steps of the Madeleine. As if they were maneuvering between the shell craters of a battlefield, the empty autobusses picked their way cautiously through the entanglements and the groups of soldiers. The same spectacle on the *grands boulevards*; everywhere we saw heavy troop concentrations and but few civilians. In the sidewalk cafés on the Boulevard des Capucines some American officers were sitting around a *brasier*, an open-air stove. They looked as glum and mournful as people with a bad conscience waiting for Gabriel's trumpet call. Paris seemed deserted or confined to barracks. A regiment of dragoons clattered by, and then more infantry and still more infantry. All those soldiers carried their bayonets at the fix. The day had begun in rain, it now advanced to brief gleams of sunshine which, passing up and down the long streams of bay-onets, lighted up the waving lines like a silver cornfield.

We walked as far as the Porte St. Denis and turned left into the Boule-vard de Strasbourg till we came to the Gare de l'Est. The gates of the railway station's vast outer court were closed. Through the iron bars we saw that the entire court was packed with troops. Sentries paced nervously back and forth on the outside. Parked against the sidewalk stood a row of armored cars. A lieutenant sitting on the hood of one of these *chars d'assaut* was, not very successfully, trying to roll himself a cigarette from a sack of Bull Durham.

"Here," I said, "try one of these," and held out the package I had pur-chased a few hours before at the canteen in the Hotel d'Iéna.

"Oh, thank you very much! *Vous êtes bien aimable!*"

"The atmosphere seems kind of tense in Paris," I said. "We've just come in from Belgium. We thought we'd find the people still dancing in the streets in celebration of the victory."

"Victory?" he sneered. "A country that counts one dead in every family does not celebrate, *mon ami*. There's no need to proclaim either victory or defeat. Everybody with eyes in his head can see it: *La France est fichue!* We're in trouble. France is finished...."

"But all these soldiers? The sight made us think perhaps that the Boche had made about turn, and was heading this way once more."

This made him laugh. "If that were only true," he said, "we'd know what to do. As things stand it's all very miserable. Nobody knows what's going to happen!"

"Then what's up?"

"A general strike is about to go into effect. But that isn't all. Twenty of our own divisions are reported to be marching on Paris. They've given up trailing the Germans and are coming to join the revolution...."

"The revolution? Great God! Is there likely to be any shooting?"

"Not if we can help it. I for one certainly don't feel like shooting my own people. Would you fire on your own brothers? *Je suis Parigot, moi!* I'm a Parisian!"

"Come and have a drink at the café across the street."

"I can't leave." The lieutenant shook his head. "I'm stuck here...."

"Then take a pull from this flask," said Gordon, producing our last bottle of cognac from his knapsack.

"*Ah, ça je veux bien....* I don't mind if I do. It's chilly hanging around in the streets. We've been here since dawn."

In the distance, from the direction of the Rue des Récollets, a long column of workers hove in sight. Rain-soaked red flags led off the procession. A few of the flags were covered with black crape....

Some of the paraders sang *La jeune garde qui descend sur le pavé, sur le pavé,* "The young guard which comes to take possession of the streets." Masses of police and republican guards armed with carbines followed in open trucks at the tail end of the procession.

"Now, if I was ordered to fire on those punks, I wouldn't hesitate a moment," said the lieutenant, contemptuously motioning his chin towards the police. "*Sales vaches! Salauds!* Vile, rotten scum! ..."

A bugle's shrill call sounded somewhere in the station's courtyard, and the soldiers halfheartedly picked up their rifles from the stacks. Our lieutenant climbed aboard his armored car. "*Merci, hein!*" He waved his hand as he ducked inside.

"This needs some explanation," I said to Gordon. "Do you think we'll get any wiser from reading the newspapers? Let's buy some!"

But there were no newspapers on sale; all the stands were closed. For another day or so we were forced to continue our road through life in utter ignorance of what was going on in the world. I had hardly seen a newspaper in two years. When I did see one occasionally it contained at best some cryptic bulletin or communiqué drawn up by the ineffable Maxime Weygand who had a reputation, given him by Foch, of being the greatest communiqué writer since Napoleon Bonaparte.

The day and evening passed without a sign of Pinay. Around midnight Gordon and I were sitting in a sidewalk café on the opposite side of the street facing our hotel, debating whether or not we should go back to the neighborhood where we lost our master baker and institute a search for him, when we saw his bedraggled figure stagger up the steps. He was walking in his bare feet.

"How did you get here?"

"I walked," he said. "I have no money, not a cent.... Mr. Gilchrist," he turned to Gordon, "did I give you some of my money to keep for me?"

"You did not!"

"Then it's all gone!"

"How much?"

"Two thousand francs!"

"Where did you get so much money in the first place?"

"Didn't I bake cakes for all of you? Those bastards took everything: my money, my papers, my watch, my shoes, my greatcoat, my underwear, my socks. . . . "

"Who robbed you?"

"That whore and her pimp!"

"How?"

"How, you ask?"

"Yes, how? Did you just let them frisk you? . . . "

"No, that's not the way it went. After I left you, the girl and I first went to a bistro near the station. . . . I had a glass of Pernod. . . . I got very sleepy. . . . I remember walking to a small hotel with her, up two flights of stairs. . . . In the room I fell smack on the bed, and that's all. . . . That's all I remember. . . . I woke up with the bums. . . . "

"What do you mean, the bums?"

"I didn't wake up in that hotel. . . . I woke up under a bridge. There were half a dozen guys lying there. All drunk as hell. . . . "

"Any of our fellows there?"

"No, just bums. . . . They puked and stank. . . . I got sick, too. . . . "

"How did you get under the bridge?"

"How should I know? I don't remember a thing. . . . But they got my transportation ticket, too! For Christ's sake, you are not going to write home about this, are you?" he anxiously inquired.

"Don't worry! My letter-writing days are over! First have something to eat. Then we'll go up to the room and call Raoul and decide what's to be done. . . . "

Liliane's lover boy proved unavailable till next morning.

"Sergeant Pinay, you are a disgrace to the British uniform and a damn fool," Raoul blurted out the moment he stamped into our room while the prodigal still sat rubbing his eyes on the edge of the cot where he had slept.

"Stand to attention, man, when I speak to you. You are a damn fool!"

"Yes, sir!"

"Say that you are a damn fool! Say it!"

"I am a damn fool, sir!" Shorty agreed, and started to whimper.

"That's alright then. . . . Blow your nose. . . . Not on the rug, you damn peasant! ... We'll have some coffee brought up. Then we'll go downstairs and try to get you a pair of shoes and an overcoat. We have no quartermaster store in Paris. There are some imperial M.P.'s around, but if we take those guys into our confidence, they're bound to start an investigation, and we're apt to land in the clink.... Don't forget we're not supposed to be in Paris...."

"Have they a clink here?" asked the still blubbering Pinay.

"Of that you may be sure," said Raoul, "if the imperials have anything at all, they'll have a clink! We'll have to try the Americans.... Pierre, you talk to the Y.M.C.A. wallah downstairs.... Just give him a cock-and-bull story about the bums robbing Shorty here. Leave the whore and pimp out of the picture. The Y.M.C.A. is prejudiced against people who consort with whores...."

"But I didn't consort with any whore!" said Pinay in a pitiful voice. "I never touched that girl!"

"You never touched her? Then you're a still bigger damn fool than I thought you were...."

In less than an hour Shorty had a pair of secondhand American service boots. "Such things are happening all the time," remarked the desk man. "But you needn't do any beating about the bush with me. We know perfectly well what happened. Ten to one it was a woman who lured the sergeant. She slipped him a mickey, and he woke up under a bridge somewhere. Isn't that the truth?"

Since the remorseful Pinay was determined to go to Rouen as soon as possible, the whole day was spent in rehabilitating him. Liliane and Raoul supplied the money for the rail ticket, and the next morning our baker departed, swearing on the heads of his nine children that in future he'd drink nothing stronger than water.... To make sure that he wouldn't fall under the spell of another sweet siren's song, we accompanied him to the station and put him safely aboard the train. We never saw our sergeant again. When Raoul and I turned up at Rouen's base hospital a few weeks later, nobody could tell us what had become of him, or whether he had reached the place at all. There was no record....

Lieutenant Gilchrist did not accompany us to the station. He was taking a bath and repeating the stunt with the six whisky and sodas on the bathtub's rim.

"I'm going to get drunk twice a day as long as my money lasts," he announced. "Once in the morning and again in the evening. I'm sorry the war is over. I don't know how to get along without it. . . ."

That was just double talk. The truth was that he wanted to get rid of us. He wanted to go it alone in Paris. His wish was fulfilled a few days later when he met up with a Scottish WAAC. The two went on a sight-seeing trip to the châteaux on the Loire, at least so they said. We never saw Gilchrist again either. . . .

His departure soon forced me to look for more modest quarters. I had received 30 pounds sterling from the army paymaster just before starting from the Brussels-South station. This amount had dwindled to 25 pounds in less than a week's time. At this rate, I figured, my financial situation would soon become catastrophic, and so I decided to retrench. Without informing Raoul, since he would almost certainly have objected and insisted on pitching in from his own or Liliane's affluence, I moved to a small room on the Rue Soufflot near the Luxembourg Gardens in the heart of the Latin Quarter. After storing my equipment in my new abode, I sent Raoul a *pneumatique,** telling him of my whereabouts. I paid the equivalent of two and a half dollars a week for the room which was located on the sixth floor. I need hardly say that it wasn't a penthouse in the modern sense of the word.

My room had no windows; the only light, a few feeble rays, percolated through a grime-covered, iron-framed set of four glass panes in the ceiling. This skylight could be pushed up and when in that position afforded me, while standing on the rickety bed, an inspiring view of the Left Bank's sea of roofs, mansards and chimney pots. To the right, when looking out, I could see within a stone's throw the impressive dome of the Panthéon. My eyesight was then still so perfect that I was able to decipher without difficulty the lettering on the band just above the massive Corinthian columns: *Aux Grands Hommes La Patrie Reconnaissante.***

If the Panthéon remained an object of recurrent pilgrimage to me, it was for one reason only: to verify how much the wear and tear of the years has contributed to the deterioration of my visual powers, and whether or not I must move any nearer than was the case in A.D. 1918 to decipher

*A *pneumatique* is a special delivery letter which is shot through a pneumatic tube and guaranteed to reach its destination within one hour anywhere in Paris.

**"A grateful fatherland to its great men." Mirabeau, Voltaire, Diderot, Jean Jacques Rousseau, Victor Hugo, Emile Zola and Jean Jaurès are some of the immortals sleeping in the granite tombs in the crypt.

the inscription above the portico. It may be objected that I might just as easily and at far less cost have my eyes tested in an optician's shop. Perhaps so! But then, every man has his idiosyncrasies; the contemplation of the Panthéon's façade is as good an excuse to visit Paris as any.

For breakfast, which was included in the price of the room, I had some hot water with chicory that went by the name of coffee. It was dished up in a bowl, very much chipped and cracked, and smeared with a brown gluey rim left over from former collations. With the coffee came a piece of unbuttered stale bread, stale bread being cheaper. The concierge's husband insisted on carrying the breakfast up all six slippery flights of stairs. This journey, a very arduous undertaking for a man stomping around on a cork leg, was not, however, inspired by any altruistic motivation on his part. As I was to learn to my sorrow, he climbed all those stairs in his line of duty as an *indicateur de police*. In other words: he kept an eye on things.

After he stumbled upstairs with the coffee, Jules Vignon—such was the informer's name—told me how he came to lose his leg. The story came not all in one piece, but in installments, a little more every morning after a brief synopsis like the old-time *feuilleton* in the family newspaper. The mishap occurred, Vignon said, during the Battle of the Marne in September, 1914. He was one of the 100,000 men who were rushed at a moment's notice from the streets of Paris to the battlefield.

According to Vignon, Papa Joffre was still asleep at nine o'clock that morning of September 4, when General Galliéni, the military governor of Paris, telephoned:

" 'Look Joffre, it's time . . . . '

" 'To get up? Already?'

" 'No, it's time to attack! You'll never get such a chance again. Von Kluck is out of breath. . . . He's staggering with exhaustion. . . . '

" 'Leave me alone!' replied Joffre. 'I haven't the men, I can't attack! I'm going back to sleep!'

" 'Come on, Joffre, for God's sake, wake up! I'll send you the men,' the governor pleaded. 'I am calling 100,000 Parisians. . . . I am sending them up in taxicabs. . . . '

" 'What'll you arm them with?'

" 'With knives if needs be! If the knives prove insufficient they'll use their teeth. . . . ' "

"Is that the way the battle was won?" I asked Jules. "With knives?"

"Yes," he nodded, "*c'était formidable, fantastique.* We literally waded in blood.... The battlefield was a porridge of guts and *merde....* The river..."

"... flowed red with the blood of the Germans," I interjected.

"How d'you know? Were you there?"

"No, but I heard...."

"You heard right.... Believe me, that's something to see, a river of blood.... We slaughtered the Boche where he stood...."

"Didn't he fight back?"

"He didn't have time.... We were too quick for him. I myself cut down half a dozen of the slobs, maybe a dozen. I don't know, I lost count. *Zit! Zit! Zit!* I slashed right and left, never missing."

"How then did you get wounded?"

"When they retreated the *Allemands* raked us with artillery fire. One piece of shrapnel carried away my left leg. I thought I was done for.... But, as you see, I'm still hopping around.... Here"—he took a medal from his pocket—"look, this is what I got for my services, the *croix de guerre* and a gold palm."

"Why don't you wear it?"

"I am not the bragging kind."

As soon as I finished my coffee, Jules Vignon returned downstairs and donned a cocked hat with a red, white and blue cockade in front, and left for his major job as messenger boy for some brokerage house in the vicinity of the Bourse. When, in the course of my wanderings in Paris that month, I encountered him one day accidentally in the neighborhood of the Bourse, I learned that in the financial quarter he went by the nickname of Jo-Jo....

The concierge, Madame Gaetan, was a lady with reddish-brown hair, a *café-crème* complexion, and big slow-moving dark eyes. She wore a perpetual black shawl around her shoulders. There could be no doubt that once, not so long ago, she had been a very attractive person. She talked in a soft purring tone of voice and walked, or rather tripped, with the quick capering steps of a *danseuse*. She had a peculiar way of rubbing her chin while subjecting me to a little questioning whenever I passed her *loge*, the one-roomed, partially glass-enclosed quarters she occupied on the ground floor next to the staircase.

Nobody can say that the surveillance in that house left anything to be desired. It was an all around the clock service, for Jo-Jo slept on a cot under the staircase, and you had to declare, more often shout, your name to him before he pulled the cord that let you in after dark.

Also on the ground floor, but reached by a separate entrance, was a bookshop, owned by Monsieur Jacques Fourier. Monsieur Fourier happened to be a widower, a circumstance which may have gone far to explain his incredibly unkempt appearance. During the morning hours he wore a bathrobe and a sort of turban on his head. Both the bathrobe and the turban were so deeply buried under a layer of grease that their original color could no longer be distinguished with the naked eye. At noon he changed clothes; he put on a yellow dust coat over the bathrobe. In the place of the turban he wore a black skullcap with a green tassel dangling from the rear.

The bookseller must have been in his sixties, a lanky, dried-out individual with a goatee, a glittering pince-nez, and a set of badly fitting false teeth. The set, habitually referred to as his *râtelier*, caused him unendurable pain. For this reason he carried it most of the time in the pocket of his bathrobe.

He slept in a small oblong room in the rear of his shop where he also cooked his meals and had a washroom from which emanated an aroma not exactly atar of roses. However, as he remarked more than once: the great Erasmus already complained about the smells of Paris five hundred years earlier and still managed to live out a long and useful life. Why should he, Jacques Fourier, complain and lose a lot of time while the drains were repaired when he had important work to do?

Most of his waking hours Monsieur Fourier sat by a desk which was buried under a load of newspapers, trade journals, catalogues and other paperasserie. Above his desk hung a sign in red and black letters: *Notre temps est bref, soyez bref*. "Our time is short; you, too, be short." In such and suchlike slogans, he informed me, lay the secret source of the success of great American businessmen who kept these signs constantly before their eyes by reason of their subtle inspirational and creative impulse.

One narrow strip of his desk was kept scrupulously clear. In that space stood an inkwell and lay two books, one an account book, the other a weighty ledger, three inches thick, in which he wrote a few lines every day. In that book Monsieur Fourier made notes which were to serve him at a later date in the compilation of a history of all the wells, springs, fountains and pumps of Paris from the earliest times to the modern era. He had been at this task for thirty odd years and told me, as I could well imagine, that it involved a great deal of research. When completed he expected the work in two volumes to be crowned by the Academy of Archaeological Inscriptions.

It was his life's task to describe all the subterranean watercourses, where they originated or who dug them, the Druids, the Gauls, the Christian missionaries, the early kings and so on; further, after which nymphs, fauns, satyrs or saints they were named and why; which prominent person drank from them; who was drowned in them, accidentally or otherwise, not omitting the curative and therapeutic value of certain waters, as well as the sinister pestilence-breeding capacities of some of them; in short: a book most apt and suitable to make the mouths of amateurs water.

In the evening, after sundown, Fourier stepped outside for a little air and to place the shutters in front of his shop's single display window. After that hour not a glimmer of light was visible from the outside and the place resembled a tomb. Once a week he was joined in the evening by a friend, and the two went out to dinner. The first time I saw them go out, I hardly recognized Monsieur Fourier. He was dressed fit to kill: a black suit, a bowler hat, a tie in which sparkled a jewel, a thick gold watch chain and an umbrella. It wasn't till my second or third week that he had enough confidence in me to inform me that they did not really go to dinner, but attended a meeting of the masonic lodge, "Virtue and Fortitude," located in a dark alley off the Rue de Rennes.

In his shop were to be found practically all the French classics with separate shelves for modern novelists and poets. All pages of the novels were cut because he read everything before selling it. The largest section consisted of books dealing with "occultism," the subject in which Monsieur Fourier specialized: magic, soothsaying, clairvoyance, necromancy, mesmerism, sadism, sexual perversions, satanism and other subjects which he dubbed *exotique*. Since I hadn't the wherewithal to buy any of these precious volumes, the proprietor graciously allowed me to borrow whatever I liked. The only condition was that I refrain from carrying the books off the premises, which meant that I read them in bed under the feeble glow of the 25-watt bulb dangling from the ceiling in my garret. . . .

One afternoon when the cold rain drove me indoors, and I took refuge in Fourier's bookshop, a customer came in. He was a gentleman got up in the style of the *ancien régime*, a monocle, striped trousers, spats, a black overcoat with fur collar and a walking stick. Fourier jumped up like a jack-in-the-box, quickly put the *râtelier* in its rightful place, and pirouetted around the personage, bowing and scraping and addressing him alternately as Excellency and *Monsieur le Ministre*.

Then with a furtive glance in my direction, he went to the rear of his shop and opened a door which I had theretofore imagined to be that of a cupboard. It wasn't a cupboard: that door led into another room full of books. I caught a glimpse of the room's interior as he switched on the light before he and his distinguished client disappeared inside. After a quarter hour the two men emerged, Fourier carrying two or three gold-tooled volumes bound in fine blue leather. The books were wrapped up in an old newspaper, some money changed hands, and the visitor, after tipping his hat to Monsieur Fourier, rejoined his waiting limousine and chauffeur at the curb.

"*Eh bien*," said the bookseller when he returned from seeing his customer out, "now that you know my secret, I might as well show you what I have in that room. You didn't think," he remarked contemptuously, as we passed by the shelves containing the aforementioned occult literature, "you didn't think, I hope, that I make my living selling this crap.... Here," he showed me into the secret chamber, "here are my treasures!"

There must have been a thousand volumes in the room. In contrast with the outer shop, the inner sanctum appeared as neat and tidy as an American housewife's kitchen. There was even a rug on the floor. The books were ranged with the *savoir-faire* and loving kindness of a connoisseur.

What he showed me was the largest illustrated collection of erotica I've ever seen or heard of in my life. Monsieur Fourier pulled out one volume which bore the title *The Forty Ways of Making Love As Taught by a Galilean Courtesan of Distinction* (meaning Mary Magdalen).

"This volume," he explained, "is from the pen of Marcel Daniel, the pictures are from the hand of an unknown master; that is, the illustrator is unknown to the public, though he is very well known to me. ... Do you wish to see the blue, gold and red miniatures of Abraham and Sarah disporting themselves in the cool sands of the desert at eventide? Here they are! They're excellently realistic, don't you think? ... What is your opinion of this portfolio of engravings of Cardinal Dubois and his concubines? Rather crude work, isn't it? Alas, yes, it's eighteenth century! It took time to reach our present-day state of erotic perfection. ... All ages and all nations are represented in my collection: the Greeks, the Romans, the Persians, the Hindus, the Bulgarians, all of them, and each nation, as you may easily verify, has had some original or piquant contribution to make to the cult of Priapus...."

"Any Dutch pictures?" I asked.

"Monsieur," he replied, visibly shocked by my ignorance, "how can you ask such a question? The Dutch were never blessed with the necessary imagination to produce this particular kind of art, though I'll grant that they're strong in certain other directions."

"What other directions, for instance?"

"For instance: theology! ...

"By the way, he added, as we regained the outer shop and he turned the key in the lock of the treasure chamber, "I consider it my duty to warn you against the *unijambiste** next door. I have noticed you talking to him now and then. For your own welfare, I pray you, avoid Monsieur Jules Vignon as much as possible. The man is a monster of depravity; he'd sell his own mother and probably did. He's hand in glove with the *brigade mondaine*, the vice squad; I need say no more. I am a patriot, but I have so high a regard for our noble allies that I shouldn't wish you to have more contact than you can help with that one-legged piece of *ordure*...."

"But Monsieur Fourier," I objected, "how can you talk that way about a man of valor like Jules Vignon? ... True, he seems a little boastful by nature, but one must make allowances for the fact that he is a war invalid...."

"*Un invalide de guerre*? Who? Jo-Jo?"

"Yes, he told me the circumstances in which he lost his leg, throwing back the Germans in the Battle of the Marne...."

"Who was at the Marne? Jo-Jo? Did he tell you that?"

"He did. I have all the details.... He showed me his decoration...."

Monsieur Fourier started to laugh. He laughed like a maniac. He slapped his bathrobe in merriment and almost lost his balance.... "That's a good one," he coughed when he finally recovered his composure. "What would you say if I told you that I know Jo-Jo since he was that high.... He lost his leg when it was crushed by the wheels of an autobus at the age of five or six. It happened right in this street. I helped carry him indoors myself.... But tell me, how in the name of all that's reasonable did you ever come to rent a room in the hole above my shop?"

Unijambiste: from *une*-one, and *jambe*-leg: a man with one leg.

Fourier asked after he dried his tears with the slip of his bathrobe.

"I saw an ad in the window of a renting office, and took a chance. . . . "

"Where is your room located?"

"On the sixth floor."

"Ah, so it's you who occupy Mademoiselle Germaine's room!"

"Mademoiselle Germaine?"

"Yes, the girl that was murdered six months ago. . . . That was a mystery which has never been cleared up. . . . The *flics* ransacked the house from top to bottom, even took photographs and everybody was subjected to the humiliation of fingerprinting, myself included. What indignity! What barbarism! What will the republican police think up next to violate the Declaration of the Rights of Man?. . . Though the *rechercheurs* didn't find a single clue, they nevertheless informed the newspapers that they knew for sure that the assassin or assassins had entered Mademoiselle Germaine's room through the skylight. How do you like that for logic? Absolutely no clues, and still they knew! Our criminal police is very strong on logic. Myself, I have no logic, but I have my theories. In fact I worked out one theory which furnishes me with indisputable evidence as to the murderer's identity. . . . "

"Why don't you tell the police?"

"Monsieur," he replied, "crime and religion are matters of the individual conscience. Nor do I want to have my throat slit. I'm fairly certain that the murderer lives in this very neighborhood. The least suspicion on his part that I am aware of his identity and he'll strike again. *Pfuit!* Just like that! One stroke across the throat. . . . Incidentally, Madame Gaetan must be happy to have rented the room at last. It's been vacant ever since the murder. That's on account of the condition of the floor, of course."

"What's wrong with the floor?"

"Didn't you notice? You had better watch your step. . . . The old boards are rotting away. . . . They were soaked in blood. . . . The poor girl bled so much that her blood seeped through the ceiling into the room below. That's where the prince lives, in the room below Mademoiselle Germaine's. . . . "

"The prince, you say?"

"Yes, he's a prince, Monsieur Youriev. There can be no doubt about it; he's an authentic prince. . . . He woke up when the blood drops fell on his face. . . . "

"So it was the prince who notified the police?"

"He did not! The *unijambiste* did that. The prince only laughed his silly laugh. I haven't told you that he is totally demented. The poor man is as crazy as a loon. And not he alone, but all his cronies who are princes, too."

"All princes? You surprise me, Monsieur Fourier, aristocrats in this place?"

"*Si*, they're Russian princes who fled the revolution. They were very highly placed personages in their native land. We have at least one ex-general and two former governors of provinces in this house. There is hardly a stick of furniture in that room of theirs. They sleep on mattresses lying on the floor. In the evening they get drunk and run a contest of spitting at the blood stains on the ceiling. . . . That's the sole sport they engage in. . . ."

"Don't they ever work? How do they live?"

"*On dit*, 't is said, that they have some jewels stashed away. But then," he shrugged his shoulders, "this is said of every *émigré* noble. . . . Once in a while they go to the Halles, and work at unloading vegetables and fish!"

"Haven't they any family?"

"No, they have a girl that cooks for them, but she's not Russian. The girl is the daughter of the professor who occupies the room next to the prince. . . ."

"A real professor?"

"Of course, a real professor; a professor of music, piano! . . . "

"I haven't heard any sound of piano-playing so far."

"That's a profound observation. The reason you hear no piano is that there is no piano. The professor hasn't touched a piano for years. He plays on a wooden board on which the keys are painted black and white, a a make-believe keyboard. . . ."

"*Quelle misère!*"

"Why? It's no misery at all. In fact, he's very happy, the professor! He feels quite certain that an invisible audience listens to his inaudible music. . . . The professor and his daughter are accompanying the princes when they return to their beloved native country. They weep together when they hear the church bells of Nizhnii Novgorod ring in their heads. They all want to see the dear *moujiks* again, too. . . . "

"When are they returning to Russia?"

"Ah, don't worry, it's only a dream. . . . Those gentlemen will never go back. Lenin and Trotsky cooked their goose. But in their case the dream is stronger than the dreamer! ...

"Since I'm introducing you to your neighbors, I may as well tell you that just below the professor lives a couple who hail from the Low Countries. I am but imperfectly informed on their affairs. They don't talk much. To tell the truth, we know nothing about their business, but they do have money, and they spend it liberally. Every Sunday they go to the country and walk in the forest of Meudon."

"Well, that shouldn't be so expensive. Meudon isn't very far!"

"Not expensive? Do you think that riding out to Meudon in a taxicab isn't expensive? Just try it once. You'll find that in a time like this the rates are ruinous, and the taxi chauffeurs worse than Sicilian bandits.... The couple I am speaking of are in mourning.... You'll see them sooner or later, very decent and sedate bourgeois people.... They had a boy who was killed by the explosion of a Big Bertha shell.* If you turn to the left on leaving the Rue Soufflot and follow the Boulevard St. Michel as far as the School of Mines, you may see with your own eyes where the bomb struck that killed the little boy. The façade of the school is pitted with holes made by the shell's fragments. The explosion tore the boy to shreds. They picked up the pieces in a blanket.... The authorities proposed that the child's remains be cremated.... But the parents objected. For what reason do you suppose?"

"I have no idea!"

"They were afraid that if the body was reduced to ashes, the child would not hear the archangel's call on the day of judgment. ... Upon my soul, I'm not joking. The parents were afraid that the child would miss the resurrection, so to speak. A grisly prospect, don't you think?"

"What's grisly about it?"

"That boy rising from the grave all in pieces—wouldn't you call that grisly? I can't imagine where people pick up such lugubrious notions...."

"There's nothing grisly about this," I observed, as we saw a young lady entering the large door next to the bookshop.

"I take due notice," replied Fourier, smiling his toothless smile, "that the eternal snows of Canada have not blinded you to the glorious reality of Dédé. ... That's the name of this goddess, this blonde *poule* you just saw enter Madame Gaetan's doleful cavern. ... That girl is the joy of my eyes, and of all our eyes, I may well say, all of us on this street, and many

*The giant gun with which the Germans bombarded Paris.

others. . . . It's a mixed world we live in, isn't it? Maniacs and murderers on the one hand, and angelic innocence, snow-white immaculateness on the other. Aren't they a bizarre lot, our contemporaries?"

"But I thought you said she was a *poule?*"

"There isn't any contradiction in my estimates. She's the loveliest child in Paris, my dear sir. Her figure is divine. I have had the honor and privilege to gaze upon it. Oh, not in the way you imagine perhaps! I only want to say that aesthetically her body is a masterpiece, definitely the crown of creation. God did Himself proud when He made that creature. Yes, I'll not withhold praise where praise is due; the Lord puts out superb workmanship when the fancy strikes Him. What I sincerely deplore is that this doesn't happen more often. . . ."

"The Lord probably grows weary. . . . He's been at it so long. . . ."

"Not weary, Monsieur, disgusted He gets, thoroughly disgusted with all the *cochonnerie,* swinishness, in which His human creations indulge. . . . But as I was saying, it came about this way—I mean the time I saw her disrobe. Dédé was struck by a taxicab, not seriously, thank heaven—she wasn't hurt in the least. But the police officer on duty in front of the Panthéon thought she'd better accompany him to the precinct house located to the right of the great building at the end of our street. I was on my way back from delivering a volume from my treasure chamber, when I noticed Dédé being escorted into the police station. I immediately inquired what was wrong. The policeman said that he took her in to have her examined by the physician on duty.

"Though I had not seen the accident, I came along as a witness, as a friend of the victim, as is my right and duty as a citizen of our *république* one and indivisible. . . . *Eh bien,* the doctor and the commissaire questioned Dédé. When she said she wasn't hurt and did not wish to prefer charges against the chauffeur, the doctor asked her to show her shoulder and more particularly the spot where she was slightly bruised by her brush with the cab.

"*Ah, mon Dieu, mon Dieu,* what a spectacle! What a revelation! What an apotheosis! What we saw was something to make the gods gasp! She dropped her gown right down to the waist: 'Look,' she said, '*vraiment, ce n'est rien!* It's nothing, really!'

"We couldn't answer, Monsieur. 'It's nothing,' she said. Fact is, it was everything. We couldn't find words. We could only stare. The vision before our eyes was one of dazzling Praxitelean inspiration. The doctor, the commissaire, the chauffeur and myself, we had to swallow hard as our throats had suddenly gone dry. The aspect of Dédé's be-all reduced us to silence, a religious silence, I may well say.... Such a *gorge,* such a bust, such a miracle of perfection! We were all men of experience, men of the world, but we hadn't the faintest idea that such a wonder of beauty existed here below.... That's our little Dédé who just went by.... She lives on the second floor in the rear."

"What does Mademoiselle Dédé do for a living?"

"She's an artist's model!"

"Lucky artist!"

"You wouldn't say that if you knew the man. He's the unluckiest, unhappiest person alive, perhaps the man most to be pitied in the whole world...."

"Why?"

"He's a eunuch!"

"A Turk?"

"No, he is not a Turk, he's a Frenchman, Parisian born and bred. He lives on the Rue Lepic in Montmartre, on the hill of the martyrs, very aptly so called in his case. He became a eunuch through the ravages of war. He was grievously wounded at Douaumont in the vicinity of Verdun. One razorlike sweep by a shell fragment and, horrors, the most essential part of his anatomy flew off.... The peculiarity of it is, perhaps it's a biological curiosity, in less than a year's time he lost all his hair, he is totally bald. Even the hair of his eyebrows he lost. His vocal powers degenerated into the piping, fluting sound we expect in a castrate.... But loyal! Ah, what loyalty that man displays.... He's like a watchdog over Dédé.... He fetches her in the morning and brings her home again in a taxicab. The comfortable thought about his attentions is that Dédé is perfectly safe with him...."

On weekdays I was usually out of the house by seven o'clock. I had no definite travel plans; I just walked where chance and the spirit led me. It has often been said that Paris is composed of many cities. There are at least twenty *mairies* or borough halls within the circle of the old fortifications. I visited every one of them and found that every *arrondissement,* every district and quarter has its own distinctive physiognomy, its own poetry, its own sadness, its own moral climate. Paris even has its own dialect. I haven't seen a copy for years, but I do recall once buying a pocket dictionary of Parisian *argot* with the meaning of the words in official French on the opposite page.

I traveled but seldom by bus, though I used the subway, the famous *métro* several times. On one of my first outings I emerged from the underground at the end of the line and found myself in front of the Donjon, the castled fortress of Vincennes. A Tonkinese sentry at the gate let me pass unchallenged. I walked to the grassy moat in the rear of the castle to the spot where my erstwhile compatriot, a Frisian girl by the name of Margaretha Zelle, better known as Mata-Hari, faced the firing squad the year before on October 17th.

"Was she guilty?" I asked a gray-haired quartermaster officer who was strolling about with his hands behind his back, watching me carefully as I stood looking at the three black-painted stakes at the end of the field.

"The evidence produced at her trial," he replied, "showed that she had the death of at least 21,000 French soldiers on her conscience.... As an actress she traveled up and down between Paris and Madrid. In Paris she learned from careless French officers how many of our troops were to be dispatched to the Salonika front, and when. This information she carried to Spain and communicated to the German consular authorities. The consuls in turn notified the commanders of the German U-boats lying in various Spanish ports. And they, of course, swooped down on our troopships sailing out of Marseilles and Toulon...."

"My name is Choisy," he said, putting out his hand. "I am pleased to meet you! I have my quarters here in the Donjon. I've lived here eleven years."

"*Mon adjudant*," I asked, "did you ever see Mata-Hari? Was she as beautiful as they say she was?"

"I saw her carriage pass through the Donjon's gate at five in the morning on the day of her execution.... She sat between two nuns.... I caught a glimpse of her eyes only as the carriage passed by the lanterns in the covered gate.... A few minutes later I heard the shots and was called over to the moat because one of our men serving on the firing squad had fainted...."

"She was dead then?"

"No, evidently she wasn't quite dead. The officer commanding the firing squad was bending over her and discharged his revolver.... I didn't care to look at her face after that...."

"But why," the quartermaster suddenly asked, "why should you, a Russian, be interested in this woman?"

"A Russian, I? I am not a Russian. Why do you take me for a Russian? This has happened before. Others have taken me for a Russian." I thought of the first time Raoul and I met General de St. Gervais on the beach at Paris-Plage when old Red Pants also mistook us for Russians. . . .

"You needn't worry about me," Choisy nodded reassuringly. "I respect your secret. . . . I took you for a Russian because of your greatcoat. . . . I thought perhaps you were one of the Russians who escaped the massacre. . . ."

"What massacre? What greatcoat? I don't know what you are talking about. . . ." I unbuttoned my coat and showed him the shoulder straps on my tunic with the word Canada and the letters C.G. (Corps of Guides) embroidered in gold on the collar. . . . "*Voilà*, there is no secret! Only I don't understand what you mean when you speak of the massacre. . . ."

"Don't you know about the ten thousand Russian soldiers who came to France to fight on the Western front?"

"I never heard of them! How did they get here? Break through the German lines?"

"No, they sailed around the world from Vladivostok and landed in Marseilles."

"Did they go to the front?"

"Yes, they went to the front and gave a fine account of themselves under Mangin in the first offensive on the Chemin des Dames. . . ."

"Were they massacred in that battle?"

"They were massacred—executed would be a better word—when they declared their solidarity with the Russian revolution in October last year. They downed arms and demanded to be sent back to Russia. . . . Their camp was then surrounded by units of the French battle police, and they were machine-gunned to death to the last man. . . . No, not to the last man, a few are thought to have escaped and to be hiding in Paris. . . ."

"Why were they killed?" I asked. "We had a few hundred Russians in the Canadian army who also downed arms at the time of the Russian revolution. They weren't shot. They were sent to work camps in southern France. They'll probably be dishonorably discharged, but that's all."

"Clemenceau ordered the ten thousand executed because he feared their influence on French morale. Do you realize that the spirit of defeatism was so strong that just before the Armistice there was but one division between Paris and the front on which the government could place absolute reliance. . . . Just one division! All the rest were ready to quit.

Had the Boche waited two or three more days before carrying the white flag over to our lines in the Rhetondes forest, he would have found that the bulk of our soldiers had followed the Russian example and gone home. . . . "

"So the German surrender came just in time?"

"In the nick of time!"

"A light begins to dawn," I said. "I begin to understand now why there is so much tension in Paris. There is more brewing than a general strike. . . ."

"*Ça gronde partout!*" he came back. "The volcano is rumbling everywhere. The general strike has been called off, postponed for the time being. . . . It's in a month or two that we'll be up to our necks in the worst crisis since 1871. . . ."

I visited all the *faubourgs,* the old revolutionary Faubourg St. Antoine, the aristocratic St. Honoré, the drab but multitudinous Faubourg du Temple, the site of the Bastille and the Trocadéro which has since disappeared. One of my longest walks led me to the Père-Lachaise cemetery and the Mur des Fédérés, the wall where the last defenders of the Commune died before General Galliffet's firing squads in 1871. The wall was covered with fresh wreaths of poppies and red roses, a sure sign that the revolutionary fever in Paris was on the way up. I climbed the steps of one of the towers of Notre Dame and a day later went up in the elevator to the top of the Eiffel Tower where I sat down to eat a freshly baked brioche in Gustave Eiffel's private chamber at the very summit. That day the wind was so strong that you could feel the gigantic structure sway in the breeze.

It was the first time in many months that I marched unencumbered save for an insatiable curiosity and a love for the city which has grown stronger ever since. It is from that first visit to Paris that I retained the habit of looking into the churches of every city I visited in afteryears, be it Rome, Warsaw, Moscow, Copenhagen, Kiev, London, Sevilla, Trondheim, Constantinople or Jerusalem. I still like the churches of France best, especially the country churches. Their interiors are so dark and mystical, so neglected and poor; poor as the church should be, impotent, helpless in the face of the world; without "form or comeliness."

From the Madeleine which served as a "Temple of Victory" during the Revolution and which is not so much a church as a religious salon, though its red plush boxes and alcoves are growing seedier-looking every year, I walked to the Sacré Coeur on the summit of Montmartre, the hill of the martyrs where St. Denis was beheaded in the good old days when the Church had no cathedrals but was a persecuted minority whose members gathered in catacombs.

If the towers of the Sacré Coeur look from the distance like a set of champagne bottles, the resemblance is by no means intended to be symbolical of the traditional gayety of "Montmartre by Night." The church was erected after the national defeat of 1871 as a protest on the part of the Catholic party against the godlessness of the republicans who brought the third empire to a fall and drove the fanatical war-mongering Empress Eugénie into exile.

Ever since the Sacré Coeur has remained the monumental symbol of Catholic opposition to the inroads of laicism and secularism. On the other hand, the anticlericals, represented by the Masonic Order and such political leaders as Waldeck-Rousseau, Clemenceau, Briand, Sarraut, Herriot and Daladier, had their revenge in such a way as to render the great basilica almost anathema to the faithful. Right in front of the church they erected a statue to the Chevalier de la Barre who has no other claim to immortality save the fact that he was the last man to be executed in France for refusing to kneel before a procession carrying the sacred host. Thus the two adversaries, clerical and anticlerical, continue to confront each other on Montmartre's hilltop, albeit only in stone. . . .

If I had little difficulty in identifying the great monuments and edifices of Paris, this was largely due to the old stereoscope which had its place on a small polished table in my mother's "best" or "Sunday room." On special occasions the children were permitted to see "the wonders of the world" through the two tiny magnifying windows in this delightful contraption. The longer you looked through the stereoscope, the clearer became the outline of the sites and façades of Europe's greatest buildings. As far as I remember there was but one view from America in the set of about 120 photographs. This view represented Niagara Falls. Since we were not permitted to open a book or do the least homework on Sundays, the stereoscope helped mightily to while away the most tedious hours of our Calvinist sabbath. There were some photos of London, Rome, Milan, Florence and Naples, but Parisian scenes predominated.

When I walked around in the Seine city in December, 1918, it was merely a case of verifying the exactitude of the stereoscopic pictures.

I greeted all those sites as old acquaintances: the Opera, the Palais Royal, Palais Bourbon, Petit Palais, Grand Palais, the Louvre, the Luxembourg, the Tower of St. Jacques and the Bridge Alexander III with its golden eagles which was built in honor of the last Russian Czar but one. Alexander was also the first to cross the bridge. So great was the fear of assassination that the police did not allow another living creature on the bridge while the Czar's carriage started to cross. Yet, to the stupefaction of the authorities and the huge crowds, a gentleman was seen to climb over the railing. He had been hiding beneath. The gentleman, whose identity was never established, walked up to the imperial carriage, politely swept off his hat and said to Czar Alexander: *"Vive la Pologne, Monsieur!"*

Every corner of Paris became alive for me. I would have liked a guidebook, a *Baedeker* or something, but for such things I was not financially equipped, so I let the stones speak for me. The stones of the Concorde bridge, next in line to the Pont Alexandre, I knew, were taken from the pile left behind when the revolutionaries pulled down the Bastille. I sat in the graveyard of the Church of St. Julien-le-Pauvre wondering which old stone Dante used as a pillow five hundred years before when he was a penniless and a very hungry student in Paris. In the Panthéon quarter, at number 12 Rue Valette, I found the house in which John Calvin lived while studying Hebrew at the Collège Fortet. There was a picture in the room once occupied by the Reformer. It showed a young man, dressed like a sixteenth century dandy, gloves in hand, a blond beard and a large beret of the kind the artists wear. Right behind the Panthéon I entered the Church of St. Etienne-du-Mont, perhaps the oldest, surely the finest little church in all Paris. Behind the altar in an alcovelike chapel sat a group of Carmelite nuns absolutely motionless in "perpetual adoration" before the Holy Sacrament. Every few hours these girls were relieved by another batch of sisters who marched in close formation through the narrow streets of that part of Paris which is now the Chinese quarter. On the floor, amongst the tombstones, I saw the grave of Clovis, the King of the Franks, and the epitaphs of Jean Racine and Blaise Pascal.

At the Prison du Cherche Midi, where Dreyfus was incarcerated, I was first refused admission, but later called back from the street and told that I could come in and look around. It's almost incredible that such a primitive structure with rat-infested corridors and bare cells, really ice-cold stone cages without much light, has continued to exist in the very heart of Paris till the present day. At the time of my visit the prisoners were all soldiers who had refused military service for religious reasons. I asked the officer who presented the visitors' book to me if I could write a word of observation. "Please do!" he said. I wrote: "This prison is a disgrace to France and to humanity...."

"I'm surprised that you don't have a torture chamber," I said.

"If you want to see a torture chamber," he said, mistaking my sentiments, "you should take a look at the cellars under the Place du Châtelet. There they'll show you the iron chair with a grated seat under which a fire was stoked to cook the heretic sitting in it.... They have five-pronged grapplers equipped with claws. With those things a woman heretic's breast could be squeezed off in one single twist.... But don't pull such a horror-stricken face. They don't use those instruments any longer. ..."

I left the prison by a rear door and came out into a courtyard where stood a small church, absolutely invisible from the street side. I walked through a tiny narrow street, the Rue Dupin, and emerged in the Rue de Sèvres where a crowd of women milled about a large fruit and vegetable stand. Against the wall, looking on, stood a very old man in the old-fashioned clerical garb, a large white bib with black borders instead of a modern-day Roman collar. His mouth hung open like a child's looking through the window of a toyshop as his gaze turned slowly from the apples and pears to the magnificent grapes. Finally he approached the stall and bought himself a bunch of soup greens.

"Is this all you buy, *Monsieur l'Abbé?*" I asked.

"It's all I can afford," he came back with a shrug of the shoulders and a pathetic smile.

"In that case *faites-moi la grâce,* do me the pleasure of accepting some of these muscat grapes."

"Ah, but what will madame say if you come home without them?"

He accepted the paper bag and pulling me by the hand went a short distance up the street where he made me sit on a bench by his side. I have never seen another person eat grapes in just the same manner as that old priest. He put six, eight, ten grapes in his mouth, chewed for a while and then spat out the skins.

"It's a day I won't soon forget," he said, as he rose to his feet. "I haven't eaten such excellent grapes since I was ten years old."

"Where was that?"

"In the village of Moissac on the Garonne River. That's where I was born, eighty-three years ago. My parents died before I was twelve. I was placed in an orphanage and that's where I am today. I am now *directeur de conscience* to the nuns who run the orphanage down this street. Their convent stands behind the chapel of St. Vincent de Paul. . . . This was his district, you know."

"Ah, it must be a source of deep satisfaction to you to work in the same district where once lived so great a saint and humanitarian."

"Would you like to come in and see the convent and the orphanage? I have my room there. It's not much of a room, it's located in the cellar. . . . But it's in Paris, that's all that matters. It's really a pity that you can't come with me. From my room you can hear the weirdest sounds, especially at nights. . . ."

"What kind of sounds?"

"You can hear the voices of the dead. . . ."

"The dead?"

"*Si, mais il n'y a rien à craindre,* they have a good time. They do an awful lot of laughing while they work."

"The dead are working, you say?"

"Yes, it's only a theory of mine, but I believe, not without some evidence, that the dead are constantly excavating the territory beneath our feet. They are undermining the foundations of the world. They are always digging, scraping and hollowing out the earth. There is really not much more left but a thin shell. One of these days the shell will crack and that'll be the end."

"The end of Paris?"

"No, they are digging everywhere. The earth's crust under London, Vienna and Moscow is just as thin. The entire world is going to crumble in the dust. This will be the revenge of the young men who died in all the senseless wars of history. . . ."

Only one structure, perhaps the most interesting of all, I did not recognize. I refer to the ruins on the Boulevard St. Michel, in the very heart of the oldest part of Paris. This building made of the flat long bricks used by the Romans in the construction of their temples, baths and aqueducts, could not be entered. It was and is separated from the street by a fence of iron staves the original of which the *sans-culottes* removed during the Revolution to use as weapons and pikes. On those pikes they carried the severed heads of the aristocrats.

In the rear of the ruins stands the Musée de Cluny. This was open to the public and there I learned that the house in front was once inhabited by that Julian the Apostate who, since schooldays, was one of the most fascinating figures in history to me. In that place Julian sat writing his books, dressed in a philosopher's gown, his face adorned with the philosopher's beard.

Here came the legionnaires one stormy night to inform him that he had been chosen Caesar Augustus. When he refused the diadem, the soldiers threatened to kill Julian, and he gave in. The imperial purple was thrown over his shoulders and he was raised on a shield amidst the wild acclaim of the troops. Julian forthwith marched back to Rome where he proclaimed the abolition of Christianity as the state religion.

No matter what the Church historians* say to the contrary, Julian did not persecute the Christians. He detested them, that's true enough. As a student of philosophy in Antioch, he one day climbed the wall of the garden where he walked and meditated. On the other side of the wall ran the avenue of the gods adorned with a long row of statues from the chisels of Pheidias and Praxiteles. As Julian looked on, he saw the Christian mob break up those priceless works of art with hammers. "I despise myself," he said, "for being of the same flesh and blood as these utter barbarians. . . ."

No human language can express the emotion which rises when one comes to a spot of which it can be said with reasonable certainty: "Here once stood a *man*! Here once an act of greatness was performed! Here a word of truth or wisdom was spoken!"

The novelist and critic Ludwig Lewisohn,** in whose neighborhood I lived in Paris in later years, reproached me for visiting the Chapel of the Invalides and Napoleon's tomb on the day when the annual Mass of Requiem is said for the repose of the Emperor's soul. Lewisohn called Napoleon "the greatest vulgarian of all times."

I have never been able to make up my mind whether Napoleon was a soldier of liberty, the bearer of the Revolution or merely the last flare-up of the dying theocratic military order. I have read I don't know how many biographies of the man, but to say that I have seen his face or caught a glimpse of the inner recesses of his soul, I cannot. Nor can anyone else, it seems, for though there are no less than 40,000 biographies of the Corsican, we still do not know him. We know a good deal about his wars,

*Alzog, Auer, Luebker and others.
**The Island Within, Criticism in America, etc.

his policies, his marshals, his ministers and administration, his wives and mistresses, and we have some information on himself. But the more there is written, the less we seem to know the man. Forty thousand volumes like so many tombstones cover that Unknown Soldier.

The seventeen year old Russian poet Lermontov, who had never seen Napoleon, perhaps understood him best when he wrote: "Napoleon was a stranger to this world. . . . Everything in him was mystery!"

The little children of France still sing: *Parlez-nous de lui, grandmère, parlez-nous de lui!* "Speak to us of him, grandmother, tell us about him. . . ."

The last time I visited the Chapel of the Invalides, I noticed the white coffin containing the remains of the Duke of Reichstadt standing in one of the niches. The Duke of Reichstadt was the curly-headed little King of Rome, Napoleon's son by Marie Louise, who wanted to share his father's exile on St. Helena. The strange thing about the coffin is that it was Adolf Hitler who ordered it shipped from Vienna to Paris and placed near the immense porphyry sarcophagus where the Emperor sleeps. It's the one and only known act of kindness the Fuehrer ever performed in his life. Was Hitler perhaps another man nobody knows?

The book barrows along the Seine quays were closed and locked on account of the bad weather. But I found one library, the Bibliothèque des Huguenots, on the Rue des Saints-Pères. In that place where I was often the one solitary reader, I met the editor of the organ of the Christian socialists, *Christianisme Social*. I became the correspondent of that periodical and remained so till 1960. . . .

After a day's tramping, I was glad to get back to my ultimate port of call on the Rue Soufflot. If I reached the premises before closing time, I sat for an hour or so in Monsieur Fourier's bookshop where a number of the proprietor's neighbors and friends dropped in for a chat during the cocktail hour. Not that we drank cocktails! One visitor, Dr. Roger Curand, condemned cocktails as "poisonous filth" which, in his opinion, not only ruined five million French stomachs a year, but produced sexual impotency in men and sterility in women. White wine was the sole beverage he approved of; so it was white wine we drank with roasted chestnuts from a paper bag which I usually brought along from one of the peddlers' stalls at the entrance to the Luxembourg Gardens.

Dr. Curand was a gynecologist, fiftyish, graying hair, and a cigar smoker. When I say that he was a cigar smoker, I mean he sucked away on a stogie of the Voltigeur brand, which when set alight reeked like a mixture of tarred rope and dried camel dung. He had no private practice, but functioned as an obstetrician at the maternity ward of the Hôtel-Dieu, the great hospital near the Notre Dame church. When he turned the door knob of the bookshop, his friends would look up and almost unanimously say: "Ah, there's the good Doctor Vaginette!"*

As soon as Dr. Curand let himself down with a big sigh in one of Fourier's prehistoric armchairs, the proprietor or someone else would ask: "And, *cher docteur*, what was the harvest like today?"

"Just a moment, please," he'd reply, "let me consult my logbook! ... Now, let me see; one, two, three ... Three females! One, two, three, four, five ... six, seven, eight, nine ... Nine males! That's the score today! See for yourself! The tiny circles in my notebook stand for the girls, the circles with the dots in the center for the boys I delivered today."

"You must have delivered a thousand babies in your day, judging by all those pages filled with circles!. . ."

"Alas, yes, not just one thousand, but many thousands. And a sad business it is when you come to consider that all of them were born to suffer and die an early death.... What does Homer say? 'Of all that breathes and walks upon the earth, or creeps, naught is more wretched than the unhappy race of man....'"

"*Docteur*, you are a pessimist," remarked Fourier. "Nine males! That's not such a bad day for France! That'll mean nine good soldiers twenty years hence!"

"Why do you say twenty years hence? Do you expect another war by then?" asked Monsieur Eugène Linsolas, the proprietor of an electrical shop a few houses further up the street.

"Twenty, thirty years, that's about the rate, isn't it?" returned Fourier. "We count 1918 now, in twenty years it'll be 1938.... Yes, I imagine just about 1938 we'll be sliding into another war...."

"If I thought you were right," protested the doctor, "I'd sterilize all the females of the species I could lay my hands on."

"That would be a criminal offense!"

*The nickname corresponds to a certain four-letter word in English. For this reason the doctor's friends made sure that he never heard them say it.

"Not at all! It would be a boon for humanity.... The only way to make the statesmen stop waging war is to place them before a *fait accompli*: no more babies, no more soldiers, no more wars. Isn't that logical?"

"I wish you would practice your logic and sterilization tricks across the Rhine," said Fourier. "Here in France your radical proposition sounds defeatist, unpatriotic.... What do *you* say, Monsieur Linsolas?"

"I say nothing." The electrician dolefully shook his head. "I have my own troubles...."

"Troubles, you? A man with such a flourishing business? How is that possible?"

While Fourier said this, he signaled to me to pay attention, for they were merely trying to draw the electrician out in order to amuse themselves.

"Pray, Monsieur Linsolas, tell our transatlantic visitor about your troubles! He is sure to be amazed!"

"Well," said Linsolas, eager to comply with his friends' suggestion, "have you noticed a lady walking around in this neighborhood with blood-shot eyes and the face of a bulldog?"

"Not that I remember," I said. "I have seen many ladies, of course, but none answering your particular description...."

"A woman with a large bust, broad shoulders, a mustache and the gait of a dragoon!"

The doctor taking his stand behind Linsolas' chair motioned to me to reply in the affirmative.

"Yes, yes, such a lady I seem to recall...."

"You see, you *have* seen her! In fact, you couldn't miss her! That person is my wife, Monsieur. Do you know why she is so big up in front? Do you know what she carries in that enormous bosom of hers? Make a guess!"

"I cannot guess...."

"I'll tell you," went on Linsolas, "it's no secret anyway. These gentlemen know what she carries around with her.... That's my money she has there. Yes, my money! Whole packets of one thousand franc notes, all pinned down to her chemise!... That is the reason her bosom is so large.... What do you think of that? Two hundred thousand francs she took with her when she left me, all the money I had."

"The last time you told us it was three hundred thousand francs!" interrupted Dr. Curand.

"That's true, but the franc has been devaluated since, as you well know. . . . It's all in those packages on her bosom. It's ten years since she left me. She still parades around with that money on her person and passes my shop half a dozen times a day just to aggravate me, just to wreck my nerves. . . . "

"Why didn't you put your money in the bank?" I asked. "Madame couldn't have touched it without your consent!"

The doctor nodded vigorous assent. "*Très bien, très bien!* Very good, very good!"

"Monsieur Linsolas comes from the Pyrenees country," explained Fourier, "from the city of Pau. They don't believe in banks down there! They don't believe in anything! The only thing they believe in is Henri IV, the King of Navarre, who became King of France."

"The best king France ever had!" retorted Monsieur Linsolas with a ring of defiance in his voice.

"Certainly, certainly," assented Fourier, "if we may believe Gabrielle d'Estrées. Gabrielle swore that Henri was as formidable in love as he was in war. . . . "

"I maintain that Henri IV was our greatest king!" returned Linsolas heatedly.

"Ah no!" contradicted Fourier. "There you are wrong, *mon ami.* It's Louis XIV who was our greatest king. There can be no doubt about that, the Sun King who said: '*L'état, c'est moi!* The State? I am the State!'"

"Do you know what the people of Pau thought about your confounded Louis XIV?" shot back Linsolas. "They petitioned Louis to permit them to erect a statue to Henri IV, because Henri was born in Pau. For a long time Louis did not reply. Then, one day, a statue arrived; a statue of Louis himself. Can you beat that for arrogance? The statue had been cast in Paris and dragged all the way down to Pau, eight hundred kilometers. Do you know what the people of Pau did? They put the statue of Louis XIV on a marble pedestal and placed it in the main square, where it still stands. But they did not put Louis' name on it. On the pedestal they had a sculptor chisel the words: *Celui-ci est le petit-fils de notre bon Henri!* 'This one here is the grandson of our good Henri!'"

The doctor and Fourier roared with laughter, though they must have heard the account of Pau's statue a hundred times.

"The men of Pau must be very clever!" I commented.

"Cunning would be a better word," interjected Fourier.

"Thank you for your tribute to my native city," Linsolas bowed in acknowledgment. "Your opinion does you great honor.... But I'm leaving.... I see that these gentlemen can only laugh! How beastly rude can you get! To laugh over a man's domestic tragedy is the height of uncivilized behavior! *Au revoir!* Till tomorrow night! . . . "

What lured me to "Montmartre by Night" one evening was a burning curiosity to see something which I found advertised in the theatrical paper *Comoedia* as a spectacle "tantalizingly philosophical and superbly satanic" to be given at the Théâtre du Grand Guignol. Let me say at once that I came away nauseatingly disappointed and feeling ridiculously gypped.

The first of four short plays showed a young man in the act of digging a grave by the light of a lantern. At least such was the first impression I gained from the tombstones and crosses standing about pêle-mêle. What the young fellow actually did was disinter a corpse, the corpse, as it turned out, of a well shaped damsel, somewhat in the style of the currently beauteous B. B. After a time, as he dug deeper and deeper, the digger became invisible to the audience, but his cries and groans and sighs of rapture could still be heard rising from the depths. From his passionate exclamations uttered in an appropriately hoarse voice it became evident, first, that there wasn't any coffin, and second, that the buried damsel's name was Yvonne.

"At last I've found you back, *m'amour.*... So they buried you, my beloved Yvonne, in this cold, cold earth!"

The digger hoisted the body onto the stage floor and picked some tiny lumps of clay from the region of the breast and elsewhere. This gesture earned the actor a wave of applause. The dead Yvonne lolled in her lover's arms like a big kewpie doll, eyes half shut, arms limp, with a big painted smile on her lips. Though dead she still seemed to enjoy the touch of the digger's roving fingers. Then came what I suspect to have been the philosophical part as advertised: the moment supreme. The lover twisted Yvonne's neck corkscrew fashion, and off came the head. As can well be imagined the decapitation scene made the audience shudder... with pleasure. The disinterrer tore the mop of red hair from the corpse's head and buried his face in the curly locks. Then he threw the body back into the hole and jumped in after Yvonne screaming like a maniac: *O m'amour, quels délices, quels délices!* . . . "

The second tableau showed a much gayer scene: a middle-aged surgeon in his clinic. This gentleman was in the habit of luring young ladies into his office, strapping them to the operating table and neatly slicing off their upper eyelids. On a board on the wall he had a whole collection of severed eyelids, brown, white, black and even green. He sat contemplating his collection like any other amateur of butterflies or postage stamps.

In the course of the action he got suspicious of his wife who was having an affair with his assistant, a much younger surgeon. Just at the moment when he was going to strap her to the operating table to remove her eyelids, the young doctor came to the rescue and instead they both put the old man on the table. They went to work on him with lancets and scalpels till the blood spouted forth like a fountain gone haywire. The victim screamed like a pig that has its throat cut by the pork butcher. Then I had enough!

When the lights went on, I walked through a door next to the stage marked "emergency exit." Passing a dressing room I saw the actress and the actors wiping their hands and faces. The young lady called: "Did you enjoy yourself?"

"I should say I did! Very high art; *madame, mes hommages!*"

"Are you alone?" asked the usherette who opened the street door for me.

"Yes, all alone!"

"Won't you wait for me? I'll be through after the next act.... We could go to a *cinéma bleu* on the next street.... It's very good they say, very obscene...."

"No, thank you, I must be leaving.... I have a date...."

"Where?" she asked.

"In the Montmartre cemetery!"

"*Ah, quelle horreur!*" she exclaimed. "*Vous êtes vraiment vicieux.* You do have a dirty mind, don't you?"

I sauntered leisurely down the Rue Pigalle. It took me almost till daylight to reach Madame Gaetan's emporium. At every corner, in doorways, under rusty old awnings and staircased streets, in alleys too narrow for a cat to squeeze through, the prostitutes were on the prowl.

"Won't you come up?"

"It's too cold!"

"But it's warm in my room.... I can light a fire. Have pity on me. I've been on my feet since four o'clock. My shoes are killing me. They're soaking wet.... Can't you see that I'm a widow?"

"I see that you are in mourning. Was your husband a soldier?"

"He was killed on the Salonika front, *mon pauvre mari....* I weep for him every night.... And two *gosses* I have. They're orphans now.... Don't think, please, that I'm doing this to amuse myself.... I do it to keep from *crever de faim*, croaking from hunger...."

The same tale of woe on the next block; two of them, both widows with husbands killed on the Salonika front, both starving to death, both with children boarding out in the country somewhere....

I don't recall how many times I heard the Salonika front mentioned that night. It was never the Verdun front or the Somme or any other front but Salonika.

On the corner of the Rue Clichy, I entered a bistro for a glass of coffee. There were no seats available. The leather-backed benches under the mirrors against the wall were occupied by card-playing cigarette-smoking pimps. I stood at the *zinc*. Four or five girls also leaned their elbows on the counter.

"Can I have something? I'm so hungry!" said a little one, very young and pretty, a whiff of whose breath indicated a very empty stomach.

"Sure, what'll you have?"

She named some brand of apéritif.

"Don't drink that muck. It isn't good for you. Rather have a glass of wine or coffee and a sandwich...." She grabbed a big sandwich from the basket in front of her and bit into it like a tiger.

"You have strong teeth!" I said.

"Ahhh, is that what you like? Would you want me to bite you a little, just a little?"

"Ho, what's this? Why the favoritism?" challenged a tall brunette who had taken off her wet shoes. "Why can't I have a sandwich like Denise? Am I not as good-looking as she?"

"Have one," I said. She was already eating it.

One of the pimps sneaked up from behind and was on the point of performing the old hat-snatching trick when I caught sight of him in the mirror back of the bar and saved my cap just in time. The idea is to force you to buy your cap back from the snatcher, probably another ten francs.

Those women and their keepers operated on the principle that all foreigners are fools. I was a particularly big fool: I had given away something for nothing. I paid the sad-faced double-chinned bartender and made for the door. The little one joined me in the street where she put up her umbrella.

"That was a good sandwich," she said. "I'll accompany you wherever you want. You may not believe me, but I'm a widow. My poor husband. . . . "

"I know. . . . Salonika front, wasn't it?"

From the corner of my eye I could see her pander in the bistro's doorway looking after us to see if his protégée made the contact. We advanced a few steps when another woman bobbed up from some hole in the wall and screamed at the girl by my side: "You can't have him. . . . This is not your territory. . . . You stay in your own place."

For answer the little one gave the newcomer a whack over the head with her umbrella. Just then a group of American soldiers came into the street from an alley. At their sight both females deserted me.

Every second house in that neighborhood was a bistro, a bar or a taproom. In between were small walk-up hotels with broken down electric signs advertising "running water and all comforts." Vegetable and grocery shops had a frontage no wider than six feet. It was the first time that I became aware that Parisian butcher shops keep their light burning at nights and also that they have no doors. They are separated from the street by sets of iron bars; for what reason I do not know and never found out. Here was a *boucherie chevaline*, a horse butcher. A little further down the street a *boucherie hippophagique*. What's hippophagique? The Greek-sounding name is a trick to fool the foreigners. It also means a horse meat shop. How many tourists eat horse meat in Paris while imagining they have a thick juicy *chateaubriand* in front of them? You order a *bifteck* and you hear the waiter shout into the kitchen: "*Une boule!*" (A ball or a lump.) He doesn't mean you, he's not as impolite as all that; he is notifying the chef to dish up a piece of horse meat made up to look like a *tournedos* with a thin slice of fat around it held together by a piece of string. In every restaurant I passed I saw American servicemen eating mighty beefsteaks.

The further I walked down the Rue de Clichy, the fewer became the tiny dance halls and dives with low-burning lights. I still met widows whose husbands had fallen on the field of honor at Salonika, but they were on their way home now, weary, dragging their high-heeled professional shoes. At the foot of the street, near the Trinity church a window stood open. In passing I looked inside the fully lighted room and saw an enormously fat individual stark naked doing his physical exercises.

"Come in," he invited, "and join me."

"I'm in a hurry," I replied. "There's a cop fifty paces behind me."

"Thanks for the tip, *copain!*" He shut the window with a bang.

At the deserted tables of a darkened sidewalk café on the Rue de la Chaussée d'Antin I saw three or four ragpickers assorting the day's loot from the garbage cans. One man in a tattered overcoat, his worn-down shoes tied with a rope, turned up his bearded face at me as I passed.

"Want to buy some tobacco?" he asked.

"Is that what you have there, tobacco?"

"*Si*, I pick up cigarette butts all day. At nights I come here to remove what's left of the tobacco from the butts. . . ." He had a heap of shag tobacco in front of him on the marble table top and was making small paper bags from old newspaper sheets lying on a chair beside him.

"How much?" I asked.

"Fifty *centimes* a bag," he said.

A man in a postal employee's uniform passed by. He greeted me with a grunt. As he was going in my direction, I walked by his side. When I approached a wastepaper basket for the purpose of disposing of my tobacco, my companion held me back: "Give it to me if you don't mind."

Ahead of us staggered a drunken vagabond. He was singing at the top of his voice. He sang the famous song about the station master and his wife. . . .

"*Ça va ta gueule?* Shut your trap," the postman said.

The singer stopped dead and asked: "Can't a citizen sing when he feels like it?"

"Sure, you can, but not that song. . . . Not in public at least. It's forbidden. . . police regulation."

"Police regulation?" asked the drunk. "Well, isn't that funny? I'll sing twice as loud now that you've told me. That's as much as I care for the police." He snapped his fingers disdainfully and began to bray the "Carmagnole":

> *Ça ira, ça ira, ça ira*
> *Tous les bourgeois on les aura. . . .*
> *Vive le son, vive le son,*
> *Vive le son de l'explosion!*

On the bridge leading into the Boulevard du Palais, a man who was doing some midnight angling with the aid of a lantern held up his hand to us as we approached. At the same time he pulled up his tackle and a tiny fish, no larger than a lead pencil, flopped on the pavement.

"You see," he said, "I have a catch.... Pardon me for stopping you. I was afraid that the sound of your footsteps would scare away the herring."

"That's a good sign," remarked the postman.

"What's a good sign?"

"To see a man catch a fish. Didn't you know? It means good fortune for both of us. I can stand a little luck. My wife is sick with consumption.... The kids, too, have it. *C'est triste la vie, hein*? Life is sad, isn't it?"

From far away came the sound of a church bell. The postman counted the strokes. When the bell stopped the man crossed himself. "Do me the favor of crossing yourself, too," he said.

"Why?"

"The ringing of that bell means that a priest is lifting the chalice before the altar somewhere...."

"Isn't it rather early for Mass?"

"Not in the monasteries. The monks pray for us all the time, night and day. If we make the sign of the cross now, we join their prayers for my wife and kids...."

"Alright! It's done!"

"Thank you very much, *frère!*"

We walked past the Conciergerie, the old prison where Marie Antoinette spent the last hours with her two children before being pushed into the tumbrel, her hands tied behind her back, to be driven to the Place de la Concorde where thousands of Parisian women sat knitting and watching the heads of aristocrats plop into the executioner's basket.

"Danton, too, had his head chopped off," remarked the postman. "He was a great man, *un chef*, we haven't got men like him nowadays.... Marie Antoinette was an Austrian bitch; she got what she deserved...."

"What about *her* two children?" I asked.

"Just royal scum! ... They vanished, they were probably dumped into the Seine, drowned like rats!" he laughed.

With these words the postman left me while I continued my way past the statue of Voltaire. Under the street light I noticed that the lips were curled up in a sneer. Incidentally, Adolf Hitler ordered Voltaire's statue removed. It isn't there any more. I marched up the Rue Bonaparte as far as the old abbey church of St. Germain-des-Prés and the Café des Deux

Magots which was dark and deserted. Two more clandestine tobacconists were occupied disembowling cigarette butts on the marble-topped tables on the sidewalk.

In this neighborhood are more bookshops than in the whole rest of France, and lecture halls and publishing houses and antique shops and secondhand furniture dealers. How in heaven's name all these shop-keepers make a living is more than I can understand. But they have been there for hundreds of years through war and peace and student mobs in the window-smashing mood. Every bookshop specializes in one or more particular branches of literature: geography, history, classic languages, political science, archaeology, poetry.... Because of the prox-imity of the School of Medicine, there are several shops vending surgical instruments, human skulls and skeletons. In one display window between two human skulls I noticed a large gray cat, its front paws placidly folded under its body, staring into the street where a rat scurried in the gutter.

An old woman lay sleeping in a doorway not far from Danton's statue which has also disappeared, also on Hitler's order. "To dare, to dare still more, to dare always more," read the inscription beneath the statue. At the corner of the Boul' Mich' two cycling *sergents de ville** passed me. They looked me over intently and then talked between themselves. Ideas about escaped Russians must have crossed their minds. One of them called out: "*Quelle nationalité?*"

"*Britannique!*"

"*Ça va bien!*" Both men saluted.

On the Rue Soufflot, Monsieur Fourier was out taking down the shutters. "Better come inside," he said, "and have some coffee. Get the dampness out of your bones...."

"You're early!"

"I couldn't sleep.... I knew you were out. It worried me...."

Towards evening I came down to the bookshop again and gave an account to the Messrs. Fourier, Linsolas and Curand of my expedition to the district of joy. Dr. Curand listened attentively when I told of the postman who prayed for his wife and children suffering from tuberculosis.

"Outrageous!" exclaimed Fourier before the doctor could say any-thing.... "It's with this kind of superstition that the priests keep our people in subjection. How long will it go on, this prolongation of the Middle Ages into the twentieth century?"

Sergents de ville-night police.

"Till the last priest is strangled with the guts of the last king," said Linsolas.

"Well spoken, Monsieur Linsolas!" nodded Fourier.

The doctor chuckled. "Monsieur Linsolas quotes from Pierre Joseph Proudhon. The words are apocryphal, but the tuberculosis is real enough. It is the worst scourge France has ever been visited with, France, and particularly Paris. . . . "

"Is it something in the climate or environment?" I asked. "Germs? A virus perhaps?"

"Not at all. Its main source is malnutrition, dietetic insufficiency—in other words, low wages and poverty. Look what the Parisian working class gives its children for breakfast. A cup of coffee and a piece of bread and butter. This is all the average Parisian family can afford. It is not substantial enough. . . . Don't the children look poorly, anemic, weak?"

"I can't deny it, but perhaps that is the result of four years of war and food scarcity."

"It's that way in peacetime as well," said the doctor.

"The thing that struck me most painfully," I said, "was the sight of the young girls standing on the sidewalks in front of the big department stores—the salesgirls, I mean, who serve the sidewalk customers. Yesterday it was cold and it rained. Many of those girls were sick of cold and exposure. Their faces and hands were blue and raw. Can nothing be done about such conditions? You seem to be breeding tuberculosis on every hand."

"That's not the worst," said the doctor. "None of those children—for that's all they are, children—earns enough money to pay for her board and lodging. Girls like that are compelled to look for supplementary income from lovers or pickups. It's customary, it's our way of life, it is expected of them. It's the same sad business all around. Poverty is at the base of it all, the unequal distribution of wealth. You say you found Montmartre a gay place? Well, our police prefect calls it the whorehouse of Europe. . . . That's the correct name for it. It's a phony, artificial, make-believe gayety. It's all put on for the benefit of the foreigners. Vice is big business. French people don't go to Montmartre. The average Parisian goes to bed at ten o'clock, not later. Fundamentally, Paris is the most puritanical parish in the world. You must not count Montmartre or the great boulevards. There's some night life there, to be sure. But what can you expect with thousands of licensed prostitutes on the streets? They start work at four or five in the afternoon and most of them go home hungry by midnight or thereabouts. They enjoy something of a windfall at present with so much foreign military around. Still, most of the girls are poor starving creatures. This accounts for more tuberculosis and more physical deterioration.... Come with me some morning to the health department and see with your own eyes. I am dutybound to spend two mornings a week examining the card-carrying prostitutes.... The sight is so degrading, humanly degrading and disgusting as to make one almost nauseous. Of course, I'm used to it by now. I no longer notice the ugliness and misery. I have been examining harlots for nearly thirty years."

A few mornings later I did accompany Dr. Curand to that section of the health department which was then installed in the basement of the Palace of Justice. We entered a large bare hall electrically lit and with a rough concrete floor. Along one side of the huge room ran an iron bar of the kind on which ballet dancers rest their feet and flex their muscles. The metal bar was approximately twenty yards long; a wooden step-up elevation, about two feet high, ran in front of the iron bar. At the door stood three or four policemen near a glass-enclosed booth marked "cashier."

"These policemen are members of the *brigade mondaine*, the morals squad," explained Dr. Curand.

The doctor went into a side room and presently returned wearing a white coat. With him were two younger medical men similarly dressed. Some women came in. They showed identification papers to the police sergeant sitting in the cashier's booth, and walked to the side of the room opposite the long iron bar. There they undressed and left their clothing on chairs and benches standing against the wall.

When there were about thirty to forty women in the room, a policeman called out: "*Attention les filles!* Alright girls, line up! You can keep your shoes on!"

The girls marched across the room. They hadn't a stitch of clothing on. Every one of them shivered; the hall was as cold as an icebox.

"Alright, step on the platform! Bend over, all of you!" ordered the policeman.

The women bent over the iron bar.

"No talking now! No talking!"

The two young doctors walked to opposite sides of the room and began their examination with a flashlight and a surgical instrument known as a speculum. Some girls were told to stand up straight and face the examining physician.

"What's going on?" I asked Monsieur Curand.

"Those girls will have to be more closely examined at the hospital. They're suspect. . . ."

"Suspect of what?"

"Of disease! They go to the Hospital Saint Louis for observation. I wouldn't advise you to go to St. Louis. The sight is unbearable. Some of the leprosy and elephantiasis patients at St. Louis are simply rotting away. . . ."

More girls came in as Dr. Curand was called over to the line-up bar for a consultation. The newcomers undressed and took their place by the metal bar. When the doctor returned I asked: "Are these girls the inmates of brothels?"

"No, the brothel girls are due tomorrow. These here are streetwalkers, licensed streetwalkers. They pay ten francs for a monthly examination."

"How many are there in Paris?"

"I don't know exactly, several thousand, I expect. Of course, there are also a good many who never come here. They are the free lancers, ladies who try to make a little extra money. They are the most dangerous from a sanitary point of view."

"How can they be told apart?"

"These girls here are good girls, they carry a card."

"What happens if they don't show up for examination?"

"Eventually they will be picked up by the morals squad and they lose their card. Before leaving here they have their cards stamped at the booth where their names are checked off too. A red card signifies that a girl is certified clean, a yellow card that she has been diseased once but has been cured. Under police bylaw the women are required to show their cards on demand to prospective customers."

Two girls were crying as they were led away into a side room by a policeman.

"They're sick," said Dr. Curand. "They're off to St. Louis. . . ."

Other girls were still coming in. They undressed and bent over the bar, twenty, thirty at the time, fat ones, lean ones, old hags, fresh young things, not older than seventeen or eighteen. Their skin was discolored, blue and raw from the cold. With all those women bending over the bar, the hall looked like a stable for human cattle. . . .

I accompanied Dr. Curand to the Hôtel-Dieu. "What do you say now about human dignity?" he asked. I bade him *adieu* at the door of the maternity ward.

I often saw the doctor in afteryears when I came to reside permanently in Paris. All his days he remained a man of candor, good sense and compassionate interest in his fellows.... "We must work while it is yet day," was his counsel, "no matter how distasteful the work at times. *Le jour viendra*, the day will come when disease will be no more...."

In 1926 Curand sponsored my admission to the masonic lodge on the Rue Cadet. If you are interested you may see his name on a small bronze plaque with the names of eleven others attached to the façade of a house on the Rue Soufflot. Beneath their names appear the words: *N'Oubliez Jamais*, "Never Forget!" The twelve men, all physicians, were executed as hostages by order of General von Stuelpnagel, the Nazi governor of Paris in the spring of 1944. Dr. Curand was 82 years of age at the time of his death....

The trip to Chartres to see the great cathedral was made in a chauffeur-driven Renault belonging to Liliane's grandfather. It was about one o'clock in the afternoon on a Sunday in mid-December, that Liliane and Raoul picked me up at the corner of the Rue Soufflot and the Boulevard St. Michel. As I stepped in the car, I noticed from the corner of my eye that Jo-Jo, the one-legged stool pigeon, had followed me and was casually glancing at the automobile's license plates. The informer was soon forgotten as we fell to chatting of the sights I had seen and of the theaters the two lovers had visited.

We did not, however, get as far as Chartres that day. Halfway we left the main road and stopped near the small town of Saint-Cyr where the French have their military academy, the equivalent of our West Point. The idea was Liliane's; she suggested that, before going to Chartres, we drop in to pay our respects to Anatole France who lived in an old remodeled farmhouse, known as La Béchellerie, just west of Versailles.

"Are you sure he'll receive us?" I asked. "It seems a bit of an imposition."

"He keeps open house on Sundays," Liliane reassured. "You'll find La Béchellerie full of American soldiers. He's as vain as a peacock and likes playing the role of showpiece. It'll flatter his ego no end that two Canadians have come halfway around the globe to pay homage to the first literary man of France. But we must bring him a present, anything at all, else he will be peeved. I think we had better double back to Versailles and buy him a box of chocolates."

"Chocolates? There aren't any!"

"Oh, yes, the Americans are importing shiploads of chocolates. They're buying up half the women of Paris with them."

And so it came to pass that Liliane got out of the car and bought a large box of assorted candy in a shop across the street from the Church of St. Louis in Versailles.

The Maître, thus he was addressed by everybody, opened the door himself. He waved us inside. Looking at Liliane with the eye of a connoisseur, he rubbed his hands and bowed very ceremoniously.

"Canadians! Ah, that's something new for me!" were his first words. He went on talking rapidly: "You represent a virile race, a tragic race perhaps, but better days are in store for you. The British, who are our allies now, defeated the poor French farmers of Canada on the Plains of Abraham. . . . That was in 1759, if I am not mistaken. The people of Quebec lost their country and their courage at the same time. What to do? What stratagem to employ to get the conquerors out? Once the rude Godons burnt Joan of Arc; what might their descendants not do to the gentle women of Acadia and Laurentia? We all remember Monsieur Longfellow's poem about Evangeline. . . . Nobody had an idea how to proceed. That's the way it generally is in an emergency.

"But the priests, leave it to them, hit upon a solution: '*Au lit!*' they told the dispirited *habitants* of Quebec. 'To bed! To bed!' Here in France we sing in 'The Marseillaise' about the day of glory having arrived. In Quebec the priests said: 'The night of glory has come. . . . Go to bed! Make children! Make as many children as you can. In a hundred years we will not only recoup our losses, but outnumber the British ten to one. . . .' Isn't that the whole history of French Canada in a nutshell? Isn't that the way providence has most graciously ordered things for your country, Madame?" he asked Liliane as he bent to kiss her hand the second time. . . .

"I am informed that the French Canadians have enormously large families. . . . How many have you, Madame? Is this your husband?" He pointed to Raoul. "He seems quite capable, this young man. What is your rank, my child? A lieutenant? Well, to work, *mon lieutenant!* There's work to be done! But at least it's pleasant work! With me it's altogether different. For me the night has come when man can work no longer, not the kind of work I'm talking about, anyway. When you grow as old as I am it's unbelievably sad. . . . One wants to love, but cannot! The last time I tried it made me very ill. *C'est à pleurer*! I could weep! Why am I so sad today? It's the sight of your beautiful shoulders, Madame. It's the *tristesse* of love. It's the abyss of regrets that rises in my soul. . . . Have I said enough? Can I now have that package which I see you hold in your dear hand?"

"Maître," said Liliane, "we brought you some chocolates." He affected to be surprised and opened wide his eyes.

"Chocolates, you say? Please, let me have them at once. I haven't tasted chocolates in years. It's perfectly horrid the way we have been deprived of everything good by that confounded Clemenceau. . . . "

He stuffed a bonbon into his mouth and began carrying the box away. "I'm going to hide these," he called back. "If I show them around everybody will want some. You brought them for me, didn't you? Well, to me they go, all of them! My infinite gratitude, Madame, for your kindness in filling an old man's heart with joy and his mouth with sweetness. . . . "

In spite of his seventy-four years, the Maître still walked erect. He seemed tall and lean, but his beard and the hair on his head were white as snow. He wore a black velvet jacket and a spotless white shirt with a loose flowing tie, a so-called *lavallière*. When he returned from hiding his box of chocolates, he shepherded us into the salon where a few guests were assembled. He gently pushed me in the direction of three gentlemen standing together in a corner of the room.

"This is Dr. Couchoud," he introduced. "Monsieur Couchoud is the enemy of St. Paul. . . . This other gentleman is Monsieur Vaillant-Couturier, a deputy to the Chamber. He's just out of the army. . . . Politics called him home. And this gentleman," he continued, "is my dear old friend, Monsieur Jean Longuet. Monsieur Longuet is a legitimate grandson of Karl Marx. . . . Yes, of *the* Karl Marx!" he repeated. Monsieur Longuet's mother was born Jenny Marx. . . . "

Longuet was the only one to shake hands with me. The other guests just stared at Liliane.

"Tell me," whispered Anatole France, "who is this woman you brought with you?"

"She's the granddaughter of General de St. Gervais," I said.

"A French general?"

"Yes, a French general!"

"*Pas possible!* Unbelievable!"

"Are you an enemy of St. Paul?" I asked Dr. Couchoud.

"Not an enemy!" he laughed. "I don't think that such a person at St. Paul ever existed. The figure which goes by that name in the books is a sort of a prop to hold up the Christ myth. . . ."

"Oh, now I know you, you are Dr. Couchoud, the *mythologue!*" I gasped. All at once I recognized his name as that of one of the most radical New Testament critics. "We have heard of you in Canada," I said, " of your theories, that is. Your work is well known in Holland, too. . . . I was a theological student before entering the army. . . ."

"So was I, chimed in Vaillant-Couturier. "My father is a Huguenot pastor."

"And you? A pastor, too?"

"I'm a socialist deputy to the Chamber. Jean Longuet is one of the editors of *Humanité.*

"The paper founded by Jean Jaurès?"

"Precisely!"

"But this is a most fortunate meeting. I am an old admirer of Jaurès. . . . If only he had lived. If Jaurès had lived this war would probably never have taken place. . . . "

"That's going a little too far," Longuet interrupted. "Jaurès could not have prevented the war's outbreak. . . . But you may safely say this: had Jaurès lived, this war would have been over two years earlier at least. . . . "

"Well, it's over, anyway!" I said somewhat lamely.

"Monsieur," said Longuet, "you depart from a false premise. . . . The war is not over. It has only begun. Or rather we are moving headlong into a new war. . . ."

"Well, there is no peace treaty as yet, only an armistice, if that is what you mean. . . . For the time being the Germans are done for, aren't they? They were thoroughly defeated."

"Were they? By whom were they defeated? Not by us, surely."

"The Kaiser fled to Holland," I said. "Ludendorff has fled to Sweden. Hindenburg is a doddering old sergeant major. All the fighting spirit has gone out of him. . . . "

"No, Monsieur," said Longuet, "you are positively wrong, and I'll tell you why. With the consent and approval of the allied high command, the doddering old field marshal is at this very moment under our very noses pulling one of the greatest mystifications of history.... What he is doing is nothing less than a stroke of genius.... God the father Hindenburg is bringing his children safely home.... When you say they are done for, you overlook the fact that the German army is not in flight. It is undefeated. It is intact. It is making a perfectly orderly withdrawal. It is retreating like a machine that's put in reverse. The organization of the withdrawal across the Rhine is a marvel of German efficiency. Not one unit goes astray. Every man knows exactly what route to take and to what garrison town or military depot he is to direct himself...."

"Even so," I said, "they'll be demobilized the moment they pass the Rhine...."

"Have you heard," asked Longuet, "that the Germans are taking everything with them they brought into France and Belgium, all the guns and tanks and weapons, plus the loot from a hundred thousand private dwellings, factories and public institutions? They're buying up horses in Holland and Denmark to pull their overloaded caravans of household material, machinery and foodstuffs. It all goes like clockwork. They're stripping northern France bare...."

"They'll be made to pay for it!"

"Pay? By whom? Hindenburg will be fêted as the savior of the fatherland, the supreme benefactor, the navigator who steered the ship safely back into harbor.... The allies trail behind him on the homeward trek till they reach the Rhine.... That's the armistice agreement, isn't it? There's no customhouse or control system on the Rhine to see what the Germans take out...."

"Monsieur Longuet," I said, "you speak as if the Germans were the victors.... My impression is different. Their army is definitely *kaput*. If they do not carry out the armistice terms punctually, the Americans will surely cross the Rhine and bring them to their senses...."

"*Jamais de la vie!* Never on your life!" almost fiercely interrupted Vaillant-Couturier. "Evidently, you don't know what's going on."

"I know a little of what goes on. The Americans clinched our victory. This is undeniable...."

"It is true," Vaillant-Couturier agreed, "that the Americans brought the war to an end. But you are positively wrong if you imagine that the Americans have come to put or keep the Germans in their place. That's not their plan or purpose. The American armies are in Europe to prevent the revolution. . . . They are here to save German big business and French big business from collapse. . . . "

"Do you mean to say," I asked, "that American big business is in some way in cahoots with German big business?"

"You are a big child, Monsieur." Anatole France entered the conversation at this point. "I mean: you talk like a child, all innocence, all good faith. But you are terribly naïve. Didn't Monsieur Longuet just tell you that if Jaurès had lived the war would have been over at least two years earlier? Do you know why Monsieur Longuet said that? He said that because all through the war till the year 1917, German and French diplomats and military men and representatives of German big business and French big business met on the neutral soil of Switzerland to confer, not on how to bring the war to an end, but how to keep it going without running the risk of arousing the wrath of the people on both sides, the popular masses who were doing the bleeding and the dying. . . . "

"Is there proof of this? If true, it is abominable!"

"There is ample proof," observed Vaillant-Couturier. "Don't you read the papers? . . . It was revealed in our *Journal Officiel* that till the beginning of 1917 the firm of Krupp of Essen shipped 250,000 tons of steel per month through Switzerland to the Comité des Forges, here in France. In exchange for this German steel, the French high command undertook not to bomb the iron ore mines and smelters of Briey which is French territory of course, but was occupied by the German army at the time. . . . It was not till the beginning of 1917 that the growing social unrest in France forced our government to take energetic measures to put an end to these murderous arrangements between the general staffs. . . . "

"Clemenceau took those measures?"

"Yes, but not till Romain Rolland unmasked the whole vile intrigue in the *Journal de Genève*. . . . Rolland was the first to dare tell the truth about the war and refute the lies of the bourgeois press. . . . "

"So all the woe and misery of the war was endured for the sake of keeping the capitalist system afloat? Is this what you mean to tell me? . . . Do you think," I asked, "that there's an awareness amongst the American soldiers of what you say is the real purpose of their presence in France?"

"Did the British air force ever bomb the Krupp works on the Ruhr?" Longuet asked in turn. "Or the munition plants at Liège under German occupation, or the Skoda cannon factories in Bohemia?"

"Not that I know of! . . . I'm shocked beyond belief," I said.

Even if these men exaggerated, as I thought then, I was bowled over by what they told me. That the war had never been an idealistic struggle to make the world, in Woodrow Wilson's phrase, "safe for democracy," I had long suspected. I never realized what sordid, naked, slimy mammonism it had been. I looked at Anatole France with a questioning glance, but he only nodded his head gravely: "It's true!" he said. *"On croit mourir pour la patrie, on meurt pour les industriels."**

His hands behind his back, Anatole France paced back and forth amongst his guests, starting a conversation here, asking a question there, but never lingering very long with anyone. Without any apparent effort the Maître made everyone feel that he or she was the subject of a particular preference. He took a few of us out of the house and led us to the pavillion where he had his library. In that cottage he resumed his pacing. I noticed that whenever he passed the fireplace he looked up for an instant at the fine eleventh century tapestry which occupied the entire wall space from the mantelpiece to the ceiling. No matter how many times he went by the enormous bookcases, he never failed to brush the costly bindings with his fingertips. The paintings and engravings on the walls of both the salon and library, as well as other *objets d'art*, were all of perfect style and taste, not spectacular but quiet and somewhat solemn.

It having become too late to continue our journey to Chartres—the cathedral is closed after sundown—Liliane's chauffeur dropped Dr. Couchoud off at his home in the Passy quarter of Paris, and the two socialists at the offices of L'Humanité on the Rue Montmarte.

I don't think that a French general's official car would stop to let two editors of *L'Humanité* off in front of their office today. In 1918, however, *L'Humanité* was not a communist paper: there was no French communist party in existence. Founded by Jean Jaurès, who was assassinated on July 31, 1914, by the wretched half-wit Robert Vilain, whose mind had been inflamed by false reports that Jaurès' efforts to preserve the peace of Europe proved the socialist leader to be in the pay of the German Kaiser, *L'Humanité* at this time was the official organ of the Section Française de l'Internationale Ouvrière (SFIO), the French section of the International of Labor.

The split in the socialist ranks did not occur till the party congress at Tours in 1920 when the extreme left wing broke away and entered the

*"People imagine they die for their country, in reality they die for big business."

newly founded, Moscow directed Third International, better known as the Comintern. The communists took *L'Humanité* with them when they split off. The socialists remaining in the old Second or Amsterdam International then issued a new journal, *Le Populaire*, of which Léon Blum was the editor in chief. For this paper I wrote many articles, amongst them a series on F.D.R.'s New Deal under the pseudonym Pierre Laurusse, which, I should say, is really not a pseudonym at all, but an excerpt from the long name my parents gave me at the baptismal font.

I paid two or three visits to the offices of *L'Humanité*. It was a long walk from Madame Gaetan on the Rue Soufflot to Montmartre, but well worth the trouble. I met some men whom I will always remember: Pietro Nenni, who is still the leader of the Italian socialist party; Henri Barbusse, in whose company I made a trip to Russia on a Soviet ship through the Kiel canal in 1934. With Barbusse and Nenni I was associated in the Comité Franco-Ethiopien under the chairmanship of Pierre Cot, minister of aviation in the Popular Front government. We thought we could prevent the outbreak of the Italo-Ethiopian war by publicizing the underhand intrigues of Pierre Laval with Mussolini, an effort which turned out disastrously in my case. Pierre Laval never forgot; he requisitioned the house where I lived in Maisons-Laffitte when the war broke out in 1939, and forced me to leave the country.

Others with whom I became acquainted were André Marty, the man who headed the mutiny of the French Mediterranean fleet when ordered to bombard Odessa in 1919; Marcel Cachin, senator of France, at whose request I wrote a series of dispatches from Berlin in April, 1933, when Hitler was appointed chancellor. My first dispatch, signed "P.v.P.," was printed on the front page under an eight-column banner: HITLER: C'EST LA GUERRE EN MOINS DE DIX ANS! ("Hitler's access to power means war in less than ten years.")

Not a bad guess!

But was it a mere guess? It was no more a guess than my announcement in *Le Populaire* in 1935 that Austria would be the first country to be attacked by the Nazis, and Czechoslovakia would follow in short order. These things sounded incredible at the time of publication and I was duly covered with ridicule and all the scurrility, venom and slime the Fascists could muster.

Où sont les neiges d'antan? "Where are the snows of yesteryear?" Save for Pietro Nenni, all these men have been carried away on the ever-rolling

stream of time. In memory they come back at times in the too-little-known
lines of Landor:

> The leaves of perhaps our last autumn are falling,
> Half spent is the fire that must soon cease to burn,
> How many are absent who heed not our calling?
> Alas! and how many who cannot return?

As the year 1918 moved to its close, the weather turned uncommonly
cold. But it was not the vigorous, blood-warming cold of Frisia or the
Canadian forest. It had a soggy, bone-chilling quality that made me
sweat and caused my teeth to chatter at the same time. Nearly every
morning the world was enveloped in a blanket of fog. The milky white
vapor penetrated the cracked roof tiles in the top of my room with the
result that the moisture ran down the walls and stood in puddles on
the floor. The old crazy quilt on my bed soaked up the dampness like a
sponge. On a day of high wind, it is true, the room dried out a little, but
if it rained the situation became too dreary for words. I could not afford
to close the skylight, for when sealed off the garret reeked so strong of
rotting plaster and decay that I became nauseated.

I began to lie awake at nights listening to the rain gurgle in the gutters
and counting the strokes of the clock tower of the nearby church of St.
Etienne-du-Mont. I cannot say that after the day's noisy scenes in the
streets, the hushed quietness of the night came as a release. Restlessness,
boredom and anxiety are the fate of those confined to enclosures where
absolute silence prevails. My garret was as silent as a tomb. I was as tired
in the morning as when I went to bed. Nothing was more welcome than
Jo-Jo's stomping footfall at the peep of dawn.

Not that the city itself bored me. That never happened. Paris was even
then getting into my senses and working its way into my blood, and has
remained there ever since. There were generally a few hours of sunshine
around noon when the light sprinkled the gray façades and the dead trees
in the parks with a powder of soft gold. This brief surcease from the rain-
sodden drabness compensated almost miraculously for the dreary hours
of night.

A strange, yet startlingly realistic image of things rose in my mind. I felt
as if I stood on the top of a hill looking backward and in one all-
encompassing glance took in the entire road through life which I had

covered so swiftly. Was I dreaming? Was I sick? Did I suffer from hallucinations? No, for my eyes remained wide open. Still, whatever their nature, dreams or imaginings, they left an uncomfortable, haunting aftermath of futility. One moment, I recall, I was plunged into sadness over the death of Ross MacDonald. Where was he now? Could he see me? As if he had heard my question, his face rose before me as I last saw it on the morning of the Armistice with that intense gaze of surprise and horror. "Are you in pain now?" I asked. The gaze softened into tenderness and vanished. . . .

Homer calls that part of tne day the solemn hour when the sun stands highest and the market places are still and deserted. Isn't there a solemn hour also in the night? The dead seemed so near me that I thought I could hear them murmur: "Tomorrow, tomorrow, we will meet again!"

Since I had so few people to talk to, I had begun to talk to myself. Luckily, I discovered a clubhouse for students of the Free Protestant faculty on the Rue de Tournon, not far from the Luxembourg Museum, and often dropped in there in the evening. But in that place, as I soon found out, I went too far in the other direction; I talked so much and so long that I got ravenously hungry and was forced to dip into my fast diminishing exchequer for an extra meal before retiring. Evidently, my position of the half-tourist, half-deserter vagabond was becoming untenable. I had no idea though that the next step would be forced on me by events over which I had no control. . . .

It was towards dusk on a Tuesday evening, about the time when the official bugler makes his rounds in the Luxembourg Gardens, blowing the sad signal for all lovers lingering in the dark avenues to break it up, that I turned for the last time into the Rue Soufflot. When I noticed that the light in the window of Fourier's bookshop was burning brightly, I sensed at once that something unusual was afoot. The proprietor himself was standing behind the door peering through the rivulets of drizzle running down the glass panel. The moment he caught sight of me, he opened, and with a discreet motion of the hand he beckoned me inside. When I gave him a word of greeting, he placed his index finger on his lips and whispered: "We had better go into the treasure chamber so as not to be overheard. . . . Will you do me the honor of drinking a little glass with me? I have just opened a new bottle." He poured me "two fingers" of old Armagnac and downed his own with a mighty click of the tongue.

"*Courage, Monsieur, courage,*" began Fourier after shutting the door of the inner sanctum behind us. "I am a blunt person.... I feel honor-bound to inform you that you are in danger!"

"Danger? What are you talking about? What danger?"

"Your room has been searched in your absence by a representative of the Ministry of the Interior!"

"The Ministry of the Interior? That's the political police, isn't it? What do they want from me?"

"I am not quite sure whether the visitor was from the Ministry of the Interior or from the prefecture of police. But that he was a *mouchard,* a plain-clothes man, of that there can be no doubt whatsoever. I cannot deny that he had a somewhat human face and certain other human attributes, still I discerned in his features and general deportment inescapable evidence of a soul distorted by the most powerful evil passions: terror, greed and cruelty...."

"Monsieur Fourier, please come to the point.... You frighten me...."

"I beg your forgiveness; such is not my intention. To the contrary: I believe that it would be a grave error of judgment on your part to show the least sign of alarm or nervousness.... That uncouth individual I just mentioned talked with the *unijambiste* and with Madame the concierge. I overheard at least part of their conversation...."

"Were you present at the interview?"

"I can answer both yes and no," he chuckled. "Just allow me to explain: like every citizen I have had to take measures to protect myself against prowlers and Peeping Toms; that is to say, in the rear of my shop, above the water closet, there is a loose panel in the wall. By standing on the toilet and applying my ear to the wainscoting, I am able to overhear whatever is said above a whisper in Madame Gaetan's loge. When the light burns in her room, I can also see what goes on. However, with the sordid details of what I have witnessed there over the years, I will not detain you for the present...."

"Oh, please, do tell me what you heard!"

"You want the truth? Well, here it is: I heard that you are suspected of being a spy!"

"A spy? Who accuses me of being a spy?"

"The fake hero, the phony war invalid, our one-legged friend, the odious Jo-Jo! Nobody else!"

"Jo-Jo's crazy. I'm not a spy. He has no evidence...."

"Don't speak hastily, Monsieur, nor in anger. As I told you before, the man is evil incarnate. It's his business to fabricate false evidence. That's what he gets paid for. It was he who called in the police inspector and denounced you in the first place. That much I gathered readily enough from their conversation."

"But in what dirty deal does this scoundrel seek to involve me?"

"Ah, there's the crux of the matter; it appears that Jo-Jo saw you enter an automobile two weeks ago last Sunday at the corner of our street and the Boulevard St. Michel. . . . And further that the ownership of this automobile has been traced to a French general. . . . "

"Is that all?"

"No, it isn't all by any means. The general has made a statement denying all knowledge of you. He says he did not loan out his limousine or place it at anyone's disposal."

"The general is in his second childhood. . . . He suffers from an enlarged prostate gland and his brain has turned to putty. He doesn't even know that he owns an automobile. Still that limousine can be easily explained. . . . The general's granddaughter, the Countess de Jouvenceau, treated a friend of mine and myself to a ride in her grandfather's automobile."

"If you will permit me to give you a bit of sound advice, leave the lady's name out of your explanations if ever they should have to be made before an official body. . . . "

"Well, we visited the home of Anatole France that Sunday afternoon. I told you so at the time. That certainly can easily be verified. . . . "

"That has already been verified! But the limousine, recognized by its license plates, has also been observed standing in front of the publishing offices of *L'Humanité.*"

"Why sure! We gave the editor a lift back to Paris from La Béchellerie at Saint-Cyr. . . . That's no crime, is it?"

"And the fortress of Mont Valérien? What was the limousine doing there?"

"Oh, that's true, I forgot all about that. My friend and I visited the old fortress one afternoon last week. . . . "

"That's serious, Monsieur," said Fourier, gravely nodding his head, "that's very serious. . . . No foreigners are permitted inside that military strong place under wartime regulations which, as you must know, are still in force. Why did you go to Mont Valérien? Why expose yourself to suspicions? ... Don't you realize that your visit to Mont Valérien may be used to weave a net of circumstantial evidence around you?"

"Monsieur Fourier, the fortress has some historical significance. Didn't it figure prominently in the Dreyfus affair? Didn't Colonel Henry, the accomplice of Esterhazy, commit suicide there? The general's granddaughter obtained a permit for us to enter...."

"That makes no difference.... The lady's name will never figure in the evidence...."

"But you say that the mouchard and Jo-Jo searched my room. They certainly didn't find anything incriminating there?"

"The inspector carried some articles away with him!"

"What? My steel hat, my sewing kit?"

"I have no idea."

"What will happen now?"

"When you go into the house presently, Jo-Jo or Madame Gaetan will ask you to fill out a sheet of paper giving all the details of your *état civil*, date of birth, names of parents, grandparents, nationality, color of eyes, the shape of your big toenail, what side you part your hair on, birthmarks, your entire *curriculum vitae*.... Signed by you, that paper will be taken to police headquarters this very night yet by Jo-Jo. You yourself, no doubt, will also be summoned, probably tomorrow, or the day after, or even this very night, who knows? ..."

Things passed off precisely as Monsieur Fourier foretold. I answered all the questions on both sides of the long sheet of paper and signed it. Madame Gaetan handed me a receipt signed by "Georges Gougerot, Inspector," stating that he had taken away from my room the following articles: one gold ring engraved with a tiny Prussian eagle (the gift from the *Oberleutnant* at Seneffe); further, a spare set of brass buttons and two Mills' bombs.

Then I went out and raced by taxicab to the Place d'Iéna.

"Why did you carry the hand grenades with you?" asked Raoul.

"They were in my haversack, I guess. I completely forgot they were in there. I should have turned them in after Mons...."

"Anyway," he said, "bombs or no bombs, this is the end. *Finita la commedia!* We're picking up your things right now and you'll spend the night in the Hotel d'Iéna. We'll go to Rouen either tomorrow or Thursday...."

We were back on the Rue Soufflot in less than an hour's time and parked the general's Renault at the curb. I went upstairs while Raoul stood talking to Madame Gaetan. As expected, Jo-Jo was absent. I brought all my equipment down and was about to dump it in the car when Monsieur Fourier stepped outside.

"You are leaving us, I see!"

"Yes, I am going to Rouen."

"Monsieur," said Fourier, "it has been a pleasure and an honor.... Do me the favor, I beg of you, to accept in souvenir of your stay amongst us this beautiful volume with my respectful homage...."

He handed me a splendidly bound book. It's title was: *The Secrets of King Solomon's Harem.*

I thanked him for all his kindnesses and his hospitality, and he gave me the *accolade.*

That was the last time I saw the bookseller. I corresponded a little with him, but did not tell him that the book he gave me was stolen from my bunk on the troopship *Aquitania* on the homeward journey, even before I had time to delve into wise old Solomon's secrets. In 1922 I received a death notice, a card framed in deep black borders: *Priez pour l'âme de Monsieur Jacques Fourier, décédé à son domicile... muni des Saints Sacrements de l'Eglise....* "Pray for the soul of Mr. Jacques Fourier, who died at his home, fortified with the holy sacraments of the Church...."

It must have been a deathbed conversion for the old Jacobin, who swore to me that he would never retreat before the Pope.

The last night in Paris, Raoul and I spent in the Opera quarter. The chauffeur carried my belongings to the Hotel d'Iéna, and we two went to dinner at the Café de la Régence opposite the Comédie Française. The place was crowded with American service men and a few British staff officers, recognizable by the red tabs on their lapels. One of these, Captain Ferdinand Tuohy of the intelligence service, introduced himself and joined us for a drink and then another drink and still another, till I don't recall how we ever managed to get to the Rue de Caumartin and the bar of the Hotel St. Petersbourg. The barroom was crowded; men were standing eight, ten deep in front of the dispensing counter. All drank whisky and soda, the atmosphere was tense with the spirit of battle.

"D'you know what the senators told Sims?" shouted a Yank officer in my ear as I walked in.

"No, I don't, and I couldn't care less!"

"Well, I'll tell you, anyway," he insisted. "Just before Admiral Sims took the American fleet into the Atlantic to beat the Jerry submarines, the senators in Washington warned him: 'Look, Sims!' they said, 'don't let the damn British pull the wool over your eyes!' That's what they told him. Wasn't that a good one? . . ."

"Why did they tell Sims that?" asked Tuohy.

"Search me!" said the Yankee.

"Because the British are no damn good, see!" a red-faced major spoke up. "I'm Boston Irish. I ought to know."

"I'm Irish, too," said Tuohy, "but from Ireland, from Armagh. Did you ever hear of the place?"

"No, I haven't," said the major. "But who won the war, you or we? Tell me that, you Redcoat!"

"Oh," I said, "don't let's start that! Who cares? Let's have another drink."

All at once the whole room changed from buzzing into an uproar. "You started the war and we finished it for you," the major shouted at Tuohy.

"You don't think we could have finished it by ourselves?"

"No, you couldn't! Neither you nor the frogs, nor all of you put together! You were stuck!"

"Then why the hell did you wait so long before you came to help out?"

"It wasn't our war! It was the British who dragged America in. . . . We would just as lief have . . ."

"Shut up, you idiot!" several Americans admonished their overheated companion.

"Gentlemen," I said, "let's talk of something else. Anything! Mademoiselle from Armentières, for instance! . . ."

"The hell with you!" the major interrupted me. "I say the British bastards are to blame for everything. . . ."

"Don't call me a bastard, you son of a bitch!" Tuohy said threateningly.

He and the Boston major were blazing into each other's faces, two fighting cocks, ready to start slugging. They tried to put their glasses down, but couldn't reach the bar on account of the mob.

A short white-haired man in the front rank, leaning his arms on the bar, the only person in civilian clothes in the room, suddenly asked:

"Isn't there anyone here who has a good word for the British?"

"I have," I said, turning to the man in the tuxedo. "I like them."

"Why?" he asked.

"They are decent people," I said.

"Right!" he came back. "Have a drink! The name is French!"

Tuohy prodded me in the ribs. "You're talking to General Sir John French . . ." he said in a hiccup that was intended as a whisper.

"I don't care if he's the Lord God Almighty," I said. "The British are decent people!"

"*You* say that?" asked Raoul. "Have you forgotten what you told me about the South African Boers?"

"To hell with the Boers!"

"Right again!" broke in the gentleman in the tuxedo. "Have another drink!"

"Okay, so we'll all have a drink!" chimed in the American major. Everyone in the room was aware by now of the civilian's identity.

"Gentlemen," spoke up Sir John, "I drink to the health of President Wilson and . . . His Majesty the King!"

"The King! The King! . . . For he's a jolly good fellow," the Americans sang as if to the manner born.

"I'm proud of you, *vieux!*" said Raoul as we rolled to the Place d'Iéna. "I only wish Old Mac could have heard you. . . ."

"He and Cyril are sitting right here between us in this cab," I said. "We couldn't let them down, could we? . . ."

And so we both cried!

We drove in the general's car to Rouen the next afternoon. It was Christmas day, 1918.

CHAPTER VI

Short Stand in Dixieland

I DID NOT ACTUALLY go in search of my newspaper job; I was assigned to it by the army, or rather by the government's Bureau of Soldiers' Civil Re-establishment. When I informed the last medical board before demobilization that I felt no inclination to return to church work, the three board members awarded me a pension of $5 per month in compensation for my shattered left arm plus a $1000 gratuity, plus "a farm" of 160 acres, a so-called veteran's lot, located in North Ontario. An Indian guide from Cochrane's land office showed me the approximate location of my farm, which looked like one solid pile of rock grown over by a forest of stunted pine trees. I came, I looked, but left the conquest of the wilderness to more competent hands. I returned to Toronto and mingled with the "returned" soldiers who swarmed in their thousands in the downtown area; very restless, very much in need of a program of action. In one Canadian city they went so far as to hoist the red flag on the city hall and to enforce a general strike of ten days' duration.

In the absence of a school of journalism, the Bureau of Soldiers' Civil Re-establishment suggested that I go and sit in a newspaper office for a year or so at the government's expense, and learn the trade. This seemed not an unpleasant prospect and I called at *The Star, The Telegram, The News* and *The World*, saw the managing editors of these papers and put the proposition to them. They wouldn't take a chance; there were long waiting lists, and besides members of their permanent staffs were still overseas. I was about to give up the quest when I happened to pass the offices of *The Globe*, the foremost liberal paper of Canada. I did not expect any better reception at *The Globe* but, as fate would have it, in the hallway upstairs I met a gentleman wearing a high silk hat.

"Show me your discharge papers!"

The man studied my credentials for a while and suddenly looking up said: "For what you have done for Canada, we all owe you a debt.... You may come here as soon as you like.... I'm the editor in chief." He put out his hand. "My name is Thomas Stewart Lyon...."

The same evening, after talking with Fred Mears, the city editor, I went to work. "The main thing in newspaper work is accuracy," said Mears. "I mean, you've got to spell people's names correctly.... There are MacDonalds and McDonalds in this world, some spell their name with a capital 'D,' others with a small 'd.' If we get it wrong, we're in a heluva lot of trouble.... Watch yourself, especially in writing obituaries.... The bereaved are our worst enemies...."

For a time I accompanied veteran reporters on their assignments to the law courts, inquests at the morgue, city council and Ontario parliament meetings, police stations, the old labor temple, familiar from days gone by, the headquarters of the Canadian Manufacturers' Association, the Board of Trade and other such uninspiring spots. This went on for two months when a fierce blizzard struck Toronto one evening in December, 1920. I was sitting in the waiting room of the old Union Station watching the passengers go to and fro when a Roman Catholic priest came up to me and asked in broken English whether I could tell him the hour of departure of the delayed train for Montreal.

"You're French, *mon père*," I said. "Old country French. I seem to detect a Gascon flavor in your speech...."

"Yes," he replied, "I am a Gascon, and my colleague here—" he pointed to another priest "—is German. We're missionaries going home after twenty years in the jungles of Borneo south of Sarawak...."

"So you were stationed in Dutch colonial territory? Did you see any head-hunters in Borneo?"

"No, we didn't. Most of the head-hunters are on the island of New Guinea...."

"It will be quite an experience to see France after all those years?"

"Yes, we are both anxious to see our homelands again. We spent the duration of the war in total ignorance of the fact that it was going on.... We only heard two years ago that France had been invaded. A trader who passed our way told us about the destruction and devastation and the battles of Verdun and the Chemin des Dames.... But when the man told us the fighting had already stopped..."

"Amazing!"

"Amazing and atrocious. We had a hard time of it after learning of the invasion...."

"How so?"

"Well, my colleague is German as I told you, and I am French. . . . Suddenly we found ourselves at daggers drawn. The Germans had carried out a ruthless campaign of destruction in France. . . . The news struck us with a sort of paralysis of the senses. We actually hated each other. . . . We couldn't talk. . . . We couldn't eat. . . . We couldn't sleep. . . . We couldn't look each other in the face. . . . The tension was terrible. We both suffered agonies compared to which the awful heat and the swamps and fevers were as nothing. . . . We who had lived and worked together as brothers for twenty years were suddenly separated as by the whole world's width. . . . We were estranged in one blow. . . . We were enemies. . . . "

"How did it end, your estrangement?"

"One Sunday morning I saw my colleague walk across the sun-drenched clearing from the hut which he occupied. He was on his way to say Mass at our small chapel. I could see that he was weeping. So I ran out to meet him. When I came near, my friend knelt down and asked my forgiveness for what the German army had done to France and the French people. . . . We fell into each others' arms. . . . There was no more question of German and French, either then or ever afterwards. . . . The love of Christ wiped out all our differences, swept away all our hate. . . . That morning we rang the church bell together laughing like two schoolboys. . . . "

After seeing the two clerics to their train, I sauntered back to the *Globe* office which was but a few minutes' walking distance. As I entered the local room and stood by the city desk, Fred Mears asked me the usual: "Anything doing?"

I told him of my meeting with the two priests. Mears listened attentively, but the further I got, the more excited he became. He had a curious habit of pulling out the hairs on his head one by one while reading copy. Now he was pulling them out so rapidly that the other copy editors pricked up their ears. . . .

"Tell your story to Paul Reading," said Mears. "He'll put it in shape for you." Reading, I should say, was a rewrite man. Mears himself walked off and entered the *sanctum sanctorum* where Stewart Lyon was writing a late editorial.

A few moments later Mears returned to the local room. "Go in there." He pointed to the editor's office. "The chief wants to see you!"

When I told Lyon about the two priests, he asked: "Are you writing that story?"

"No, sir," I said, "Mr. Reading is writing it. He is waiting for me now!"

"Nothing of the sort!" returned Mr. Lyon. "You write that story in your own words. Hand the copy to me when you get through, I'll edit it myself."

After typing the story, which lasted about an hour, I took it to the editor. As a rule Stewart Lyon went home about ten o'clock. It was now ten to twelve. A few minutes later he came out and, rolling my manuscript into a tube, shot it up to the composing room.

"Tell the army," he said, "that they needn't pay you any longer.... You are from now on a member of the staff of Canada's National Newspaper.... I hope I spelt your name correctly in the by-line, two a's; and two s's, isn't it? Change it, if necessary, when the proof comes down...."

The representatives of the Montreal papers and the telegraph agencies met the two missionaries the next morning at Windsor station, verified their statements and flashed the word over the length and breadth of Canada. After that, I was no longer assigned to any particular task, I was free to write whatever I liked and my daily piece appeared as a feature in the right-hand lower corner of *The Globe*'s front page.

Because he was the first of the prominent persons I interviewed I recall most vividly Bramwell Booth, the General of the Salvation Army. The interview took place in a combination club-sleeping car standing on a siding in the yard of the Canadian National Railway in the vicinity of Toronto's Exhibition grounds. As the general insisted on detaining me for dinner, the meeting lasted no less than six hours, from five in the afternoon till eleven in the evening.

Bramwell Booth was a fluent and fascinating talker, a man of dignified, even regal bearing, imbued with that "passion for souls" which is characteristic of the Salvation Army's spirit and endeavors till this day. However, it was not I who did the questioning. Placing his hands on my shoulders as I entered the railroad car, his first question was: "Before anything else let me ask you: How does it stand with your own soul?" Though I did not resent the question as coming from him, I replied somewhat flippantly that I had lost it in the mud somewhere between Péronne and Bapaume on the Somme front. The general threw up his hands in a gesture of alarm and immediately went down on his knees to ask God kindly to help me find my soul back.

Although an absolute newcomer to journalism, I realized (by instinct, I suppose) that this episode would not make the slightest impression on

Fred Mears. Fortunately, when Bramwell Booth, having risen to his feet, proceeded to predict a cataclysm that might well signify the end of the world "in our time," I felt mightily reassured and on much firmer and familiar ground.

The newspaper for which I worked styled itself "Canada's National Newspaper," but was commonly referred to as "The Scotchman's Bible." The owner and publisher, Mr. Will Jaffe, was a Calvinist of the old stamp in whose ears, if he ran true to form, the news of coming world catastrophes would probably sound like so much sweet music. I therefore listened carefully as the general made a startling forecast of the nature of the calamity bearing down on us. It would, he said, take the form of "a universal conflagration, a fire of such fierce intensity as will make us all shrivel up like so much tissue paper in a roaring furnace." He described the disaster so realistically that it almost seemed as if he had a premonition of Hiroshima. On "that awful day of wrath," he predicted, "the waters of Lake Ontario will seethe and boil and the steam arising from it will choke millions to death. . . . The mountains will catch fire, the very heavens will be rolled up. . . ."

In an attempt to turn him from pursuing his horrible story to the bitter end, I ventured to mention that as a boy I had seen and heard his illustrious father, General William Booth, on the occasion of that gentleman's visit to Rotterdam in the spring of 1911. Bramwell Booth took this bit of information so kindly that he dropped his apocalyptic prognostications and told me the whole fascinating story of the Salvation Army's rise from the slums of London's "darkest wilderness" to the world-wide and universally respected missionary and rescue movement which we know today.

Probably wanting to test either my memory or my veracity he suddenly asked if perchance I remembered the names of any of the Army's officers who accompanied his father on that preaching mission to Holland.

"I remember the names of two men who were on the platform with your father in Rotterdam's old Doelen hall," I said. "Commissioner Thomas E. Estill and Colonel Lawley. . . . Colonel Lawley was a tall man of a deadly facial pallor and a coal-black beard. Of him it was said that he had been picked from the gutter by General William Booth himself. Seven times Lawley slipped back into the drink habit and seven times he was sought out by General Booth in one of London's shabbiest flophouses and brought back to the Army. In the end Lawley became one of the most eloquent and persuasive 'fishers of men' who was constantly by the general's side in that moment of supreme importance in the Army's services when sinners are asked to step forward and kneel at the mercy seat...."

"You have a good memory," said Bramwell Booth, "and a good understanding of my father's concern for the world's outcasts and the victims of drink.... It is true, my father never despaired no matter how low a person had sunk. He never gave up hope.... It's also true that Lawley had an extremely pale face. For years he was in agonizing pain: he suffered and died of cancer of the stomach...." Then the general talked with gentle wistfulness and admiration of his mother, Catherine Booth, somehow giving me the impression that his father came quite a poor second in his affections....

The interview with Bramwell Booth established me so firmly in the publisher's confidence that I was assigned to the "hotels and rails" beat which meant keeping an eye on the registry blotters of various Toronto hotels for persons who visited the city to give lectures or concerts or perform some other task. In rapid succession I talked with Margot Asquith, the wife of the prime minister who declared war on Germany in 1914; Frank Swinnerton, the author of *Nocturne* and other novels; Cardinal Mercier, the Primate of Belgium; Hilaire Belloc; Gilbert K. Chesterton; Belgium's socialist leader Henri de Man, who turned collaborator during the Second World War; Sir Philip Gibbs, the famed war correspondent and author; H. G. Wells, the snootiest snob I ever met in my life; and Field Marshal Jan Christiaan Smuts, nicknamed *Slim Jannie*, "Clever Johnny," by the Boers, who is still bitterly spoken of in South Africa's nationalist press as "Smuts the traitor" because of his swift transfer of allegiance to Britain after the Anglo-Boer War.

In Sir Arthur Conan Doyle, I met one of the saddest, most mixed up men I ever came across. Sir Arthur was in Toronto to lecture, but not on the subject of crime detection or any related topic. He spoke on the possibility of communicating with the dead.

I began by telling him as much as I knew about the case of a certain local theatrical entrepreneur, Alexander Small, who had disappeared without leaving a trace. I suggested to Sir Arthur that he interest himself in the case.

"I can solve only those crimes," said Conan Doyle, "which I have plotted myself.... All others are beyond my capacity. But what may not be beyond my capacity," he continued, "at least I hope it is not, is to see my boy again, or perhaps hear him speak...."

"Did you say your boy, Sir Arthur? Wasn't he one of the gallant guard officers who fell in battle?"

"Yes, a most gallant and dear boy Kingsley was.... He is now trying to get in touch with me from the other side. I have hopes of finding here in Canada a spiritualist medium able to establish the connection with my son.... I am much encouraged by what I have learned about one particular woman medium who resides here in Toronto.... She is said to have brought many people in touch with their beloved dead...." He fell silent, but then suddenly asked me: "Do you think she will succeed in putting me in touch with him?"

It's horrible enough to see a woman weep. But to see a strong man, a calm and unemotional man like Sir Arthur Conan Doyle, who wrote without the least trace of sentimentalism about the atrocities in the Congo and the sufferings in the Anglo-Boer War, break down and sob like a child is unendurable....

He walked over to where I sat in the chair facing him and took my hand.... "Promise me," he said, "that you'll help me. Promise me that you'll go to the medium with me...."

"I promise you, Sir Arthur. I'll do whatever I can...."

"Please, excuse my emotion," he added. "I can't get over my boy's death. ..."

On Sundays, like most of the senior reporters and editors, I went to church. Religion was news at *The Globe*, which wasn't called "The Scotchman's Bible" for nothing. We turned in a brief synopsis of the sermon we heard. There was a wide choice, for Toronto, if I am not mistaken, counted no less than 500 churches, large and small. I turned up frequently at the Church of the Ascension where my friend of the first hour, Henri Roche, was the rector, and his father, Papa Roche, the top-degree Orangeman, one of the vestrymen. Once only I visited the Unitarian Church on Jarvis Street where the minister gave a talk of such sound common sense that I wrote two columns. But that report got me into plenty of hot water with the publisher.

Mr. Jaffe sent for me, and lectured me in somewhat the following terms: "Your reports on sermons are a great comfort to me, and, I dare say, to tens of thousands of our readers. I also agree that we must have broad sympathies with others so that I do not mind if you report an Anglo-Catholic service and sermon occasionally. But we must draw the line somewhere. The Latter-day Saints? Well, they might pass in a pinch, though not too often, if you don't mind. . . . On the other hand I don't see why we should give the liberal Catholic Church any space. There are no liberal Catholics, as you well know, so that all their hocus-pocus is pure eyewash. I'd leave them stew in their own juice if I were you. . . .

"But the Unitarians," he went on as his face suddenly hardened, "I am sorry to have to tell you; they get no space in my paper. They are Arians, Socinians, pagans, heretics, godless materialists, worse than Jews! The Jews are damned and doomed on their own say-so. They called God's curse on their own heads when they shouted at Pontius Pilate when he was judging our Lord and finding Him innocent: 'Crucify Him! Let His blood be upon us and upon our children!' If they are persecuted they have only themselves to blame. Still, we must be patient with them for God's word commands us to! But the Unitarians. . . . "

"The Unitarians do not stand far from liberal Judaism," I said.

"That's just it!" exclaimed Jaffe. "They are Judaizers. They deny our Lord's divinity. . . . But whereas the Jews sin unknowingly, their minds and hearts having been closed to the truth of Christ, the Unitarians know the truth but reject it. They sin against the light, and they know it. I never want to see another Unitarian sermon reported in *The Globe*. Never! That piece you had in the paper this morning was an insult to every believing Christian. . . . What will people think we are, heathens? . . . And as to yourself, a Calvinist, born in a Calvinist country, aren't you ashamed of yourself? You have betrayed your Lord! Are you aware of that?"

"But that Unitarian minister did not say anything that could offend an orthodox Christian; in fact I agreed with a good deal he said."

Jaffe sank back in his chair. His anger grew into a towering rage. He rose and advanced upon me with pointed finger.

"Young man," he shouted, "if you go back to that Unitarian charnel house, you may lose your chance of salvation. Do you realize what's in store for you? You are going to get a red-hot seat in hell between Satan and Judas Iscariot. . . . "

With this harrowing, though not wholly uninteresting prospect staring me in the face, the end could not be far off. And it wasn't. I was assigned to cover the revolt of the Six Nations' Indians at Brantford, Ontario. On that reservation I saw the sharpshooters again who reduced the German snipers to silence with the exception of their leader Ruby who, as I learned, had been killed in action. For the sake of *old lang syne* I was permitted to sit in at the convocation of the Indian parliament and touch the sacred wampum belt.

The parliament of the Six Nations was in session to deliberate on the advisability of seceding from the Dominion of Canada because the Ottawa government in proposing to modernize the reservation by introducing the public school system and making other innovations had, in the Indians' opinion, broken its word and all its solemn pledges to let the red man choose and follow his own way of life. In the night I attended a session at the Long House, and learned to my astonishment that the Indians still clung to their ancient tribal religious practices.

By the light of torches, the medicine man, who wore an ugly mask, slaughtered a few chickens. When the decapitated birds ran around flapping their wings and scattering drops of blood all around, the braves went into a frenzy of excitement. Unable to understand their language, I did not fathom the symbolism of the sacrifice, and hence could not make out what they howled and shrieked about. The celebration ended with a dance. It wasn't lurid or sensational; it was about the silliest thing I ever witnessed, though, who knows, it might well have been full of meaning. . . .

The Indian parliament served an ultimatum on the government intimating that at the first sign of the Royal Mounted Police on the reservation the braves would shoot. I was commissioned by the chiefs to proceed to Brantford to notify the authorities of the state of affairs on the reservation. When I brought back word that the police did not seem to attach much importance to their warlike declarations and preparations, the Indians promptly got drunk and declared war. Some of them became so angry with me for bringing back bad news that I was arrested and locked up in the Long House. One fellow informed me that I was being held as a hostage and an enemy agent. The incarceration lasted two days and two nights. For food I had what was left over from the sacrificial chickens, but had nothing to drink. In the course of the second night the population had another celebration. What the occasion was I do not know. Those people celebrated at the drop of a hat. During the festivities so much whisky was consumed that my jailer, the medicine man, lost interest and went to sleep on the floor of the Long House. I took the key from his pocket and walked out, reaching Brantford without any further trouble about daybreak.

Eventually peace and order were restored on the reservation. But not before a royal commission of inquiry disclosed that the Indians were systematically neglected and left to succumb to the ravages of tuberculosis, rickets and similar diseases of malnutrition and faulty diet. The only physician on the reservation was the native medicine man.

Their resistance against the government's plans to modernize the reservation was not just a momentary fit of unwillingness to assimilate. The Indians were *a priori* suspicious of the white man. They nourished an enduring hatred for him and this, we may well add, not without good reason. For, if we want to be honest, we must recognize that the history of the relationships between the white man and the Indian all over the North and South American continents is a horrible record of word- and treaty-breaking, unprovoked attacks, expulsions, deliberate starvation and massacres ... on the part of the white man.

As a boy I read the Indian stories by James Fenimore Cooper and Karl May. As a result I had expected to find a manly, courageous, proud race on the reservation. I was never so disillusioned as when I saw the depth of degradation into which the Indians had sunk. Here indeed was a race of people broken in spirit. Something had gone out of them. In frustration and dumb hopelessness many had become chronic alcoholics. Others were virtually dying on their feet. Naturally, many of the young folk had left and were constantly leaving to find their way in the white man's world. Some Indians had opened law offices in Brantford and other Ontario towns or hung out their shingles as medical practitioners, but the old people who stayed behind were a sorry lot indeed, physically speaking. The children looked anemic, undernourished and were so weak that their voices scarcely rose above a whisper. The reservation was a joyless, dreary place. Blank faces stared in stupid inertia at the occasional visitor. . . .

I was busy at the *Globe* office writing a series of articles on the human condition on the reservation when a letter arrived from Clark Howell,* the owner and publisher of *The Atlanta Constitution*, inviting me to come to Georgia and work as a feature writer. The time was March or April, 1922. After a week or so of deliberation I decided to accept. Save for a brief visit to Morristown, New York, while on military service at Brockville on the Canadian side of the St. Lawrence River, I had never set

---

*Clark Howell, national democratic committeeman for Georgia, was the delegate who placed Franklin D. Roosevelt's name in nomination at the democratic convention in 1932.

foot on United States soil. It was more a case of wanting to see something of the world than a desire to change my employers or habitat that I took the step. I told Stewart Lyon that I would be back shortly, since I considered Canada my country and Toronto my home; Atlanta was to be a mere interlude. But this is not the way things turned out. I never returned to Toronto except to lecture in that same Massey Hall where I had heard so many others.

I arrived in Atlanta on a Saturday morning, and after registering at a hotel went in search of *The Constitution*'s offices. The building was an old ramshackle structure five stories high wedged in between sections of a department store. I sat with Clark Howell in his office for an hour or so. When he asked me where I was staying and I said the Kimball House, he remarked that General Sherman resided there too "during the war." I did not know who General Sherman was, nor to which war Mr. Howell referred. But as can readily be imagined I was not for long allowed to remain in the dark on the subject. To the Atlantans there was but one war; all other wars were meaningless tempests in puny teacups. . . .

"On the morning of November 15, 1864, my father took me by the hand," said Clark Howell, "and with a number of citizens we called on General Sherman at the Kimball House. We pleaded with him to desist from his proclaimed intention to destroy the city. Absolutely to no avail! We could not bring him to change his mind. Atlanta was a railroad center, an important link in the Confederate lines of communication; it was 'the gateway to the South.' Sherman deeply regretted the step he said he was forced to take; the destruction of Atlanta was an unavoidable necessity of war. . . . The same afternoon Atlanta started to burn. The city was almost completely destroyed. . . . "

The horror of that day still made itself felt in a hundred ways in the daily life of the city. There was more animosity against Yankees, bluecoats and carpetbaggers than there was in France and Belgium against the Kaiser and the Germans, though the Civil War lay nearly three quarters of a century in the past and the city had entirely been rebuilt. There being but few Yankees about, the resentment against the North for the ruthlessness displayed seemed to have been transferred to the Negroes who made up one-third of the city's population.

There is scarcely a trace left today of the unimaginable squalor of

Atlanta's Negro quarters. Under the drive and impulse of Roosevelt's New Deal all the shanty towns and slums were wiped out and replaced with modern dwellings. In 1922, though, the city's Negro sections were labyrinths of unpaved narrow streets, tumble-down shacks with corrugated iron roofs and a teeming population of loose laborers, their wives and children and so many drunken harlots that by comparison Cairo's old Fish Market seemed a model of puritan respectability.

Even so, my first assignment lay in quite another direction. In one of Atlanta's suburbs stood a home for veterans of the Civil War. It was a palatial structure in red brick with a broad lawn of such pure emerald green as if a portion of the mythical Elysian fields had been transferred to the here and now. Above the lawn floated the flag of the Confederacy and in the shade of its rich old elm and laurel trees sat the last remaining "boys of the old brigade," the erstwhile comrades-in-arms of Generals Lee, "Stonewall" Jackson and Bragg still wearing their gray uniforms and broad-rimmed campaign hats. These veterans, daydreaming on the white benches dispersed over the length and breadth of the lawn, were not only Atlanta's pride, they were the object of all of Dixieland's love and veneration. Delegations of southerners from far and wide visited the home to pay tribute and homage to the tired old battlers in "the lost cause."

Now it was a custom at *The Constitution* newspaper to mark the birthdays of these old campaigners with a visit by a photographer and a reporter. It really meant no more than that since most of the old soldiers were fading away so fast they were no longer capable of giving a coherent account of their exploits or reminiscences. The oldest inmate of the home was far past the century mark and the youngest not much behind. It so happened that just at the time of my arrival one of the most tempestuous of the southern army commanders celebrated his ninety-second birthday. Everybody on the staff, from Clark Howell to the youngest reporters, felt that I should go out to the veterans' home for the occasion. I think they all expected some fun.

"You've seen famous French and British generals, now you'll see the victor in the battle of Chattanooga," said the publisher. "If you can make him talk, you'll have the biggest story of the year."

I think the general's name was Calhoun, but I may be mistaken. The superintendent of the home took the lensman and myself all through Dixieland's Valhalla looking for the day's celebrant.

At last we found our man. He sat hunched forward resting his chin on the knob of a hefty shilelagh, his snow-white beard touching his knees. He didn't even look up when we stood still in front of him. I congratulated him on his birthday and said something about the beauty of his surroundings and the fine Dixie weather we were having. He looked up at me and at the superintendent whom he seemed to recognize, but did not say a word. I asked him if he remembered anything about the great fight he put up in the Shenandoah valley at Richmond and at Chattanooga. There was no answer. I tried four or five more questions with the same negative result. At last seeing the futility of my efforts the superintendent came to my aid: "Just stand back a little," he said, "I'll make him talk!"

"General Calhoun, sah, I have a damn Yankee here who says he can lick you!"

The old boy jumped to his feet like an eighteen year old. When he straightened out, he appeared very tall, powerfully built, as erect as a candle. He put me in mind of my great-grandfather Amos, the tugboat commander.

"Where is the son of a bitch, sah?"

"Right here in front of you, sah, ready to fight you."

I didn't wait; I made a run for it. Friend reader, I have served in the Canadian infantry alongside Australia's diggers. I've watched at close quarters the riot of the Australians on the Rue des Gallions in Le Havre on New Year's day in 1919 when they tossed the harlots up in blankets and first disarmed and then stripped the pants of an entire regiment of Portuguese military police. In other words I have heard such profanity as could not be surpassed, at least so I thought. But the Confederate general went beyond all previously established records. I withdrew as fast as I could up the sloping lawn in order to escape the shilelagh which my would-be assailant swung about his head like old Goliath his spear. Looking around for an instant I saw the general stumble and fall to the ground. I ran back and picked him up.

"Did you see any damn Yankees here just now?" he asked when I lifted him to his feet.

"Yes, sir, I did, but they were running like hell. . . ."

"That's what I thought," he came back. "I can lick any dozen of them any day." He laughed like a goat that has the hiccups. . . .

To familiarize myself with my new environment it was suggested that

I visit the police court on Monday morning; not to report, of course, only to have a look. The court was located on Marietta Street in the heart of the Negro quarter. On Monday mornings the men and women were tried who had been arrested over the weekend. A judge or magistrate sat on the bench which was a large table placed on an elevation. A dozen cops in shirt sleeves rested their elbows on the judicial rostrum. The judge, a shriveled up little man with blackened teeth stumps and a drooping mustache, wore a soiled linen jacket and had unfastened his collar, for it was stifling hot in the courtroom. On the side stood the prisoners closely packed together, all Negroes. They were waiting to be tried, or rather to be sentenced, and were called one by one to face the man on the bench.

"Joe Smith," called out a cop.

The man answering to that name approached the magistrate.

"Nigger, what was you doing in that woman's room Saturday night?"

"Judge, I wasn't in no woman's room. . . ."

"Thirty days! Next!"

"Fred Hastings!" called out another cop.

"Haven't I seen you here before, nigger?"

"No, sir, Judge, I never. . . ."

"Thirty days! Next!"

"Elsie Gibson!"

"Your name Elsie? You scratched your landlady's face? . . . Was you drunk, Elsie?"

"No sir, Your Honor, I wasn't drunk. . . ."

"Thirty days!"

"Charles Newman!"

"Nigger, you were caught with a knife in your hand, threatening an officer. . . ."

"Your Honor, that wasn't no knife!"

"You carried a deadly weapon! Thirty days on the chain gang!"

"But Your Honor, I was peeling potatoes when the officer walked in. . . . And it wasn't no knife. . . ."

"Don't talk back! Sixty days!"

"Sixty days, Your Honor! What for?"

"Shut up, nigger, ninety days on the chain gang. The trouble with you is that you talk too much. . . ."

"Jeez, Your Honor, it was the victrola that was playing. I wasn't doin' no talkin'!"

"You talked yourself into a year on the chain gang, nigger. You used profane language in court.... Take that blabbermouth away.... Next! ..."

I am not exaggerating; such was the normal procedure at the Atlanta police court day after day and especially on Monday mornings when the number of arrests sometimes ran up to a hundred or more as a result of the raids carried out by the police in the Negro section on Saturday nights. The prisoners were not even asked whether they pleaded guilty or not. But seldom were they represented by counsel, and even more rarely was anyone discharged as not guilty. It was the sheerest travesty of justice and a negation of those very Anglo-Saxon traditions of fair play on which the whites as pure lineal descendants of the English settlers under Oglethorpe so highly prided themselves.

The "niggah" simply did not fall in the human category. And newcomer that I was, I did not understand what it was all about.

"Would you want your sister to marry one of these monkeys?" I was asked when I spoke critically of the sessions in the courtroom. "Don't you know that the niggers have but one thought in mind: to rape a white woman?"

"Is that why you see so many half-colored people around here?" I asked in turn.

"Stay a while," said Clark Howell, "I'll buy you a house, and you'll learn to love the South." Had I accepted the offer, I would almost certainly have fallen victim to the depradations of the Ku Klux Klan of which Atlanta was then the headquarters and the managing editor's brother, Edward Y. Clarke, the Kleagel or Grand Master.

The Jewish community of Atlanta at that time seemed to live under a cloud. Several years previously one of its members, Leo Frank, had been lynched as he was being transferred from the Fulton Tower Prison in Atlanta to Milledgeville for trial on a charge of having raped and murdered a little girl in his warehouse which stood right opposite the *Constitution* building. Many Jewish citizens who recalled the lynching were unanimous in assuring me that Frank was innocent of the crime.

I took to reading all the evidence pro and con in the record department at the courthouse. Before long I came upon an envelope containing a sheaf of papers and a number of X-ray photographs showing teeth indentures. The murdered girl had been bitten on the left shoulder and neck before being strangled. But the X-ray photos of the teeth marks on her body did not correspond with Leo Frank's set of teeth of which several photos were included. If those photos had been published at the time of the murder, as they should have been, the lynching would probably not have taken place.

Though, as I said, the man died several years before, it was not too late, I thought, to rehabilitate his memory and perhaps restore the good name of his family. I showed Clark Howell the evidence establishing Frank's innocence and asked permission to run a series of articles dealing with the case and especially with the evidence just uncovered. Mr. Howell immediately concurred, but the most prominent Jewish lawyer in the city, Mr. Harry Alexander, whom I consulted with a view to have him present the new evidence to the grand jury, demurred. He said Frank had not even been tried. Hence no new trial could be requested. Moreover, the Jewish community in its entirety still felt nervous about the incident. If I wrote the articles old resentments might be stirred up and, who knows, some of the unknown lynchers might recognize themselves as participants in my description of the lynching. It was better, Mr. Alexander thought, to leave sleeping lions alone. Some local rabbis were drawn into the discussion and they actually pleaded with Clark Howell to stop me from reviving interest in the Frank case as this was bound to have evil repercussions on the Jewish community.

That someone had blabbed out of school became quite evident when I received a printed warning saying: "Lay off the Frank case if you want to keep healthy." The unsigned warning was reinforced one night or, rather, early one morning when I was driving home. A large automobile drove up alongside of me and forced me into the track of a fast-moving streetcar coming from the opposite direction. My car was demolished, but I escaped without a scratch. . . .

It was on a Sunday afternoon that I sat in the local room alone with Robert Moran, the assistant city editor, when the telephone rang. Moran answered and after hanging up the receiver turned to me: "There's a murder near Fort McClellan. . . . Will you go out and see? . . ."

On a side road near the Fort McClellan suburb I came on the scene of the murder. A Negro man lay on his back in the middle of a dirt road. He had been shot through the head. Two policemen were trying to move the body out of the way. They rolled the dead man over with their feet. There were about twenty or thirty people standing about, all Negroes.

"Has someone called for an ambulance or a doctor?" I asked the by-standers. Nobody answered.

One cop was saying to the other: "Ain't that a fine shot? Right between the eyes. That nigger must have had a hell of a big surprise." Both police-men laughed.

"What's this man's name?" I asked, pointing to the dead Negro.

"Who wants to know?"

"The Constitution!"

"You from *The Constitution*, bud?" one of the policemen asked me, and, turning to his partner: "D'you believe he's from *The Constitution*?"

"Who shot this man?" I insisted.

"What business is that of yours?"

"I told you I am a reporter from *The Constitution*. I'd like to know. I want to turn in a report...."

"You do, heh? A report? Now ain't that nice!... We'll do all the reporting that's to be done, bud. Just go about your business!"

"What's your name?"

"What do you want my name for?"

"I want to print the name of the man who kicked the corpse...."

"You do? What'll you print if I kick you the hell out of here?"

"It'll be the last time in your life that you lift your foot, copper...."

"Say that again!"

Both policemen advanced on me. One man raised his baton and the other fumbled for his revolver in his hip pocket. The bystanders came nearer, too. One elderly Negro man said to me: "I'll give you all the details.... Come away with me. You have no chance here. Those fel-lows will kill you...."

I walked away from the dead man's side. The stranger told me that the man was killed by his own wife. "They were both drunk. He aimed the pistol at her, but she grabbed it from his hand, and off went the gun. That's all there is to it!"

It was nearing six o'clock. Knowing that the first edition of the morning paper would be on the street by eight in the evening, I thought it better to telephone the story of the murder from a corner drugstore. Hilyard Wimpe, one of the rewrite men, took the message.

Then I drove back to the office. The paper came out. The first copies arrived in the local room via a belt conveyer from the press room in the basement. I looked for my story, but found no trace of it. When the hubbub in the local room subsided somewhat, I went up to the city desk and asked Robert Moran: "Was there anything wrong with my story about the murder?"

"What murder?" came back the assistant city editor.

"The murder at Fort McClellan this afternoon. You sent me out yourself. . . . I telephoned it to Mr. Wimpe. . . ."

"Wimpe," Moran called out in great alarm at the rewrite man who sat typing something with a set of earphones clamped about his head, "Wimpe, what about that murder at Fort McClellan?"

"That was no murder, Bob, that was a nigger!"

"What's your name again, sir?" Moran asked me. I gave it to him. "Mr. van Paassen," he said, "we never report the killing of niggers in this paper. . . . And please, don't forget that the word Negro is never spelt with a capital 'N' in this part of the world. . . . Atlanta is a beautiful city, isn't it? Let's not spoil it. . . . You don't want to get to be known as a nigger lover, do you? It might do you great harm, you know. . . . Quite a few members of the staff here belong to the Klan. . . ."

"Well, I'm going back to Canada," I told Clark Howell the next day. "I know I can't do anything to change the situation with regard to the colored people. . . . But I don't *have* to live here. . . . I'd explode if I had to witness any more of what I've seen so far in the police court and on that road at Fort McClellan."

"Don't run away yet," came back the publisher. "I will take you off the local staff and put you in a room by yourself. You'll write some editorials and some feature stories. . . . One of these days I'll show you that we know how to appreciate a good darky when we see one. . . . I am sending in to you George Washington Carver. George is quite a boy. He was born a slave, but he has studied and done a good deal to improve the soil of Georgia by eradicating certain plant diseases. George is a good darky who makes no pretense of being anything else. . . ."

That "good darky" came into the room to which Clark Howell transferred me, holding his hat in his hand and bowing to me as if I were the Shah of Persia on his peacock throne.

"Come in, Dr. Carver, please have a seat!" I said to the world-famous agronomist, member of the Royal Society of Arts, who served as professor at the Agricultural Institute of Tuskegee.

"I'll gladly come in, sir, but I won't take a seat," he replied. "Not that I wouldn't like to sit down, but somebody is apt to see me sitting in a white man's room and that wouldn't do."

"In that case, I'll stand too, Dr. Carver, or if you like we can go down and sit in my car."

In the room to which I was transferred stood two desks of ancient and dilapidated vintage. At the other desk sat Frank L. Stanton, a remarkable man about seventy years of age, a little waggly on the legs, but for the rest still hale and hearty. Stanton had been publisher of a weekly country paper, *The Dahlonega Nugget*, but never in his life, as he told me, set foot outside the territory of the state of Georgia. On *The Constitution* he succeeded Joel Chandler Harris, the "cornfield" writer and creator of the "Uncle Remus" stories. Stanton wrote one editorial a day and one poem.

"The Poet of the Soil," as Frank Stanton was known, is perhaps best remembered for his:

> Sweetest little fellow,
> Everybody knows,
> Don't know what to call him,
> But he's mighty like a rose. . . .

a sentimental song which, like several of his compositions, was set to music and sung by a make-believe Negro on the vaudeville stage all over the country.

Frank Stanton and the publisher lived in a permanent state of undeclared war. Each in his own way was constantly wondering who would be the first to be called on the long journey from which there is no return.

"He can't last much longer," Stanton would tell me, speaking of Clark Howell, "his neck is too short. . . . People with short necks never make the grade. . . . They are destined to die in infancy. Our dear employer has long since passed the limit. . . ."

"Frank," the publisher would say as he sauntered into our office, "I just came down from the composing room and saw the poem you wrote for next Sunday. . . . It's too long, Frank. I cut off two lines. . . ."

"At the top or the bottom?"

"At the top! But they aren't lost. Your poem for next Tuesday I found too short. I added the two Sunday lines to Tuesday's piece. . . ."

"At the top or the bottom?"

"It doesn't matter. The poem makes no sense either way!"

When Clark Howell left the room, Frank Stanton looked at me in dumb despair. "Now you know," he'd remark, "why General Sherman said that war is hell. He discovered it here in Georgia.... There is nothing for it but to get a pint and drown my sorrows. It's the only way to drum up enough inspiration for the next poem....

"Theodore Roosevelt Gibson!" he called out to the Negro boy in the hallway. "Theodore, go out and get me a pint!"

He meant a pint of corn liquor, aptly called "Georgia mule" because of the devastating wallop it carried. Stanton drank the pint in one gulp and with one big groan. "If the Muse doesn't come now," he said, "I'll get me a second pint, though I'll probably have to be driven home in a hearse as happened more than once through the kindness of my friend, Mr. Strachey, the undertaker...."

Stanton always left a little liquor in the bottom of the bottle. This he carefully poured into a saucer and placed on the floor. In no time the saucer was surrounded, invaded and swamped by a host of cockroaches which came running from all directions, from the cracks in the walls and the ceiling, and... from the drawers of our desks. They were of all sizes, big whoppers and tiny ones, really too small to become victims of the drink habit at so tender an age.

"I don't see General Grant this morning," Stanton would say looking at the gathering of the roach clan. "He's the granddaddy of them all and usually comes first to my roll-call. I see Sherman, Sheridan and Fighting Joe Hooker.... He's the big one over there that's pushing everybody else around. Now watch how they get drunk and go staggering all over the place.... Good God, if we only had had some of this Georgia mule we could have won the war. It would have blown the damn Yankees sky-high...."

This was no exaggeration: Georgia corn was not only a drink it was also a high explosive. Although I could not stomach the stuff, which tasted like spoilt carbolic acid, I thought that by mixing it with some cream, sugar and beaten eggs, and boiling it, something like an eggnog could be concocted. I took a pint home to make the experiment and put it on the kitchen stove to boil.... It didn't boil. It practically exploded.

Many of the reporters got their supply of "corn" by driving out into the country in the small hours of the morning after the paper had been put to bed. I accompanied them several times on these nocturnal expeditions which took us in the general direction of Stone Mountain where the renowned sculptor Gutzon Borglum was carving the gigantic figures of

Jefferson Davis, General Robert E. Lee and other southern heroes on the face of that promontory. On top of Stone Mountain the Ku Klux Klan frequently met in conclave and burnt fiery crosses to warn Catholics, Negroes and Jews not to intrude on white Protestantism's sacred preserves.

One day Clark Howell said to me: "The darky was better off under slavery than he is now.... When he was a slave, he represented a valuable piece of property. His master looked after him, clothed him, fed him and got him a wife. When he fell sick, it was in his master's interest to make him well or else lose him as a productive force.... Since the emancipation he has been on his own, and you can see for yourself what he has made of his freedom. Most of the darkies would become gangsters and bums if the police didn't keep them in bounds.... The Negro districts of Atlanta are breeding grounds of crime, vice and Bolshevism...."

I brought Clark Howell's attitude to the attention of the Negro clergy and asked them what their view was. One of the bishops of the Afro-American Methodist Church seemed more afraid of me than of the Kluxers. I dare say he suspected me of being a spy or informer trying to draw him out. Not one man amongst the professors and instructors of Atlanta's Negro university dared probe, at least in public, the dismal situation of his people. Nor did a single Negro ever complain to me about the social discrimination of which he was the victim.

In fact, the southern Negroes put me very much in mind of that tribe of Pigmies which Stanley encountered on his voyage across Africa in search of Livingstone and which he mentions in his book *Zanzibar*. These tribesmen lived in a forest so dense that the sun's rays never penetrated. They fed on ants and grass roots. They disinterred the corpses of some of Stanley's companions who had succumbed to the heat and other rigors of the climate and were on the point of eating them when the explorer intervened. Stanley sought to convince them that beyond their dark forest was sunshine and light and open fields, rivers and lakes. He invited them to follow him. But the Pigmies waved their arms: "All the world is like our forest, dark, dark, dark with the menace of wild beasts lurking in every corner.... We pray to our god, Yer, when he sends thunder and lightning and say: 'Why are you angry with us, Yer? We are content with the portion you gave us.'"

Thus also spoke Atlanta's Negro bishop: "We Negroes," he said, "do not believe that we are placed in this world merely to be happy, but to prepare for heavenly glory." The same man, Dr. Howard Brown, died of a heart attack within a month after I had talked with him. Though I wasn't assigned to it, I attended the funeral service in what was said to be the largest Negro Methodist church in the world.

I was the only white person in that vast congregation. The white clergy evidently drew the color line even in the case of death of a brother *in Christo*. The coffin containing the bishop's body stood in front of the pulpit and was almost buried under a mass of white lilies and pine branches. The dead man's face was visible and except for a pair of gold spectacles resembled that of a Roman senator in its fine symmetry and dignity. A scarlet-robed choir of 100 voices, male and female, accompanied by a first-class organ, sang: "Swing low, sweet chariot...."

Another bishop, the dead man's successor, a powerfully built individual with the voice of Boanerges, preached the sermon.

"Brother Brown!" called out the bishop, looking directly in the dead man's face. "Brother Brown, Brother Brown, can you hear me?

"Last Thursday evening," the preacher went on, turning to the congregation, "an angel came to Brother Brown as he was sitting in his study and says to him: 'Brother Brown, come along, you gotta get packed. You're goin' on a big long trip....'

" 'No, angel man, please,' replied Brother Brown, 'I can't leave just now. I got so much work to do here.... I'm up to my ears in a revival campaign and fighting the devil for all I'm worth....'

"But the big angel he insists and Brother Brown he packs his trunk and he goes on the train and he rolls through Georgia and through Alabama and Germany and Russia and China and all those places till he come to the river....

"And Brother Brown he gets into the boat and the boat sails away. And it is dark on the river. Oooh, is it dark? It's so dark that Brother Brown he can't see his own feet.... He can see nothing, nothing but darkness in front of him and darkness behind him and all around him.... And the waves they roar, and the waters of the river of death they rise up and they bang and beat against the boat. And Brother Brown gets scared and calls out: 'Oh, Jesus, Jesus, save me, for my bark is so small and the waves are so big....'

"But at last Brother Brown he sees a small light, a weeny, teeny light. He knows now that he's bound for Canaan's shore and soon will stand where bright angel feet have trod....

"And then," continued the bishop, "Brother Brown sees a man in a white gown and as the light grows stronger, Brother Brown he can see that it is Jesus standing there on the other shore and peering into the darkness.

"And Jesus, He too sees Brother Brown, and He calls out:

" 'Hello, Brother Brown!'

" 'Hello, Jesus!' "

"Jesus! Jesus!" The congregation took up the cry and it was as if the church would burst with pent-up emotion and fervor.

" 'Come on, Brother Brown, get a move on! We're all waiting for you,' Jesus calls out. 'The apostles and the prophets are waiting for you. And the angels are waiting for you with the golden crown and My father is waiting for you to hug you in His big arms.... We're having a picnic here on the golden street by the side of the glassy sea that flows from the throne of God....'

"There's a dance going on in heaven now," the preacher assured the congregation. "And Jesus He's dancing. He's dancing with Brother Brown. And God He shakes with laughter and He, too, joins in the dance.

"Dance people of God! Dance children of the Most High! Dance! Shout for joy! All your tears will be wiped away! All your chains they will be broken.... They are even now melting in the hands of God's love! ... "

It was a beautiful and fascinating picture the speaker drew of a white-robed Christ and a laughing God dancing on golden streets, but it was also infinitely pathetic and naïve. I told a gathering of the most "liberal" white ministers at their weekly ministerial meeting that Bishop Brown's funeral service was a dishonest, mean, unchristian trick to divert the people's attention from the real issues at stake in society.

They listened in silence, but at the end of my talk, one of the brethren neatly turned the tables on me by accusing the Dutch of standing at the source and origin of the Negro's woes in America.

"Your Dutch slave merchants," he said, "were the most active in bringing the Negro to America.... Have you never heard of Wagner's opera *The Flying Dutchman*, which deals with the cursed slave ship and its godless captain who raided Africa's shores, clamped irons on tens of thousands of blacks and brought them to America to sell them to the planters? ... You have no right to talk, brother," he added. "It's your nation which for filthy lucre's sake sold its soul to the devil and dumped the Negro problem in America's lap.... "

I should not like to leave anyone with the impression that I thought the South and Atlanta in particular a place of unmitigated squalor and misery, or an intellectual desert. This would be misleading. There was unquestionably a certain backwardness, a standstill in development, but this could truthfully be ascribed to the consequences of the Civil War. For the North not only conquered the South, it also ruined its economy and thwarted its recovery. For more than half a century the South's path led through purgatory. Its most gracious flowers were uprooted. An endless chain of perpetually repeated and unmeaning torments bound the people's destiny in nostalgic and tragical unity. . . .

The truth is that I found Atlanta a beautiful city with fine parks, extensive flower gardens, shaded avenues and stately homes. In the downtown section stood a cluster of skyscrapers housing banks, hotels and insurance companies, a magnificent city hall, a legislative assembly building and dozens of churches including a Roman Catholic and a Protestant Episcopal cathedral. Atlanta had many institutions for the higher education of both white and colored students. The Georgia Institute of Technology which is a part of the state university is of world-wide renown.

Here and there I also came upon small groups of men and women whose consciences were disquieted in the presence of social contradictions which were growing more acute as time went on. In the Protestant churches a small minority seemed aware that the Church's theologizing period had long since come to a close and that the social question would inevitably become the foremost subject of discussion and dispute even in Atlanta. . . .

If conditions, especially among the Negroes, have improved enormously since my stay in the city, it is in no small measure due to the reforming zeal of the same newspaper where I worked for a couple of years. Its ramshackle old building has come down and the offices transferred across the street to a splendid, modern office of which even much larger cities might well be proud. If a new spirit has come to prevail this is in the main due to the unflagging devotion of *The Constitution*'s young editor, Ralph McGill, whose example of liberalism has set the whole community in motion to such an extent that the partial integration of the Negro came about without any noticeable shock in Atlanta, though a hard fight had to be waged and the editor's life was more than once in acute danger. The "cracker" know-nothing mentality based on deep fundamentalism in religion had to give way, albeit reluctantly and still fighting a stubborn rear-guard action, before the irresistible advance of enlightenment and social democracy.

In this respect Atlanta has conformed to the general pattern of what the humanitarian and Christian social philosophers would probably ascribe to a profound change of heart in America. But this is an illusion. There was but a small dose of altruism involved in the movement to improve the human condition of the millions of "submerged" whom Roosevelt inherited from previous regimes.

What has really happened in our day, I think, is this: the modern capitalist state has brought to fruition a good deal of what was mere theory or doctrinary aspiration on the part of socialism at the beginning of this century. America, the last stamping ground of "rugged individualism" has nilly-willy moved in a direction which, verbally at least, still remains to the entrenched reaction anathema, Utopian foolishness, softness and weakening of the national fiber. Social security, popular health, socialized medicine, popular education have more and more become the concern of the government. Forty years ago these socialization measures were still regarded and denounced by the public opinion molders as crass subversion of the competitive system which was camouflaged under the nice-sounding name of "The American Way of Life," the way of life which "made the country great."

Slowly an awareness grew that the American way of life is not an unalterable, solidly and eternally fixed Rock of Gibraltar, but rather a great ship on the move in the teeth of social and economic storms buffeting the entire world. Where the humanitarians were wrong was in propounding the notion that the improvements of the last quarter century were undertaken for the sake of lifting the souls of men.

The first and foremost motivation was one of expediency; the interests of the state and society. The modern state simply cannot afford the colossal waste of the people's strength, capacities and potential technical and intellectual skill as was the case under half-feudal and autocratic systems such as czarism or early capitalism or even the initial stages of the communist regime in the Soviet Union. The state cannot function properly if its human material is deficient.

If the state wants to remain strong, capable of engaging in competition, capable of waging war too, it must become social. It must raise the status of popular health, liquidate illiteracy, encourage talent, instill hope of a better life and, in general, give the under-privileged, the propertyless masses, a chance to raise themselves to a higher economic level.

Marx thought that this was a moral question which capitalism would be incapable of solving because of the clash of interests between the possessing classes on the one hand, and the aspirations of the proletariat on the other. On this point Marx was most certainly in error. It's the capitalist state which has proven that in self-interest it can—because it must—raise the general status of well-being.

The socialization measures introduced in recent years are, therefore, not, as is sometimes said, a form of "creeping socialism." They are designed and operate as supports of the capitalist order. And Roosevelt under whose New Deal a beginning was made in socializing America—only a beginning, for the process will, because it must, go much further—was not a traitor to his class as he is often still decried in ultraconservative circles, but its savior. . . . "I am trying to keep the millionaires from committing suicide," he said once, explaining his program of social renovation.

In 1942, Atlanta's Oglethorpe University built a memorial tower and in the vault placed a number of articles dating from that year. One of the articles in the vault is a book of mine entitled *Days of Our Years*. In A.D. 2042, one hundred years after the sealing of the vault, it is to be opened. In addition to the book, I was asked to give a letter with a prediction. My prediction ran this way:

"*Eppur si muove!* In A.D. 2042 when Oglethorpe's vault is opened, there will be a socialist president in Washington. He will be a Negro!"

CHAPTER VII

Going To and Fro in the Earth

WHILE STILL a resident of Atlanta and a member of *The Constitution*'s editorial staff, I started to write a daily column under the general heading "The World's Window." This column did not deal with strictly local affairs, but was made up of semieditorial comment on men and events abroad, anecdotes about the great and near-great, brief notes on books published in various European countries, and, generally speaking, of incidents marginal to the flowing tide of world history. In addition to printing this column, *The Constitution*'s management syndicated it and in a few months' time sold it for publication to some 30 newspapers in the United States and Canada. The strange part of this syndication enterprise was that I was left completely in the dark about it so that the column had been running regularly in the *Evening World* of New York for some four or five months before I became aware of the fact.

About the same time, April or May, 1923, Mr. Isaac Carmel, an organizer for the Zionist Organization of America, who visited Atlanta to present a certain Dr. Joseph Silverman, rabbi emeritus of Temple Emanu-El in New York to the local Jewish community, called on *The Constitution*'s publisher to ask for an editorial to draw attention to Dr. Silverman's visit. Clark Howell referred the organizer to me and I wrote the requested editorial. The novelty about Dr. Silverman's position was that he, a rabbi in the Reform branch of American Judaism, after a lifelong opposition to the rebuilding of Palestine on a national-political basis, had been converted to the Zionist ideal following a visit to the Holy Land where he had seen the initial stages of the land redemption program which in our day has flowered into the progressive democratic State of Israel.

Since the *Constitution* seemed to approve of the cause represented by Dr. Silverman, not only the local Jews, but virtually all of Atlanta's Protestant clergy attended the mass meeting which was held in the largest theater in town. After hearing Dr. Silverman I wrote a second editorial in which I expressed the view that a reconstituted "national home for the Jewish people in Palestine" was one of the most worthwhile and hopeful changes in the international scene to issue from the Great War. To this I added a word of hope: that our generation might yet see the lamps on Zion's hill rekindled and, according to the prophet's vision, that Torah, i.e. teaching, enlightenment and inspiration for all mankind go forth from Zion once more.

With that I passed to the order of the day and thought no more about Palestine till the local Jewish community invited me to speak in one of their synagogues. The editorials evidently had fallen on fertile soil. I received invitations to lecture from New Orleans, Memphis, Chattanooga, Birmingham, San Francisco, Syracuse, Buffalo, and other cities where my column appeared. One invitation which I accepted eagerly came from New York. This led directly to my departure from Atlanta.

In New York I lectured right and left, not only in synagogues and Jewish centers, but a good deal also in the old Dutch Reformed churches up and down the Hudson valley, in New Jersey and Michigan; Detroit, Grand Rapids, Kalamazoo and towns with rather large populations of Dutch origin. In the city of Albany it was Mr. Gorham Rice, onetime American ambassador to the Netherlands, and author of "The Singing Towers of the Netherlands," who did me the honor to preside at the meetings which I addressed. Save for the minister of New York's Community Church, Dr. John Haynes Holmes, I was, I suspect, the only non-Jewish Zionist in America at the time. And not only was I a Zionist, I was passionately imbued with the ideal of Zion Restored as the beginning of the triumph of justice in all humanity.

Others soon followed, amongst them: Charles Edward Russell, American high commissioner in Britain during the First World War; Dr. Amos I. Dushaw, a Presbyterian divine in Brooklyn; and Dr. James E. Freeman, the Episcopal bishop of Washington, D.C. Before long we enlisted the collaboration of about 500 Protestant clergymen and set up an organization known as the Pro-Palestine Federation of America which also published a journal, the *Pro-Palestine Herald*. When I say that we published this *Herald*, I mean that we came out three or four times a year or whenever a man or a woman of means gave us a helping hand. There was no pecuniary compensation and not even the editorial factotum and general secretary of the Federation, Dr. Aaron Ben Elias, received the slightest remuneration.

For the study of the history of Zionism, its ideology and philosophy, I turned to some of the most eminent Jews of the day: Reuben Brainin, the dean of Hebrew letters in America, who was the living refutation of Renan's assertion that Hebrew as the language of the prophets could never be turned to profane or modern use. Brainin remained a friend till the end of his days and was, much more than any of the contemporary Zionist leaders, steeped in every phase of European culture, a lover of the Russian poets and the German philosophers, and an essayist of distinction. Professor Mordecai M. Kaplan, the promoter of "Judaism as a Civilization," the first to title me "a friend of the Jewish renascence," remains till this day in spite of his advanced age, through his vast erudition and his capacity for work and study, one of the greatest living Jewish scholars.

There were also Dr. Shimon Bernstein, the authority on medieval Hebrew poetry and Louis Lipsky, the peculiarly American interpreter of Zionism, a brilliant writer and great orator; Dr. Stephen S. Wise, the liberalizer of liberal Judaism, founder of the Free Synagogue and of a rabbinical school, the Jewish Institute of Religion. It was in Dr. Wise's pulpit at Carnegie Hall that I preached my first sermon from a Hebrew text: *Hoy, kol-tsame lechu lmayim,* "Ho, everyone that thirsteth, come ye to the waters!"

By Louis D. Brandeis, Associate Justice of the Supreme Court, I was encouraged with many letters in his meticulous handwriting. When I published my first book, *Days of Our Years,* in 1940, Justice Brandeis bought the chapter dealing with Palestine and Zionism from the publisher and distributed, at his own expense in pamphlet form, a hundred thousand copies. He declared that the Palestine chapter marked "the turning point in Zionist endeavors in America in that a non-Jew had finally brought the issue into the open." A compliment which coming from him was as good as, if not better, than the poet's: "Praise from Sir Hubert is praise indeed!"

Sometimes the situation became a little ticklish in the Pro-Palestine Federation by reason of the fact that most of its clergymen members were Christian fundamentalists who undoubtedly nourished a secret hope that our movement might somehow or other be instrumental in bringing Jews to the foot of the cross. Others, believers in the millennium, supported

Zionism on the basis of their eschatological expectations that the Jewish people's return to Palestine was the *conditio sine qua non* for Christ's reappearance on the clouds of heaven. This sentiment I discouraged as much as I could. Of course, the brethren were perfectly free to tell their own congregations whatever they liked. In our official conferences, however, the subject of Jesus was taboo in deference to the sensibilities of any Jew who might happen to be present. The Jewish people have suffered too much to be reminded of Jesus in whose name or because of whom most of the horrors of their tragic history have been inflicted upon them.

As might be expected, we non-Jewish pro-Palestinians also met with a good deal of opposition. Several persons of national prominence upon whom we thought we could confidently call for moral support turned us down flat. Two of these, Mrs. Eleanor Roosevelt and Dr. James G. McDonald, refused us their patronage on the grounds that Jews should strive to be good American citizens rather than meddle in foreign affairs, as if every man in this world has not at least one other, perhaps a higher loyalty than to the country in which he happens to be born or reside. Haven't we all two fatherlands: our own country and the City of God?

While it is true that both these distinguished citizens in the course of time became ardent supporters of the State of Israel, the first as one of the chief fund raisers for Israeli causes, the second as America's first ambassador to Israel, they did not do so till the battle for Israel's independence had been won.

Personally, I met with strong opposition in the *World*'s editorial office. Herbert Bayard Swope, the director general of the two *World* papers, reproached me for mentioning Palestine too often in my column. The truth is that he would rather not have seen it mentioned at all. Once he had me on the carpet to charge me with patriotic laxity for not having become an American citizen which, it had to be pointed out to him, was an impossibility with only a couple of years' residence in the U.S.A. At another time Mr. Swope went so far as to order a discontinuation of my column because of what he called its pro-Zionist slant. There seemed to him something un-American about Zionism. Nor were the harassed European Jewish masses fit or desirous, he argued, to set up a commonwealth of their own in the wastes of the ancient Holy Land.

In his case, too, I lived to see the day when he—gingerly, it is true— climbed on the band wagon. Was he converted to Zionism? I hardly think so. I could never fathom the mentality of assimilationist Jews of his kind. Nobody asked them to transfer their political allegiance to Palestine or go and reside in that country. Still they behaved as if they were asked to commit an act of high treason when summoned to support the rebuilding of the land of their fathers. What were they afraid of? Were they ashamed of the land which produced the prophets and psalmists, that extraordinary body of men which stands at the head of the chain of those who have made Americans differ from the slaves who crouch beneath despotic scepters? Were they fearful of the reactivation of those values and beliefs which sprang from Israel's soil and made the Hebraic culture one of the parent streams of Western civilization? I could not then, and still cannot see why it should be un-American to support any nation, people or individual suffering injustice.

The controversy came to a head in a Reform temple in the city of Cincinnati where I was to address a congregation which filled every nook and corner of the edifice long before my arrival. In Cincinnati Reform Judaism had, and still has, its training school for the rabbinate, the Hebrew Union College. Back in the 1920s that college was one of the bastions of anti-Zionism in America, though amongst its professors were also some of the most brilliant exponents of different schools of the Zionist philosophy: Neumark, Maximon, Margolis, Schloessinger. . . . Dr. David Philipson, the rabbi of the temple where I was to speak, was considered a bitter anti-Zionist. He was a native of Germany and preached exclusively in German till the outbreak of World War I.

The chairman of the evening was State Senator Alfred M. Cohen, president of the International Order of B'nai B'rith. When I found myself in his company in the robing room behind the Ark, I noticed that he was nervous and apprehensive. "Yes," he admitted, "I have heard that you sometimes mention that country in Asia Minor [Palestine]. I beg of you not to do so in your lecture this evening. Frankly, we are not interested. The congregation is anti-Zionist. . . ."

"But," I asked, "isn't the audience made up of Jews? And don't Jews pray three times a day for the rebuilding of Jerusalem?"

"Not these Jews," he replied. "We have dropped all references to Palestine from our prayer books! Besides, there are several Christian clergymen present."

"Palestine is also the Christian's holy land. . . . What would the situa-

tion be like if the audience were made up of Hollanders or people of
Dutch descent, and that at this time Holland was in trouble and Hollanders at home were trying to rebuild their country, what would they
think of me if I kept silent about a matter in which they would unquestionably be deeply interested?"

"Heavens! I foresee a lot of trouble here this evening," exclaimed
Senator Cohen, throwing up his hands in alarm. It being time, however,
to start the meeting we walked out onto the platform. He introduced
me and said that I would discuss the Rapallo Treaty between Soviet
Russia and the Weimar Republic and turned the pulpit over to me.

I thought: I will have to make myself clear once and for all. For I did
not speak to convince; I spoke because of my faith in divine prophecy.
"I feel greatly honored to be in this rabbinical city and to stand in the
presence of so many scholars and students of Judaism, but though not a
Jew myself," I added, perhaps a little melodramatically, *"le ma'an Tsion lo
echsheh,* For Zion's sake I shall not keep silent. . . . "

The students started to applaud and the battle, for that night at least,
was over. Not till a Christian minister rose in the question period was
there any disharmony. This person called out in an angry challenging
voice: "By what right has Britain given Palestine to the Jews?"

I had to point out to this brother that Britain had neither the right nor
the desire to give away anything that did not belong to her. Palestine
was under a League of Nations' mandate, just as Syria and Iraq, Trans-
jordan, Tanganyika and German West Africa. Britain merely administered
the Palestine mandate on behalf of the League. She was required under
the mandate's terms (ratified by 52 league members and by one non-
member, the government of the United States) to institute such conditions, political, social and economic, in Palestine as would in the course
of time lead to the establishment of "a national home for the Jewish
people" with the proviso that nothing be undertaken against the civil and
religious rights of peoples (Arabs and Druses) already resident in the
country. . . .

It was around the issue of the spiritual allegiance of American Jewry
to the land of their fathers and its rebuilding as a means to revivify and
revitalize the Hebraic tradition wherever Jews dwelt, that the debates
and controversies generally revolved.

One evening I filled a speaking engagement in a Presbyterian church in Brooklyn. In the course of my address I said that certain observers of the international scene warned that the skies were darkening once more in Europe and that a new armed conflict seemed to be in the making. There was a reporter present in the meeting and the next day one of the newspapers carried word that I had predicted the outbreak of a new world war. John H. Tennant, the managing editor of the *Evening World* sent for me: "On what do you base your prediction of war?"

"I made no such prediction," I said. "I merely cited the opinions of men like Romain Rolland, Barthélemy de Ligt, Judah M. Magnes and Stefan Zweig who believe that the danger of a new armed conflict is growing."

"Who are they? Who is this Rolland you are talking about?"

"He was awarded the Nobel prize for literature for his book *Jean-Christophe*. He's a professor of the history of art at the Ecole Normale Superieure in Paris."

"Never heard of Rolland." Mr. Tennant shook his head. "Where does he get his information anyway?"

"Who knows? Maybe from the gypsies!"

"The gypsies?"

"Yes, there was a gypsy woman once who foretold the course of Germany's history for a hundred years to come. She foresaw wars and revolutions and great upheavals."

"Write me the gypsy's story!"

"You're sure you do not want something about Rolland? He's one of the truly great men of our time, as great as Tolstoy perhaps."

"I'm not interested in the guy. Write about the gypsy!"

"But it's a very old story, nearly a hundred years old. I read it at least twenty years ago in a magazine which was itself perhaps fifty years old. . . . "

"She predicted war, did she?"

"She did that, yes."

"Write it, man! Gypsy stories are always good. . . . "

Here in brief is the story. The year was 1849 when the gypsy's prediction was made to William, the second son of the King of Prussia, Frederick William III. Prince William was not directly in line for the succession to the throne, his eldest brother Frederick, who was still alive, bore the title of crown prince. William had been in charge of the Prussian troops in the revolutionary year 1848 when riots occurred in Berlin and the barri-

cades went up in half a dozen European countries. Prince William acted
with such severity in repressing the revolt in Berlin that he became
very unpopular and was given the nickname "Billy Cartridge." His father
thought it advisable to send him abroad till the wave of popular dissatis-
faction should have blown over.

William went to Switzerland and stopped in the city of Interlaken.
Strolling along the lake front one day a gypsy woman approached him
and greeted him as "Your Imperial Highness."

"Woman, are you out of your mind? Imperial Highness of what empire?" asked William with a sneer.

"Of the German empire," she said.

"But my good woman, there is no such thing as a German empire."

"It will come," said the gypsy.

"When?"

"Just write down the figures of the present year 1849 and add the numbers vertically, thus:

$$
\begin{array}{r}
1849 \\
1 \\
8 \\
4 \\
9 \\
\hline
1871
\end{array}
$$

"That's the year," she said, "1871, when the German empire will be
born. . . . And you will be the emperor."

"That's interesting," said William. "How long will I remain emperor?"

"Make another addition in the same way:

$$
\begin{array}{r}
1871 \\
1 \\
8 \\
7 \\
1 \\
\hline
1888
\end{array}
$$

"That's the year when you will cease to reign," said the gypsy.

"The year of my death?"

"Yes, that's the year of your death!"

"Will the German empire go on existing?"

"Certainly!"

"For how long?"

"Add up the figures again:

$$
\begin{array}{r}
1888 \\
1 \\
8 \\
8 \\
8 \\
\hline
1913
\end{array}
$$

"1913 marks the beginning of the end for the German empire," said the woman. "The empire will be defeated in war. But Germany will remain united."

"That's one consolation at least," observed William. "And how long will this condition last?"

"Just add the numbers once more," suggested the gypsy:

$$
\begin{array}{r}
1913 \\
1 \\
9 \\
1 \\
3 \\
\hline
1927
\end{array}
$$

"The year 1927 is the beginning of a new time of troubles for Germany."

"But some day there's an end to all troubles, isn't there? Shall I add up once more?" asked William.

"You may add if you like, but I wouldn't if I were you, for the outcome of your addition will give you the year when Germany in its entirety will lie in ruins."

1927
1
9
2
7
———
1946

"I'm going to add up once more," laughed the prince. "I won't leave Germany in the horrible state you just mentioned."

1946
1
9
4
6
———
1966

"What's going to happen in the year 1966?" asked William. "I don't know," shrugged the woman. "I don't recognize what I see. . . . Germany isn't Germany any more. . . ."

"I wonder if you couldn't go to Europe for us," said Jack Tennant a day or so after publication of the gypsy story. There must be plenty of that kind of stories lying around. It's human interest stories I am looking for. I don't want any political stuff. Who the hell cares about Rapallo and San Remo and all that diplomatic blah which don't mean a damn thing to our readers anyway? I'd like to find out who that guy Mussolini sleeps with, and that other fellow Briand [he pronounced the name Bryant]. They say he's quite a skirt chaser. . . . We don't do badly ourselves here in New York, but don't they have the juiciest murders in France? I mean those *crimes passionelles* as they call them. All I get is politics and more politics. Who cares? Besides, the telegraphic agencies supply us with all the political gossip we need. It's damned dull stuff, if you ask me. . . . Go upstairs and see Arthur Krock. He wants to see you."

That's how I became a foreign correspondent for the *New York Evening World*. Mr. Krock, who still functions as an editorial columnist for *The New York Times*, supplied me with letters of introduction to the (Morning) *World's* correspondents resident in Paris, London, Rome, Geneva, Moscow and Berlin, requesting them to place the facilities of their offices at my disposal. I was to be a roving correspondent and could go wherever I liked. And so I was off on the S.S. *Mauretania.*

From the day I arrived in Paris my life was split in twain. Jack Tennant wanted anecdotes and other trivialities. He got them. But I also had my own life to live and it was more valuable to me than a hundred thousand *Evening Worlds.* The first thing I did in Paris was to inscribe myself at the Sorbonne as a student in the Ecole Pratique des Hautes Etudes. The men who received me and under whom I graduated some years later was Charles Guignebert, professor of the history of Christianity.

Before going any further, I must say that I was not alone in Paris; Cornelia Machelina, who has been my companion through joy and sorrow from her youth till this very day, stood by my side then as she does now. Everything of value I received in life is but dust and ashes compared with what she gave me. Love is so mutilated in our time, so profaned and turned to such banality that it has become virtually impossible to pronounce the word love. There are all sorts of love and they are all related, sexual or erotic love, caritative and sympathetic love, but there is also the kind of love of which the Apostle Paul speaks: the unconditioned giving of one's self to another. That love is timeless and rises above all conventionalities and legalities. This love was ours and, I am happy to say, remains ours today when silver threads have begun to appear amongst the gold. . . .

After a day or so, Paris looked as familiar as in that month of December, 1918, when Raoul Desormeaux and I spent our last war days in the city. Before settling down to work I made a quick trip to Holland, going by train as far as Antwerp and walking the rest of the way through Flanders and re-entering the land of my birth at the customs post of Wuustwezel.

My grandparents had passed away in the dozen years of my absence. My uncle Kees had been drowned in the Rhine. My other relatives, uncles, aunts, cousins, etc., were so infuriated with me for having served in the Canadian army and to have borne arms against what they called "your own German brothers" that I came away in a hurry. One of my cousins who has since risen to the position of theology professor in Utrecht University, proceeded to give me such a dressing down for my "militaristic insanity" that I left his house without saying a word. The family had to wait till 1939 before becoming convinced what a nightmare a united Germany is and always will be to Holland and the rest of Europe.

I wrote a few articles for Mr. Tennant about the dykes and the plans for the draining of the Zuyder Sea, and on the way back to Paris stopped over for a few hours in the city of Ghent to take a look at the new Flemish National University. On the Street of the Bears, near a bridge across the river Lys which bisects the city, I found a restaurant which seemed to be frequented exclusively by instructors and students of the nearby Athenaeum. There was a prolonged, somewhat embarrassing lull in the buzzing conversation when I entered the dining room so that everybody present could hear me plainly as I ordered something from the waiter who presented himself with the menu. Quite inadvertently I spoke to the waiter in French and immediately I was in trouble. Two of the students came over and politely inquired: "Do you not speak Dutch? [Netherlandish, they said.] You don't look like a Frenchman."

"I am not a Frenchman," I replied in Dutch.

"In that case, will you be kind enough to speak your own language in Flanders?" they asked. "Any language in the world except French. . . ."

"Do you hate French that much? I thought Belgium was bilingual."

"Quite right, Belgium *is* bilingual, but Flanders is not bilingual. Flanders is unilingual. Flanders is Dutch [Netherlandish] and does not want to be anything else but Dutch. We are trying to get rid of French, not of French itself, but of French as the language that is forced on the Flemish people. The policy of forcing the Flemish people to speak a foreign language which has been in operation for nearly a century cut the common people from the source of its culture and literature and has caused Flanders to sink to the intellectual level of a Balkan peasant country."

"But you yourselves broke away from Holland, the source of your culture, in 1830. You live in a separate state called Belgium. You have an army, a judiciary, and all the paraphernalia of separate statehood. You even have a national anthem which is the only national anthem in the world which carries an insult to the ruling house of a neighboring nation. Don't you sing in the "Brabançonne," your national anthem: *La mitraille a écrasé l'orange de l'arbre de la liberté* [With our grapeshot we have knocked the orange off the tree of liberty]? That's a reference to the House of Orange and an insult to Queen Wilhelmina, who is the Princess of Orange and the sovereign lady of Holland."

"We never sing that Belgian piece of *Dreck*. It's not the anthem of Flanders. We don't uncover our heads when we hear it sung or played. We would like to get rid of the whole Belgian caboodle; state, king, army and officialdom. Have you ever heard of any other state which seeks to denationalize the majority of its population, its principal ethnic group? Our Flemish boys are commanded in French in the army. The courts use only French. All official documents are drawn up in that foreign language...."

By that time a dozen or more students had gathered around. They talked and talked while the evening wore away. When they finally accompanied me to the Hôtel de la Poste on the Place d'Armes, it was two o'clock in the morning. But it wasn't wasted time entirely: for one thing I discovered the reason why the British Intelligence had prevented me from going to Flanders right after the Armistice in November, 1918.

In that month the Belgian government, which spent the four years of World War I in exile in the city of Le Havre, returned to Brussels and broke up the Flemish nationalist movement. During the occupation, the German governor general, Von Bissing, allowed or rather urged the Flemish nationalists to set up a Council of Flanders under the presidency of Dr. August Borms and thus virtually made Flanders autonomous. In the event of a German victory Flanders was to be either an independent republic or to be reunited with Holland, whatever the people favored.

The mistake of Dr. Borms and his Council of Flanders was that they allowed the Germans to bring their nationalist aspirations temporarily to fruition. The Flemings were certainly entitled to autonomy and self-determination, but it was neither politic nor wise to have these rights established for them by the occupying power. As soon as King Albert and Queen Elizabeth returned from Le Havre, Dr. Borms and the members of the Council of Flanders were arrested, tried and sentenced to death. Many of the most prominent Flemish leaders fled to Holland and the whole country was thrown into turmoil.

With the Germans under General von Bissing as their friends and protectors as long as the occupation lasted, the Flemish nationalist groups came to look upon the British who were fighting the Germans as their enemies also. Here lay the source of that animosity and anti-British sentiment which our soldiers felt on every side while fighting in Flanders. The Flemings did not hate the British *per se*. They hated the Belgian state; the ally of the British. They resented the British presence in their land because if and when victorious the British would almost certainly contribute to a restoration of the *status quo ante* in Belgium, which would mean that the French-speaking Belgian bureaucracy would rule Flanders again as if it were a conquered province.

From the day that Flanders was torn away from Holland in 1830 by the intervention of a French army, the policy of the emerging Belgian state had been directed towards the denationalization of the Flemings. In a hundred years' time, the Belgian government figured, there would be no more Flemings. All the inhabitants of Belgium would speak French and the Flemish question would be a thing of the past.

As things turned out, the present-day situation in Belgium is precisely the reverse. The French-speaking Belgians, known as Walloons, are in a hopeless minority. The population increase in Catholic Flanders has been infinitely greater than that in liberal and socialistic Wallonia. The two peoples did not merge; they remained two separate nations in two separate countries lying side by side: Dutch-speaking Flanders and French-speaking Wallonia.

The main issue at stake between the two remains the city of Brussels where 87 per cent of the people are Flemings. Being the administrative capital, however, Brussels is in Walloon hands.

It is on the issue of Brussels that the Belgian state may yet fall apart. Indications are that the struggle is entering a new and more disquieting phase. It's the Walloons who want to split off now; some of them want to be integrated into or attached to France and have done with Flanders for good. That would mean the end of the Belgian state. . . .

I promised the students in Ghent that I would keep in touch and, if at all possible, bring the situation in Flanders to the attention of world public opinion. Before I left I asked them the names of some of the Flemish nationalist leaders. They gave me a dozen names, but insisted that the man most likely to be of help to me was: Brandt van Varewyk.

"Where does he live?"

"He lives in Holland, just across the border in the village of Heerlen near the city of Maastricht. He is forbidden to come into Flanders by the alien Belgian government, but he comes to see us nevertheless from time to time."

"In disguise?"

They all laughed. "Yes, in disguise more or less. . . ."

"What's the joke?"

"There is no joke. You'll find out who he is when you see him. . . . "

Before continuing my trip back to Paris, I took a bus from Ghent to Brussels, then another one to Liège. A third bus took me to Maastricht in Holland and the fourth bus brought me to the village of Heerlen.

It was pitch dark and pouring rain when I found the house. The young lady who opened the door exclaimed: "Oh, there you are at last. Uncle has been waiting for you all day. He had almost given you up."

"How did you know that I was coming?"

"Uncle received a telegram from the Flemish university in Ghent. . . . "

When she led me into the study I stood face to face with a Roman Catholic prelate.

"Are you Brandt van Varewyk?" I asked.

"Sometimes," he laughed. "It's my pen name. My real name is Robrecht de Smet. I am the papal prothonotary for the Scandinavian countries."

"What does that mean?"

"I am preparing the restoration of the Catholic episcopate in Sweden, Norway and Denmark. . . . I can see that you are surprised. . . . "

"Indeed I am. I had not expected to meet a Roman Catholic dignitary. . . . Had I known I would probably not have come. . . . You see, I am a Protestant. . . . "

"I know, I know, your family lives here in Holland. They are of Flemish origin!"

"Quite right! They moved north into Holland when the Inquisition exterminated Protestantism in Flanders. . . . "

Monseigneur de Smet must have been in his fifties, a tall man with pale blue eyes shielded by a pair of thick glasses. Before dinner we sat a few minutes in his study where hung a Flemish national flag and a painting of . . . Queen Wilhelmina of Holland. When I remarked that I was distressed by the intellectual decline amongst the Flemish people, adding that the deterioration was almost inconceivable in a people which produced the later renaissance, Monseigneur de Smet said: "This is the policy of the criminal Belgian state; impoverish the Flemings intellectually before denationalizing them altogether. It's a scandal that cries to high heaven for redress. . . *Belgica delenda esse.* . . . "

I have never met another person who hated Belgium so thoroughly as Monseigneur de Smet, and not only Belgium but France as well and the whole Latin or Mediterranean civilization. If his duties did not call him to Rome from time to time, he said, he would never go there. On the other hand, anything Germanic, Scandinavian or Nordic could not be praised enough. The character of the Teutonic peoples was marked by honesty, frankness and straightforward dealing. Unlike the decadent French and the amoral Italians, the Nordic peoples were the salt of the earth. The Belgian state was a monstrosity, a bastard state which, at the behest of France, was doing its utmost to destroy the national spirit and language of Flanders. . . .

Though I could not, of course, agree *in toto* with these outrageous propositions, I felt a deep sympathy for the degraded and, the word is not too strong, the downtrodden and oppressed section of the Netherlands' people living in Flanders. When De Smet asked me, I promised to help him in the Flemish liberation movement with the understanding that no violence was to be used or advocated. By regular parliamentary and democratic methods and by virtue of the universally recognized Wilsonian doctrine of the right of self-determination for small peoples, the Flemings could not fail to win out in the end. It was a matter of education and of inculcating a will to freedom and independence in the Flemish masses.

Monseigneur de Smet revealed that he was publishing a paper called *Vlaanderen* (Flanders) which he smuggled into the land of his birth and distributed amongst the students of Louvain University and the Flemish National University in Ghent. The great obstacle to the diffusion of this paper lay at the border. Edition after edition had been seized and confiscated by the Belgian customs officers. He wondered if I could not have the paper printed in France and smuggled into Belgium from the south. "It will take the Belgian authorities a long time to discover that the source of Flemish nationalist propaganda lies in France. Here," he said, "is the last copy of *Vlaanderen*. Take a look!"

I took a look. Across the front page ran an eight column banner headline: *Flemings never forget, Belgium is NOT your fatherland.* In an article on the same page, "Brandt van Varewyk" referred to King Albert of the Belgians as "the French prefect [provincial governor] in the Flemish city of Brussels. . . ."

The greatest difficulty lay not in the smuggling. It was the printing of the paper which caused me the most trouble. French printers print French well enough, I dare say. It was a different matter to get French printers to print Dutch correctly. I was proofreader, make-up editor and sometimes typesetter (by hand) in a rat-infested attic on the Rue du Croissant in the Montmartre quarter. One thousand copies of the journal were smuggled out of France by passing them through the property of a nobleman, half of whose estate lay in France and half in Belgium.

Rather than following personal experiences in chronological order at this point, I would like to show how my association with the Flemish nationalist movement continued for some years and then abruptly terminated with the assassination of the President of France, Paul Doumer, in 1932. In the publication of *Vlaanderen* I had the assistance of four Flemish young men residing in Paris: one a schoolteacher, two seminarists and one man, a painter, named Vlaminck who rose to world fame.

In addition to supervising the printing, shipping and smuggling, I wrote a regular article for the periodical dealing with the struggle or the movements for national liberation in other parts of the world. Catalonia sought freedom from Spain, Brittany from France, the Basque nationalists clamored for liberation from both the Spanish and the French tutelage. The Jewish people were maltreated in Poland, Rumania and in the little Baltic states who had, along with Finland, been given their freedom by the Soviet government following the revolution of 1917. In Alsace a movement had sprung up directed against the centralizing tendencies of the French state, the suppression of the German language which is the mother tongue of 90 per cent of the Alsatian people and against the replacement of the old Catholic parochial school system with the neutral, laic school of the Third Republic into which Alsace was incorporated at the close of the war in 1918.

Some of the leaders of these nationalist and activist groups came to Paris from time to time to supply me with news or to ask questions till the idea gained ground that these movements of national liberation should all band together and thus not merely represent some nuisance value, but exercise a definite and constructive influence on the course of events. Henri Barbusse accompanied by Panaït Istrati, the Rumanian novelist, came to see me and proposed the integration of all the movements for national liberation or autonomy into the "League against Imperialism."

Now the League against Imperialism was a communist-controlled organization. Barbusse served as its international chairman. Ilya Ehrenburg was one of its officers and likewise, I think, the gentle and scholarly Christian Rakowsky, the Soviet ambassador in Paris who was expelled from France precisely for participating in the anti-imperialist league's activities.

I pointed out to these men that even if I should accept the proposition, there wasn't a chance in the world of bringing the Flemish nationalist movement, where a great many Roman priests were amongst the active members, into a communist-controlled organization by whatever name it went. The same objection held for the Catalans, the Basques, the Alsatians and the Bretons. The membership of all these groups was predominantly Catholic.

When the negotiations failed Barbusse wrote me a letter: "Not one of your nationalist movements will ever achieve national liberation; it is the Third International which will set humanity free." At the same time he went full speed ahead with an attempt to extend communist control over the various nationalist movements in Europe. He launched a weekly paper called *Monde* and appointed Auguste Habaru, a Flemish nationalist, who had formerly been with us, its editor.

In riposte Monseigneur de Smet and I set up "The International of Oppressed Nations," and issued a monthly bulletin in French under the same title. My house in St. Germain-en-Laye served as headquarters of the new International. The meeting place for the executive was the back room of a bistro on the Place de Rennes in Paris facing the Montparnasse railway station. The bistro which was owned and operated by an ex-schoolmaster from Alsace, Erich Matmueller, put up a sign: *Au Rendez-Vous des Nations Opprimées*, "Meeting Place of the Oppressed Nations."

Of course we were no match for Barbusse and his associates. They put out a fine, attractive paper and soon gained a wide circulation. Barbusse, Istrati and Habaru, moreover, were excellent writers. We had no writers worth mentioning. We had no money either. There were neither salaries, nor expense accounts, nor subsidies of any kind. Barbusse's journal received a large subsidy from the French communist party which was at the time on the way up with a membership in the millions and more than a hundred deputies in the French parliament. Had I not been paid a salary by the *Evening World*, it is quite safe to say that we would not have come out with a single issue of our *Bulletin des Nations Opprimées*.

On top of that our International received a blow which nearly put us out of commission. This happened when the chief of our Alsatian section, Friedrich Roos, and some of his companions resorted to direct action. They bombed some newly installed French public schools in Colmar, Strasbourg and Muehlhausen. In court Roos sought to put the blame on our International. We, he declared, had sent him instructions to take the bull by the horns and start an anti-French revolution in Alsace. Monseigneur de

Smet's name could not be disclosed to the police, so I had to take the responsibility for our defense. I had no difficulty in showing the French political police that neither as an individual nor as the secretary-general of the International was I in any way involved in the terroristic activities in Alsace. It was a stroke of good fortune that the Minister of the Interior at the time was Anatole de Monzie with whom I had previously made a public appearance in the Salle Wagram in behalf of the reconstruction work in Palestine.

Then months and months went by. I was absent successively in Syria, Poland, Russia, Palestine, Rumania and Italy, but on the day of my return to Paris a Russian terrorist, Gorgulov, shot and killed the aged President Paul Doumer, the most inoffensive and innocuous President the Third Republic ever had, which is saying a good deal. André Tardieu, editor in chief of *Le Temps*, the great Parisian daily, brought out a special edition with a headline: *The communist assassins have killed Doumer!* The communist newspaper *L'Humanité* came back a few hours later with a special edition of its own. On *L'Humanité*'s front page appeared only the words: *Tardieu a Menti!* "Tardieu is a liar!"

However, on an inside page *L'Humanité* supplied the information that Gorgulov had confessed at a preliminary hearing before the police magistrate that he was a member of the Green International. The communists, who knew better, charged that the Green International was *our* International. In reality the Green International was an association of peasant parties, Rumanian, Ukrainian, Bessarabian, Bulgarian and so forth. But the name of our International had been mentioned in public and its link with the anti-Belgian Flemish nationalist movement disclosed. Our secret was out.

French-speaking Belgians resident in Paris held a demonstration in the Place de l'Opéra to express their indignation over the murder of Doumer *...by us!* I attended the demonstration and asked to speak. I wanted to tell the crowd that the Flemish nationalists had nothing whatever to do with the assassination. I hadn't spoken five minutes when someone struck me a blow on the head from behind and then a mob of Belgian ex-servicemen—at least they wore Belgium's military uniform—set about to give me a drubbing. It rained blows and kicks, but finally I managed to break away from the lynchers and jumped into a cab which drove me at a furious rate to the house of an old friend, Marvin Lowenthal,* on the

*Author of *A Civilization Passed By, Montaigne*, etc.

Quai de Béthune, who not only bandaged my head, but gave me so much vermouth to pick me up that I sallied forth from his place a couple of hours later in high spirits.

After that the International of Oppressed Nations died of inanition. The association of different nationalist movements in an international organization is not only a contradiction in terms; it is an impossibility. The different parties either become internationalist, socialist or communist, or they fight each other. Neither course was practicable. Matmuehler changed the sign on his bistro to *Au Rendez-Vous des Chauffeurs*, and I notified Monseigneur de Smet that my participation in the Flemish activist movement must come to an end by reason of other pressing business.

As I said, I was a roving reporter and hence frequently absent from France. The first trip abroad was made in 1926 when I attempted to keep the vow I made in 1918 to go on a pilgrimage to the Holy Land.

Ever since the death of Colonel MacDonald, who had promised to go to Palestine with me, I had been worrying how I could get to the Holy Land. With my appointment in Paris I felt I came within view of my project. I wrote Jack Tennant a letter saying that if he would furnish the funds I would undertake a journey to the Arabian desert where, I lied, certain archaeologists were reported to have found a remnant of "the ten lost tribes of Israel."

Mr. Tennant pondered the matter for a while and finally replied by cable: DONT BOTHER STOP FIVE LOST TRIBES LOCATED HERE RESIDING OCEAN PARKWAY BROOKLYN OTHER FIVE TRIBES BRONX. That put it squarely up to me to find my way to Palestine, at my own expense. To cut down the cost of transportation I took the cheapest boat available out of Marseilles, the S.S. *Lotus* of the Messageries Maritimes whose first port of call was Oran in Algeria; second, Alexandria, Egypt; third, Jaffa, Palestine; and fourth, Beirut in Lebanon which country was then still a vilayet or province of Greater Syria.

The *Lotus* passengers were divided into four classes. In first class traveled a pilgrimage of about 200 Irishmen under their bishop. In second class I was lodged in a cabin next door to two Dominicans, Father Joseph Marie Lagrange, the head of the School of Biblical Research in Jerusalem and one of his assistants, the world-famous scholar and chief of the Vatican's Biblical Commission, Father Pierre Dhorme.

Below in the hold, third class or steerage, was an entire company of African infantry on their way to Syria where the Druses were in revolt. On the forward deck (fourth class) in the open, slept, ate and prayed a motley crowd of Moslems whom we picked up at Oran in Algeria. These men, old and feeble and some actually on the point of death, hoped to debark at Jaffa and from there proceed to Amman in Transjordania in order to travel by the old Hedjah Railway as far as Medina from which city they intended to continue by camel-back to Mecca, Islam's holy city. These men literally went out to die in the comforting nearness of the Kaaba. Not all reached their Meccan destination. One old fellow, who suffered more from hunger than from any disease, expired on deck. His body was wrapped in a canvas shroud before the rats could get at it. Weighed down by stones, it sank out of sight in the vicinity of Stromboli which happened to be in eruption.

The rumble of the volcano, which sent up puffs of fire and smoke and huge rocks at regular twenty-minute intervals, frightened the African troops below deck so much that they howled and screamed in distress. They were not allowed to come on deck. They were locked in the hold. A door with heavy iron bars separated their quarters from a stairway. On account of the terrific heat in the hold, the soldiers had taken off their clothes. You could see them hunched down stark naked behind the bars and hear them screaming obscenities, the only words in the French language they had learned.

We had twenty-nine nationalities on board and seven representatives of the world's leading religions. In second class we ate at one common table presided over by the ship's doctor who was flanked by the two Dominican Fathers. Next to Father Lagrange sat the Marquis de Chaunessy, a cavalry officer on his way to fight the Druses in Syria; next to the marquis three ladies, one the madam of an *établissement* in Beirut called "High Life" which she pronounced "Ee Leef," the other two to take up positions in that selfsame establishment which was, according to the proprietress, reserved "for officers only." On one side of me sat a Greek merchant of *loukoum* on his way back from New York to his home town of Smyrna, and on my right a terrific fundamentalist bore, Elmer Brocklebank, who was employed by the Sudan Inland Mission. His town of origin was Wichita, Kansas. He was setting forth for the second time in his life on the utterly futile errand of trying to convert little Moslem *mullahs* to our sacred Christian religion. He said grace before meals in a voice intentionally loud and offensive to the Roman Catholic priests, but not before our two waiters had temporarily removed the bottles of red wine. Our Kansan fellow traveler was a teetotaler and refused to pray so long as there remained strong drink on the table. In revenge or disgust, but to everybody's intense satisfaction, one of the waiters, a good-looking boy from Nice, spilled some soup now and then down the fanatic's neck or over his clerical vest.

We also had three or four Jews and their families in second class, but they did not eat with us. They brought their own kosher provisions which ran out because of the delay in crossing the Mediterranean. In the Strait of Messina something went wrong with one of the ship's screws and we lay motionless for three days and nights opposite Messina, the famous city ruined in the earthquake of 1908. We were so close to the shore that we could see the Sicilian signorinas stroll along the brilliantly illuminated boulevard at night. We could even hear a band playing in one of the parks.

In Port Said, where we crawled into port for another layover of twenty-four hours, an Arab wearing a fez and a nightshirt attached himself to me along with a small army of shoeshiners, self-styled guides, touts, pimps and their "little sisters," *hashish* peddlers and a voluminous assortment of pickpockets and cutthroats of indeterminate nationality. In order to get away from this reception committee, I entered the Hotel of the Nile where the staff was Greek and ate a meal with a predominant taste of olive oil. I considered taking a room, but on lifting the mattress, I noticed such a large number of crawling things that I retreated to the *Lotus* and its legion of cockroaches and rats which, at any rate, didn't get into bed with you.

In Jaffa the *Lotus* did not touch land. It lay about a mile off shore. The passengers were taken off one by one in the following manner: after a section of the railing of the *Lotus'* lower deck was removed, you stood in the open space. Down below an Arab rowboat could be seen dancing up and down on the swelling waves. When the boat rose to the level of the deck, an Arab standing astride the rowboat's gunwales on his bare feet seized you by the waist, lifted you bodily from the *Lotus* and deposited you safe and sound in his boat, which simultaneously dropped back between the waves with the speed of a falling elevator. This maneuver was repeated till the boat was full.

Once ashore the boatmen started to haggle about the price of debarkation. I offered the chief of the rowers a half pound Egyptian. He said: "Excellency, count, baron, my prince, I have five babies...." I cut him short: "I am not His Excellency, I am only His Excellency's secretary. His Excellency is just coming ashore now with the next boat," and I pointed to the Reverend Elmer Brocklebank. A dozen Arabs stormed in the direction of the Kansan D.D. Father Dhorme tapped me on the shoulder: "You are coming with us in the automobile. Father Lagrange invites you to be our guest at the Convent of St. Stephen in Jerusalem...."

And so it came to pass that on my first visit to the Holy City I was the guest of the Dominicans. I slept in a cell like any monk, rose for mattins and again for early Mass, and even rang the bell once or twice for the brother bell ringer. With Father Lagrange I sat many hours in his library. He was a tall man with a small graying beard. His eyes sparkled with enthusiasm and goodness as he discussed the Gospel of St. John on which he had spent a lifetime of study. He was positively convinced, he said, that St. John's is the oldest of the four gospels. When his book on St. John came out a few years later in Paris, I rushed out to buy a copy. To my amazement I saw that St. Matthew was indicated as the writer of the first of the gospel booklets. The Vatican had threatened Lagrange with suspension from his function as dean of the School of Biblical Research if he went on insisting on St. John's priority. Lagrange submitted; he was an old man. Like Galileo, at the sight of the Inquisition's thumbscrews, he gave in.

I stayed ten days in Jerusalem, saw all the *soi-disant* holy places, such as the Via Dolorosa, Pontius Pilate's pretorium, the Upper Room where the Last Supper was eaten by Jesus and His disciples, the Garden of Gethsemane, the Basilica of the Holy Sepulchre, the valleys of Hinnum and Josephat, and the spot where once lay those marvelous gardens of Solomon where the wise king received the Queen of Sheba and made her the ancestress of the Ethiopian emperors.

In the Arab village of Bethany, on the eastern slope of Mount Olive, I paid ten *piasters* for the privilege of sitting down in the house, a mere hovel, where once dwelt Mary and Martha and their brother Lazarus who was raised from the dead. The attendant Franciscan monk was a Frenchman. He told me the story of the miracle. In turn I told him the story which Oscar Wilde was fond of telling: "When Lazarus came home from the grave where he had lain three days, Jesus took him aside: 'Well,

Lazarus, tell me something of your experiences. What did you see? With whom did you speak while you were dead? What did heaven look like?' Lazarus shook his head: 'I heard nothing and saw nothing. There was nothing, absolutely nothing!'

" 'Are you sure?'

" 'Absolutely sure!'

" 'In that case,' said Jesus (according to Oscar Wilde) 'see to it that you never breathe a word about this to any living soul!' "

Not being a Jew, I was permitted to enter the Mosque of Omar after putting on a colossal pair of slippers over my shoes. I stood gazing at the rock jutting from the floor on which Abraham is said to have tied his son Isaac for the sacrifice which was prevented by an angel of the Lord. . . . The mosque is built on the site where Mohammed's horse, Al Borak, rested for an hour on its flight to heaven. . . .

All those so-called holy places have to be taken not merely with a grain, but with a whole sack of salt. None is genuine or authentic. The most phony place of all is the Church of the Holy Sepulchre which contains the alleged tomb of Christ as well as the hill of Calvary. As late as the year 325 A.D. absolutely nobody knew where the tomb was located. It was the Empress Helen, mother of Constantine the Great, who found it buried sixty feet under a heap of rubble and rock. The site was revealed to her in a dream, a method of research of which modern archaeologists cannot avail themselves. It is she who also built the Basilica or part of it, as well as the Church of the Nativity in Bethlehem above the grotto where Jesus was most certainly *not* born.

The journey to Bethlehem, as per vow, was begun on my bare feet. I put my shoes on again near Rachel's Tomb, another spurious site, and marched the rest of the way in comfort. My fellow traveler was Father Georges Thibault, a Basque, who went from St. Stephen's Convent in Jerusalem to take up a new position in the city of David. Father Thibault's luggage lay astride the back of a donkey which he pulled by a rope. The donkey not only stopped repeatedly, he bolted twice, thus forcing us to go after him in the sweltering heat and bring him back to the narrow path. When we reached Bethlehem at last, Father Thibault was pulling and I was pushing the donkey.

I spent the night in a pilgrim hotel which was run by a Greek who told me that he had made his money in Rochester, N.Y. "I'm returning to

America as soon as I can," he said. "This Bethlehem is not what it is cracked up to be!"

"What's wrong with Bethlehem?"

"Too damn many Greeks, my dear sir! Too damn many Greeks by far!"

I walked on to Hebron the following morning and on the way inspected the ruins of the palace of Machaerus in the dungeon of which Herod's son imprisoned John the Baptist and Salome danced the dance which cost John his head. In Hebron I entered the mosque which is built over the cave of Machpelah containing the tombs of the Hebrew patriarchs and their wives, with the exception of Rachel. At the police post, Captain Edgar Saunders of the Palestinian Military Police introduced me to an Armenian gentleman who owned "a limousine" of the Ford variety. Then back to Jerusalem via the western shore of the Dead Sea and through Hebron and Bethlehem once more.

In Tel Aviv I stayed at the home of Marek Schwartz. Schwartz was an ex-officer who served in the Austrian artillery attached to the Turkish army in Palestine during the First World War. If ever the Israelis get to the point where they honor the memory of their heroes, they ought to bear Marek Schwartz in mind.

Schwartz was ordered by Jamal Pasha to train his batteries on Jerusalem in 1917 and to blow the Holy City to smithereens at the precise moment when General Allenby and his staff would walk in through the Jaffa Gate. In the course of the preceding night Schwartz spiked all the Turkish guns and then ran over to the British lines to surrender. The British promptly arrested him and locked him up. But Schwartz escaped and hid for a year in that ruined Crusaders' castle which stands at the top of the Jordan valley east of Lake Huleh.

At Schwartz' home I met Dr. Shmaryahu Levin, onetime member of the first Russian Duma and Meyer Dizengoff, the first mayor of Tel Aviv, who in 1929 conferred honorary citizenship on me. He took me for a stroll through the city and showed me the surroundings from the top of a hill. It is hard to believe that back in 1926 I saw nothing but sand as far as the eye could reach. Today the city has grown to metropolitan size with shops and apartment houses, banks, schools, a university, many first-class theaters and with a population approaching the million figure while the reddish sand hills outside are now overgrown with orange groves and plantations of all kinds.

From Tel Aviv I walked to Nazareth. On the way to Nazareth in the middle of the Emek valley, then still largely a malarial swamp but now the great agricultural center of Israel with villages and *kibbutzim* stretching in a long string from Mount Carmel to the shores of the Jordan, I heard a British bugle sound the mail call—"A letter from lousy Lou, boys!"—and I entered an old Turkish blockhouse in which was quartered a company of the King's African Rifles, the famous Green Howards. The commanding officer was Captain W. C. Cowper, D.S.O. When he heard that I served in the Guides in the Great War, he exclaimed: "Wasn't Ross MacDonald your colonel? A marvelous soldier, your colonel, but socially impossible!" I spent two days with Cowper and ate British army rations once more.

From Nazareth I walked clear around Lake Galilee and found my way to the confluence of the Jordan and Yarmuk Rivers where Pinchus Ruttenberg had built the first hydroelectric station.

Ruttenberg drove me back south to Jericho and Petra. On the way, following the eastern bank of the river, Ruttenberg told me an episode from his life's story. I had noticed that he always kept his gloves on; at table during mealtime, in the automobile again. I had seen only one person before who had this habit, Georges Clemenceau, who kept his gloves on even in the Chamber of Deputies when he spoke from the rostrum. Monsieur Clemenceau may have suffered from some skin disease, but I dared not ask Ruttenberg the reason why he constantly hid his hands. I had to wait till he told me.

Ruttenberg was a member of the presidium of the social revolutionary party in Russia at the time of the 1905 revolution. In the beginning of that year he and his party decided to petition Czar Nicholas II to grant Russia a modern constitution and a democratically elected parliament. One of their fellow members on the executive committee was a Russian Orthodox priest by the name of Georgii Gapon, a handsome, black-haired individual dressed in a splendid cassock who enjoyed immense popularity amongst the workers as well as in governmental circles.

Father Gapon and Ruttenberg headed the procession of a hundred thousand to the Winter Palace in St. Petersburg where the petition was to be presented to the Czar. The country was seething with discontent. There were strikes everywhere and demands for reform. With religious banners flying and ikons borne aloft, the procession halted before the main entrance to the Winter Palace. Here the vast crowd went on its knees to sing the national anthem. The palace major-domo came out to inform the multitude that only Father Gapon would be permitted to enter for the purpose of presenting the petition to Nicholas.

No sooner had Gapon gone inside and the door was shut behind him when the approaches to the Winter Palace Square were closed off by squadrons of Cossacks. Infantry mounted on the roofs of adjoining buildings trained their Gatling guns on the crowd and began to fire while the Cossacks rushed in swinging their swords and long leather nagaikas. . . . Thousands of innocent people were mowed down.

This happened on January 22, 1905, which is known in Russian history as Bloody Sunday.

Ruttenberg and the other members of the social revolutionary executive fled across the Finnish border and took up residence in a deserted hunting lodge near Terioki. There they remained in hiding till one day Gapon put in an appearance and greeted them as if nothing had happened. They realized at once that their hiding place had been discovered and that Gapon would soon be followed by the police or that he would attempt to lure them back onto Russian soil.

Pinchus Ruttenberg and his companions seized the priest and, constituting themselves into a revolutionary tribunal, accused him of being a secret police agent, convicted him of treason and sentenced him to death by hanging. A rope was tied around his neck and the end thrown over a rafter in the ceiling of the hunting lodge.

But the rope broke and Gapon fell back on the floor. The priest was struggling to his feet when Ruttenberg threw himself on Gapon and after a brief struggle choked him to death.

"From that day [April 11, 1906] till now," the engineer said as we drove through Transjordania, "I have not been able to look at my hands. I have tried to live without gloves, but every time I do I become ill, and would go insane if I persisted in looking at my hands."

With Ruttenberg at the wheel we drove through Transjordania as far as Petra, the mysterious deserted city of the Nabataeans which is entirely palaces, temples and houses, carved from the rock. Then back north as far as the legendary site of the cities of Sodom and Gomorrah.

There are no words to describe the godforsaken dreariness of the area just south of the Dead Sea where Sodom is located. One is 1200 feet below sea level, deeper than any submarine has ever dived below the ocean's surface. It's the "abomination of desolation," mountains of salt standing in a burning desert, the sun so hot that it cuts off your breath like a two-edged sword and no living creature in sight save for some lizards and other creeping things. At nights we could hear the jackals howl from close proximity.

But at dawn it was bitter cold and our sleeping bags were covered with a thin layer of hoarfrost. From the east blew a wind carrying the smell of jasmine.

When I walked in that blistering heat south and west of Sodom, I could not by the widest stretch of the imagination envisage even a thousandth part of the work of reclamation and soil redemption that has been accomplished in that part of the Land of Israel now called the Negev. At the time of my first visit the Negev was still called Turkish crown land. And there is no use saying that Jews of great vision foresaw the future development of the Negev, for they definitely did not. The directors of the Jewish land development agency in Jerusalem to whom I spoke about the Negev shook their heads: "Absolutely nothing can be done with the Negev!" they assured me.

We raced back to Amman, crossed the Allenby Bridge over the Jordan River; I was back in Jerusalem in time to meet Captain Cowper, who transferred me to his own car and carried me to Haifa and along the hard sand beach to Beirut in Syria. In that beautiful city I was the guest of General Maurice Sarrail in the Hotel Unger next door to the Cercle Militaire, the officers' club. The headquarters of the French Expeditionary Force was in the Grand Sérail, the former harem palace of the Turkish governors.

Though petering out, the revolt of the Druses was still a serious matter in Syria. The French had suffered several thousand casualties. Patrols were still being ambushed and having their throats slit. The Druses who had filtered into Damascus in small parties were blown out of the city by a fierce artillery bombardment. Sarrail had called in the Foreign Legion to mop up the countryside. The legionnaires went to work with such savagery as was perhaps never known in French colonial warfare till Algiers in 1961. Seventy-five per cent of the Foreign Legionnaires were Germans. These German boys in French uniforms were taking revenge on the Arabs and Druses for the massacre of German prisoners of war in 1918 at the close of the war against Turkey.

Captain Charles Henriet, adjutant to Sarrail, drove me to Damascus. On the way he showed me how every well and farmhouse was stuffed with dead Arabs and Druses. The corpses lay rotting in piles. The sky was darkened with clouds of flies. . . . The Meiad quarter of Damascus lay in ruins.

When I returned to Beirut, General Sarrail had just been notified that he was recalled. He received me in the Grand Sérail. To a question as to how the Druses had been able to amass so much ammunition and guns as to stage so powerful a revolt, the General took me to a window of his room which looked upon the port.

"Do you see that flag?" he asked pointing to a boat flying the Union Jack.

"That flag," he said, "is the flag of the enemy of France. . . . Without British supplies, the Druse tribesmen could not have lasted a month. Every Druse warrior has a Lee-Enfield rifle and carries a supply of British manufactured hand grenades. Every Druse woman has a string of British gold sovereigns around her neck. . . . And this is the reason I am recalled. I have told the truth about the treacherous machinations of our British allies in stirring up the Druse revolt and carrying on with a ferocity of which the world has no conception. . . . These things are going on behind the scenes, behind the official screens of *entente cordiale* and eternal Anglo-French friendship. . . . "

Back in Paris, while going over the twenty odd daily newspapers one morning, my eye caught an item in the theatrical journal *Comoedia* containing a very peculiar request by the editor. He asked any possible reader who had seen the film *The Big Parade* in the United States to communicate with him immediately. According to rumors, he said, the version of the film as shown in America differed considerably from that of *Le Grande Parade* running at the Cinéma de la Madeleine on the boulevard of the same name. The American version, he claimed, showed an incident which was intended as a slap in the face to the whole French nation. In the American film a French officer was seen to tremble at the sight of an oncoming German infantry attack.

I had seen the picture in New York just a few days prior to my departure and I could not remember any such scene. Perhaps it will be recalled that *The Big Parade*, starring John Gilbert and Renée Adorée, from the script by Laurence Stallings,* dealt with an episode in the battle of Château-Thierry where American troops were heavily engaged in World War I. I wrote *Comoedia* that the rumors were obviously false. No American movie company, I wrote, let alone Laurence Stallings, who was himself grievously wounded in the course of that battle, would knowingly have portrayed anything detrimental to the honor of the French people or army.

*Book reviewer at the *New York World*.

"There is no trembling French officer in the American picture. I even doubt if there exists a special American version of the film at all."

My letter was published in *Comoedia* a few days later. But another letter followed mine in the same column signed by a person with a Scandinavian-sounding name. The second letter writer affirmed that he too had seen *The Big Parade* in New York and that he had been shocked by the disdain for the French army as shown in "the American version." *Comoedia's* editor added a postscript in which he set forth the opinion that his Swedish correspondent was "obviously right" and I just as "obviously wrong." To this he added a few uncomplimentary remarks about the American army.

I wrote back: "*S'il y eût*. . . . If there really was a French officer in the American version who trembled, it was clearly not a case of fear of the Germans, but a deep concern for the young American soldiers whom he saw, without much preparation, throw themselves into the fight against the battle-hardened German veterans of three years' campaigning. . . ."

In printing my second letter *Comoedia's* editor doctored it up a little by leaving off the conditional "*si*" (if), so that in the paper I was made to say the very opposite of what I intended to convey. In his closing paragraph he spoke of my "apology" and "admission" that I had made a mistake.

Again I wrote, but this time a little sharper. I said that I had made no apology and no mistake either. "There was definitely no French officer who trembled." I furthermore advised the *Comoedia* man to stop waving the flag, and challenged the French movie people to produce at least one war picture as good as *The Big Parade*. And that was the end of the debate, at least so I thought.

I went off to the Near East and only learned upon my return that a police inspector had called at the office to ask about my whereabouts, my family relations, country of birth and so forth, the usual rigmarole. Many months went by till one day, as I was about to board a train at the Gare de l'Est, a man with a mustache à la Groucho Marx, dressed in a black suit and wearing a derby hat, handed me a sheaf of papers.

When the train moved off, I sat down to read the document and saw to my amazement that I had an "Act of Accusation" in my hands. *Au nom de la République,* I was charged with having launched "vile insinuations" 1°. against the French people; 2°. against the Actors Equity Society; 3°. against the Association of Scenario Writers; 4°. against the employees of the various French movie companies. . . . I had abused French hospitality, expressed disdain for republican institutions, scoffed at the honor of French womanhood.... In short, or rather not in short for the document was seven pages long, I saw myself described as an undesirable alien and was summoned to appear in police court... "to hear sentence pronounced."

In the police court I lined up with a number of prowlers charged with having committed offenses against public morals in the Bois de Boulogne the night before and heard them sentenced to various stretches in prison. I was fined 10,000 francs for defamation, libel and derogation of the French national character "with costs" which brought the total up to the considerable sum of 20,000 francs, something like $1,000 at the current rate of exchange. My attorneys, Patrick Morgan, an American, and Pierre Goupy, a Frenchman, went into the basement of the Palace of Justice with me and signed a request for an appeal.

Two years passed as French justice ran its course, sending half a dozen individuals to the guillotine and I don't know how many to Devil's Island, when my turn came at last to face the court of appeal.

There were five judges sitting on the bench at the end of the room. On the left of them, in a box all by himself, throned Monsieur le Procureur de la République.

The procureur rose and addressed himself to the chief prosecuting attorney: "*Maître Lémery vous avez la parole.*" My own lawyer bent forward to whisper in my ear: "He is Senator Lémery. He sits in the senate for the island of Haiti. He is particularly vicious when it comes to America or things American.... He was once a candidate for the French ambassadorship to Washington, but was turned down because of a few drops of colored blood in his veins. At least, so it is said.... Whatever you do, keep calm. He will say the most outrageous things in order to make you lose your temper.... That's his usual tactic...."

Maître Lémery walked to the center of the forum, bowed to the judges, and, pointing his finger in my direction: "Gentlemen, I show you the accused: born in Holland; an adherent of a false religion; a citizen of the British empire; employed by an American newspaper; a resident of France; just returned from a journey to Syria; *quel mélange de brutalité*, what a mixture of brutality!"

I jumped to my feet, though the gendarmes tried to push me back into my little bench. "Monsieur," I called out, "my life is an open book. There is nothing unavowable in my life...."

The procureur shouted: "Do you realize to whom you are speaking?"

"Sure I do. I am speaking to him over there, the fellow in the button shoes. . . . "

"Accused, observe the amenities. . . . You are speaking to a senator of France. . . . "

"*Je demande pardon,* I thought the senate assembled in the Palais du Luxembourg. . . . "

From the audience which, I became suddenly aware, was for the greater part made up of cinema actresses and other "arteestes" came shouts of "*A bas le Ku Klux Klan!* Down with the Ku Klux Klan! . . . *Le sale mété-que,* the dirty foreigner!" and so forth.

When order was restored, Maître Lémery once more bowed to the procureur and the judges, and began his discourse by stressing the demoralizing effect of American films on pure and innocent boys and girls. According to him, American movies dealt chiefly with violence, corruption, alcoholism, adultery, crime, perversion, murder and sudden death.

"I point to the accused and show you a typical specimen of the degrading influence of American films. . . . "

My attorney, Maître Goupy, interrupted him at this point: "Is my learned friend aware that my client does not represent the American movie industry?"

"He is a hireling of the yellow Yankee press which is just as evil as the American movies," shot back Lémery.

Loud cheers from the audience!

Then amidst the astonished silence of the judges and everyone else in the courtroom, Lémery revealed to what depths of ignominy and vilification Hollywood descended in its portrayal of life in France.

"When the Americans," exclaimed the Haitian senator, "present a particularly lewd female on their cinematographic screens, they make sure to give her a French name or a French accent. They paint her face, dye her hair and arrange her coiffure in a way which they imagine to be typically French or Parisian. . . . When they picture a debased criminal, a pickpocket, a gigolo, or a lecherous *débauché,* they select an actor whom they can easily, by various false tricks of make-up and travesty, pass off as a Frenchman. . . . Do they want to titillate their audiences with a taste of fiendish sadism, they pounce upon the French Foreign Legion and show our glorious soldiers in the act of cutting the throats of Moroccans, Berbers and Senegalese or practicing other unmentionable cruelties upon their writhing bodies. . . . These brutes," he pointed at me again, "transfer their own beastly instincts to the people of France and draw a psychological compensation from this ignoble substitution.... All they know about Paris, or rather all they tell their American audiences through the medium of the cinema about Paris, is the abject Rue Mouffetard and its neighborhood with its brothels, streetwalkers, male prostitutes, apaches, *souteneurs, voyous,* peddlers of dirty pictures and organizers of nauseating sexual orgies....

"*Voilà l'image de la France* as shown the world by the money-grubbing crowd of Hollywood's film directors," declared Maître Lémery.

He received a thunderous ovation from the courtroom spectators and shouts of "Bravo, bravo!" which the procureur allowed to pass without a word of rebuke or remonstrance.

Lémery had been orating and gesticulating for nearly two hours. The sun was sinking, the shadows in the courtroom lengthened. The slightly discolored spot above the judges' heads, where once hung the crucifix back in the days before the separation of Church and state, had merged with the drab grayness of the plastered wall. Two of the judges were struggling against sleep by rubbing their eyes when the presiding official suddenly interrupted:

"Maître Lémery, you have given the court a most fascinating and learned exposé of the way in which certain foreign interests calumniate and defame all that is good and decent in France.... Yours has been a truly astounding revelation. I trust that the stenographers have noted down your words most carefully so that we may see them reproduced in our great journals of opinion, though I hardly think they will be appreciated at their true value in certain countries across the Atlantic. [Laughter in the courtroom and female shouts of 'Vive Lémery, Vive la France!']

"But Maître Lémery," continued the presiding judge, "may I ask you one question: Do you charge that the accused is personally responsible for all those horrible and in fact uncouth and worthless movies which you have so truly depicted and courageously castigated? ... You have not said a word about the film called *The Big Parade*, nor about the accused's fantastic nerve in daring to use his pen against France and distinguished French artists. . . ."

"Mr. President, I was just coming to that," replied Lémery. "I will presently call the accused and question him concerning his, let me say it mildly, his villainous, scandalous conduct." (Renewed acclaim from the bleachers.)

"Mr. President," I called out, "Maître Lémery goes too far. . . . " The two gendarmes tried to hold me down, but I was on my feet. "Am I not here in a hall of justice in the land of the Declaration of the Rights of Man? Are not the shades of Zola, Condorcet and Voltaire looking down upon us? May I not expect to be treated in a civilized manner in France, the most civilized country in the world? . . . "

"*Silence!*" thundered the procureur. "If you don't keep silent you will be cited for contempt of court."

"Sit down! For heaven's sake, sit down!" urged my counselor. "If you lose your temper that way, only the opposition will benefit. . . . "

"*A bas le Ku Klux Klan! . . . Le salaud Yanqui!*" blared the chorus.

The presiding judge rose and rang a bell to restore order. "Court is adjourned," he said, "till one month from today at two o'clock in the afternoon. At the next session, Maître Lémery, you will kindly conclude your argument, and Maître Goupy, you will take up the defense. . . . "

During the month's delay Pierre Goupy prepared the defense; that is, he made me write the war department in London for a copy of my military discharge papers.

The finale came a month later. It was so typically, comically and at the same time generously French that I recollect it with the greatest satisfaction. While walking to the Palace of Justice on the day of the trial, I asked my attorneys, Goupy and Morgan, what they planned. "Are you going to refute Lémery's attacks on the American movie industry?"

"If the American movie industry is offended or feels itself libeled, let its legal representatives take appropriate action. I am not defending Hollywood, I am defending you!"

"How?"

"We'll let events take their course. But remember one thing: when you are asked to stand up and testify, be sure to keep your left hand in your trouser pocket. And keep it there! Don't let the procureur or anyone else bulldoze you. Keep your hand in your pocket! That's all! Understand?"

Lémery resumed his argument as soon as the proceedings reopened. But he was brief. He merely referred to the word *indigne* (unworthy) which I had used in my last letter to *Comoedia*. I had written: "It is *indigne*, unworthy of you, Mr. Editor, to mutilate and falsify my letter in leaving out the conjunction *si* [if] with which I began my epistle." Lémery sought to insinuate that *indigne* meant something sinister, something criminal or treasonable. A sworn interpreter was summoned and he informed the court that the the word *indigne* meant unworthy and nothing else.

Then Maître Lémery took up his stand before the judges and asked the procureur to call me to the bar of judgment.

"*Accusé, levez-vous!* Accused, stand up!" called the procureur.

I walked over from my poor sinner's bench to the little semicircular fencelike contraption facing the judges.

"*Tirez votre main de votre poche!* Take your hand from your pocket," ordered the procureur. He repeated the command twice more. Lémery, seeing me keep my hand in my pocket, spoke up: "I move," he said solemnly, "that the accused be cited for contempt of court. I have never in all my life seen such unseemly and insolent behavior in a court of law."

These were the last words he spoke.

My lawyer, Pierre Goupy, advanced to the bar and turning half to the judges and half to Lémery and his clique of *gens de robe* and his claque in the courtroom: "*Messieurs,* I present my client, *un soldat de France,* a soldier of France...." And then in a high voice: "He is incapable of taking his hand from his pocket. . . . That hand, *messieurs,* he gave for France.... Native of a neutral country, he volunteered for service in the cause of France.... His hand was shattered in the battle of Villeneuve St. Vaast, which is, as we all know, a village in France.... He placed his very life in the balance for France, I repeat, *messieurs,* for France. . . . I have here a document from the British War Office citing his acts of bravery. He served in an army of a country that was and remains forever *terre française,* French soil, the never-forgotten, dearly loved, ever glorious land of Canada...."

There was nothing in my discharge papers about acts of bravery or any other acts. I had never in my life been in Villeneuve St. Vaast. My left hand, though once crushed, was as good as ever. I had never thought of my military service as performed for France.... I trembled lest the opposition enter into a detailed questioning, but I needn't have worried....

The presiding judge turned to Pierre Goupy: "Maître, I thank you!" To Lémery: "Maître Lémery, the case is dismissed!"

From the rear of the Villa Gabrielle, the house which we rented in St. Germain-en-Laye, twelve miles from Paris, I caught a glimpse now and then of an extremely tall old gentleman with a small white chin beard who walked up and down a beautiful garden with his hands behind his back and his head bent forward in deep meditation. From other neighbors I learned that this solitary giant was the Grand Duke Nikolai Nikolaievich, uncle to Czar Nicholas II and onetime commander in chief of the Russian armies. He waved his hand in friendly salutation whenever he spotted me, and once, on one of his rare appearances in the streets, stopped to chat for a few moments.

Because of the Grand Duke's residence, St. Germain was filled with Russian nobility, princes and princesses, counts and countesses, generals, ambassadors, marshals and such, all ex-, of course, and nearly all reduced to penury and even to near starvation. They lived in garrets and tumble-down old houses dispersed through the various quarters of the town.

His mansion was a meeting place for Russian *émigrés* of the top social rank from all over Western Europe. If not for its poor secondhand furniture, rugs and drapes, one might have called it the last court of the Romanovs. The visitors, as I noticed on the two evenings when I was invited over as a neighbor of His Imperial Highness, still observed the rules of etiquette to which they and their fathers had been accustomed for centuries in the palaces of St. Petersburg, Kiev and Moscow.

About the Russian nobility there was one peculiarity which distinguished them from the nobility of certain other countries I know: they were the least snobbish of all and they liked to talk. In fact each and every one was just burning to tell you his or her life story. We met on the famous terrace or in the Café de la Débarcadère where they dropped in for a glass of coffee or to play a game of cards. In this way I came to know the Count Obudiuwo, Prince Gallitzin, General Miller, General Kutiepov, Prince Piotr Troubetzkoi and Prince Ilya Gorchakov, the last two mere boys, both orphans and straws in the tempest that swept over their country. Both boys studied in Paris at the expense of the Jesuit Order.

The Jesuits looked after the Russian youths in gratitude to the Empress Catherine II who, when Pope Clement XIV dissolved the Society of Jesus in 1775 and every country in Europe, even Spain, expelled its members, gave the Jesuits asylum in Russia. Many of the Russian boys became Roman Catholics and even priests to form a band of missionaries to accompany the armies which some day, they fervently believed, would lead them back to Mother Russia to convert the Slavs from *Pravoslavnaya* to Roman Catholicism.

Though the figure is probably greatly exaggerated, there were, it is said, nearly a million White Russians in Paris in the '20s and '30s. They had their societies and clubs and, of course, their veteran organizations. From Piotr Troubetzkoi I learned that he belonged to a military formation which gathered on Sundays in the forest of Rambouillet where the President of

France has his country house. They drilled with real rifles and machine guns and maneuvered with secondhand armored cars. Who paid for these military operations and equipment? Not the *émigrés* themselves, of course, for they were on the whole as poor as church mice. André Tardieu was their protector and benefactor. An orphan from birth, Tardieu was brought up by Georges Clemenceau and inherited not only the Tiger's aptitude for statesmanship but his hatred of the Bolsheviks.

One Sunday afternoon, in the fall of 1927, all the Russian *émigré* societies in France assembled in Paris, the military phalanx included. They marched up the Champs Elysées to place a wreath on the tomb of the Unknown Soldier under the Arch of Triumph. The hetman of the Don Cossacks and about a hundred of his men, followed by a score of Pre-obrazhensky Guard officers, led off the parade. It was a grand show; especially the patriarch and his staff of censer-swinging and banner-toting archimandrites in their splendid copes made a fine impression on the Parisian working class, the so-called *popu*, which, as everyone knows who has lived in Paris for any length of time, considers the downtown streets and boulevards its private reserve on Sundays.

All might have gone well had not the old generals and the mitred abbots intoned the czarist anthem when they arrived at the Arch.

"*Qu'est-ce que c'est que ça?* What's that?" the workers asked themselves. Since nobody knew, the hymn was taken for a Fascist rallying cry. There was a brief skirmish. The Russians retired in disorder without having accomplished the pious mission on which they had come. The demonstration, perhaps five to ten thousand strong, dispersed ingloriously into the side streets.

As he wandered mournfully down the Avenue Kléber General Eugène Miller from St. Germain spotted me and told me something which brought the tears to his eyes. "In August, 1914," he said, "the French army was defeated at Charleroi and retreated on the Marne. There seemed no way to stem the German avalanche under Von Kluck and the Crown Prince. In that moment of great peril for France, the Czar began his offensive against East Prussia, though the Russian mobilization was by no means complete. This forced the Kaiser to withdraw three whole army corps from the Western front and transfer them to the Eastern front. The Russian army was sacrificed for the sake of France. And France virtually won the war at the Marne.... Hadn't we the right," he asked me, "to commemorate our share in the victory this afternoon?"

After the demonstration's failure on the Champs Elysées, the Russian military formation broke up. The generals waited for "the coming opportunity" and in the meantime grew too old and wobbly on their legs to think of any offensive except on paper. Also they quarreled fiercely amongst themselves. Should they or should they not move to Germany and line up with the Nazis whose Fuehrer already then screamed that he was going to wipe the Bolshevik subhuman creatures off the face of the earth.

Many nobles returned to Russia when the Soviet government declared the doors open to repentant "Whites." Prince Dmitri Mirsky, the fine literary critic, was about the first to go. Alexander Kuprin, author of *Yama* (The Pit), I visited one day together with the Russia-born Joseph Loewinsohn of Atlanta. Kuprin said his nostalgia for Russia was killing him. He soon followed Mirsky and many others. One Russian woman in St. Germain, the Countess Alexandra Tierwin, told me, as we traveled on the commuters' train from Paris one day, that there wasn't a night when she didn't weep out her eyes for Russia. She too went home.

The Russian philosopher and lay theologian, Nikolai Berdiaiev, who did not live in St. Germain, but in the working-class suburb of Clamart, gave me a glimpse of what kind of life the half-starved exiled families left behind. He himself did not run away, but was first imprisoned and then expelled by the Soviet government from the family estate of Belaia Tserkowi owned by his aunt the Countess Branitsky. He said the estate was really a feudal dukedom with a court and tens of thousands of people who lived from the court. There were racing stables with 500 horses on the estate. In springtime hunting parties, dances, reunions and plays were given for the benefit of hundreds of members of the aristocracy of South West Russia. All these nobles, their wives and children, ate in the estate's summer palace: fifteen-course dinners prepared by expert French and Polish cooks and served by a staff of 250 liveried servants and a majordomo. For many families a private house was available the year around. Though Berdiaiev's ancestors were all generals and field marshals and personal friends of the emperors, and he himself in his youth served in the imperial corps of pages, members of the reigning imperial family were never invited to Belaia Tserkowi. The Countess Branitsky and Berdiaiev's mother looked upon the Romanovs as too plebeian and vulgar a crowd to associate with.

Berdiaiev had no sympathy with the monarchist exiles. He believed in socialism "because," as he said, "I understand socialism." He was one of the most prolific writers on Christian ethics and philosophy. His books have been translated into a dozen languages. With the aid of that great and good American, John R. Mott, the head of the Y.M.C.A., Berdiaiev set up the Academy of Philosophy in Paris, which still exists. To this place he invited both Catholic and Protestant scholars and thus may be said to have brought about the first genuine ecumenical encounter.

As a speaker Berdiaiev also appeared frequently at the Union de la Verité where I saw amongst his hearers such men as Paul Claudel, Stafford Cripps, Paul Valéry, Jacques Maritain, André Gide, Etienne Gilson, Emmanuel Mounier, Leonhard Ragaz and many other philosophers, theologians and statesmen, French, German, Swiss and British, but never an American, though the sessions were open to the public.

One day as we strolled in the Parc Monceau, Berdiaiev said: "There are two great organizations in this world which seek the Kingdom of God, the Christian Church and the communist party, but of the two only the communist party works at it.

"Communism always imitates its bitterest opponents; it has become a church in turn. The communist who is wholly wrapped up in the service of the idea, capable of immense sacrifices and of a disinterested enthusiasm, is the heir of that Christian education in which our Western society has been steeped for ages. . . . Everything in the communist movement, its methodology, its proselytizing, its totalitarianism, its doctrinaire infallibility and intolerance has been taken from the Church. . . . "

In mentioning Berdiaiev I merely want to show how valuable was my wholly unsought acquaintance with different groups of Russian exiles. When Sunday night came around and the *World's* correspondents, Arno Dosch-Fleurot, Alfred Murray and Georges Rudlov gathered in the office at number 47 Avenue de l'Opéra to bemoan the scarcity of news, I was often instrumental in cooking up a good and true Russian story for "Blue Monday." I don't know how many times I transmitted an announcement from the Russian general staff in exile or the Orthodox patriarchate, also in exile, that important events were about to transpire in Russia or amongst the Russian exiles in Turkey, Yugoslavia and France. It was nearly always: in another month, in another week, in another day or so that the White armies would assemble somewhere in Eastern Europe to launch the grand crusade for the liberation of Mother Russia.

I called for Berdiaiev one evening and took him from his cottage in

Clamart to the Salle Cadet to hear Ilya Ehrenburg who was going to explain the situation inside Russia to the members of the International Committee of Writers and Artists. Berdiaiev and I sat in the second row between André Gide on one side and Andrée Viollis, the famous newspaper correspondent, on the other.

Gide chain-smoked Gauloises Jaunes, the cheapest cigarettes obtainable. The chairman of the evening was Louis Aragon, the poet. Next to him sat Paul Vaillant-Couturier, Pierre Drieu la Rochelle and Ehrenburg.

Instead of discussing conditions in the Soviet Union, Ehrenburg attacked Drieu for being a Fascist. Gide eyed *Izvestia's* correspondent (Ehrenburg) with looks of unconcealed contempt. Though admittedly an excellent writer, he was classed by his own fellow communists as *un fils à papa*, "papa's darling boy." He was suspected of being in direct touch with Stalin. . . .

Unlike the others who advanced to the rostrum to speak, Ehrenburg remained seated when his turn came. He insisted on being addressed as *Maître*. He sneered at the old Russian intelligentsia and attributed a purely social function to literature by saying that a pair of shoes was of infinitely greater value than Shakespeare and Tolstoy. He jumped from one subject to another, but seemed most concerned about a lecture he had given at the Lycée Duruy where the students had dared to snicker a little at his French pronunciation. Gide could not stand the man's snobbishness and arrogance. He got up and left, snorting with indignation. . . .

At the close of the meeting Paul Vaillant-Couturier came down from the platform to shake hands. "Did you hear that Gide is going to visit the Soviet Union? When he returns he will join the French communist party. . . . Isn't that significant?"

"He will probably go to Russia, but don't be too sure that he will join your party."

"Why not?"

"Have you ever been to Gide's house?"

"No, have you?"

"I have, and I can tell you that the inhabitant of such an apartment will not quickly find himself at ease in the Soviet Union. Gide has been accustomed to great luxury from his youth. No matter how much he sympathizes with the Russian revolution, the material conditions and the lack of freedom of expression in Russia are bound to disgust him. . . ."

"*Ah, non!* Not Gide!"

"*On verra!* We will see!"

We did see. Gide went to Russia and wrote one of the most scathing attacks on Stalin and the Stalinist period ever published.

My first meeting with André Gide came about when I received a cable from Meyer W. Weisgal, the editor of *The New Palestine*, the house organ of the Zionist Organization of America: "Please ask Gide for an article on Palestine." His telephone did not answer, so I went to his home. Gide lived then on the Rue des Champs just off the Boulevard St. Michel near the top of the Luxembourg Gardens. He opened the door himself. We soon laughed heartily about my mistake.

"Obviously you've come to the wrong Gide. I have never been to Palestine and I never write articles for magazines. It's my uncle Charles who, as professor of social economy at the Sorbonne and president of the Christian socialist movement, takes a deep interest in the Palestine question.... I understand he has just recently paid a visit to the Holy Land.... But let me warn you, if you see *l'oncle* Charles, you had better not mention that you spoke to his nephew...."

"Why shouldn't I?"

"*L'oncle* Charles is a strict Calvinist.... I am not, I'm afraid...."

That is also the way (by requesting articles) that I met Joseph Caillaux, prime minister and minister of finance in different cabinets; Anatole de Monzie, rector of the university; Aristide Briand, the foreign minister; André Spire, the poet; Edmond Fleg, another poet who is still living in one of the most beautiful apartments in Paris on the Quai aux Fleurs from where he looks on the whole expanse of the Cathedral of Notre Dame across the river; and Ferdinand Buisson, a Nobel peace prize winner, who was the author of a book on Castellio, Calvin's opponent. The Nazis traced and burnt every copy of Buisson's book but two. One of the remaining copies is in the library of St. Pierre's Cathedral in Geneva; the other stands right in front of me as I write these words.

The *World*'s Sunday editor, Louis Weitzenkorn, published articles by all these men. The other correspondents were reluctant to go and ask for articles because of the miserably low compensation they were allowed to offer the authors. Letters requesting articles received no reply. I took it upon myself to call on the authors in person, first to ask for an article, later to bring them their checks. Everyone received me with the most exquisite courtesy especially when they got their reward, except, I must say, Joseph

Caillaux; he raved like a wild man because the *World*'s editor by way of introducing one of his articles had prefaced it with a brief biographical note in which the fact was mentioned that Caillaux' wife had shot and killed Gaston Calmette, the editor of *Figaro*.

The relationship with Daladier and Herriot was a different one; we were *frères maçons*, lodge brothers. What this meant in the days of the Popular Front, of which they were the leaders, can be imagined when I say that in the lodge they frequently gave the brethren the low-down on the international situation.

Theodore Dreiser I saw several times at the home of Ludwig Lewisohn. James Joyce we all went to see one evening in the dining room of the Hotel Lutetia on the Boulevard Raspail. It was like watching the animals at the zoo. Joyce didn't say a word and I couldn't blame him, it was all too ridiculous for words: half a dozen reporters with notebooks poised waiting to hear him ask for the salt shaker. His Irish voice was said to be a marvel. Nobody, not even a genius like Joyce, can drop pearls of wisdom with an Irish flavor at the word of command.

Sholem Asch, on the other hand, invited a number of friends to his home in Bellevue near the Meudon forest whenever he was about to finish a book. One night he read us snatches from *The Nazarene* in Yiddish: *Reb Jeshuah hot ongeton sein groessen weissen talis.* In Maurice Samuel's English translation this phrase became: "The Lord put on his great white robe." Quite a difference! But it was this difference which made the book!

The historian Hendrik Willem van Loon never failed to look us up when he came to Paris. During the '20s and '30s he commuted between New York and the town of Veere on the island of Walcheren in Holland's Zealand province where he dwelt in a house dating from the Middle Ages. Van Loon was of enormous physique, but his heart was still bigger. When in trouble every broken-down Dutch sailor or ship jumper in New York went automatically in search of Van Loon. He was never too busy to cross over to Ellis Island to help them get straightened out with the immigration authorities. I don't know another person in the whole world who had so many destitute individuals of all nationalities on his pay roll. Several remained on his staff, so to speak, for years. When he died he bequeathed half a dozen of his most deserving customers to me, or, rather, they bequeathed themselves. They still come to tell me stories about the good Dr. van Loon.

Once in a while I visited an upstairs room at the Closerie des Lilas at the corner of the Montparnasse and St. Michel boulevards with some artists of my acquaintance: Leopold Gottlieb, Arthur Szyk, Soutine, Cassou, Pascin, Vlaminck, Zucker and Piet Mondrian. Except for Jacques Zucker who now lives in New York and Jean Cassou who became director of the Musée de l'Art Moderne, these men have all preceded me to "the land o' the leal."

"There's nae sorrow there, John.... The day is aye fair, John, in the land o' the leal," sang Carolina Nairne. I hope that painters of genius like Mondrian meet with a little more appreciation in the land o' the leal than they got in the paradise of mediocrity and smugness which our world has become. The fate of the truly great artists is enough to make one shudder. Rembrandt was buried at the expense of the "commissioners for the poor." Van Gogh died of starvation. Pascin killed himself. Soutine was carried in a coffin to the hospital for an operation when it was too late. Modigliani's girl friend jumped from the roof.... Mondrian would willingly have given one of his masterpieces for one cup of coffee and a bun....

The best friend I had amongst the artists was Max Band, who is listed in the art encyclopedias as one of the "founders of the Ecole de Paris." He is still with us, *baruch ha Shem*. But Max Band was also at a low ebb when a committee of Americans residing in Paris back in 1934 commissioned him to do a portrait of F.D.R. In 1940 he escaped as by miracle from Paris and made his way to the U.S.A.

What's peculiar about Max Band's art? Like Van Gogh he is a God-seeker. Every still life of his conveys the feeling of a religious poem. He has this in common with Rembrandt, that in the amazing blend of light and dark every child he paints seems to step straight from the pages of the Bible. From the luminous eyes of his men and women goes forth a stream of sorrow and *Weltschmerz*. His art has that indefinable quality which the Bible calls the beauty of holiness. When Mrs. Roosevelt saw Band's portrait of her husband she stood silent for a time and then said: "Here is something nobody else ever caught: the President's inner smile."

When you come to his cottage in Hollywood, whether it is Martin Buber, Joseph Schildkraut, Mordecai Kaplan, Gregor Piatigorsky or Bruno Walter that's sitting for him, you will, even before you enter, be struck by the noise of laughter and joy. For Band is the greatest raconteur I know, in seven languages at that.

On my way back from the Near East to Paris, I landed at Naples and at once proceeded to Rome where Filippo Turati, the secretary-general of the Fascist party, took me to the Palazzo Venezia. In the Venezia, Turati turned me over to Emilio Mascia, the chief of the press department of the Ministry of Foreign Affairs. Mascia led me to the Duce's chamber and left me, without a word of introduction, standing alone in Mussolini's presence. When I said: *"Bonjour, Excellence!"* the Duce looked up from his desk and barked at me: "Why do you have a correspondent in Lugano? Why all the mystery-mongering? You Americans, you think you are very sly, but you can't fool me. . . ."

He referred to George Slocum of the *London Daily Herald* who was on the lookout at Lugano just across the Swiss border for prominent Italian liberals and socialists fleeing from Fascist daggers.

"Slocum reported to your paper that Fascist gangsters, Fascist *gangsters*, mind you, broke into the homes of Italian scholars and destroyed their private libraries. This is a lie! Nobody was maltreated. Besides, we don't burn books. We write them. The entire Italian nation is writing a new page in history. When you foreign correspondents want to find out what goes on in Italy, why don't you come to Rome? We have nothing to hide. Why do you pick up rumors and gossip from runaway cowards in Switzerland? Here in Rome is the place to come for information. . . ."

"Well, as you can see for yourself, Signor Mussolini, I have come to Rome, here I am. . . ."

"Oh, no! You don't get an interview out of me that way. I gave an interview to Bolitho,* and look what he made of it. A series of twelve articles in the *New York World* on 'The Truth About Fascism'. . . . Lies, lies, lies from beginning to end. . . . I tell you the interview is dead. The bad journalist Bolitho killed it."

"Whose head is that, Signor Mussolini?" I asked, pointing to a human skull grinning at me from the corner of the Duce's enormous writing table.

He laughed a big round boyish laugh. "No, it's not Bolitho's skull, if that is what you thought. . . . And more's the pity. The fellow ought to have his head chopped off. . . . Incidentally, what is that woman correspondent of yours doing here in Rome? What's her name. . .Miss Baskerville. . . . She writes pretty good detective stories, I understand. What else does she write?"

*William Bolitho, author of *Twelve Against the Gods, The Trial Of Landru,* and other books.

"She's mainly occupied with Vatican affairs!"

"What is there to write about the Vatican?"

"Your Excellency ought to know, you wrote a whole book about the Vatican. . . ."

"You mean my book *The Cardinal's Mistress?* Don't mention it! It's gone and forgotten. . . ."

"Where did Your Excellency learn to speak French so flawlessly? I am really astonished. Most Italians do a lot of oo-ooing like Napoleon's mother who said *'pourvou que cela doure'* [instead of *pourvu que cela dure*], if only this lasts!"

This brought another big laugh. . . . "It takes practice," said Mussolini. "I lived in Switzerland. I had public debates in Lausanne and Geneva with Emile van der Velde (secretary-general of the Second International), with Lenin, with De Brouckère, with Trotsky, with Eduard Bernstein. . . . I wiped the floor with all of them."

"But you were on their side then as a socialist, weren't you?"

"Yes, but those men lacked the courage of their convictions. . . . They were without initiative. . . . I alone took the bull by the horns. . . . I am the only man to have consummated a great revolution without accepting the revolutionary doctrine of Marx. . . . Were you in Italy before my assuming the direction of things? No? Well, people who were here before 1921 do not recognize the country. It's a new nation that has come upon the scene. . . . What do you really want to know of me? Let me rather ask you a question: What do you think of the Italian people? No, not about their souls or their philosophy. What do you think of their looks, their appearance? Did you see any beggars on the streets of Naples?"

"Now that you ask, Signor Mussolini, I must confess, here in Rome I've a feeling that everybody is dressed in his Sunday best. The Romans seem much better dressed than the Parisians."

"I am glad you said that. That's the esthetic sense of the Italians. . . . No other people has so high an artistic sense, so refined a taste. . . . Only this national quality, it must be taken into account, has both its good points and its drawbacks. It's bad for instance when you have to build an army, as I am doing now. I need an army of lions. All I get is regiments of opera singers. . . . Every Italian rear-rank buck private wants to look like a stage admiral. . . . It's impossible to gratify their ambitions. . . . Italy represents the proletarian amongst the nations of the earth. We are the poorest country in Europe. We have no coal, no wheat to speak of, no steel, no oil, no colonies, except some worthless deserts in Africa. The others have all the wealth, all the well-being.... Look at England.... She owns half the world.... She has far more than she can take care of...."

"Signor Mussolini, I am to confine myself to writing about your private life, your family, your hobbies, things of that sort. No politics!"

"*Va bene*! Because I said that about England, please, don't put me down as an Anglophobe. I'm not an Anglophobe. I am an Anglomaniac. I admire the English tremendously, I envy them.... My family? Well, you know where I was born of course. I was born in Predappio and my father was a blacksmith, Alessandro Mussolini, a great and good man and a revolutionary. Do you know that my father once planned to emigrate to America? What do you think would have become of me in that event?"

"An actor, a journalist, a politician maybe...."

"Not President of the United States?"

"No, that would be impossible: a President of the U.S.A. must be native-born.... That's the law...."

"What about breaking the law? I did it here in Italy...."

"I wouldn't try it in America.... They don't joke about such things in the United States.... America is a democracy...."

"So what? Democracies come and go.... I talked about democracy myself as long as it suited my purpose. But the impetus of my policy is not derived from democratic or philanthropic principles. I admit that I am animated solely by my love of glory and of Italy. Democrats have the same ambitions, but they are hypocrites. They won't own up to it. They talk of the common weal, but they feather their own nests first. We can't afford such waste in a poor country like Italy.... I advance straight to my goal. I eliminated all my adversaries because their ambitions and aspirations stood in the way to my own power and fame.... You remember the story of Caesar looking down from the Pyrenees on a Spanish village when someone asked: 'Wouldn't you rather be first in that village than second in Rome?' Caesar replied: '*Aut Caesar, aut nullus*. Either Caesar or nothing....' That's my motto also....

"You can form an estimate of my father's character when you consider that he named me after Benito Juarez, the Mexican revolutionary leader. My brother Arnaldo was named for Arnaldo da Brescia, a great adversary of the temporal power of the Popes and a republican....

"You want to know about my hobbies? I have many hobbies," he went on in the same breathless tempo, as he rose from his chair and started to pace up and down the room. I saw that in spite of his elevated boots he was but a short stocky peasant with the bent legs of a worker of the soil.

"I like to play with the lions in the zoo, that's one of my hobbies. They communicate something of the fearlessness of their spirit to me.... And then, I have one great hobby, which I've had all my life, I read one canto of Dante before going to sleep.... But I've never yet been able to stop with one canto.... One hour with the divine poet and I forget all my troubles; I am a new man every morning.... Of course, I also play the violin...."

"Signor Mussolini, this is absolutely new. I'm sure nobody in the whole world knows about this...."

"What is that you say? Nobody knows? Let me call for my violin.... I'll play for you...."

"Could we have a picture of yourself in the act of playing the violin?"

"Certainly! I'll call Mascia. He will summon a photographer...."

He put the violin under his chin and played Tartini's *Adagio*. The next day a courier brought a photograph to the Albergo d'Inghilterra, the hotel where I was staying. It showed the Duce fiddling while Rome... didn't burn as yet. On the side was written: *A mon cher collègue*... "To my dear colleague...." The autograph I cut off, but even then the picture was too large for any mailbox. It had to be rolled up and was duly published in the *Evening World* full-page size....

To visit me at the Albergo d'Inghilterra came the Duce's brother, Arnaldo, who was to commit suicide a few years later. Unlike his brother, Arnaldo Mussolini had remained a socialist. He told me with a sad face that all the talk about Fascism's imperial grandeur and invincibility was a sorry illusion. About his brother's ambitions of power and conquest he could only shake his head: "The future of Fascism? Blood, blood, blood ... the whole experiment will end in a terrible blood bath."

"Why should it?" I asked. "The Duce seems to enjoy the confidence of some of the world's leading statesmen.... Winston Churchill said that if he was an Italian he would certainly be a follower of Mussolini.... Austin Chamberlain calls himself the Duce's friend. The British press lords—Northcliffe, Rothermere, Beaverbrook—show great sympathy for your brother's views. Even Bernard Shaw gives him high recommendation...."

"What good is that?" asked Arnaldo in turn. "Benito will be deserted by everybody when the chips are finally down. He will stand all alone. You watch!"

I did watch. I visited Rome several times in years to come. Outwardly the pomp and circumstance went into ever higher gear; glorious parades, wonderful military bands, arches of triumph, fiery discourses from the Venezia's balcony and boiling multitudes shouting: "Duce, Duce, Duce!" When he was gradually but irresistibly forced into Hitler's camp by the persistent refusal of the Western statesmen to pay the slightest heed to Italy's needs in her deteriorating social and economic condition, the Duce's face hardened. He lost his sense of humor. The chin went up higher and higher. It was like keeping a stiff upper lip. It is true, of course, that he always pulled a stern face in public. But that was mere make-believe, part of the game, part of the role he played. After Hitler's accession to power, Mussolini became uneasy, nervous, visibly ill at ease. Long before others he saw the abject role he would be called upon to play under Hitler, a stooge of the Gestapo which was ordered to plunge a dagger into France's back. But he could no longer break away from the fateful alliance. With sadistic glee Ribbentrop ordered Mussolini to execute his favorite daughter's husband, Galeazzo Ciano, and wept as much as Ciano when told that as a traitor he must stand with his back to the firing squad.

In spite of all his histrionics, I must say that I rather liked Mussolini personally. Especially in the beginning of his reign. He was always ready to talk, always accommodating, always genial. "I won't have you stay at that Albergo d'Inghilterra again. Do you like it there? I know the place. It's full of German monsignori and such people.... Go to the Hotel Excelsior.... Tell them from me that you are the guest of the Italian government. Wait a minute till I give you a note to the management...."

It was not only to me that he was kind; he liked to talk with newspapermen in general. I know at least a dozen journalists, not necessarily Fascists themselves, who were captivated by the Duce's charm and brilliant conversation. It was quite evident that he had read a book or two, unlike Hitler who boasted that he read only Karl May's stories of North American Indians. In 1928 he did me the great favor of informing me that Cardinal Pietro Gasparri, the papal secretary of state, and he were negotiating to bring the so-called Roman Question to an end, so that I was able to announce the outline of the Lateran Treaty of 1929 nearly six months before the Pope's isolation in the Apostolic Palace was brought to a termination.

An incident that has been totally forgotten, or at least never been publicized, occurred in 1934, a few weeks after Adolf Hitler murdered Ernst Roehm and others of his associates in the Nazi party. I asked the Duce about his reference to Adolf Hitler as *ein schwaetzeriger Moench*, a monkish blabbermouth, which he had made to the correspondent of the *Reichpost* of Vienna. I learned then of the immense service he had rendered France and was also convinced that Mussolini would much sooner have stood on the side of France in the bloody disturbance that was soon to follow.

In July, 1934, the Fuehrer suddenly flew to Italy, met Mussolini at the airport of Venice, and after two hours' conversation raced back to Berlin. On that occasion Hitler solicited Mussolini's aid and co-operation in a venture that, had the Duce accepted, would have sent the world spinning out of its course. The Fuehrer proposed nothing less than a nocturnal attack by the combined German and Italian air forces on Paris and Lyons, the harbors of Saint-Nazaire, Le Havre and Marseilles, the Longwy-Briey steel manufacturing district, the Schneider-Creusot armament mills and France's chief centers of communication. Paris itself was to be blanketed with poison gas while the fleet of bombers rained showers of incendiary and high explosive bombs. The larger part of the population, the government and the employees in the service were to be exterminated in a six hour bombardment, the bombers moving up in waves at twenty-minute intervals.

Mussolini indignantly refused to be a partner in this undertaking and dismissed Hitler with the prediction that such an attack would be followed by a world rising in arms against Germany and such a commotion in the German soul that the young Nazi regime would be swept into the garbage can.

As he came from the airport Mussolini was met by some newspaper correspondents, the *Reichpost*'s correspondent amongst them to whom he remarked that he had just talked to *ein schwaetzeriger Moench*.

"And you notified France?" I asked.

"I notified Henri Franklin-Bouillon [the leader of one of the right-wing parties in France] whom I knew to be staying at the Lido-Venice at the time. M. Bouillon rushed to Paris and in turn informed the French prime minister and foreign minister Pierre Laval."

In return for this information Laval gave Mussolini a free hand in the conquest of Ethiopia, and when the Italo-Ethiopian war broke out it was Laval who, to the entire world's amazement, refused the British navy the use of the French harbors of Toulon and Bastia (on Corsica) as bases for an eventual anti-Italian blockade.

The French people never learned of the Fuehrer's planned sneak attack till after the Second World War. But by then all the dramatis personae, Hitler, Goering, Laval and Mussolini had died violent deaths.

At one time Mussolini said: "Tell me honestly: do the Jews in Palestine really talk their ancient language again?" When I said that the little children in Jerusalem's streets call each other in the language of Isaiah, Mussolini exclaimed: "Unbelievable. . . . That nation is the most unpredictable in history. They were the toughest people to handle in the days of the Roman empire. . . . In Russia, which was overrun by the Mongols, the conquerors withdrew leaving not one soldier behind. Yet for hundreds of years the Russians paid their tribute annually. A caravan loaded with treasure made the trip to Karakorum once a year. . . . On the other hand, the Romans were always in trouble with the Jews. The best legions had to be stationed in ancient Palestine to keep the Jews from revolting. . . . The ablest Roman generals had to be summoned from the ends of the earth, from Britain even, to suppress the Jewish revolt when it did break out. . . . Funny thing, I had a man here from Palestine the other day, a journalist, Ittamar Ben Avi, who told me to take down the Arch of Titus because of the inscription *Judea Capta*. He wanted me to change the words to *Judea Liberata*.

" 'And if I don't?' I asked him.

" 'If you don't, we Jews will come and do it ourselves some day,' replied Ben Avi."

He always inquired about the circumstances in which his old socialist friends lived in their Parisian exile. When Laval and Pétain took over the government in France for Adolf Hitler and shipped the Italian exiles back to their homeland in the expectation that Mussolini would do like Francisco Franco, the Duce let Laval believe that they were executed. In reality, Pietro Nenni, Malatesta, Augusto Turati and many others were given cottages and villas in the Tivoli district where Mussolini frequently visited his old comrades at nights. . . .

The only time that the Duce left Italian territory (before he made his pact with Hitler) was on the occasion of the International Conference at Lausanne. There must have been 50 foreign newspapermen on the railway platform to see him arrive. We were all frisked for arms by the

Swiss police. As Mussolini hove in sight followed by Grandi, Ciano, De Bono and all the other members of his cabinet, he walked close by the ranks of the spectators. He greeted many newspapermen by name. When he spotted George Slocum, whom he couldn't miss because of the (London) *Herald* correspondent's fiery red beard, Mussolini exclaimed: "Hello, Signor Slocum! How are the Bolsheviks?"

"We're not Bolsheviks!" Slocum called back.

"Oh, I must be wrong!" said the Duce, shrugging his shoulders.

"You certainly are wrong," retorted Slocum, "and this is not the first time.... Nor will it be the last time, I am afraid...."

CHAPTER VIII

Shadow of Coming Events

As DID NEARLY EVERYONE else in the France of 1927, I believed that the Weimar Republic had completely disarmed. All the troops had been demobilized and a great deal of war materiel destroyed. The German fleet lay at the bottom of Scapa Flow. No new keels were put down and the shipyards were idle. Allied control commissions, going up and down the country, certified to their governments that their inspections had brought to light nothing that could be interpreted as violation of the terms of the Versailles Treaty. German popular sentiment was definitely antiwar if not antimilitaristic. Ludendorff had started a movement among reactionary war veterans preaching revenge, but his mobs of nationalists were chased off the streets of Munich and Berlin. There was never before such a stream of peace literature—books, pamphlets and periodicals—as came out of Germany in the mid-'20s. Huge German pilgrimages visited the French battlefields to swear solemnly on the graves of their own and the former enemy's war dead that there would never again be war.

In the summer of 1927 the myth of a reborn peaceful Germany exploded with a loud bang. A German of aristocratic ancestry, who served as professor of political science and philosophy at the University of Zurich, blew it wide open. This man, Dr. Friedrich Wilhelm Foerster, today a resident of New York, placed a pamphlet of his own composition entitled *Germany's Secret Rearmament* before every delegate to the League of Nations' general assembly in Geneva ten minutes before the session opened.

Germany's foreign minister, Dr. Gustav Stresemann, almost had an apoplectic fit when he read Dr. Foerster's pamphlet and the meeting broke up in confusion. Dr. Foerster revealed that for several years Germany had been busy manufacturing tanks in...Russia, notably at the Krupp Works in Kazan on the Volga which started operating immediately after the conclusion of the Rapallo Pact between the Soviet Union and Germany in 1921. Under cover of the peaceful democratic Republic of Weimar, German big business had worked out and set in motion a vast plan of rearmament and remilitarization. Not only was Krupp manufacturing tanks in Russia, but also guns and airplanes and turning out a vast quantity of small arms.

Foerster's revelations met with a wild outburst of denunciation and invective on the part of the German Right, which was in 1927, as it is now, made up of the Rhineland's big business concerns, the banks and the Centrum Party of which Konrad Adenauer's Christian Democratic Union is the latter-day offspring. A few years later in 1935, Josef Goebbels, Hitler's propaganda minister, referred to Dr. Foerster's revelations in a mass meeting in Berlin where, amidst a storm of laughter and applause, he praised Germany for having led the whole world by the nose as early as 1927 by rebuilding its army in secret.

I was in Zurich at the home of Leonhard Ragaz, the leader of Europe's religious socialist movement, when the storm over Foerster's revelations broke. Though a pastor of great promise at the Basler Munster and a professor of theology at the University of Zurich, Ragaz had quit his mansion on the Zuercher Berg and gone to dwell in a working-class district. He resigned his professorship and opened a People's University in the garden of the tenement house where he took up residence.

To him flocked students and scholars from all over Europe. He brought Thomas Masaryk to lecture in Zurich; also Martin Buber, Gustav Landauer, Bertrand Russell, Barthélemy de Ligt, Henri Roser, Rauschenbusch and Karl Barth. Barth was amongst the first collaborators on the *Neue Wege*, the periodical which Ragaz founded, edited and published for 40 years.

"Unless the allies take prompt action," said Ragaz when the Foerster revelations hit the newsstands, "the remilitarization of Germany will go from strength to strength and another world war becomes a virtual certainty. . . . " Ragaz' hope was vested in the League of Nations and in men like Lord Robert Cecil, George Lansbury, the British labor leader, and Thomas Masaryk of Czechoslovakia, whose country, Ragaz predicted even then, would be one of the first to be put under pressure by a new German militarism. Ragaz thought that an aroused public opinion could still rally the nations against the German militarists and prevent them from carrying their conspiracy to its logical conclusion. But on this point he was proven wrong.

The world turned against Friedrich Wilhelm Foerster. Germany was the poor benighted victim whose genuine peaceful aspirations and striving had been called into question. Even Robert Dell, the Paris correspondent of the *Manchester Guardian* and *The Nation* of New York, a man of great influence at that time, called Foerster to task for having disturbed the growing atmosphere of peace.

"The world *wants* to be fooled," says an old German adage. And so the world *was* fooled! The German Right succeeded in a very short time in burying the Foerster revelations out of sight. And the secret rearmament of Germany went on till Hitler came to power in 1933 when it was no longer secret.

I was only half convinced and went on from Zurich to Berlin. Although tanks and planes were being constructed in faraway Kazan, I thought something of the resurgent militarism must be visible here and there in the Reich also. I saw absolutely nothing in a military way to cause alarm. I smelled poverty in Germany and saw it, mass misery and hopelessness on all sides. Considering that years had elapsed since the termination of the First World War, I was struck by the sight of the large number of crippled, blind and invalid soldiers still dressed in their tattered uniforms dragging themselves around on small pushcarts or hobbling on crutches. In Paris the authorities kept the so-called *Gueules Cassées* out of sight because of their hideous aspect. In Berlin it was the other way around. The maimed, the halt and the blind seemed everywhere; they mingled with the crowds on the busy streets, walked in the parks, stood at street corners with hands outstretched or a tin cup at their feet waiting for alms from passers-by. People were hungry, children were hungry. Even a sackful of deflated marks did not suffice to buy one cup of coffee. If you sat in a restaurant close to the street window, men and women going by threw a furtive look in your direction, making you feel ashamed of your own affluence. A man walked up to me in the vicinity of the Schlesinger railway station. He wore a neat dark suit, though threadbare and shiny. On his lapel was the ribbon of the Iron Cross first class. "I've been following you," he said. "It took me an hour to work up enough courage to address you. But I cannot go on. I am too weak. And I wouldn't ask for help if it were not for my wife and children. We have literally not a crumb of bread in the house. . . . "

I thought: these people have learned their lesson; they will never go to war again. I noticed that many who were evidently veterans wore the emblem of the tiny bronze rifle broken in twain on their lapels, denoting membership in the *Nie Wieder Krieg* (Never Again War) movement. If a secret army was in course of formation where was it?

Under the terms of the peace treaty, the Reichswehr was permitted to keep only 100,000 men under arms. Divided over the barracks of a hundred cities through the length and breadth of the country there could hardly be more than a couple of thousand soldiers in Berlin. Every day around noon, a Reichswehr company marched up and down Unter den Linden from the Brandenburger Tor to the vicinity of the old palace where President von Hindenburg was in residence in a house which flew the republican flag. Nobody stopped to look at the changing of the guard.

There were hardly any civilians at the ceremony in midtown at the small Grecian temple east of the Friedrichstrasse-Linden intersection where they once buried their Unknown Soldier. It was a day of commemoration of the Battle of Tannenberg, in which Hindenburg destroyed the Russian armies in the first months of the Great War. A *Schupo* said: "If you want to see the President, stand right here." Presently a black-helmeted Reichswehr detachment, about two hundred strong, marched down the street and took up a position in front of the Unknown Soldier's shrine. Almost immediately a limousine arrived and discharged Hindenburg and General von Mackensen. The President wore the old-fashioned spiked helmet, the *Pickelhaube*. The handle of his saber lay in the crook of his left arm. Mackensen wore the busby with the *Totenkopf* emblem of the Death-Head hussars, and a uniform with blue horizontal stripes across the chest.

A bugle sounded. A monocled infantry lieutenant, whose torso seemed squeezed in a corset, stepped into the center of the *carré* and called the parade to attention in a voice unmistakably Prussian. It rasped like a knife on the grindstone. Four or five officers unsheathed their sabers, advanced and saluted the President. Not a word was spoken. Then five notes on the bugle and, in a movement of such perfect precision as to take my breath away, the troops presented arms. They stood absolutely motionless like so many statues, their white gloves on the butt end of their rifles bisecting their bodies in a straight unbroken line. Stolid, impassive, Hindenburg entered the shrine. Somebody handed him a wreath of roses which he laid on the tombstone in the center. Then the band struck up: "Der gute Kamerad." The civilian bystanders uncovered their heads, some women daubed their eyes with their handkerchiefs. Now, I thought, will come "Deutschland, Deutschland Ueber Alles," but there was no more music. Hindenburg and Mackensen merely saluted the tomb by lifting their marshals' batons, and walked back to their car. The ceremony was over. The war spirit is dead, I said to myself.

My next call was at the press department of the foreign office on the Wilhelmstrasse where I was shown into the office of a *Ministerialdirektor*. The gentleman asked me: "Have you also come to probe our wounds?" He asked the question in Dutch. But it was spoken in such perfect grammatical Netherlandish, each syllable so carefully enunciated as no native Hollander could ever imitate without feeling ridiculous.

I asked: "Are you a Hollander?"

"No," replied the *Ministerialdirektor*, "but I served as an attaché at the German embassy in The Hague. I married a daughter of Mynheer Staal, the leader of the liberal democratic representation in the Dutch parliament." He then asked: "What's your dominant impression?"

"I have been only a day or so in Berlin," I said, "but I am profoundly depressed. It's horrible to see a great people in such a state of humiliation and destitution."

"A great people? Aren't we *aller Welt Feind*, the whole world's enemy?"

"I don't look upon Germany as an enemy. All of us, all nations, are debtors one to another. I don't care a hoot what revanchists or disappointed generals either here or in France or wherever have to say. It's your poets and thinkers that I would like to hear again. They speak the heart of the nation. Cardinal Newman's motto was: *Cor ad cor loquitur*. Only if the heart speaks to the heart will misunderstandings vanish.... To me Germany is still the land of *Denker und Dichter*. The world cannot do without Germany. If you suffer, as you do now, all the world is bound to suffer in the end...."

"You do not hate Germany?"

"Not in the least, and never did! But will you kindly tell me: what are we to make of these rumors that Germany is secretly arming, building tanks and airplanes in Russia... building naval units in Scandinavia... laying up vast stores of oil? What about these national socialists we hear about? Wasn't there a whole crop of political murders beginning with Rathenau and others who stood for European reconciliation? Isn't there a secret so-called Black Reichswehr which seeks to revive the spirit of revenge and war?"

"I won't deny it," he said. "But these elements are leftovers from the Ruhr occupation of 1921 and '22 which caused deep resentment in

Germany. Those national socialists you mention are mere hooligans. They are unemployed bums and loafers. Their movement will die a natural death as the nation gets back on its feet. There's no denying that we are bankrupt today. We are stagnating in the lowest depths of an economic slump. But we are straining all our efforts to get to work again. Work is the only cure for the present situation. . . ."

But what kind of work, I wondered, as I strolled back along the Friedrichstrasse to my hotel on the banks of the Spree. In the newsstand in the Friedrichstrasse railway station I bought myself a book: *The Kaiser Left, but the Generals Stayed On.* And before the night was over I knew from reading this book that, however disillusioned and peace-loving now, Germany would sooner or later rearm and remilitarize and some day fight another war because such was the will of the international merchants of death.

"Proletarians of all countries unite," said Marx. They were as disunited as ever. But the *petrolarians*, the international oil trusts—the common market of death—were getting together with Krupp, Thyssen, Hugenberg, Siemens, Frowein, the Ruhr steel magnates, the banks and the general staff, and their unity spelt disaster for the whole world.

Every foreign newspaper represented in Paris had received an invitation to send a correspondent to Poland to see the "miracle" of *Polonia Restituta*, the resurrection of Poland in the few short years since that country's triple liberation from German, Austrian and Russian domination. In the *World's* Paris bureau we had drawn lots for the opportunity to make the trip to Poland which was to be on a grand scale at the expense of none other than Marshal Josef Pilsudski, the President of the Polish Republic. The winning matchstick had indicated me as the prospective Polish traveler. Thus it happened that I continued my journey from Berlin to the capital city of Warsaw where I put up at the famous Bristol Hotel.

One hears it said that the communists show a foreign tourist only what they want him to see in Russia. If this is so, I can tell from whom the communists learned the trick. It's the Poles who are their teachers and masters in this respect. On my three journeys through Russia I was each time accompanied by a guide supplied by the Intourist Bureau. In Poland I had two superintendents, two robust young honey-blondes of the Amazon type, Anna and Marta, who spoke French *comme une vache espagnole*. These girls never let me out of their sight. They even came with me into the office of Marshal Pilsudski in the Belvedere Palace when I was granted an audience by the old Bazi-Bazouk. Though I hadn't said a word about my intentions or desires, it was Anna who told the chief of state where I wanted to go and what to see. It seems that I was simply burning up with impatience to lay eyes on the new port city of Gdynia, the cotton-spinning factories at Lodz and the brand-new coal mines in the districts bordering on German Silesia. When at last I managed to get a word in edgeways by asking if I would have a chance to see the city of Przemysl, Pilsudski's heavy brows contracted; he couldn't make out what I meant.

After some discussion about the correct pronunciation of that impossible word, President Pilsudski asked me: "Why Przemysl?"

"I was brought up in a fortress city myself; isn't Przemysl the place which changed hands sixteen times in the course of the Great War?"

"Seventeen times," the marshal corrected, and proceeded to give me the dates of the takes and retakes which one of the girls dutifully noted down.

But he didn't really want to talk about the Great War. "Every country has its own rivers, mountains, monuments and heroes," he said, "and also its own wars. Our greatest war was fought in 1920 against Stalin. Stalin was in command of the Red army column which came nearest Warsaw. Budenny commanded the Red cavalry. They were rolled back with heavy losses. Every foreign invader has been thrown back from Poland's borders. ...Everyone...."

"Were you in command of the Polish forces in 1920, *Monsieur le Maréchal?*"

"No, the Virgin Mary, the patroness of Poland, gained the victory for us."

"But it was General Weygand of France who brought up the guns."

"Yes, Weygand was in charge of the artillery.... Herbert Hoover of America supervised the food supply for our army and the *papal nuncio*, Cardinal Achille Ratti, who is Pope today under the name of Pius XI, fired the troops with his enthusiasm...."

"Does His Holiness speak Polish?"

"I don't think so. He speaks Latin though. . . . Poland is the furthest outpost of Latin civilization in the Slavic world. That's our great historic vocation: to keep the Slavs in their place. Poland is the bulwark of Latin civilization. . . . We are the traditional enemies of Pan-Slavism. We hold the Slavs at bay as once we kept the Turks out of Central Europe. . . ."

"But in the case of Przemysl the business worked both ways, by rotation you might almost say. One day you Poles were in command of the city, the next day the Russians. . . ."

The President laughed. "Let me tell you about Przemysl," he said. "That's a different case entirely. It has always been a peculiar situation in Przemysl. In peacetime, before the great war between Austria and Russia, the Austrian officers of the Przemysl garrison crossed the border once a week into Russia to dine with the officers of the Russian garrison in Getorsk. The next week it was the other way around: the Russians visited Przemysl. It was an ancient custom established way back in the days of Catherine the Great and the Austrian Empress Maria Theresa. . . . The two countries entertained the most cordial relations then. . . . As a result of those military visits there were perhaps as many babies with Russian fathers born in Przemysl as there were babies of Austrian paternity in Getorsk. . . . Were you ever a soldier?"

When I said yes, the marshal remarked: "Well, in that case I don't need to tell you. You know how things go in the army. . . ."

"I'm sorry," I said, "the battalion in which I served never experienced such a pleasant concurrence of circumstances. . . ."

"This is a question of personal initiative," said Pilsudski. "All I can say is that I don't think you were a very good soldier. . . ."

Pilsudski, a former socialist, who came to power by a *Putsch* engineered by a group of younger officers headed by Colonel Josef Beck, assured me that Poland need fear no foe since he had taken the reins of government personally in hand. German rearmament he pooh-poohed, the growing strength of the Soviet Union he dismissed as so much propaganda: Poland was ready for any contingency. Moreover, Poland was allied with France and the combination seemed invincible to the marshal. He gave me notes of introduction to foreign minister Colonel Josef Beck and the chief of staff General Rydz-Smigly. These two gentlemen laughed heartily when I told them of my fears regarding the remilitarization program that had just gotten under way in Germany. "Just let them try," said Rydz-Smigly. "The Polish army will be in Berlin *and* Moscow in no time. . . . Poland is invincible!"

That day of the audience as we were about to leave the marshal's office, Pilsudski reminded Anna and Marta to be sure to show me the Cathedral of the Holy Trinity, a remark which made the girls burst into laughter and me very curious. Forthwith they took me to the center of the city and showed me a field of mud. "This is Holy Trinity," they said, still laughing at my surprise. On the site of that sea of mud stood for two centuries the Russian Orthodox Cathedral of the Holy Trinity and the palace of the Russian governors general. The first thing the Poles did after the liberation of their country in 1918 was to demolish these structures which in their eyes symbolized their long subjection to Russia.

One evening Anna and Marta took me to a combination restaurant-dance hall near the riverside where two bands were playing in different pavillions and the smallest meal was a seven-course dinner costing I do not know how many *zloty*. Marta paid for everything. The place was packed with Polish officers eating, drinking and dancing. *En passant*, I must make mention of a peculiar art in which, I think, the Poles are the masters. It's in the department of medals that they excel. Polish generals don't just wear ribbons. They wear real medals, row upon row, all the way up to their collars and down to the region of the navel. When the generals in that restaurant danced they jingled like Salvation Army tambourines. Before quitting Poland I came to the conclusion that if the Poles would have ten thousand times less medals, but instead one, just one good solid well-paved road, they might stand half a chance in any future war. In Poland the country roads were made of mud; not just plain everyday ordinary mud, but a slimy mire sucking carts and wagons and horses down like pools of quicksand.

"Would you like to talk to some of the officers?" Anna asked me as we sat in the restaurant-dance hall.

"I would like it very much!"

"With whom?"

"There's a fine-looking officer over there," I said. "He seems to be all alone. . . . Could you ask him? . . ."

"Not him!" said Anna, drawing up her nose. "Look, he has only one row of medals. . . . He's only a *poprrycnik*, a second lieutenant . . ."

"A lieutenant may be a general some day, Annouchka. You should not discourage the lower ranks."

The lieutenant came over. He was Ignace Stanislas Kowalski of the artillery and was as hungry and thirsty as if he had just crossed the Sahara Desert on an empty stomach. But he turned out a mine of information, not alone on the military situation, which he pronounced deplorable, "our artillery is a joke," but on the love life of the high brass as well. He invited me to visit the town of Kalisz where he lay in garrison. I promised to stop over in Kalisz on my way back to Western Europe.

The girls showed me the port of Gdynia and the cotton factories, the new coal mines, steel plants and oil wells. I have always been deeply interested in steel mills. But there is one peculiarity about steel mills that must have struck others ere this: when you have seen one steel mill, you have seen them all.

In Cracow I saw the Stanislaw Cathedral, the Panthéon of Poland. Here the Kings of Poland were crowned and many of them buried, as well as the national heroes and poets, Thaddaeus, Kosciuszko, Adam Mickiewicz and others. Above the sepulchre of St. Stanislaw, the patron saint of Poland, burnt a perpetual light. A group of nuns dressed in black and wearing black shrouds drawn over their heads kept up a day and night vigil while chanting in Polish a mournful lament which had such a depressing effect on me that it spooked through my head for days.

Unlike Cracow, Warsaw is a magnificent city, or at least it was. University buildings, libraries, cathedrals, governmental departments, banks, theaters, opera, all were sumptuous structures. The architecture was conspicuously German, late Gothic, splendid and rich. The churches contained many art treasures and much gold. . . .

It was not till my second Sunday in Poland that I slipped away from my chaperones and set out to look around with my own eyes. After attending service at the surprisingly large and beautiful Reformed church, I strolled down the Ujazdowska Aleja, the Champs Elysées of Warsaw, planted with fine rows of lime trees and bordered by cafés and places of amusement. I came out in the Lazienki Park, which, next to the Saxony Garden of the same city, is unquestionably one of the finest in Europe. In the Church of the Holy Ghost I stood still for a moment and bowed my head before the monuments of Copernicus and Frédéric Chopin.

To the north of Sigismund Square with its palaces and churches, I landed in the Stare Miasto, the old quarter, which is the ghetto. The spectacle of squalor and destitution that I beheld in this area shocked me as nothing else ever did. In the Stare Miasto lived "Jews without money," 300,000 of them, in conditions that can be only described as the lowest depth of human degradation. Squalid tenement houses, narrow alleys with the fetid odor of open sewers, unpaved streets, mud everywhere, heaps of uncollected garbage, and narrow-chested, pale-faced children in rags wan-

13. Count Ciano, who expelled the author from Eritrea in 1936

Pierre Laval, who expelled the author from France in 1934

14. Joseph Goebbels, who expelled the author from Germany in 1933

15. Eduard Daladier, speaking, and left, seated, Edouard Herriot,
    in 1937 with other leaders of the Popular Front

16. Mr. and Mrs. Léon Blum, 1936

dering about in sunless passageways. The walls of the alleys were lined with peddlers: peddlers of matches, of shoelaces, of bagels, of lead pencils, thread and needles. All their stock in trade the peddlers carried on a sort a tray which hung by strings around their necks. When a *droshky* came tearing into one of the alleys it bespattered them and me from head to toe with mud.

It was about four o'clock in the afternoon as I passed a house from which issued a crowd of teen-age boys dressed in ragged black overcoats. On their heads they wore small round black caps (not skullcaps). From under the caps peeped long strands of hair curled over their cheeks denoting their Jewish identity. I stopped to speak with some: "Can any of you direct me to the Palestine immigration office? There is such an office, isn't there?" Twenty, thirty boys accompanied me to a dilapidated community center where a crowd of men, women and children were getting something to eat from a soup kitchen. In the office I saw Dr. Shmaryahu Levin, the one-time member of the Russian Duma whom I had met earlier in Jerusalem.

"Explain to me, please," I said, "what the meaning is of all this misery. How do all these Jews live? Nobody seems to have a job in this neighborhood. . . . All that the men seem to do is stand or walk about in the streets or just sit in the doorways of these stinking holes in the wall which for lack of a better word one still must call houses, I suppose. . . ."

We went to a restaurant to drink tea. The tea, slightly yellow-colored hot water, was served in tall thin tumblers. Dr. Levin produced a lump of sugar from his pocket and drank the tea scalding hot, so hot in fact that he had to wrap his handkerchief around his glass for fear of burning his fingers.

"Now you've caught a glimpse," said Dr. Levin, " of the Jewish condition in Poland. But only a glimpse; conditions in half a dozen smaller cities are far worse. Of the 80,000 Jewish men in Lodz, 60,000 are unemployed. They are weavers by trade. But the Russian market of prayer shawls and *zizith** which they formerly supplied is closed since the Bolsheviks took over in Russia."

"Can't they move out, emigrate?"

"They would like nothing better, but the doors of America are only ajar now. Hardly a thousand a year can go to America on account of the new immigration laws. . . ."

"What about Palestine?"

*Fringes which observing Jews wear around their waists (Deut. 22:12).

"The British administration in Palestine declares that the absorptive capacity of the country is too limited to permit more than a few thousand Jews to enter the Land of Israel. . . . "

"But Britain pledged to make Palestine "a national home for the Jewish people!"

"*Ja, ja, ja!* Sounds good doesn't it, especially here in Poland! But the truth is that the outlook is very dark. The [British] Palestine administration is keeping the doors of the Jewish national home closed to Jews. . . ."

"But Poland is booming. I have just been told by the highest authorities in the state that the New Poland is riding high on a wave of prosperity unheard of. Isn't the Jewish population to share in this prosperity? The Jews are Polish citizens, aren't they?"

"*Ja, ja, ja!* But there is no difference between starving as a citizen and starving as an alien. There is no hope for the 'Polish citizens of the Jewish faith.' No hope at all. They are doomed. . . . "

"How many are there?"

"More than three million!"

"What will become of them?"

"The majority is going to perish!"

For five days I walked around in the Warsaw ghetto, climbed the stairs of tenement houses, spoke to men, women and children; everywhere the same story: they were all poverty-stricken, all the Jews in the sixty or seventy city blocks, which made up the ghetto; three hundred thousand pauperized Jews. It was the same all over Poland, in the towns and villages, masses of ruined Jewish middle-class people. The misery of the three million Polish Jews beggared all description.

And why was this? Why this ruination and squalor? Was all this accidental or unavoidable? So long as Poland was under the Czar, Jews constituted a class of traders, merchants, cattle dealers, shop and tavern keepers, teachers and foresters; in short, they were the middlemen. With the glorious resurrection of the Polish state, the Poles became the masters and started to build a middle class of their own, entirely composed of non-Jewish citizens. The new middle class was built, unavoidably—I was quite frankly told in official places and governmental circles—on the systematic and calculated ruination of the Jewish population. There was no alternative. It was a question of life and death for the new Poland to destroy the old middle class or get rid of it. There were three million Jews too many in the country. Ultimately they would have to perish or be evacuated, go elsewhere, anywhere. The Polish authorities did not care where they went. In Poland they were unwanted.

I talked with dozens of former middle-class Jews who told me all the same story. They were ruined, living in the worst slums in the world. Formerly—ten, twenty years before—they had been quite well to do. Nearly all those fine shops on the main streets of Warsaw, the Marszalkowska and the Ujazdowska, were formerly Jewish owned. Their proprietors had been taxed out of existence and driven into the proletariat. Seeing no way out of their troubles, the younger element had turned socialist or communist. This was a new cause of vexation and irritation to the Polish authorities: the Jews were Reds now and because Reds they were also enemies of Poland, of religion and of free enterprise. When you want to beat a dog it isn't hard to find a stick. . . .

Whole families lived in one room with a couple of rickety beds, a table and an oilstove the only furniture. I found an entire family, consisting of a father, mother, three sons and one girl, squatting on the floor. They had neither chairs nor table. All of them were sewing buttons on khaki army overcoats. A few houses further down the street I glanced into a room where a baby was being born in one bed while in another bed an old man moaned and groaned in the last stage of a mortal disease. People showed me family albums with photographs of themselves younger and in better circumstances, men carrying golden watch chains on their vests, some even wearing top hats, women in silk dresses with necklaces and bracelets on their wrists. There were pictures of confirmation and wedding parties, the men in neat cloth suits and the women in their sabbath best, the children fresh and clean.

They wanted to prove to me that they had not always been as I saw them now, destitute and impoverished. One man showed me a photograph of the big dairy products store he once owned in one of the main shopping districts of Warsaw. The man's neighbor had been a prosperous timber merchant. He was ruined now. He once had offices in different cities and agents all over the country. "There isn't one office left today," he said, "Jews are no longer employed as land agents or cattle traders. . . ."

One mother showed me a photograph of her youngest son. "This is Misha," she said. "Misha lives in Eretz Israel. . . . He walked to Palestine. . . ."

"He walked?"

"Yes, he walked. He had no money and no passport. He was notified one day that he must serve in the Polish army. He said he wouldn't serve in the army of a country which denied his people bread and life. He disappeared. Several months we were in fear and trembling that something had happened to him. Then at last came a letter from Misha. He had safely arrived in the Holy Land. He is saving up money now to take us all there. . . ."

"You will all go," I said.

"No." An old Jew shook his head. "We'll never see Eretz Israel. It isn't possible. We are lost, all the old people are lost. But it doesn't matter so long as our children may go to the Land. . . ."

Getting not the least satisfaction in official Polish circles, but expressions about "very regrettable circumstances," "unavoidable social trasformations" and "unassimilable minorities," I called as a last resort on His Grace, the Archbishop of Warsaw. The prelate poured me a glass of wine and proceeded to tell me that "after all, we should not be too surprised to see the Jews suffer."

"Not surprised in *la nouvelle Pologne*; a land bursting with prosperity and new wealth?"

"You forget the Bible, *mon fils*, you forget that they crucified Our Lord! The Jews killed God's only Son, our Saviour. . . . They cried out to Pontius Pilate: 'Crucify Him, let His blood be upon us and upon our children. . . .' It has come down upon them, hasn't it? God took them at their word! You see how true the Bible is. . . ."

I don't know what came over me in that moment. "Monseigneur," I said, "Your Grace has the reputation of being a fine biblical scholar, but Your Grace is guilty of willful obscurantism. . . . You have just now invoked a text which of all the false texts in the New Testament is unquestionably *le plus faux*, the most spurious and corrupt. . . ."

"*Mais mon fils*, have you forgotten how the Jews massacred the inhabitants of the land of Canaan?"

"Does Your Grace mean to tell me that the government of your country in ruining and persecuting the Jews is taking revenge for what happened four thousand years ago to Moabites, Edomites and Philistines? . . . Are you aware that you are speaking of something that never really happened at all. . . . Those accounts in the Book of Joshua about the entry of the Hebraic tribes into Canaan are mere wishful thinking. They are the work of the prophetic, Yahveistic school, which flourished five hundred years after the Hebraic infiltration into Canaan. The writers wanted to preserve the Jews from contact with the Baal and Astarte worshippers in their midst, who hadn't been massacred, obviously. . . ."

"But there is no proof of this!" objected the Polish prelate.

"Yes, there is, Monseigneur! Three hundred years after the Hebraic tribes entered the Holy Land, Jerusalem was still the capital of the Jebusites. . . . Your Grace quoted a text; I will also quote you a text. You look in Ecclesiasticus and you will read there: 'The inhabitants of the land [Canaan] had sinned against thee, o Yahweh, but *thou didst spare* them for they were human. . . .'"

The last thing I saw of Poland was the city of Kalisz where I visited with Lieutenant Kowalski. The library of the military club where I stayed contained all the back copies of the two pornographic weeklies, *La Vie Parisienne* and *Le Sourire de France*, but not much else to remind one of Latin civilization. When Poprrycnik Kowalski took me to the railway station we saw how the yards were taken by storm as a wild crowd of Jewish men, women and children clamored around some carloads of spoilt potatoes which had been rejected by the military commissariat as unfit for comsumption by the troops. And they, too, those Jews had once, not so long ago, been fairly prosperous tradespeople, shopkeepers, professional men.

Upon my return to Paris I wrote the story of my first visit to Palestine for the *Evening World*; nine articles on Palestine and three on the Jewish condition in Poland. I contrasted the two: on the one hand, a virtually empty country crying out for workers and farmers, scientists and teachers. On the other hand, the overpopulated ghettos of Poland with all their human misery and hopelessness.

The typewritten articles were 1500 words each in length. They made quite a package of paper. I sent them off and waited. After two months I received a notification that the articles would not be published. Mr. Tennant and Mr. Swope had submitted them "for verification" to Louis Marshall, a well-known attorney in New York, who was frequently designated in the press as "the spokesman of the American Jewish community."

Mr. Marshall's report, seventeen pages long, drawn up in the pompous style of a lawyer's brief, stated that whereas and whereas and whereas . . . I "must be regarded as having been too pessimistic about the Jews of Poland" and "too optimistic about Palestine as a haven of refuge." His,

Marshall's, private sources of information in both countries did not lead him to believe that the situation in Poland was "half as bad" as I pictured it. "Van Paassen's report about the Palestine groves shipping 600 boxes of oranges to Australia and New Zealand [in 1926]," I read, "is a foolish exaggeration. Palestine couldn't possibly export 100 boxes of oranges per year. The land is too poor for citrus culture," wrote Mr. Marshall.*

And so the articles were not published, not in the *Evening World* at any rate. But I sent copies to other papers and they must have been published after all, though I had forgotten all about them in the years during which three million Polish Jews were trapped and done to death.

On February 16, 1962, in Temple Israel in Jamaica, Long Island, where I preached the Purim sermon, the chairman of the Cultural Activities Committee, Dr. Rudolph Halley, introduced me to the congregation.

I transcribe here part of his introductory remarks:

"We will tonight hear the man who back in 1927, thirty-five years ago, wrote the following warning: 'The Jews should be evacuated from Poland and from all Eastern Europe at no matter what cost. . . . They should be directed to Palestine in their hundreds of thousands, in their millions if possible. . . . Just as there has been a total evacuation of Greeks from Anatolia and of Turks from Grecian Thrace under the supervision of the League of Nations, so the Jews should be transferred from Poland to their Palestinian homeland by land and sea in the shortest possible time. . . . No matter whether Palestine can absorb them or not; let them be temporarily housed—for a whole decade if needs be!—in camps and tents till they can be integrated in the growing economy of that country. . . .

" 'But save them! Save their lives! . . . There is no time to lose. . . . If left in Eastern Europe masses of Jews are doomed to die if not of hunger then by persecution. . . .' "

I do not mean to claim credit for having been a prophet of doom. I would much sooner have been utterly repudiated by events. Nor, must I add, was I the first to point to the situation of the Jews of Poland laden with hazard and danger as it was. Already in 1895 Theodore Herzl, the founder of the Zionist Organization, hearing the mobs on the Parisian boulevards shouting *"Mort aux Juifs!"* remarked: "If this can happen in France, the most enlightened country in the world, what can we expect

*In 1962 Israel exported eleven million boxes of oranges.

in certain countries of Eastern Europe which have not reached the position which France occupied a hundred years earlier?"

Max Nordau, the correspondent of the Vienna *Neue Freie Presse* in Paris wrote in the same year: "The world should seriously consider the evacuation of the Jews from Eastern Europe. . . . If left in Poland, Russia, Hungary and Rumania they will perish in the great upheavals that stand before the door. . . ."

As late as 1930 Vladimir Jabotinsky started a movement in Poland to walk the Jews out in a great exodus. He actually got a few thousand young Jews to follow him on the long trek to the Holy Land when a few miles outside Warsaw the Polish government stopped the march and the military drove the Jews back into their ghettos. At that time certain respectable Jewish individuals and organizations in the United States amused themselves by deriding Jabotinsky's act of desperation as that of a Fascist Fuehrer without followers, a self-styled saviour and publicity seeker.

In 1930 the Nazi party had an office in the Kaiserhof Hotel on the Wilhelmstrasse. The hotel was headquarters for *Gau* Berlin; Dr. Goebbels was the *Gauleiter*. The main headquarters were still in Munich. I do not know If Horst Wessel had an official position in the Nazi party. He did not wear the brown shirt. He hung around cafés where foreign newspapermen foregathered. Guido Enderis of *The New York Times* introduced me to him one evening in the Vaterland Café. There was a disturbance in front of the coffeehouse that evening; the city police was picking up homosexuals on the streets and in the cafés and charging them with "solicitation of men by men" which had just been forbidden under a new city ordinance.

Herr Wessel explained to us that this police action was an outrage initiated against the national socialist party by the Jews and Marxists.

"As German citizens," he said, "we homosexuals have our rights. . . . We will not stand for the curtailment of our freedom by such Asiatic intruders as Jews and communists. There is going to be a showdown one of these days. To begin with we plan a tremendous protest meeting in the Turnhalle. The Berlin municipal government simply has to revoke this bylaw against the freedom of the streets. . . . It's an outright scandal and provocation. Women are *not* forbidden to solicit, but men are. We are going to put a stop to this disgraceful injustice. . . ."

"Who's we?"

"The Maenner societies and clubs. . . ."

"Has the Nazi party as such anything to do with the fight for homosexual freedom?"

"No, though there are some very distinguished Nazis in our elite societies. . . ."

"Elite societies?"

"Yes, elite societies! We homosexuals are the elite of the German nation. We are the creative elements, the poets, the artists, the defenders of masculinity, the champions of German morality. We are the *Edel-Germanen.* Homosexuals always appear on the scene when a given civilization reaches its highest pinnacle. . . . The great Greek philosophers, soldiers, builders were all homosexuals, Socrates, Pericles, Alcibiades. . . . The Romans, too: Caesar, Pompey, Augustus. The Renaissance flourished as a result of greater sexual freedom. . . ."

"Is Herr Hitler a member of one of your elite societies? . . ."

"No, the Fuehrer is indifferent on the subject."

"Who knows the Fuehrer best? Is it Goebbels? Or Roehm?"

"No, the man who knows the Fuehrer's innermost thoughts is Ernst Hanfstaengl. Hanfstaengl's mother is the lady who gave Hitler his first chance to meet with persons of influence and distinction at her home in Munich. If you want to know something of Hitler's intimate life you ought to speak to Hanfstaengl. He's half American, a graduate of Harvard University. . . ."

"Where can he be found?"

"Wherever the Fuehrer is. . . . At present all the leaders of the party are staying at the Kaiserhof Hotel. They have all been summoned to Berlin. There's something big in the offing. There are several thousand storm troopers in Berlin for the big event. . . ."

"What big event? Are the Nazis going to seize power?"

"We will see what we will see. . . ."

Horst Wessel sold me a book of his own poetry and vanished into the night. He was murdered a few weeks later in a brawl between rival bands of pimps.

Alfred Rosenberg, later the governor of German-occupied Russia who was hanged at Nuremberg, struck a pose when I came to see him. I had been told that he was of Jewish extraction, but he did not impress me that way. He had fishy gray eyes that bulged somewhat from his forehead, and pudgy hands. He sat in a room full of books. On the table in front of him, conspicuously in sight, lay his own two volumes: *Die Talmud Juden* and *Der Mythus des 20 Jahrhunderts*. The chief aim of the national socialist party, he said, was to stand guard over the purity of the Aryan race and to seek living space for the German nation.

"In other words you want colonies!"

"No, what we want is beauty. But not beauty like the Greeks of yore, a cold sensuous beauty." Beauty of soul was the object of all Nazi striving; nobility of character, clarity of thought, a warm sense of solidarity with all members of the Aryan race.

"Of course, we want colonies too, but not in Africa or Asia. Germany's colonies lie right next door. For ages the Teutonic peoples moved West for their conquests. It was a mistake. . . . The Fuehrer will direct Germany in easterly direction. There in the East we will find all the room we need and shall not have to go as far from home as the British or the French to satisfy our needs."

"You mean you are going to march against Russia if you get a chance?"

"It will not be so much a march of conquest as taking possession of what properly belongs to us. It would be unnatural and downright criminal to leave the resources of the East in the hands of a mass of backward, illiterate and uncouth peasants."

"But Germany has a pact of friendship with the Russians: the Rapallo Pact. . . . The *moujiks* are manufacturing tanks for the Reichswehr. . . ."

"It's a lie thought up by a Bolshevik agent!"

"Is Dr. Foerster a Bolshevik agent? He is not known as such in France and Britain. He is the personal friend and counselor of prime ministers and presidents. He is rather known as a conservative Prussian of the old school and, no doubt, *ein sehr frommer Mann*, a most pious person."

"*Er ist ein Schuft* [He is a scoundrel]! This is what Stresemann called him."

"Dr. Stresemann apologized and publicly expressed regret for that remark. . . ."

"He's an enemy of the new order. . . . He stands on one line with the Jews, the Roman Catholic Church and the Marxists against German renovation and the Fuehrer."

"You forget the army, the Reichswehr. Neither President Hindenburg nor the members of the general staff such as General Schleicher or Freiherr von Fritsch seem to be very receptive to Hitler's propaganda. . . ."

"Ludendorff is. . . . He's the man that counts. . . . Frau Ludendorff's book *Zur heiligen Quelle der Deutsche Kraft,* 'The sacred source of German power,' is the Bible of the New Germany that's a-borning."

"Do you expect the Christian German nation to adopt Mathilde Ludendorff's paganism?"

"Yes, I do. When the light begins to shine the German people's eyes will be opened. They will see that they have been defrauded for ages by the priests and ministers of Christianity who, by fire and sword, have foisted a Jewish Galilean creed on them. . . . There will be one united German church, a new religion, a German religion. . . . Adolf Hitler is the Messiah of the new religion, the savior of the world. . . . He's even now throwing his fire into the world, his fire and his *Kupferwut* [his brass fury]. The sparks of Hitler's fire fly from town to town, from village to village, from farmhouse to farmhouse, from peasant cottage to peasant cottage till all the land will be on fire, till Germany boils over with holy wrath and men will draw the sword without prompting. . . . Did you know that Adolf Hitler's picture stands on the altar in many German churches?"

"I didn't know that. I haven't seen any pictures in the churches at all. . . ."

"I can give you the names and location of half a dozen Evangelical [Protestant] churches where Hitler has been elevated to the altars and is venerated as the divine redeemer. . . ."

"I don't believe it."

"You doubt my word?"

"I certainly do. I am like St. Thomas; I don't believe unless I see. . . ."

"You will see and you will believe and you will fall at Hitler's feet in adoration. . . ."

"Dr. Rosenberg, you are a student of Talmud. Do you know the story about Akiba who proclaimed Bar Kochba the Messiah? The rabbis of that time told him: the grass will sprout from your ears, Akiba, before the Messiah comes. . . . I wish you could give me the name and address of just one Protestant minister of training and education who shares your belief in Adolf Hitler as the new Messiah. . . ."

"I'll give you ten names: Dr. Buchholz of Cottbus, Dr. Schneiderman of Bremen, Pfarrer Otto Schmidt of Wolfsburg, Pfarrer Frenssen of Barlt. . . ."

"Do you mean Gustav Frenssen, the author of *Hilligenlei?*"

"Yes, that's the man!"

"Can I see him?"

"Will you believe in Hitler if Gustav Frenssen shows you the truth?"

"I am very respectful of Gustav Frenssen. It so happens that I also know something of the Frisian people of whom he writes. I lived in Frisia, in the Dutch part of Frisia. I know their language and their way of life. It would be interesting to see what influence Hitler and Nazism exercise on the mentality of a Free Frisian...."

"Go to Hamburg, change trains there for Meldorf. In Meldorf take a carriage to Barlt and you'll be at Gustav Frenssen's house in half an hour.... You'll be able to see the ships and ocean liners sailing out of Hamburg from the window of his front room...."

Knowing a little of what goes on in the minds of Protestant pastors in Frisia, I bought a fine Edam cheese, a box of cigars and a crock of Bols' gin in the Hamburg railway station, and set out in quest of the reverend gentleman whose novels *Joern Uhl, Otto Babendiek, Der Pastor von Poggsee,* and many others, dealing with Frisian and Ditmarsh folkways, I admire till this day. Barlt is but a hamlet inhabited by fishers and farmers. In front of the Frenssen home stood a flagpole with the swastika flapping in the North Sea breeze.

"Herr Pastor Frenssen?" I asked the bearded man with deep-blue eyes who opened the door.

"You can drop the Pastor stuff," he said before I could utter another word. "I have broken with the Christian Church.... Just call me Gustav. How did you know that Edam cheese on rye bread and gin is my favorite?"

"I figured it out. I am a little bit Frisian myself."

"You are of the right stock, my boy. How did you find me?"

"Dr. Rosenberg gave me your address."

"There's a man for you, a German man, *ein rassechter Germane* who dares tell the truth. Do you drink your coffee with sugar, dear Peter? That is your real name, isn't it? Let's drop the foreign, un-German names!"

"Are you no longer functioning as a minister?"

"Not for many years! It took me a lifetime to come to the truth.... Did you read my books?"

"I did, Gustav!"

"In German?"

"In German, though I've seen them in English translation too. They had quite a vogue in America! Ludwig Lewisohn translated them."

"I met him in New York. . . . A Jew, you know that, of course. But what do my books matter? We have now the greatest book ever written: *Mein Kampf.*"

"Gustav, do you mean it?"

"Do I mean it? I swear by *Mein Kampf.* . . . What a book! What power! What a hero! What do Goethe, Shakespeare, Schiller amount to when compared with Hitler. . . . *Ach*, that my old eyes have been privileged to see this miracle, this resurgence of the German spirit. Who'd have thought it possible ten years ago that Germany would rise again. What a blessing! What did the angels of Bethlehem tell the shepherds? Unto thee is born a saviour. . . . and his name is Adolf Hitler. . . ."

"You talk as if Hitler had already taken over?"

"He has taken over. He has taken over the mind and soul of the German people. . . ."

"But he's not in power!"

"He soon will be, my boy. Hitler is irresistible. He'll sweep Germany clean of all the internationalisms, Christian, Marxist and Jewish. Under Hitler Germany is going to walk in its own shoes. Nobody in the whole world will dictate to the German people the road it is to travel. The German blood is the measure of all things. It is the healing stream in which all mankind will find salvation. . . . *Trinken wir*: *Heil Hitler*! *Sieg Heil*!"

"He still faces a tough struggle. There is strong opposition. . . ."

"Not as strong as you think! All his foes are vanishing. . . . Franz von Papen, as the spokesman for the Catholics, will see to it that the Centrum party withdraws its candidates in the next national election. There will be no Catholic opposition after that. . . . With the Jews no compromise is possible. They will be eliminated. They will be transported to the island of Madagascar."

"The socialists, the liberal democrats, communists, still make a powerful opposition, don't they?"

"They're Germans, aren't they? They will see the light!"

"If they should not see the light?"

"In that case we'll have to be as ruthless as they. No mercy! Our enemies had no mercy with us. They made us a people of slaves, didn't they? Tens of thousands of German children died as a result of the hunger blockade. . . . Now the shoe goes on the other foot. Soon it will be Germany's turn to make decisions."

"Before that can happen Hitler must be in power!"

"He will be in power, in great power. Here in the Nordmark there isn't a man or a woman who opposes Hitler. That's the way it will be all over Germany. . . . Our people are growing more determined every hour that the two million German men who laid down their lives for the fatherland, for the honor of Germany, for its place in the sun, for its right to live, shall not have died in vain."

"But all this will lead to war. Are you willing to see more millions of German men and women sacrificed in a new armed conflict?"

"See, that's where you are wrong, my boy. There will be no war! Under Hitler Germany will be so strong, so united, so well organized, so well equipped with arms of all kinds, that no power on earth will dare to attack her. German preparedness will be the greatest deterrent to war that was ever devised. No war will be necessary. German authority will impose itself by its moral superiority. . . . We are at last in sight of the eternal peace predicted by our greatest German philosopher Immanuel Kant. . . ."

When I left Frenssen's home, I noticed that a stiff breeze blew from the West and the swastika flag was beginning to unravel at the edges.

CHAPTER IX

I Saw the Triumph of Evil

ALFRED HUGENBERG, a member of the board of directors of the Krupp Armament Trust and leader of the German nationalist party, took it upon himself in 1932 to collect large sums of money both inside Germany and abroad to help set the struggling Nazi party on its feet. These funds, which included some important contributions from American financiers, were to be used for propaganda purposes and to stimulate the flagging German national economy. However, before turning the money over to the Nazis, Herr Hugenberg once more tested Hitler as to his political views. One of the questions he asked the Fuehrer was: "Why do you believe in a communist danger?"

Hitler replied: *"Ich bin nicht so dumm, um selbst an eine kommunistische Bedrohung zu glauben, aber ohne Propagieren dieser Gefahr kommen wir nicht an die Macht. . . .* I am not so stupid as to believe in a communist threat myself. But without making propaganda about this danger, we will not get into power and without taking over supreme power in the state we will not be able to rearm. There is no other remedy to overcome the economic crisis than by spreading the fear of communism. We can only get popular support for rearmament by pointing to a communist danger."*

In this statement by Adolf Hitler, which motivated German big business—and certain foreign business interests—to come to his side, lies the heart and kernel of "the big lie." Hitler ordered all Prussian state papers destroyed in which appeared documentary proof that he himself did not believe in a communist menace. He threatened death to all witnesses because in the Reichstag fire trial his statement could have become very

*This statement by Hitler is found in the section of the Abegg Archives containing the *Papers of Gregor Strasser.* Gregor Strasser was one of the top Nazis who was killed on the Fuehrer's orders in the Roehm purge of July, 1934. The Abegg Archives are called after Dr. Wilhelm Abegg who was state secretary for Berlin when Hitler came to power. Dr. Alhard Gelpke of Zurich is the Achives' present-day custodian.

embarrassing to him. He had ordered the Reichstag building set on fire precisely to impress his countrymen and the world at large with a clear and present communist danger.

The charge that the communists set the Reichstag on fire was proven false in court. But this did not keep Goebbels from taking up the cry. It was one of the propaganda minister's shock tactics to influence public opinion. "The big lie" repeated over and over again was the most powerful of the Nazi weapons. It not only nearly conquered Europe for them, it still operates with mighty suggestive power as we may see by simply opening any morning or afternoon newspaper. "The big lie" leads directly to the anticommunist hysteria under which all creation still "groaneth as in pain together."

When Hitler came to power, his master plan as outlined in *Mein Kampf* looked so difficult, if not impossible of execution, that many in France and elsewhere dismissed it as the figment of a fool's imagination. What could the Fuehrer do in 1933 to upset the European balance of power? How could the Nazi Reich ever break out of its encirclement?

France had a formidable army and was linked in pacts of mutual assistance and collective security not only with the Soviet Union, but also with the Czechoslovakian and the Polish republics and with the kingdom of Yugoslavia. Though "cordiality" and depth of "understanding" between the two countries had worn pretty thin, the wartime Franco-British alliance, known as the Entente Cordiale, was still, nominally at least, in force. South of the Pyrenean border the dictatorship of Primo de Rivera had collapsed in 1931 and been replaced by a freely elected democratic republic. The Spanish republic represented no danger to France.

There was only Mussolini, the Italian dictator, who ordered his black-shirted cohorts to clamor for living space in the French protectorate of Tunisia and for a return of the city of Nice and the province of Savoy to the Italian motherland. But Mussolini was not taken seriously, nor was he Hitler's ally as yet.

"I have eight million bayonets," boasted the Duce. "Nobody and nothing in the whole world can stop them when I give the order to advance."

"Signor Mussolini seems to overlook *la douane française* [the French customs service at the border]," retorted the Parisian newspaper *L'Oeuvre*.

Moreover, France's Yugoslav sentinel stationed on Italy's northeastern borders was ready at a moment's notice to throw into action those Croat, Slovene and Serb divisions which the Duce remembered only too well from his days as a common soldier when he saw them come across the Alps in the Austrian army to inflict the defeat of Caporetto.

In March, 1934, a year after Hitler's coming to power, King Alexander of Yugoslavia was assassinated as he debarked at Marseilles for a state visit to France. The French foreign minister, Louis Barthou, the champion of the German and Italian containment policy, met his death at the same time, while General Joseph Georges, one of the younger French commanders, who was the leader of a group in the general staff which favored strengthening the French army with more armored divisions, suffered a wound from which it took him a long time to recover.

Who killed Alexander? Unquestionably it was a Croatian terrorist who fired the shots. The murderer was cut down within a minute after the shooting. But who organized the murder plot? Who stood to gain most by Alexander's disappearance? The virtual unanimity of the European press held the Duce responsible. Ex-prime minister Joseph Paul-Boncour, who was retained by the widowed Queen Marie of Yugoslavia to represent her in a court action to recover damages, would not say anything beyond: "The French government has carried out a minute investigation and knows the names of all the participants in the murder conspiracy. . . . "

Not till after the close of World War II did the Co-operative Society of German Officers disclose that the murder plot was hatched in the German embassy in Paris.

After Alexander's death Yugoslavia was thrown into chaos through inter-party warfare and terroristic activities on the part of pro-Nazi elements and fifth columnists. The surest ally of France had been knocked out.

In the fall of 1934 Germany withdrew from the League of Nations and in the spring of the following year, in defiance of the terms of the Versailles Treaty, introduced compulsory military service.

After restoring compulsory military service Adolf Hitler told six of his army commanders what was next.* "We are now free to attend to our main business: Germany is going to move in easterly direction. . . . First Austria, then Czechoslovakia. In Austria I expect no trouble. If France should show half a mind to go to Czechoslovakia's aid, I will create a social crisis of such severity inside France that the French army will be wholly occupied in suppressing internal troubles and thus, as a striking force against us, completely eliminated."

But the Fuehrer did meet with resistance in Austria. When the Reich's

*Protocol of the Nuremberg Trials.

diplomats pressed Austria to join the Nazis in the so-called Anschluss, Chancellor Engelbert Dollfuss refused and mobilized his small army.

In support of Dollfuss, Mussolini occupied the Brenner Pass and sent 50 divisions to the Austrian frontier. Hitler went into one of his tantrums. But Dollfuss was assassinated in July, 1934, by pro-Nazi elements in the Austrian capital. The labor unions, who were mobilizing to defend Austria in the event of a Nazi attack, were annihilated in a brief civil war.

Since neither France, nor Britain, nor anyone else, showed the least appreciation of the Duce's move to check Hitler's aggressive designs on Austria, Mussolini was isolated and thus forced to make up with Hitler. He came to terms with the Nazis and even concluded a pact of friendship and mutual assistance with the Fuehrer.

At the same time that Hitler tried to overrun Austria, but found his fifth column in that country not strong enough to carry the Anschluss through, Fascism raised its head in France and became a serious threat to democratic institutions and to the republican regime itself. In the beginning of 1934, the Croix de Feu (the Fiery Cross), initially an organization of nationalistic and reactionary war veterans, turned into a militant anti-democratic, anti-Semitic and pro-Fascist movement. Like the Italian Fascists in the days of the march on Rome, the members of the Croix de Feu were organized on a military or semimilitary basis.

At the head of the Croix de Feu stood Colonel Casimir François de la Rocque who made no secret of his veneration for Mussolini for having put the Italian labor unions in their place. The methods De la Rocque adopted were Hitler's. His troops paraded in the streets in military style. Gatherings of ten to twenty thousand men would appear overnight in a given place, usually one of the working-class suburbs—Montrouge, St. Denis, Malakoff, Argenteuil or Aubervilliers—and then vanish into the night. The colonel had at his disposal a vast fleet of motorcars. He also had airplanes and ambulances. From time to time his secret arsenals were discovered stocked with hundreds, in some cases, thousands of rifles, pistols and machine guns. In the four or five newspapers which sympathized with his views, De la Rocque openly announced his preparations for civil war.

In Bécon-les-Bruyères, halfway between Paris and the town of my residence, St. Germain-en-Laye, where I witnessed one of the Croix de Feu's "mobilizations," the "chief" drove up in a powerful automobile, preceded, surrounded and followed by the rolling thunder of motorcycle squads. His followers, wearing Basque berets and leather belts, greeted him with out-stretched arms, repeating his name incessantly in a sort of staccato chorus. He himself went bareheaded. He neither looked to the left nor the right. He was a man without humor, without any original ideas and was known never to smile.

De la Rocque was known to be a friend of Marshal Pétain and General Weygand, the chairman of the Supreme War Council and chief of the General Staff respectively. But he passed for an honest, patriotic, disinterested citizen, without government connections. When his movement broke in twain in 1938, the dissenters stated that De la Rocque had all along been financed by the cabinets of Gaston Doumergue, Pierre Flandin and Pierre Laval and, of course, by great industrial and financial organizations and the armament manufacturers, such as Schneider-Creusot and the Comité des Forges.

The night I heard him at Bécon, the colonel attacked the League of Human Rights and the "atheistic" Order of Free Masons who, according to the speaker, wanted to destroy the parochial school system in France and push all the *abbés*, nuns and Christian Brothers under the guillotine. After every sentence his belted minute men gave him a roaring ovation: "De la Rocque, De la Rocque, De la Rocque!" as if the colonel's name alone was the answer to every problem in the world.

Though the mass meeting, according to the posters, had been called "to examine the economic and social conditions of the French people," De la Rocque hadn't a word to say about the immense poverty, the flagrant inequality in the distribution of wealth, nor about the rotten slums in so many quarters of Paris and its suburbs where, for instance, autobus drivers lived who, at that time, earned the equivalent of $9.90 per week. Shopgirls in the great department stores were getting $5.70, less than half of what American tourists spent for lunch at Maxim's or LaRue's. The weavers in Lyons and the steel workers at St. Etienne earned a little over $10 a week, while the women at the airplane factories received $4.85. It had long been a mystery to me how people could live on such salaries without ultimately suffering physical or moral degradation.

One of De la Rocque's associates, a Sam Browne-belt-wearing big shot, the "Marquis" de la Meuse, referred briefly to the "revolutionary labor elements" and their demand for higher wages: "If the steel workers find the cost of living too high, they could save fuel by going to bed early.... Their wives are good-looking women who will surely keep them warm...."

As to the shopgirls, weren't they clever enough, he asked, "to make a little supplementary income ... by picking up a rich lover or taking a walk up and down the street now and then?" It was like the remark by Marie Antoinette to her ladies in waiting: "If the people have no bread, let them eat cake." Not even De la Rocque's faithful dared applaud these vulgarities.

On February 6, 1934, De la Rocque tried to stage a *Putsch* in Paris. All his forces, probably 50,000 men, marched down the boulevards and converged on the Place de la Concorde where they were joined by members of the Parti Populaire, headed by Jacques Doriot, a former communist member of parliament who was to die in 1942 in Hitler's service and uniform on the Russian front. The demonstration advanced in solid ranks and was heading for the Chamber of Deputies which was in session that afternoon. I readily recognized Léon Daudet, the novelist; Maxime Real del Sarte, the sculptor; Maurice Pujot, the publisher of *Action Française*; and Charles Maurras, the philosopher and editor of the same monarchist paper. They walked at the head of a contingent of their Camelots du Roi, the King's Henchmen.

Jean Chiappe, the police prefect, himself a Fascist, was present in the great square. He had just been dismissed from his post for involvement in a financial scandal, the Stavisky affair. He nevertheless gave the police the order to fall back before the surging crowd as it shouted: "Blum to the gallows! Daladier into the Seine! Pierre Cot *á la lanterne!*" The Chamber's session was suspended by its president Edouard Herriot. Herriot and the members of the cabinet appeared on the garden terrace of the Palais Bourbon which then housed the Chamber of Deputies.

A regiment of helmeted mounted police came galloping along the Quai d'Orsay, veered to the left and met the oncoming Fascist multitude on the Concorde bridge. I climbed a tree on the very spot on the Quai d'Orsay where today stands a concrete pillbox in front of the Chamber.

Instead of falling back before the cavalry, the mob produced garlands of straw soaked in pitch, set these alight and tossed the flaming hoops around the horses' necks. The first ranks of the mounted police were thrown into confusion. The horses reared and some with the burning hoops around their necks jumped in panic over the bridge railing, plunging to their deaths in the Seine. Several *cuirassiers*, who had hastily dismounted, were overwhelmed by the mob and joined their horses in the river. Steadily the Fascists were pressing onward to the left bank of the river and the parliament building. . . . It seemed but a matter of minutes till the government would be taken prisoner and the cabinet members strung up on the lamp posts. . . .

Then the cohorts of the Croix de Feu and their allies hesitated as masses of workers marching up along the quais met them head-on. Other crowds of workers, coming down the Avenue des Champs Elysées and through the Tuileries Gardens, attacked De la Rocque's "invincible legion" from two sides. De la Rocque himself, who was somewhere in the parade, backed up his automobile and, in doing so, knocked over several of his own valiants. A dozen of the Fascists on the bridge were pitched into the river. The mob surged back towards the Place de la Concorde and there the battle was fought out which ended in the complete route of the Croix de Feu and their allies. About nine in the evening a machine gun started to rattle, but I do not know where it was posted. One of its shots killed a chambermaid who was standing near one of the windows in the Crillon Hotel. On hearing the first shots I came down from my perch and dispersed, so to speak.

The following day a mountain of roses lay in the middle of the Place de la Concorde on the spot where fifteen Fascists had been killed. Women were kneeling and an abbé went around with uplifted hands blessing the ground where "the martyrs" had fallen. The Fascist papers, *Action Française, Gringoire, Le Jour, Emancipation*, henceforth spoke of Léon Blum only as "the hyena," Daladier "the killer," and Pierre Cot "the bloody scoundrel."

Within a few days after De la Rocque's unsuccessful *Putsch*, the Comité de Vigilance des Intellectuels Anti-Fascistes was formed. Its president was Jean Perrin, winner of the Nobel prize for physics and general secretary of the Académie des Sciences. Paul Langevin and Emile Borel, both members of the Institut de France, were chosen adjunct chairmen. In a month's time the Comité had five thousand members, all artists, writers, savants and professors at the Sorbonne, the Collège de France and the great lycées.

On the invitation of Félicien Challaye, professor of philosophy at the Lycée Condorcet, I joined the Vigilance Committee. This was a mistake, though not from an ideological point of view, for I was deeply convinced that the Fascists presented a universal menace who should be resisted by every democrat whether French or otherwise. My mistake was that I allowed my name to be published.

Within a month after joining I was notified by the Ministry of the

Interior that I was expected to leave French territory within forty-eight hours. I ran to the Place Beauvau and asked to see the minister, Pierre Laval.

"You occupy yourself with things that do not concern you," said Laval as he lit one cigarette with another and blew the smoke through his nostrils. I had seen him before when he came to talk to us at the Anglo-American press club in the Hotel St. Petersbourg, but never at so close a range.

"What things?" I asked. "The Vigilance Committee? But the Committee was set up in defense of the French people's liberties. Democratic freedom in France is everybody's business. Every civilized person has two countries, France and his own. It was France which poured out her own blood in the French Revolution for us all in the conquest of human rights. . . ."

"We do not need the help of foreigners. . . . Go back to America to talk of civil liberties. . . . We have more than enough of your kind here."

"What kind?"

"People who make a nuisance of themselves by blabbing about freedom. Freedom for whom? Abyssinians? . . . *Moujiks?* . . . Montenegrins? . . ."

At the Canadian embassy, Jean Désy and Pierre Dupuy, the ambassador protem and the passport officer respectively, promised to take up my case with the press department of the Foreign Office. It took them so long that I received a second note from the ministry asking when an inspector could be sent to conduct me to the border. Léon Blum advised:

"Go to the border, Belgium or Switzerland, establish residence in one of these countries, and come back on the next train. There is nothing in your expulsion document about being permanently barred from French territory. In the meantime we will investigate and try to find out for what reason Laval wants you out."

So it was done. I took Cornelia and Hugo to Brussels. But no permit of residence was granted in the Belgium capital. A Walloon official remembered my activities in the Flemish nationalist movement, and I went on to Basel. In Basel's railway station we were turned over by a French plain-clothes man, who had evidently traveled on the same train, to the Swiss immigration authorities. This kind gesture immediately rendered me suspect to the Swiss security police. I could come in as a tourist, they said, and stay as long as I liked, but for the privilege of permanent residence I must give the names of two Swiss citizens, willing to guarantee my harmlessness.

"You are expelled from France for engaging in political activities. We cannot let you go into Switzerland without some assurances that you won't do the same thing here. . . . Can you give us the names of two Swiss citizens?"

"The editor of the *Neue Zuercher Zeitung*," I said, "and Dr. Jean Schorer, minister of the cathedral of St. Pierre in Geneva. . . ." "Fine," said the inspector, "we will telephone the *Neue Zuercher Zeitung* and Dr. Schorer on condition that. . . you pay for the call. . . ." The call was made and I was at once allowed to proceed.

We lived for a year in Zurich; that is, my wife and Hugo did. I went to America to do a lecture tour hastily arranged by Morris Margulies, secretary of the Zionist Organization of America.

Upon my arrival in New York I called on J. David Stern, publisher of the *New York Post*, because the *World*, for which I had worked since 1924, had disappeared in the depression. Mr. Stern promised me a job as foreign correspondent as soon as I should have completed my lecture tour. I toured the country from New York to San Francisco, but upon my return to New York, Mr. Stern's editorial assistant, I. F. Stone, upbraided me for having given an article to Joseph V. Connelly, the manager of King Features, a newspaper syndicate.

The article in question dealt with a conversation I had on board the S.S. *Lafayette* with an Indonesian gentleman. This person told me that he was absolutely certain that Japan would at a not distant date seize the Netherlands East Indies.

"But," I said, "the Nippos won't get very far. Neither Britain nor the United States will stand for such an act of aggression. Britain has just spent hundreds of millions of pounds on a naval base at Singapore and that base will certainly keep the Japanese navy from Malaya, Burma, India and, I suppose, from Indonesia as well."

"Have you ever heard of the Isthmus of Kra?" the Indonesian asked me.

"Yes, but I don't know exactly where it is located!"

"Let's look at the map!"

"Here across this narrow strip of land at the top of the Malay Peninsula, the Japanese will dig a canal. Through that canal the Japanese fleet will sail around Singapore or, what's more likely, the Japanese army debarking at Kra will take the British base of Singapore from the landside." Thus, exactly, it came to pass in 1941!

I happened to talk of this meeting with the Indonesian to a reporter of the *Portland Oregonian* when I lectured in that city. The Portlanders showed no interest whatever in Hitler's or Mussolini's movements. Japan, on the other hand, was a different matter to people living on the Pacific shores.

The story made a sensation in Oregon and King Features wired me for details. I hadn't the faintest notion that King Features was part of the Hearst organization. But Mr. I. F. Stone did.

"We on the *Post*," he told me after my return to New York, "will not employ anyone who writes for Hearst. . . ."

Fortunately, on that lecture tour during my stay in old Toronto, Harry C. Hindmarsh and Joseph Atkinson, the managing editor and the owner of the *Toronto Star*, appointed me general European correspondent for the *Star* and the *Canadian Central Press*.

Before sailing from New York I received a cable from *le vieux militant* Jean Longuet, saying that my expulsion order had been revoked. The Comité des Intellectuels Anti-Fascistes had brought about the change.

And so we were back where we started. This time we took a house in Maisons-Laffitte and I resumed my watch of the way Hitler was working out his master plan. The leaders of the democratic parties, clubs and societies in France were negotiating to put up a common front against the growing Fascist menace, for though De la Rocque had been routed, other colored-shirt movements had come into existence. For one, the extreme right had set up a terrorist organization, known as the Cagoulards, so called after *la cagoule*, the cloak worn by monks and the masked cowl of the Ku Klux Klan. These people carried out acts of terrorism against lone individuals, masonic lodge presidents, schoolteachers, labor leaders.

The Comité de Vigilance had appointed thousands of workers to stand guard at nights and these workers promptly retaliated when a suburban city hall or labor temple was attacked. It was quite clear that the next elections would bring the parties of the Popular Front to power and that the Fascist menace would be a thing of the past.

However, just before the elections, on March 7, 1936, Hitler, frustrated in his designs to create an internal crisis in France (via De la Rocque), made an alarming move in the foreign field.

In the afternoon of that day, Radio France announced that the German army had crossed the demarcation line between the Reich and the Rhineland which was a demilitarized zone under the terms of the Versailles Treaty.

"Tomorrow afternoon at one o'clock all the members of the Supreme War Council have been summoned to the Hôtel des Invalides to deliberate on the steps to be taken to counter Germany's breach of the Versailles Treaty." In a word of comment of his own, the announcer added: "Monsieur Hitler has gone on the warpath. . . . His Thousand Year Reich teeters on the brink of the abyss. . . . *Vive la France!*"

It was a brilliant Sunday as I joined thousands of promenaders on the Esplanade des Invalides to see the military chiefs arrive. Maxime Weygand came first. In spite of his 69 years, he walked with the sprightly step of a young lieutenant. He was soon followed by Philippe Pétain, Marshal of France, and General Gamelin, the new chief of the general staff. Albert Sarraut, a member of the cabinet and chairman of the Military Affairs Committee, who was evidently going to preside, was the only official to receive an ovation from the crowd. "Albert, hold firm! don't let the *Boche* fool you!" He smiled back and waved his hand in a signal of strength and confidence.

Then we waited. At four o'clock, Sarraut's voice was heard over the radio: "German troops have entered the Rhineland in flagrant disregard of a solemn treaty. . . . The French forces in Alsace have been alerted. . . . Our first armored division is about to cross the Rhine bridge at Kehl. . . . The French people may rest assured that we will never leave the towers of Strasbourg under the menace of the German guns. . . ."

"*C'est la guerre!* This is war!" said a man next to me in the crowd.

"I agree with you, but it won't be much of a war. Hitler hasn't got the power to strike very hard. . . yet."

At nine in the evening the broadcaster said that the French troops had withdrawn from their forward positions and that there would be no interference with Hitler's occupation of the Rhineland.

What made the French government change its mind? How could they promise the French people at four in the afternoon that Strasbourg would never be allowed to come under the menace of the German guns, but five hours later withdraw their opposition and allow the Germans unobstructed passage to the borders of Alsace?

Léon Blum, in explaining the incident to me at his home, said that a telephonic consultation with the British government had failed to bring about agreement on a joint Franco-British warning to Hitler or the adoption of a common stand against the first open Nazi act of armed aggression.

We had to wait till the Nuremberg trials of 1945 to learn how alarmed the German general staff itself was on the day of Hitler's occupation of the

Rhineland. "I must acknowledge," said General Alfred Jodl, speaking from the prisoners' dock at Nuremberg, "that I felt as uncomfortable as a gambler who has placed his all on one throw of the dice. . . . "

"One French regiment," said Field Marshal Wilhelm Keitel ("with a gesture of chasing a bothersome fly from his nose"), "one French regiment could have thrown us out of the Rhineland." To which Jodl added: "Only three German battalions were involved. One went to Aix la Chapelle, one to Trier and one to Saarbruecken. . . . The French border guards could have blown us away."

Why didn't France go it alone in throwing the Nazi invaders out of the Rhineland, or at least make an attempt? Why didn't Britain lift one little finger to frustrate this breach which virtually annulled the Versailles peace treaty of 1921?

These questions are unanswerable only by those who, whether they believed it or not, spread the myth that England slept when the Nazi monster first began to show its teeth in the international sphere. They leave conveniently in the dark what Anthony Eden, to his credit, although many years too late, made quite clear in his *Memoirs*: the fact of Anglo-French disunity as the essential precondition of Hitler's career of aggression.

Right from the sessions of the Versailles peace conference, Clemenceau and Lloyd George, respectively the French and the British negotiators, were in such total disagreement on the future of Germany that once or twice they would have come to blows had not Cadorna and Woodrow Wilson kept them apart.

Lloyd George and his colleagues in the British government pursued what was with little variation essentially Britain's foreign policy in the European continent since the days of Cromwell: opposition, overt or clandestine, to any other power's predominance in Europe. Every successive rising state was knocked down by Britain, if not directly then by acting in concert with other powers. The Spanish empire was wrecked in collaboration with the Dutch Republic whose fleet bottled up the Spanish flotilla of fighting ships in the harbor of Dunkirk while the storm—"God's breath," states a commemorative medallion from 1588—threw the Armada, the battle cruisers of those days, into confusion and wrecked the major part of the Spanish navy on the coasts of Scotland and Ireland. When Holland seemed on the way to become the mightiest colonial power in the world, Britain fought four wars with the Dutch Republic, was beaten in three but victorious in the last. After Holland came Louis XIV of France whose

military supremacy in Europe was broken by the British under King William III, Prince of Orange. Napoleon and his empire were destroyed by
Britain in collaboration with Prussia, Austria and Russia. In the First World
War, Kaiser Wilhelm II and German expansionism were defeated by the
British empire and its allies and associated powers. In the years leading to
the outbreak of the Second World War, Britain isolated France from her
continental allies and thus met the Nazi grab for world power more than
halfway.

When Adolf Hitler overran the Rhineland, his generals may have held
their breath, but the Fuehrer himself showed no nervousness or anxiety
whatever. He had Joachim von Ribbentrop, his London ambassador's word
for it, that Britain not only would not budge, but would also prevent
France from interfering.

England was not asleep. The truth of the matter is that Britain had a
more or less tacit understanding with Hitler. Britain's foreign minister, Sir
John Simon, signed a naval agreement with Von Ribbentrop the year before the invasion of the Rhineland, on June 18, 1935. Under the terms of
the old Versailles Treaty Germany was not to have a battle fleet to replace
the one lying scuttled at the bottom of Scapa Flow. In a secretly negotiated
treaty, without consulting France or any other power, the British government granted Germany the right to build a new navy on a 100–35 per cent
ratio with that of Britain.

Lords John Simon and Samuel Hoare looked upon the naval pact with
Germany as a triumph for their country in that it diverted Hitler's land
hunger, his *Lebensraum* dreams, exclusively and irrevocably in easterly
direction.

With the naval treaty of 1935, Britain made a scrap of paper of the Versailles Treaty and left her *Entente* partner in the lurch.

When Hitler was asked in 1941 what was the happiest day in his life,
the Feuhrer declared that it was not the day when he was called to the
chancellorship, nor the day when he marched into Prague, nor even the
day when France begged for an armistice in June, 1940.

"The happiest day of my life was the eighteenth of June, 1935, when
Ribbentrop signed the naval agreement with Sir John Simon!"*

Not only did the naval agreement give Hitler the right to build a new
fleet, an opportunity of which he took immediate advantage by ordering

*Quoted from: *Zwischen London und Moskau* (Between London and Moscow), by
Joachim von Ribbentrop (subtitle, "Memoirs and Last Observations").

the keels laid for three battle cruisers and a score of submarines, he also ordered the construction of pocket battleships in the secret hiding places of the Norwegian fjords. The main advantage he drew from the agreement with Britain was the opportunity it afforded him to move ahead at an immensely accelerated tempo with his military preparations on land. The danger of becoming involved in a naval armament race with Britain simultaneously with the urgency to build up his land forces was eliminated.

The unopposed reoccupation of the Rhineland cannot be understood without taking into consideration the German-British naval treaty of the year before. By signing that treaty with the Nazi Reich, Britain acquiesced beforehand in any subsequent move that Hitler undertook to strengthen his position on the Continent.... It was the British government—before Churchill in 1939—which broke the back of France's military supremacy. This historic fact Charles de Gaulle was to remember when he, to the incomprehension and surprise of our "best" commentators, vetoed Britain's admission to the European Common Market in 1963. He blocked the attempt of Britain, as America's cat's-paw as he saw it, to regain her old influence on the European continent....

There is no event in the history of the Third Republic about which so many falsehoods have been told and still circulate as about the Popular Front. The Popular Front, it is charged, injected such deep dissensions in the political, social and economic manifestations of French collective life that the unity of the French nation was destroyed and France four years later became an easy victim to German aggression. The truth is the exact opposite: never, either before or after, was there such a deep sense of national unity as when the government of the Popular Front came to power in May, 1936. The three main parties constituting the Popular Front, who, on the advice of the Comité des Intellectuels Anti-Fascistes, had covenanted to stay together till the Fascist danger was over, achieved an overwhelming victory at the polls, 425 deputies out of 600. No previous government, not even the governments of national concentration of Clemenceau and Poincaré, set up in the emergency of World War I, received such widespread, almost universal support.

The new government ushered in a program of social reform which was to bring the working class and the poor peasants somewhat nearer to the standard of living long since attained by the workers of America, Britain, Germany and the Scandinavian countries. The horrible slums of the capital and other large cities, foul breeding hearths of disease and generations of anemic and tubercular human beings, were to be cleared. Higher educational facilities were to be provided for the children of the poor both in the cities and in the rural regions. The airless and sunless school buildings, erected two, three centuries before, were to be torn down and replaced with modern edifices. Clinical facilities were to be provided for the sick amongst the destitute. Maternity hospitals were planned and begun. The labor syndicates or trade-unions were conceded the right of collective bargaining. Company unions were proscribed. The number of daily working hours, still twelve and even fourteen in the mines of the Pas de Calais and in the textile plants of the Lyons and Roubaix districts, was reduced to forty-five per week, giving the workers half a day free and two weeks' vacation with pay. In a few months' time hundreds of vocational schools were opened, and the country was dotted with youth hostels to which the boys and girls from the crowded cities tramped or bicycled for week-ends and holidays.

There is no doubt in the world that the Popular Front saved France from civil war. It faced a grave situation when it came to power. In line with Adolf Hitler's avowed intention to create such a severe economic and social crisis in France as to paralyze the country and force the army to be exclusively occupied with repressing disorders, the French Fascists under De la Rocque, Marcel Déat, Maurras and Jacques Doriot deliberately brought the country to the brink of disaster in a desperate attempt to forestall the electoral victory of the Popular Front parties. The banks exported their gold abroad. The industrialists closed their plants. They refused to listen to the requests of the labor leaders for shorter work hours and the right of collective bargaining. *Agents provocateurs* were sent into the barracks and military training camps to pose as communists and foment trouble so that the Fascist elements in the general staff could point to the army's unreliability.

The first practical measure to be taken by Premier Daladier was the convocation of employers and unions for the settlement of labor questions. By December, 1936, the Matignon agreements (so called after the Hôtel Matignon, the prime minister's official residence) were concluded and a tremendous wave of joy broke over the country. There are no words to describe the mighty burst of enthusiasm that swept France from one end to the other. For the first time the workers were free on Saturday afternoon and it was on Saturday that the men, women and children of the suburbs came to Paris. The trains could not handle the crowds. When in Paris they strolled along the boulevards and sat in the cafés. There were no demonstrations, no angry chauvinist whipped-up protest meetings, not a word of rancor, not a cry of revenge. The sordid past seemed forgotten. The world of slums, of shanty towns and gutter poverty had taken on a rosier hue. It still existed but it was wrapped up in the twilight of a sinking sun. It was a regenerated France that had come upon the scene.

I have never seen such an elation of spirit, such an outburst of *joie de vivre* as a few days after the signing of the Matignon agreements. At noon Albert Einstein, invited by Paul Painlevé, one of the ministers of the government, made a speech at the Sorbonne on his favorite subject: "The reconciliation of nations and classes and the formation of a European democratic federation."

In the afternoon one million people promenaded on the boulevards. They did not march. They strolled quietly, with great dignity, from the Madeleine to the Place de la Republique and beyond to the Place de la Bastille, workers, professors, scientists, street cleaners, scrub women, shopgirls, students and soldiers. With my wife I stood at the intersection of the Boulevard de Sebastopol and the Boulevard St. Denis, seeing the real France go by, the France of the French people, the France of Robespierre, Condorcet, Lamennais, Zola and Jean Jaurès, *le pays réel.* . . .

I will never forget the moment when two rows of Catholic priests and seminarists, dressed in their cassocks, arms linked and stepping in unison, came into view. The burst of acclaim that greeted the clerics, *"Vive les camarades-abbés,"* was overwhelming.

Two of my teachers, Etienne Giran* and François Bonsirven, who passed by in a crowd of students and professors, stopped to invite us to join the moving mass.

"I dare not," I said. "I will be expelled again if I take part in a political demonstration. Please remember, I'm a foreigner. . . . "

"What are you talking about?" said Giran. "There are no more foreigners. . . . And this is not a political demonstration, *camarade.* This is the army of *la patrie humaine,* the human fatherland on the move. We are going to build schools and theaters and lay out gardens. We're going to be human. . . . "

---

*Etienne Giran, minister of the Reformed Church of France, was arrested by the Gestapo in 1942. He was promised his life if he would inject some bubbles of air into the veins of a Jewish rabbi. Giran refused and was done to death with the rabbi.

"Alright, say no more! Here we come! *Vive la patrie humaine!*"

We had to shake hands all around.

But we also took a look the same afternoon at the demonstration on the Champs Elysées where the Croix de Feu was on parade, De la Rocque in front. What did we hear there?

"Down with Blum! Down with Dreyfus! *Mort aux Youpins!* Death to the kikes!" One huge banner carried the words: "Daladier has sold France to the Bolsheviks!" Another banner proclaimed: "*Le Youpin Rothschild est Roi!*"

The *grand presse*, the respectable big papers, kept up a frenzied tom-tom of slander, attack and misrepresentation. The capacity for evil of the Popular Front's leaders was made to appear of satanic dimensions. It was as clear as daylight to the tone-setting editorialists, who had lost most of their income through the cancellation of the item for "secret funds" in the new government's budgets and now appeared at the pay windows of the big utilities as regularly as bees gather near a sugar factory, that Daladier intended to disarm France, demoralize the people and then hand the country over to Joseph Stalin and "the Mongolian hordes."

Action Française, the monarchist paper, printed lists of men who were "to be shot down like mad dogs." Blum stood at the top of the list with Pierre Cot, Edouard Daladier and Georges Mandel, Clemenceau's Minister of the Interior, who did not belong to any of the Popular Front parties. Blum was described in *Gringoire*, the paper owned by Jean Chiappe, the former police prefect, as a charter member of the executive of the Elders of Zion, a Bulgarian by birth whose real name was Garfinkel, and who was engaged at Russia's behest with Trotsky and Litvinov in the international counterfeiting business.

Léon Blum, one of the finest men I've ever known, was of Alsatian origin, a novelist of distinction, a classmate of André Gide, the last person to be called a rabble rouser. At his home it was a thrill to follow his conversation which had the range and stamp of a large and original mind. This man, a corporation lawyer by profession, was said to have given vent to his "base Semitic instincts" to bring about the demoralization and spoliation of France in the interests of some universal mythical bankers' cartel. To assist him in this undertaking he was importing the dregs of the Jewish ghettos from across the Rhine and Eastern Europe. He was said to be naturalizing the refugees from Hitler at the rate of seventy-five to one hundred thousand a year. With these "human mongrels," Blum was said to be spending his days and nights in endless carousals in the châteaux he had bought up with money stolen from the national exchequer. Fascist papers gave descriptions of banquets and feasts at which the socialist leader was said to preside that surpassed in lustful delirium the most fantastic saturnalia of the ancients. At those feasts "Jewish scum from Poland [ate] from the filched gold plate of the former kings of France and drank the health of a grateful House of Rothschild."

If anyone thinks me guilty of exaggeration let him turn up the files of the journal with the largest circulation in France, *Gringoire*, and read there the front-page articles by the "master" journalist Henri Béraud, or the outpourings of Jacques Doriot in *La Liberté* and Pierre Drieu la Rochelle in *Emancipation*, and, if he's immune to nausea, glance through a book of filth entitled *Bagatelles pour un Massacre* (Minor Reasons for a Big Massacre) by Louis-Ferdinand Céline which was scattered in tens of thousands of copies at the expense of certain large industrial concerns. Not even Julius Streicher, in his wildest paroxysms af hydrophobia, equaled Céline in obscenity and hate.

The campaign of calumny reached a crescendo when pro-Fascist sections of the British and American press treated the country of France as a boiling hotbed of anarchy, the most dangerous hearth of violent revolutionism which, with the aid of Russia, was about to set the world aflame. Although Paris and the provincial cities had remained perfectly calm and peaceful throughout the nearly two years of Popular Front supremacy, the most bloodcurdling articles and dispatches were sent out to Britain and America about tourists fearing for their lives and escaping massacre just in the nick of time, about scenes of horror, looting, lynching, raping and bloodshed, all, it goes without saying, personally witnessed, or based on the testimony of the "usually reliable sources."

The flood of misrepresentation rose so high that the French government, unable to bear the ignominy any longer, issued a communiqué saying that it could not allow the publication of "such flagrant lies" without making a categorical protest. No scenes of violence or horror had occurred in Paris, it said. "Nowhere in France has there been any rioting."

"Is this socialism you are introducing?" I asked the vice-chairman of the council of ministers, Léon Blum, one evening.

"No, it is not," he replied. "We have no mandate to introduce socialism. Like Roosevelt in America we are merely trying to extract from the capitalist system the fullest possible measure of well-being for all. We are first and foremost to raise the standard of living. We desire to create such social

Professor Leonhard Ragaz, professor of theology in Zurich and leader of the European Religious Social Movement

18. Nicolai A. Berdiaiev, Russian lay theologian and philosopher living in France

Reuben Brainin, Dean of Hebrew Letters in America who taught the author Hebrew

20. Chaim Weizmann, President of the World Zionist Organization, later first President of Israel

21. The author, second from left, with Gloria Holden, Lionel Barrymore, Mrs. Max Band and her husband, the painter, in Hollywood. The man on the extreme left is unidentified.

22. Mr. and Mrs. van Paassen at home, 1958

conditions as will make every citizen proud of the fact that he is a French-man and therefore willing and eager to defend France if a threat to her national existence should ever arise."

"But suppose," I ventured, "the people who are sometimes called the ruling class refuse to collaborate and withhold their capital or export it abroad as they have begun to do, if the high clergy and the unquestionably reactionary army officers obstruct and hinder the efforts of your government? What will you do then, employ force? Will you in that case institute a dictatorship of the proletariat as the communists did in Russia; that is, crush your opponents and liquidate them as a class?"

"Ours is not a workers' government," replied Blum, "but a government of national concentration. We are a government of all Frenchmen and of all classes. We are also the government of the bankers, the trust magnates and the press lords. It is true that these are our opponents. But I do not think that we are trespassing on their interests. Have they themselves not always insisted that France must be strong and free? How can France be strong and free if the majority of her citizens live in stinking holes where children perish from malnutrition and grown-ups are led to hate the country which is always praised as free and generous, but which denies them an elementary measure of well-being? Our program is one of national regeneration, and in this we expect all classes to collaborate for the common good."

"When you nationalized the Bank of France and the armament in-dustries, weren't you trespassing on the privileged status and the interests of the *haute bourgeoisie*? Isn't it said in certain sections of the press both here in France and abroad, in Britain and America, that you are a trail blazer for a Bolshevik revolution? Aren't you called a second Kerensky? Do not the communists charge you of being too weak, too hesitant in pushing through your reforms?"

"Yes, the communists are very critical of us. But they are not in power! They have no representation in the cabinet. They want to go faster, but they must abide by the law. They should bear in mind that a French government with a full-fledged socialist program would almost certainly meet with opposition from abroad; that there even might be foreign intervention. That's what happened in Russia. The communists ought to know this better than anyone else. . . ."

"Suppose the communists stage a *coup*? That's the way they got into power in Russia. . . ."

"The communists are no threat to our government. . . . But I will say this, if the reaction continues its present tactics, if the opposition places still greater and more obstacles in our way, if it still further discredits us abroad, I will go to the workers and I will tell them frankly: 'It cannot be done, my friends. You have enemies who deny you a place in the sun, it is up to you to decide what to do next.'"

More than once both Daladier and Blum reminded the communists in parliament and in the press that their support was desired only insofar as it affected national regeneration through social reform and military preparedness, and that the government would under no circumstances tolerate the furtherance of revolutionary aims which they might secretly harbor.

"Might secretly harbor," for in reality revolution was the furthest thing from the minds of Stalin and his followers in France. Stalin favored the maintenance of the *status quo* in Europe. He was anxiously guarding against the slightest change in the postwar situation in Europe either by a revolution or by a shift in the alliances. He did not want to embarrass France in the least. He told Pierre Laval on the occasion of that politician's visit to Moscow in 1935, to pass word to the French communists that they were to drop their opposition to the passage of military budgets in the French parliament, and zealously support any French government so long as it pursued a policy of collective security. That meant also not to play any revolutionary tricks.

It goes without saying that the French communists strictly obeyed the ukase of the Russian chief. In the days of the Popular Front the communist party conducted itself with exemplary patriotism. They were in fact more nationalistic than the nationalists and outhurrahed them in patriotic demonstrations.

By their correct attitude, or rather by overdoing it, the communists nevertheless played into Hitler's hands. The Popular Front frightened the Fuehrer. A France so solidly united, militarily so alert, politically so unanimous, was not the kind of France that could be run underfoot as easily as the Rhineland. The French communists, whom Hitler expected to disrupt the political unity by driving for a position of supremacy in the Popular Front and ultimately making an attempt to institute a communist dictatorship, did the very opposite. They toned down their revolutionary propaganda to a minimum and became the advocates of a preventative war against Nazi Germany. The communists staged their largest demonstrations and mass meetings in cities on the German border, notably in

Alsace at Strasbourg, Colmar, at Metz and Troyes and other cities.

This tactic greatly embarrassed the French cabinet. Blum, Daladier Herriot and Paul-Boncour did not want to give the world the impression that France was rearing to go to war. They still hoped for a reconciliation with Germany and to avoid a European conflict. By their tumultuous mass meetings in the German border regions, the communists, however, made it look as if France was in an aggressive mood.

Though the Popular Front alliance was still in tact, the image of a solidly united country began to pale.

Suddenly the King of the Belgians, Leopold III, fearing, as he said, that his country in the event of war between Germany and France would become the main battlefield, broke off the alliance with France and reverted to a position of neutrality. This move, which was suggested to Leopold by the British foreign office, was a serious setback for France.* The northern borders suddenly lay wide open and the Maginot Line became virtually useless if the Germans should follow the same route of invasion as in 1914 and 1870; i.e., through Belgium and the Ardennes.

Before the French high command had time to remedy the situation by building up defenses on the Franco-Belgian frontier, Adolf Hitler took a step which transferred the world's attention to an entirely different arena. A group of Spanish generals, headed by Sanjurjo, rose in revolt against the Spanish democratic republic. At first this military revolt was looked upon in France as a mere colonial brawl or *pronunciamento*. It soon booamo evident that Hitler was behind It. At the German embassy in Madrid a consignment of 140,000 revolvers from Germany was discovered. Six Italian bombing planes, carrying ten machine guns each, crashed in a storm in French Morocco. They had started from the military airdrome in Milan for Spanish Morocco three days before General Franco ferried three brigades of Moorish troops across the Straits of Gibraltar on July 18, 1936, to the Spanish mainland.

The world was informed that these patriotic Spanish generals had gone to liberate Spain from the communists. The only drawback to this assertion was that there were no communists to speak of in Spain. In the *Cortes* sat thirteen communist members out of 315 deputies. There was not a single communist in the republican cabinet. But this the world didn't

*See: *Le Roi des Belges a-t-il trahi?* (Was the King of the Belgians a Traitor?), a book published by a group of Belgian lawyers after the war.

know. Nor did the world know that Franco and the other leaders of the rebellion were men who had been banished from the mainland to the colonies for having been implicated in an insurrectionary movement in Asturia two years earlier. Any other government would have had them shot. The republic asked them to swear an oath of allegiance to the democratically elected government of Spain and gave them positions of command in the colonies, Canary Islands, Spanish Morocco and Ifni. This was their banishment.

I happened to be touring Palestine, Transjordania, Syria and Egypt following my long visit to Ethiopia when word came of the Spanish insurrection. I flew on July 25th from Alexandria to Barcelona in a machine piloted by a Belgian who carried a load of what I suspect to have been narcotics from Smyrna. I was in agony from the moment I climbed aboard this old crate till I set foot in Catalonia. Three times we almost touched the water as the one engine conked out and three times as by some miracle started up again.

When we landed in Barcelona the fighting was still going on, though the bulk of the 40,000-man garrison had gone over to the loyalist side after a three-day battle which cost about 5,000 lives. Only the commanding general, Goded, and his staff were still holding out in a tower adjacent to the Church of St. Agathe on the Plaza del Rey. They fired their machine guns into the square and the Calle Tapineria till their last bullet was spent. The church was set on fire and the general and his staff were smoked out. As they walked from the entrance they were shot down. Goded was arrested and later executed. Then the fire brigade appeared and the fire was quickly put out. This was the first glimpse I had of the so-called Spanish civil war.

I wanted to go to Madrid where the military revolt had also failed, and actually got on a train loaded with *milicianos* headed for Lerida and Saragossa. The train advanced ten kilometers, then turned back to Barcelona because unseen snipers took it under fire. On the second try we advanced fifteen kilometers and then found that the track had been dynamited. We had to wait two days before a crew of railroad workers came up from Barcelona to lay some new rails. Then we passed through Lerida, but got stuck again at Sietamo which lies a few miles southeast of the town of Huesca. In Sietamo a column of *milicianos* had made a halt prior to launching an assault on Huesca. The column's chief was Durutti, the president or chairman of the Iberian Anarchist Federation.

He had his headquarters in a freight shed on a siding. With him was his general staff made up of an English boatswain, Frank Middleton, who had jumped ship in Barcelona; Antoine Crespin, a journalist of the Parisian newspaper *Barrage;* and a certain Sěnor Panjanu, the only one of the 49 colonels of the Catalonian garrison who had not joined Goded's revolt. There was also a monk in Benedictine garb. He came from the great convent of Montserrat and seemed to have taken upon himself the role of father confessor to the badly wounded and dying. Father Ponchón was his name. He was fighting a war all of his own; for Catalonian independence. He told me he hated everything Spanish, the language most of all.

The *milicianos,* Durutti's men, carried revolvers. There were about 2,000 of them, including the batch that came on the train. There were perhaps 100 riflemen. On all sides—in the grass, under the hedges and pollard willows—lay peasants, some mere children, all waiting for supplies. The riflemen had advanced as far as the railway station, but could not get beyond. The station was under fire from the town hall and the church of Sietamo. Finally a train of flatcars came up from Barcelona. On the flatcars stood six cannons which had been removed from the fortress of Montjuich. While everybody got busy unloading the cannons, three planes came overhead and dropped bombs on the railway tracks and in the orchards. Some of the bombs must have been of the incendiary type. They set a wheat field on fire and a few barns. Everybody got up to look at the planes. Machine-gun bullets from the airplanes pecked away at the plaster walls of the cottages. One pursuit plane veered around and almost touched the roofs of the houses. It flew so low that I could see the observer swing his machine gun around.

I said to the monk: "If he comes again, you can drop him with your rifles. . . . Someone is bound to hit the gasoline tank if you give him a salvo."

"Sure we could," came the answer, "only we have no cartridges. . . ."

No cartridges, no medical supplies, no blankets, exactly two hundred old shells for the antiquated cannons. The airman flew overhead again and sprayed his bullets. The monk pulled my sleeve and made me lie down with him under an umbrella tree.

Six hours at least elapsed before the cannons were unloaded. They were placed in position to fire at the tower of Sietamo. After a dozen misses the cannons found the range and were knocking off chunks of masonry from the church's roof and belfry. Smoke puffs were issuing from the church. But nobody dared to go beyond the station where the snipers were still busy. They had been reinforced with machine guns. Some peasants were carrying the bodies of the snipers' victims past us and laid them under the trees.

An armored train rattled up. The engineer and fireman jumped off the locomotive. About twenty *milicianos* followed them.

"What do you bring us?" asked Durutti.

"A hundred rifles and a supply of shells for the artillery."

"That's enough to take Sietamo. We have to be quick though. There may be reinforcements for the Whites from Saragossa.... Unless our people have won out over there...."

The body of a boy lay slumped against the first house past the railway station. The top of his head was missing. His mouth was stuffed with bread. Death had caught him in the act of eating. In his hand he held the rest of the loaf. The bread was soaking up the blood that trickled from his head.

Suddenly a tank came lumbering towards us. It crunched over the strands of barbed wire stretching across the street. Colonel Panjanu ordered me into a rail guard's cabin. After five minutes a *miliciano* told me to come out. "It's all right. That tank is one of ours. Some peasants captured it."

Everybody crowded about the tank to look it over. The young man who drove it over was being questioned by Durutti and Panjanu. The colonel climbed on top and tumbled inside, leaving the lid open. Presently he reappeared and began handing out jute sacks containing hand grenades.

Durutti smiled: "We'll soon have as much ammunition as Sanjurjo," he said.

"Sanjurjo is dead," I said.

"How d'you know?"

"I heard it over the radio in Barcelona.... Mola and Franco have taken over...."

We were now in the main street of Sietamo. "Better walk close to the walls of the houses," said the colonel. "Get into that doorway, they're sniping. There are snipers even on the roof of this house where we are standing."

We stood in the hallway of a small apartment house. Colonel Panjanu drew his revolver and fired a few shots at the machine gunners on the roof of the house across the street.

"What do you want to do, commit suicide?" I asked.

He laughed and pulled me back further into the hall. "I am giving Durutti a signal where I can be found." As he spoke a spray of bullets from the roof ripped into the façade of the apartment house. Firing was going on in all directions. We could see *milicianos* run along the street hugging the walls of the houses. I saw one *miliciano* who seemed to stumble like a little boy who stubs his toe. His rifle flew forward and clattered on the cobblestones. As he fell his body was riddled with bullets. I sat down on my leather satchel to smoke a pipe. Colonel Panjanu moved cautiously up to the street door, threw it open and then hastily retreated into the back of the hall.

In the same instant the body of a soldier in uniform plopped into the street right in front of us. It was followed by a second and a third.

Panjanu said: "Our roof is being cleaned up. We'll soon be able to go out."

"Surely not till the roof across the street is cleared."

"It'll be done in a minute. Take a look!"

I saw a soldier lying on the edge of the roof quietly emptying the drum of his *mitraillette* into the street below. Suddenly a *miliciano*'s head appeared behind him. The soldier turned sharply and fired at the *miliciano* and brought him down. In his fall the *miliciano* grabbed the soldier and both rolled off the edge of the roof. Their bodies locked together came down with a smack in the street. A man wearing a slouch cap and slippers quietly picked up the *mitraillette*. In less than a minute it was spitting fire in the direction of the central square where the church stood.

Darkness came. Some houses in the square were on fire. The reflection of the flames through the clouds of thick smoke gave the scene a lurid, lugubrious aspect. Dark figures dashed to and fro at the spot where the street ended in the square. Only the captured tank ventured into the bullet-swept area to reconnoiter. It did not return. It stood burning and sending up thick clouds of black smoke just below the balcony which ran along the façade of the church. From all sides the *milicianos* converged on the medieval building with its massive walls, buttresses and counterforts. They fired blindly at the windows and porticos. Short wicked-looking tongues of flame leaped in answer from the sound holes in the tower and the belfry. A half dozen machine guns fired in our direction from between the pillars of the balcony.

Milicianos were dragging up two of the cannons of Montjuich.

"Why only two?" shouted Durutti.

"We have only two shells left!"

"Well, fire away, hit the balcony!"

The balcony wasn't hit, but its machine guns killed several *milicianos*.

"We'd better wait till dawn," Durutti said to the colonel. "Then we'll try the hand grenades. We must dislodge the Whites. Reinforcements for them may be here any minute."

"That all depends," came back Panjanu. "The reinforcements may well come to us. If our people won out in Huesca, the victors will come to help us out."

The firing kept up all night. By the first streaks of dawn the hand grenades were distributed. They were of German manufacture, round tin boxes fastened to wooden handles. But the hand grenades did not reach the balcony. Those who pitched them did it awkwardly. Some men hurt themselves by letting go too abruptly.

"We'll have to rush the square," said Durutti.

"It'll cost us a thousand men," objected Panjanu.

"What are you talking about, we haven't a thousand armed men here, all told. . . . "

I was showing a crowd of *milicianos* how to toss a ball of clay without causing a shock to themselves when a terrific explosion occurred in the square. All my pupils deserted me in a flash. Some men had rushed across the square and flung packs of dynamite sticks at the balcony. Two or three packages landed inside the balcony which came crashing down in chunks on the flagstones of the *parvis* in front of the church. An instant later a white flag waved from one of the louvers of the tower. A thick column of smoke issued from the bell loft. The Fascists in the bell tower were roasting to death. Those in the church came out with their hands up.

While the church flamed, the *milicianos* went around the rear and forced the municipal building in the same way as the church had been taken, by dynamite. Then a horrible discovery was made. When the last defenders came out, *milicianos* searched the building and found in the dank cellars the bodies of the hostages, the labor leaders and the liberals of the community. They lay in pools of fresh blood. The clots of brains adhering to the mildewed walls showed that they had been shot at close range.

Towards sundown the Fascist prisoners were led by. They were all soldiers, several officers amongst them. On the west side of the church they were halted and placed against the wall. A crowd of spectators gathered, women and children amongst them. Father Ponchón went along the line of prisoners with a crucifix in his hand. Each of the prisoners kissed the crucifix. Then Durutti appeared on the scene.

"Down with your rifles!" he shouted to the *milicianos* who were about to shoot the prisoners. "They executed our *compañeros*, you say? Does that mean that we have to do the same thing? . . . These prisoners are going to Barcelona or Huesca for trial. They are human even if they behaved like swine. . . ."

As the prisoners were led away, five airplanes zoomed overhead. After letting go their bombs a series of terrific explosions followed. I went to the quarter where the first bombs had fallen. Several houses had collapsed. *Milicianos* set about digging out the dead and injured whose cries could be heard from under the pulverized and smoking masonry and smashed beams. I saw a little girl and a woman brought out, both badly hurt. From the side of the square came rifle shots again. The *milicianos* were executing the prisoners after all. The friar, still holding the crucifix in his hands, sat crying on an upturned munitions box.

The journey to Madrid took eleven days. I moved by fits and starts—a few miles by rail, sometimes a lift on a truck—but most of the distance I covered on foot. It was August and the roads had turned into heaps of suffocating powdery dust, the color of ocher. My clothes, my hair and face were covered with a layer of coppery dust. At nights mist came up in clouds from the west. At daylight the gloom of night was replaced with deceptive illuminated vapors and drifting fog in which it was difficult to gauge one's progress. I slept in village inns, sometimes in a bed, more often on a wooden bench or even a table. The bread I ate was hard and stale and smelt of the dust on the roads. The wine tasted as if it had been mixed with iron. Only in one village, Taro, did I see any liveliness, a few guitars played by old men sitting under a wooden awning in front of a tavern. Three or four girls danced as about a hundred people looked on, solemnly and reverently as if watching a religious ceremony. There was also some singing.

While watching the dancers, I sat inside the inn all alone except for a very beautiful girl who set before me an excellent meal of bean soup, vegetables, bread and a flask of wine. She went in and out of the room to discuss whatever it was she discussed with an ancient character with a hard, knotted face, her father or grandfather, I imagine. For dessert she brought me some sausages which I declined. Instead she brought me some coffee and a little cheese. My request for a room and bed produced a minor sensation under the awning. After deliberating with the ancient one, the girl returned to ask if I was a Christian. When I said yes, she went into the kitchen to fetch an enormous fat female who lit a candle, took me upstairs and showed me a room with a large upholstered bed with a baldaquin. The only other piece of furniture in that chamber was a prie-dieu. On the wall hung a colored picture of the Virgin adorned with a golden aureole and a blue dress. A large bleeding heart transfixed by a sword hung by a cord around her neck.

"*Nuestra Señora*," said the woman pointing to the picture.

"*Si*," I said, "*gratia plena et benedicta inter mulieres*." My words brought a satisfied smile to the fat lady's face, the first smile I had seen in a month.

At a small third-rate hotel in Madrid not far from the Calle de Toledo I cleaned up and then went in search of Dr. Gerhard Fliedler, the Swiss pastor of the Reformed church, who acted as a sort of co-ordinator of various Protestant missions to Spain. He praised the republican government for having established freedom of religion and told me the astonishing news that since the establishment of the republic in 1931, the various Protestant denominations had won nearly 100,000 converts and opened eighty churches or chapels. They had even started a joint theological school for the training of ministers.

"The rebellion is over," said Fliedler. "We had some days of anxiety, but the fact that the people swiftly overcame the rebel garrison is indication enough that the republic will be victorious all along the line." Madrid, he said, was the heart and center of the military conspiracy and the rebellion's most formidable threat. The provinces were a mere side show where mopping-up operations were now in progress.

Two days later Dr. Fliedler introduced me to Don Miguel Azaña, president of the Council of Ministers, who in turn sent me to Indalecio Prieto and Largo Caballero, the leaders of the Frente Popular.

"Catalonia is entirely liberated," said Caballero. "And Catalonia is the crux of the situation. On Catalonia the word-breaking generals pinned their highest hopes. For in Catalonia reside twenty-five per cent of the entire population of the Spanish peninsula. The province contains fifty per cent of the natural resources of Spain and is the center of seventy-five per cent of the peninsula's light industry and commerce."

"But how many troops have the rebels? Where are they now?"

"Franco has brought across from Morocco three regiments of the Tercio, the foreign legion, and two or three brigades of Moors. We don't know exactly where they stand today, though it's quite certain that Franco has his headquarters at the moment in Sevilla. We have word that the Moors are heading for the Portuguese border line, fanning out through the valleys and forests leading towards Badajoz."

"What about the Spanish navy and air force? Can't they intercept the landings in the south?"

"The fleet lies in the Bay of Biscay ports. The crews are loyal, but about half the naval officers have deserted and several cruisers are badly damaged by saboteurs. . . . We are afraid that the rebels are under protection of Italian naval and aerial units as they cross over to the mainland."

In Madrid we listened twice a day to the voice of General Queipo de Llano, the rebel general stationed in Sevilla, the only large city where the rebellion succeeded. The first time I heard him he was telling the world that Madrid lay in shambles, all churches destroyed, all priests killed and raping parties of Marxists assaulting the nuns in the middle of the streets. But, he promised, it wouldn't be for long. Retaliation was under way. General Franco, also speaking over the radio, said that even if he had to kill off half the population of Spain, he would go through with the campaign "to restore traditional Spanish morality and religion."

When the Tercio and the Moors started their march northward, Queipo de Llano speaking on Radio Sevilla, gave the troops some highly moral advice: "Rape the women of the Frente Popular wherever you find them, rape all you want, and when you have raped them, strangle the bitches."

Fernandes de los Rios, the foreign minister, soon to go as Spanish ambassador to Washington, was the most optimistic of the loyalist leaders. He said he had faith that America and especially President Roosevelt would not leave the constitutional democratic government of Spain in the lurch. Claude Bowers,* the American ambassador to Spain, whom I had not seen since 1924 when he was an editorial writer on the *Evening World*, shook his head dolefully as he said: "The rebels have powerful friends in the democratic party."

---

*In his posthumously published book *My Life*, Bowers states that the first thing President Roosevelt said to him when he called at the White House upon his return from Spain when Madrid had fallen after a three years' siege: "God, I'm glad you're back. . . . We made a big blunder in Spain with our nonintervention policy." Like so many others Roosevelt, let me say it charitably, had been the victim of "the big lie."

Bowers was about the only foreign diplomat in Madrid to be a staunch sympathizer of the loyalist cause. He called Franco a savage and barbarian, to no avail however. Neither the President, nor Cordell Hull, nor Senator Key Pitman, the chairman of the foreign relations committee, paid any heed to his ambassadorial dispatches from Spain.

In the foreign papers still reaching Madrid, I saw that the loyalists had on the whole an extremely bad press, even before any large-scale battles were fought. In most countries the Roman Catholic Church assumed the role of propagandist and whitewasher of the rebel cause. There were, of course, notable exceptions, especially in France where some Dominicans, siding with the loyalists, issued a paper of their own, called *Sept* (Seven). In that paper the rebel generals were flatly accused of betraying not only the Spanish republic but "the cause of Christ" in the first place. What the rebels and their clerical backers found hardest to digest was the fact that the clergy of the Basqueland was solidly on the side of the republic. In return, the clerical press accused the Basque priests and bishops of being in the service of Stalin. This was a lie. François Mauriac, the editor of *Figaro*, and Emmanuel Mounier, founder and publisher of the Catholic monthly *Esprit*, who visited the Basque country before it and its people were given over to the savage murdering hordes of Franco's Moors, praised the co-operative system of the autonomous Basque republic as "the finest application of the Catholic doctrine on labor" as laid down in the encyclical *Rerum Novarum*. It didn't help; the movement was destroyed root and branch when the rebels at last reached the provinces on the Bay of Biscay.

"Why does France always have to wait for Britain to make up her mind?" I asked Léon Blum as soon as I reached Paris. "One French army corps mobilized on the Spanish border will lift the hearts of the loyalists to a pitch of enthusiasm where they will drive the rebels back to the Mediterranean shores."

"Officially we cannot intervene. Britain fears that even a partial mobilization will involve us in war with Germany and Italy."

"Without your help the Spanish republic is lost!"

"My heart bleeds as much as yours for republican Spain. I am daily pressing the British government for some decisive action, or merely to allow us—that is, France—to take some action that will redress the situation for the [loyalist] militia which is now entirely on the defensive.

"The British government proposes a policy of nonintervention," he said abruptly. "America is going to place an embargo on the shipment of arms to both sides in the Spanish civil war."

"But it isn't a civil war any more, the German Kondor Legion and the Italian Blue Division are actually fighting in the Guadarramas. They have received some hard blows, but reinforcements are constantly pouring in."

"But Russia is supporting the republic. This makes it awkward for us."

"I don't know how much munitions Russia has sent to Spain. But there are no Russian troops in Spain, of that I am sure. An embargo on arms would be an obscene farce. This wouldn't affect either Italy or Germany. If the American government puts through that measure it means that the American government has opted for Franco."

"I don't think you ought to say this; the American people certainly are not for the rebels.... The American President is under terrific pressure."

"By whom?"

"By the Vatican and the American Catholic hierarchy. The Catholic clergy is screaming blue murder. The Cardinal Secretary of State, Pacelli, has paid a personal visit to Mr. Roosevelt at his country house in Hyde Park. That some deal was pulled off, you may be sure.... In return for Catholic support in domestic affairs, the President has been maneuvered into betraying democracy in Spain...."

The only member of the French cabinet to adopt a fearless, unequivocal pro-loyalist attitude was Pierre Cot. He was the minister of aviation. He insisted that France was honorbound to make delivery of some 50 fast pursuit planes which had been ordered, contracted and paid for prior to the Franco rebellion. The delivery was held up on one excuse or other. The Fascists, Croix de Feu and Parti Populaire had stationed observers and guards around airplane factories and on the airfield at Villacoublay, to watch for shipments going out to Spain. About half the planes reached Spain nevertheless. The other half was destroyed en route by saboteurs in and outside the French air force.

At nights I attended mass meetings of the workers of Paris and suburbs. I was one of the speakers with Romain Rolland, Paul Langevin and Léon Jouhaux at a rally in the Vélodrome d'Hiver where the audience of thirty to forty thousand rose to clamor for *des avions pour l'Espagne*. In St. Denis where Jacques Doriot had been mayor and still resided, the audience marched through the streets after the meeting shouting for aid to Spain. The same thing happened in Aubervilliers where Pierre Laval was mayor.

In the Salle Wagram I followed two Catholic speakers on the rostrum. I spoke of nothing but of what I had personally witnessed in Spain. At the same time I warned that if Hitler and Mussolini were victorious in Spain, the French people would forever regret not to have gone to the aid of the Spanish republic. In the Chamber of Deputies I listened to the debate on a motion to forbid the passage through France of foreign volunteers. Pierre Cot argued that France could not prevent the debarkation of foreigners in France if they came as tourists, nor keep them from passing on to Spain. The men who went to join the International Brigade and its American sector, the Abraham Lincoln Battalion, had gone to Spain unarmed.

"*Monsieur le President,*" interrupted the rightist deputy, Tixier-Vignancour,* "let them go to Spain, accord them free passage.... The quicker they get to Spain, the quicker Franco will kill them off and save us the trouble later...."

The Chamber's session broke up in a brawl. Deputies streamed into the antechambers, pummeled each other and the ushers till la Salle des Pas Perdus looked like a battlefield.

On my last visit to Spain Dr. Fliedler gave me a list of Protestant pastors and lay preachers who had been done to death by Franco's men. "The first thing the rebels do after taking a town or village," said Fliedler, "is to look for the Protestant chapel or meeting house, set it on fire and round up the members of the congregation and shoot them out of hand...."

The dispatch of this list of Protestant martyrs to Dr. Francis McConnell, the bishop of the Methodist Church in New York, was the end of my career as a newspaperman. The American bishop published the list and the sources of my information. Every incident had been scrupulously verified. Nobody denied the accuracy of my information, but such a flood of letters from all over the continent reached the desks of the *Toronto Star* and its dozen associated newspapers that the editors gave up the struggle. A radio priest in Toronto delivered a daily blast at me. I didn't hear him, I was too far away. Only after the civil war did I learn that I had been designated as a card-carrying communist, an anarchist and atheist. My hatred of the Catholic Church was said to pass all bounds. For the sake of Bolshevik gold I was said to be slandering the Catholic

*This is the same man who defended Roger Salan, the leader of the O.A.S. at his trial in the spring of 1962 and got him off with a life sentence where everybody, including De Gaulle, had expected the death penalty.

clergy of Spain and trying to sow dissension between Catholics and Protestants in America, Timbuktu and other places en route. The *Star* discontinued printing my dispatches, but never dared inform me for what reason, till one day its circulation manager informed me that my articles had been bad for business. Elmer Balmer and Valdemar Vetluguin, the editors of *Redbook* magazine, showed me later how it's done: "Just send letters to the editor, like this pile in front of you, smearing the correspondent, and there's no publisher in America who can resist the onslaught."

In February, 1938, everybody in Paris knew that Adolf Hitler was getting ready to march into Austria and annex that country to the Reich. The leaders of the Austrian Nazis amongst whom was the infamous Arthur Seiss-Inquart, the later Nazi governor general of the Netherlands, assured the Fuehrer that the time was ripe at last and that there would be little if any opposition at all to the incorporation of the Austrian republic in the Greater German Reich. They were not wrong: the occupation of Austria came about without a hitch, except that the Nazi army showed some serious deficiencies in the quality of its equipment, especially the tanks and armored materiel. It was definitely proven to be of inferior manufacture.

At that time the French capital swarmed with German agents, most of them businessmen and *Vertrauensmaenner*, confidential agents, for German armament firms such as I. G. Farben, Rheinmetall and Vulkan with whom the French government would have made short shrift were it not for the fact that they were hobnobbing with French industrialists and bankers who were practically unanimous by now that Hitler's final aim, the elimination of the Russian menace, was in the interest of the civilized advance of mankind; that is to say, the pocketbooks of the armament manufacturers. General Hans Speidel was military attaché at the German embassy in Paris. He knew day by day and hour by hour what was being discussed and planned in the French high command. Otto von Abetz, a high-ranking Nazi, served as the Fuehrer's personal representative. His main task seemed to consist in giving parties and receptions at the German embassy and in acting *gemuetlich* in fostering Franco-German friendship and understanding for Hitler's real purpose in bringing peace to Europe. Abetz bought up journalists, writers, newspapers, news agencies and other media of communication, paying enormous sums of money to spread "the

big lie." One famous French writer I know made a million dollars writing
a series of novels with a pro-Nazi slant. Abetz bought the German rights
for these publications.

Czechoslovakia was next on the Fuehrer's list of conquests and Czechoslovakia was a full-fledged ally of France. From Jan Masaryk, then
Czechoslovakia's roving ambassador, I learned that Prague was growing
uneasy, not only about the occupation of Austria, but chiefly about certain
incidents in the German general staff. The chief of the German general
staff, General von Metzsch, and some of his colleagues had warned the
Fuehrer in March, 1938, that even though the army was ready and the
war stocks sufficient, he could not expect successfully to fight Czechoslovakia, plus France, plus the Soviet Union and possibly Britain and
Poland. His commanders gravely warned the Fuehrer against "the possibility of commotions in the German soul": far too many Germans lived
in dread of a new war which, if again fought on two fronts, might lead to a
military debacle worse that that of 1918.

The officers who took it upon themselves to impress "caution and delay"
on Hitler were immediately dismissed from the service. But the chief
of the French general staff, Maurice Gamelin, was himself disquieted to
a point where he, accompanied by eighteen staff officers, made a tour of
inspection of the military installations of Czechoslovakia and Poland.
Upon his return to Paris, Gamelin submitted a "technical report" to the
Supreme War Council and, of course, to the French government. In this
report he stated that there was no other way out of the difficulties but
to declare war on Germany and march into the Reich together with
Czechoslovakia. The French army was to cross southern Germany while
Czechoslovakia's forty divisions were to come south and make a juncture
with the French at Munich in Bavaria. Bavaria was to be detached from
the Reich and united with Austria under the crown of "His Catholic
Majesty," Otto von Hapsburg. The first effect of this military move, in
Gamelin's opinion, would be the withdrawal of the German and Italian
air force and troops from Spain and thus put an end to Franco's march
of conquest.

The new French foreign minister, Georges Bonnet, whom Daladier
had brought from Washington where he served as ambassador, immediately informed the British government of Gamelin's proposed armed
intervention, while Maxim Litvinov, the Soviet commissar for foreign
affairs, notified Prague that in the event of a German violation of the

Czech borders, Russia would throw her entire air force against Germany.

Hitler was blocked. To march against Czechoslovakia under these circumstances would be more than hazardous; it would be foolhardy. The Fuehrer had to get help. But where would he get it? It looked as if the whole world was against him. A still greater danger threatened: if Hitler got into difficulties or should fall from power, what further use would be the armament campaigns? All the national economics would suffer perhaps irreparable damage.

Herr Hitler had more friends in Europe than he counted on. The most influential opinion molders in the British press suddenly veered against Czechoslovakia. The famous J. L. Garvin, editor of the *Observer*,* denounced Czechoslovakia as "a robber state." Arnold J. Toynbee, the later author of *A Study of History*, then an official of the Royal Institute, wrote in the *Economist* that the Henlein Germans (the Germans inhabiting the Sudeten area of Czechoslovakia), who had raised the cry of "Home into the Reich," were decent patriots. It was the Czech State which oppressed and robbed them of their rights. At the same time the arch-appeaser, Lord Halifax, who was foreign secretary, busied himself in eliminating criticism of Hitler from the British press. Lord Lothian, the former Philip Kerr, onetime secretary to Lloyd George and later ambassador to Washington, joined the influential Rothermere press in expressing "nothing but contempt" for the Czechoslovakian democracy. Czechoslovakia "was an impossible caricature of statehood."** The Germans, he held were right in aiming at a Teutonic *Mittel Europa*; that is, establish a hegemony over Czechoslovakia, Yugoslavia, Rumania, Poland and Hungary, lest these states place themselves under Russian protection and thus increase the Soviet power. Britain, so ran the argument of the pro-Germans in the British press and the foreign office and its affiliates, should side with Germany and *not* back France and Russia in their "policy of Germany's encirclement."

Evidence of American support for Hitler's program of conquest of the Soviet Union came to light when in December, 1936, William C. Bullitt arrived from Moscow where he had been U. S. ambassador, to take up a similar position in Paris. Bullitt, an ex-newspaperman, one of the first, with John Reed and Lincoln Steffens, to report from Russia, was thought to be friendly disposed towards the Soviet Union. After his first tour of

Observer, February, 22, 1938.
**England's Schatten Ueber Europa (England's Shadow over Europe) by Klaus Buehler.

observation, on which President Wilson had sent him, he and Steffens returned to America to tell Herbert B. Swope, the managing editor of the *New York World*: "We have seen the future; it works!"

Appointed to the post of ambassador to the U.S.S.R. by Roosevelt, he soon came to be known as a supporter of isolationist big business interests. But nobody, I dare say, expected so complete a turnabout in his views on international affairs as became evident from the press conferences he gave on arrival in Paris. Mr. Bullitt made no bones about it that he favored an alliance between France, Britain and Germany—under American leadership—to wage war against Russia.

His sponsor in America was not President Roosevelt, but the assistant secretary of state, Sumner Wells, who often pursued a foreign policy diametrically at variance with that of his chief. Bullitt was supported in Europe by the appointment of Joseph P. Kennedy as U. S. ambassador to London and the removal from the Berlin post of William E. Dodd, an anti-Fascist liberal professor from Princeton.

At one of his press conferences, to which Robert Murphy invited me, Bullitt sharply criticized the collaboration of France, Britain and the Balkan states for the maintenance of peace. He predicted the rapid conquest of Czechoslovakia and Austria by Hitler. Czechoslovakia, he intimated, was the great obstacle in the way to a German march against the Soviet Union.

Never were the French so disillusioned and confused. Nobody knew what or whom to believe. In order to throw sand in the world's eyes, the Germans talked peace while Americans of great influence were urging a speedy breakup of Franco-Soviet friendship even if such a course clearly pointed to war. In this atmosphere of doubt, confusion and contradictory circumstances, the Popular Front lost its strong cohesive force and gradually broke up without any decree or dissolution having been pronounced. The left was in power, but the right, with powerful foreign influences at its side, ruled the roost. Blum was fully aware of the danger France ran while the Popular Front disintegrated. Daladier was a broken man because of the cruel suffering and death of his wife which occurred at the height of the Munich crisis.

In April, 1938, the Goebbels press accused the Czechoslovakian republic of having become "an aircraft carrier for Russian bombers." Czechoslovakia, it reported again and again, swarmed with Russian planes. The

Czech government not only denied these false statements, Dr. Benes formally asked the British government to send a mission of experts to investigate Goebbels' charges. Great Britain refused the request. So Goebbels went ahead propagating this part of "the big lie."

Hitler took advantage of the wavering political situation in Europe during the summer of 1938 by beginning the construction of a new Siegfried Line. One million men were set to work night and day to build an uninterrupted line of fortifications right opposite the Maginot Line inside German territory. This showed that someone had informed the Fuehrer of the existence of General Gamelin's "technical plan." The invasion of South Germany by a French army became, if not impracticable, then at least fraught with extreme hazard from that moment onward. France was completely isolated and bottled up within her own defense works. Czechoslovakia stood alone in Central Europe, for Poland declared at the League of Nations in Geneva that she would not permit a Russian army to go to the aid of Prague, nor allow Red planes to fly over her territory.

In September, 1938, the Great Powers, England and France, pulled off the greatest mystification of modern times. For ten days the world stood still. Europe was made to appear as hovering on the brink of catastrophe. Czechoslovakia mobilized. A million men poured into the Maginot Line. The civil population was evacuated from Strasbourg and the rural regions of Alsace. The British navy took up its wartime position at Skagerrak. Stock exchanges suspended operations. London and Paris were blacked out. In British and French ports, Southampton, Liverpool, Le Havre and St. Nazaire, all traffic came to a halt, except naval preparations. Not a sound was heard save the crackle of the transatlantic radio broadcasts which grew more ominous as the hours ticked away. One hasty careless move by a diplomat, it seemed, or a random shot fired by an excited peasant soldier on those borders now bristling with guns, and the continent would be aflame, great cities crumble.

Then the show was suddenly called off; Czechoslovakia surrendered. Dr. Eduard Benes of Czechoslovakia had been "persuaded" by Chamberlain's emissaries, Lords Halifax and Runciman, that it would be in the interest of world peace to hand over the Sudeten areas to Hitler. He, Benes, would be the saviour of the world, the man who made a great sacrifice to prevent the outbreak of the Second World War. Generations to come would bless his name.

Did it go as easy as all that? No, Dr. Benes wanted to resist. He counted on the Gamelin plan. But the Gamelin plan was already discarded by Pétain and Weygand on the ground that an invasion of South Germany had become impracticable by reason of the construction of a line of German forts right opposite the Maginot Line.

France and Britain reinforced their suggestion to give up the Sudeten area to Hitler with an ultimatum: if Czechoslovakia should be so bold as to defend herself against the Nazi legions standing at the borders and thus unleash war, she must not, she was told, expect any help from France or Britain. If Czechoslovakia should in desperation call on the Soviet Union for help, France and Britain would "take a serious view" of such action; in other words, France and Britain might give Hitler *carte blanche* to take over the whole of Czechoslovakia's territory and not merely the Sudeten areas.

It was under these circumstances that Benes gave in. He was *confronted with an ultimatum.* Europe's "model democracy," Czechoslovakia, was betrayed by its *staunchest* friends, the two chief democracies of Europe, France and Britain. After concluding a naval pact with the Fuehrer in 1935, and handing him the Rhineland on a silver platter, Britain and France now presented Hitler with the nigh impregnable line of Bohemian fortresses in addition to the armament and equipment of forty Czech divisions and the greatest munition plant of Europe, the Czech cannon factories of Skoda. It was quite a performance for an England which was supposed to be asleep. Hitler got what he wanted without firing a shot and all Germany sang "A Mighty Fortress Is Our God" while acclaiming Adolf "the greatest military genius of all times." Chamberlain assured the world that the cession of the Sudeten areas meant "peace in our time."

Six months later, on March 15, 1939, Hitler broke his pledge to Chamberlain and Daladier that he had no further territorial ambitions in Europe. He gave orders to occupy the rest of the Czechoslovak land.

The greatest debacle of modern times: the fall of France from the position of a first-class power was now only a matter of time. This would not have happened had not the Franco-Soviet pact been destroyed first. And the Franco-Soviet pact would not have been destroyed, had the government of the Popular Front not been eliminated first of all. Without the bastion of Czechoslovakia, which could have served as a bridge between France and the Soviet Union—a bridge from which the Russian air fleet could have bombed Germany's Ruhr industries—France could no longer be successfully defended except in the framework of the security pact she had with Russia. Repeatedly Moscow drew France's attention to the dangerous situation. German pressure on Poland was increasing in the early months and spring of 1939. Russia saw what was coming.

What could the Soviet government do? To remain faithful to the Franco-Soviet pact after Munich was to invite a German attack on France. Winston Churchill, who was not a member of the cabinet at the end of 1938 and the beginning of 1939, urged the implementation of the existing pacts with a military accord with Russia on the part of both Britain and France.

In June, 1939, Moscow asked the French government very insistently to take her agreements seriously and negotiate an immediate military accord. France accepted on condition that Britain participate in the negotiations. Britain accepted too, but with visible reluctance. Interminable notes passed between Moscow, Paris, Warsaw and London, but no accord was concluded. At last, in July, France and Britain consented to send a military mission to Russia. To show his contempt for the Soviet Union, foreign minister Pierre Flandin ordered the French mission to proceed to Britain first and from there slowly to Moscow. When the negotiators arrived they informed the Russians that they had not the power to make binding agreements, but merely exchange information. When the time came for a frank discussion of war plans, the Russian general staff realized with stupefaction that the French and British representatives either had no such plans or were concealing them. After this experience, and with Hitler's attack on Poland imminent, the Soviet government could choose only between being attacked under the worst possible conditions or signing a Russian-German nonaggression pact.

Great was the indignation in the world when the Ribbentrop-Molotov pact came into existence. Chamberlain called it "monstrous," American "liberals" denounced it as a "criminal conspiracy." It was neither the one nor the other. Closely informed by Pierre Cot, the chairman of the Vigilance Committee which had expanded into an International Committee to Prevent War (of which I was one of the first members), I knew how tirelessly M. Coulondre, the French ambassador to Berlin, and M. Suvitz, the Soviet ambassador to France, had worked to bring France and Russia together into a military accord.

The fact remains that the Soviet government did warn the French of the danger they were running. The Russians recognized Hitler's trap. When they could get no assurance from France, they realized that they must face the German attack alone. Since they were far from being prepared to withstand such an eventuality, they hastily concluded the non-aggression pact with Germany which Ribbentrop offered them. Thus the isolation of France was complete. Hitler struck at Poland and the Soviets, deeming it wiser to follow the age-old advice "If you can't lick 'em, join 'em," decided to meet the Germans halfway. They occupied the eastern part of Poland.

But when Poland was attacked by Hitler, Britain sacked Chamberlain and Halifax, the apostles of appeasement, and called Winston Churchill and Anthony Eden to the direction of national affairs. Britain and France did what they long before should have done, they declared war on Germany. But they did not attack. Britain and France with 110 divisions mobilized looked on while Germany with 25 divisions slaughtered Poland. At the Nuremberg trials General Jodl testified: "If France and Britain had struck at us in September, 1939, Germany would have lost the war five years earlier. . . . "

A British expeditionary force landed in France. The British air force dominated the sky above France. For a time it looked as if nothing more serious would follow. Then Hitler struck again, first at Denmark and Norway, then at the Netherlands, Belgium, Luxemburg and France itself. Gamelin could not prevent a break-through. The new methods of tank warfare, worked out by Colonel Charles de Gaulle, were applied by. . . the Germans. Pétain had given it as his opinion that neither tanks nor airplanes would play an important role in any future war. Instead of sending all available tanks to the front, General Weygand, who preferred fighting the workers of France to resisting the Nazis, distributed the tanks over the whole French territory to prevent an imaginary communist uprising.

All the German generals were young men who had worked out methods of co-ordination between tanks, aviation and anti-aircraft. The French army was under command of elderly, not to say antiquated, commanders who thought in terms of conditions prevailing in the 1914–1918 conflict. The Rhine and Meuse bridges were not blown up. The Maginot Line garrison was withdrawn, but, instead of being sent up north to face the Germans pouring into Belgium, was directed to the Riviera and the Gironde.

When the Germans struck and the front line was pierced, and the

British army under Field Marshal Gort withdrew towards Dunkirk, the French government moved from Paris to Tours and then to Bordeaux. Gamelin was replaced by Weygand as commander in chief.

Winston Churchill appeared in Bordeaux to suggest a merger of the two countries, Britain and France, under one single government. "If the French army is defeated, Britain will still be unconquered.... We will regroup our forces either in Brittany or North Africa...."

Weygand sneered at Churchill: *"Non, Monsieur Churchill,* France is not ready yet to surrender to Britain.... What we need is an immediate armistice with the Germans...."

"General," interjected Georges Mandel, the chief of personnel at the Ministry of the Interior, "General, why an armistice? The greatest part of the French army has not been engaged. Nothing is lost."

"Paris is lost already," said Weygand. "The communists have taken over...."

Georges Mandel interrupted again: "General Weygand, I just spoke by telephone to the police prefect in Paris. He assures me that everything is quiet in Paris. Paris will not be defended. It has been declared an open city...."

"Monsieur Mandel, I say that the communists are taking over. There is a revolution in Paris at this very moment."

"General, let me call the prefect once more!"

"Would you dare to question the word of a French officer?"

"I do question the accuracy of the statement you just made...."

Jeroboam Rothschild Mandel (Georges Mandel for short), three times Minister of the Interior and Clemenceau's most intimate collaborator, was imprisoned in a German concentration camp till 1944. When brought back to France he was turned over to Pétain's militia who assassinated him at Fontainebleau. In the eyes of the Fascists it was tantamount to crime to want to defend France against so nobly intentioned a gentleman as Adolf Hitler. "The big lie" triumphed all along the line.

In the very last hour before the outbreak of the war, the Chamberlain government sought to persuade Poland to make up with Hitler by ceding the Danzig Corridor, as Czechoslovakia had ceded the Sudeten areas. Poland did not refuse to negotiate, but Hitler was in a hurry now. The Fuehrer ordered a number of prisoners from concentration camps dressed up in Polish uniforms, and sent them to attack the border radio station of Gleiwitz. They destroyed the station with bombs and blew up a nearby bridge at Dirschau.

These two faked incidents of aggression were sufficient warrant for Adolf Hitler to launch his attack on Poland.* When Britain called upon the Reich to desist from invading Poland, Hitler lied: "Germany did *not* attack Poland; Poland attacked Germany."

In a somewhat similar way the Germans went about destroying Rotterdam. At the Nuremberg trials, Air Marshal Hermann Goering disclosed under questioning the reason for his having given the order to bomb the city of Rotterdam (causing 100,000 civilian casualties) at three o'clock on the afternoon of May 14, 1940, when a Dutch officer five hours earlier had gone into the German lines to arrange for the capitulation of the Netherlands' army.

"I sent the *Luftwaffe* to bomb Rotterdam," said Goering, "because I had information that on May tenth, ten Dutch planes threw bombs on the German city of Freiburg."

Freiburg certainly was bombed, but not by Dutch planes. Freiburg was bombed by Squadron 51, the so-called *Edelweiss* (Lion's Foot) Squadron, commanded by Josef Kammhuber. In other words, German bombers killed German people to furnish Hitler with the excuse to destroy Rotterdam in what he called retaliation for Freiburg.

The commander of the Edelweiss Squadron was in 1954 appointed chief of the new German air force by Konrad Adenauer.

That the Fuehrer did not march straight to Moscow in 1939, as was his intention all along, must be attributed to his fear of France where there might be a last minute return to the Popular Front policies, collective security and the Franco-Soviet pact. It would have meant another war on two fronts, the contingency the German general staff dreaded most. When France was eliminated in 1940 and Churchill, contrary to Hitler's expectation, did not sue for peace, the Fuehrer attacked Russia in 1941, and thus had his war on two fronts anyway. And that was his downfall!

*Testimony of German General Erwin Lahousen at Nuremberg Trials.

CHAPTER X

Last Days in France

OUR PERSONAL SITUATION in Maisons-Laffitte became downright intolerable as the date of the declaration of war approached. We were plagued and harassed day and night. Slowly it dawned upon me that someone in the political police wanted me out of the way. My friendship with certain leaders of the noncommunist left and my work in the interest of the Popular Front and the Spanish republican cause had evidently made me an "enemy" in the eyes of the rising reaction. One day in the Ministry of the Interior I happened to see four cartons filled with clippings of articles which I had sent to various periodicals in different countries. Scarcely a week passed without my being summoned to appear for questioning at the local police station where a squad of tough mobile guards had taken over from the regular gendarmerie. Three times our house was searched. For what? "*Armes blanches!*" explained the inspector. What are *armes blanches*, literally "white arms?" They are bayonets and knives. Cutlery in our case!

A division of Algerian infantry was quartered in Maisons-Laffitte and vicinity. As we stood looking on as one of its regiments marched down the Avenue Longueil, the main thoroughfare, two carbine-carrying mobile guards ordered us begone on pain of being locked up. "Aliens," said one of the men, "are forbidden to watch French troop movements. . . . "

"We are not *enemy* aliens; we are allies of France."

"Makes no difference. We have orders to keep an eye on you. . . . "

The local parish priest, Father de la Rouardaire, an old friend of ours who, in passing, overheard the mobile guard's remark, asked brusquely: "Who gave you that order?" The man did not answer. "Whoever the person is who gave that order," continued the priest, "please tell him from me, without my compliments, that I consider him and his order beneath contempt. . . . "

I was broadcasting from Paris for the National Broadcasting Company in those agonizing months of August and September, 1939. My spot before the microphone in Paris came at one in the morning, which was eight P.M. in New York. At several train halts between Maisons-Laffitte and Paris, I was forced to get off and hand over my identification papers for verification. Sometimes the train on which I had come left without me and I had to take a cab into the blacked-out capital.

In the city I had first to go to the Hotel Continental to submit my script to the military censor. Once at the Continental I was led into a waiting room and sat together with Ilya Ehrenburg, the correspondent of *Izvestia*. I thought it strange that I was left in the same room with Ehrenburg while other correspondents—British, American, Spanish, Canadian, nearly all men of my acquaintance—went freely in and out the censor's office. Could anyone in the world suspect me of being pro-Nazi? What then about Ehrenburg whose country was now associated with the Nazis in the Stalin-Ribbentrop pact and on the point of fighting together with the Nazis against the Poles?

At last I faced the censor, a young staff officer of noble birth. I handed him my script and he got busy at once with his red pencil. Every favorable reference to France or the French army in my script was roughly scratched out.

"Why?" I asked. "Why do you censor those particular sentences?"

"We owe you no explanation," he replied. "But, please remember: if you depart by one iota in your broadcast from the *corrected* script, you will be cut off the air."

"Everything is quiet in Paris," I wrote in one of my scripts just before the war broke out. "Official sources inform me that there is complete confidence that France will weather the storm if it should break. France is ready.... She has a better army than Hitler, more airplanes, more guns, just as many tanks. She has the unbreachable Maginot Line and the British navy on her side...."

"Who informed you that France is so confident?" asked the staff officer.

"The Minister of War, Monsieur Daladier," I said.

"Where did you see him? You have no pass to the War Ministry!"

"I saw the Minister at the offices of the *Grand Orient*."

"You are a Mason?"

"I am."

"Who told you that the French army was as well equipped as the Reichswehr?"

"Monsieur Léon Blum."

"*Vous êtes Juif?* Are you a Jew?"

"I am not a Jew. But Monsieur Blum honors me with his friendship. I had dinner at his home a few days ago. Isn't Monsieur Blum a good authority to consult in the present crisis? ... "

"Monsieur Blum," replied the officer, "*n'est pas Français des Français,* he is not a real Frenchman. You yourself are a Jew too. Don't deny, please! I have it right here before me in this paper." He showed me a copy of the *Angriff* dated June 23, 1933. "This article says," continued the viscount, "that you are a Jew and that you are in the pay of the Jewish international. Further, that you are one of the ten worst enemies of the German Reich."

"Who wrote the article, may I ask?"

"The Minister of Propaganda, Dr. Goebbels.

"*Je m'en fous pas mal de ce type!*" I said. "Would you mind telling me who are the other nine chief enemies of the Hitler gang?"

"Winston Churchill, Rabbi Stephen Wise, Dorothy Thompson. ... "

"Pretty good company," I said.

"Monsieur," the viscount retorted angrily, "the international Jews have for years conspired to drive France into war with Germany. ... If you think that by your broadcasts you can help the Jews take revenge for the *salaud* Dreyfus, you are mistaken. ... I cancel your script. ... In tomorrow's broadcast you will not speak of French military affairs. *Bonjour, Monsieur!* ... "

"No, it's not *bonjour,* this time it's *adieu.* You do not want a victory for France, do you? You think like Thierry Maulnier who writes in his *Gerbes de Force* that a victory for France would mean a victory for democracy in all of Europe, including Germany. You don't want democracy at all. Isn't that the whole point? ... "

"Rather Hitler than Blum!" he replied.

Such was also the thought in the back of the minds of the ecclesiastical hierarchy, the big bankers, certain members of the high command, the Weygands, Pétains, Darlans; the editors of the antidemocratic newspapers, Daudet, Maurras, Drieu, Doriot, Coty, Déat, Laval and De la Rocque, most of whom were anti-Dreyfusards in the days of the Affair. The French Fascists utilized the war of 1939 to destroy *La Gueuse* (the slut), the scurrilous epithet by which they generally designated the republic.*

*According to Daniel Guérin in his *Revolution Manquée,* Madame la Maréchale Pétain said in the spring of 1941: "My husband has never been so happy in his life as these last two years ... while liquidating the remnants of the French Republic."

They thanked God that the Popular Front was no more. They were afraid that in the hour of France's danger, the people might reunite and the Popular Front be reconstituted.

Had the Popular Front been in power in 1939, I am convinced that the war with Germany would not have taken place!

One night a dozen women and girls gathered in front of our house at No. 1, Rue Edouard VII, to shout that a light was burning in the attic. The black-out watchman for our street, who must have been just around the corner, appeared on the scene an instant later. He was a well-known Cagoulard. He went into the attic with myself following in his wake. There was no light. But the women outside kept on shouting: "We've seen the light ourselves. He's signaling to the *Boche*. He's a *Boche* himself. *Boche assassin! Boche assassin!*" The shouting woke all the dogs in the neighborhood and of barking there was no end that night.

The following day a military officer called to advise me that I must vacate the premises within ten days. "Foreign consulates are moving from Paris on account of the air raid danger.... Your house is required for the Turkish consul general.... By the way," he added, "you had better get rid of your dog. He disturbs the peace at nights. There have been many complaints.... We must preserve France's food supply. We cannot afford to feed alien dogs.... It may be a long war...."

"My dog is not an alien.... He's Alsatian."

"No matter! Tomorrow he'll be put out of the way!"

The same afternoon I watched a column of civilian prisoners walk into town. These men and women, loaded with suitcases and other luggage, were marched to the grandstand at the race track and locked up in the sheds beneath.

"Something is going on here that isn't right," I said to Jean Treille, the pastor of the Huguenot church. "I recognized three individuals among the prisoners: Lion Feuchtwanger, Ernest Toller and Leonhard Frank. These men are not enemies of France. They are fugitives from Hitler. They fought Hitler and the Nazis from the very beginning.... They are anti-Fascists to the core."

"Let's go and see the mayor," said Monsieur Treille.

At the town hall the mayor turned us over to the commandant of the mobile guards.

I began again: "Those prisoners have been legal residents of France for years.... No doubt, a mistake has been made.... The League of Human Rights ought to be notified...."

"These prisoners are Léon Blum's cronies," interrupted the commandant.

"I'm sure they have permits of residence...."

"Would you like a permit to join them under the grandstand?"

"What's going on in our France?" asked Pastor Treille when we regained the street.

"Fascism is installing itself, that seems clear enough! ... When Fascism comes in justice goes out!"

At the Police Prefecture in Paris one had to obtain an exit permit for leaving the country, and at the Finance Ministry, then located in a wing of the Louvre, a certificate that all taxes were paid. The revenue employees were very slow in their movements. Twice I lined up from ten in the morning till four in the afternoon without obtaining permits or certificates. On the third day I was finally given some attention. Sections of the Paris streets were suddenly sealed off by military police and persons caught in the sealed-off portion badgered with questions as to their identity and domicile. Many were arrested. I was caught twice and let go after being questioned and making a telephone call to Anatole de Monzie. I no longer dared call Blum or Jean Longuet....

One morning—it was in mid-September—I took the last train for Maisons-Laffitte out of the St. Lazare station at 1:40 A.M. and sat all by myself till the train set in motion and a man entered the compartment. He was well-dressed, about six feet two or three tall, and clean shaven. I glanced in his direction once or twice for, though I had some newspapers, the light in the compartment was so feeble that reading was out of the question. I thought I recognized him as a frequent traveler on the suburban line Paris–Maisons-Laffitte, but I may have been mistaken. After all, I had traveled up and down the line a thousand times and must have looked into as many faces in the course of the years.

Slowly the train rattled on, stopping at every station to let on or let off passengers: Batignolles, Clichy-Levallois, Asnières. As soon as we crossed the Seine bridge at Asnières, my fellow traveler who sat in the opposite corner near the door giving on the railway platforms, rose from his seat, reached for a package in the net above his head and unwrapped a revolver. I acted as if I did not notice but, when he sat down again, I suddenly looked him straight in the face. He had the revolver in his right hand and was pointing it in my direction.

The train stopped at Bezons. There were no passengers and we rolled on to Houilles. I was growing nervous and said pointing at his revolver: *"Qu'est ce que cela veut dire?* What does this mean?" He did not reply. He only jerked the revolver upwards pointing it at my head. As I looked at him I noticed the tiny gold emblem of the Croix de Feu on the lapel of his jacket.

"Don't make any move when we stop at Houilles," he spoke up suddenly. "I have you covered. . . . "

"Why have you got me covered?" I asked.

"That's my business," he returned. *"D'ailleurs,* you know very well! You are one of those foreign agitators who have pushed France into war with Germany. . . . "

"I have done that? Monsieur, you are mistaken. I assure you that I haven't the slightest influence in such matters. . . . "

"There's no mistake. . . . You are one of the agitators who wanted to weaken France by sending our airplanes to Spain," he said.

I did not reply; the train was slowing up for the halt at the Houilles station. I don't know what thoughts passed through my head. There was no possibility of throwing myself on the stranger for the entire compartment's width was between us, and one move on my part, so I figured, at least, would make his revolver go off.

The train stopped and, as it happened, the compartment in which I traveled halted right in front of a station platform lamp. Through the window I could see a woman carrying a basket and two station employees talking with her, the stationmaster and his assistant, the *contrôleur,* who took the tickets when passengers got off.

One of the men opened the door of the compartment and the lady entered. As she stepped inside her eye fell on my fellow traveler sitting next to the door with the gun in his hand. She let out a scream.

The train had begun to move, but the stationmaster, hearing the woman scream, blew his whistle and brought the train to a halt. He approached the door of our compartment, opened it and said to the lady: "Was that you calling?"

"Yes," she said, "look!" She pointed to the man with the revolver on his lap. . . . Before anything else could be said or done, the stranger got up, pushed the stationmaster aside, and ran for all he was worth down the platform and through the gate into the darkened street. . . .

"Who was that?" asked the railway man.

"I don't know," I said. "He's been sitting in that corner since the St. Lazare station. He pulled the gun after we left Asnières...."

"Did he point it at you?"

"He sure did."

"Did he threaten you?"

"He asked me if I still wanted French airplanes to go to Spain."

"*Ah, c'est ça!* That was one of De la Rocque's goons!"

"More likely, Laval's!" I said.

"Quite well possible," agreed the stationmaster. "That guy is another one who has sold out...."

By that time the engineer and the fireman had come into the stationmaster's office where that official proceeded to draw up a report of the incident.... The train got going again with about twenty minutes' delay. In Maisons I passed through a lot of Algerian military sentries and reached the house without any further trouble. But I never found out the name of the man who had menaced me with his gun.

I did not tell my wife for fear she would be disquieted every evening I had to go to Paris. Still, I thought it advisable to take her and Hugo to Britain. We crossed over on the last boat in the regular Channel service. At Tilbury docks, at exactly the same spot where I landed on my way to Canada in my youth, I saw them off on the S.S. *American Farmer,* sailing for New York. Back in my London hotel, I turned on the radio and heard an announcement that the *American Farmer* was stopped and searched by a German submarine crew... and, after an agonizing minute in which I felt as if the world had come to an end, learned that, while the *Farmer* flying the American flag had been allowed to proceed, another passenger liner of British nationality, the S.S. *Athenia,* had been torpedoed and many of its passengers drowned....

I had no trouble getting back to France; the Channel service was now in British hands and the steamer crowded with troops. In Paris I watched still more soldiers leave for the Belgian frontier and take up their position in the inglorious Maginot Line. The dismal mood of the departing *poilus* seized me by the throat with an agonizing grip. Without anybody telling me I knew then and there that France was lost. I never saw troops so downhearted, so dispirited, so much like dumb sheep being led to the slaughter as those French soldiers leaving for the North and East in the late summer of 1939. Their morale was not only low; there was no morale at all. The Fascist papers threw the departing troops into a still greater quandary by asking day after day whether it was really worth-while to "go and die for Poland."

After I got the old gardener in Maisons-Laffitte to help me pack the books and furniture for shipment to America, the police appeared on the scene again.

"You are not allowed to take out any books or papers," said the lieutenant as we were carrying some boxes into the garden.

"But they are my property," I objected. "Who forbids me from taking out what belongs to me?"

"I am acting on special orders of the Ministry of the Interior," he said.

"I will telephone at once."

"Whom will you telephone?"

"I will telephone Monsieur Daladier, the Minister of War. . . ."

"Your telephone has been disconnected this morning."

"I'll go to Paris right now."

"Your car has been requisitioned by the War Department. There was a brief case in it. We have saved it for you. . . . "

"What am I permitted to take out of the house?"

"One suitcase with clothes. We will give you a receipt for everything that stays behind. . . . "

I walked into the house, went through all the rooms, and in the library stood still for a minute gazing at the rows of books, all my grandfather's old books and many, many more, accumulated in the course of the years. . . . *Adieu, adieu, mes amis!*

How I ever got to Le Havre, I'll never understand. The train was so crowded that I stood on the running board outside the compartment and clung to a door for dear life's sake. In Le Havre I had a new disappointment, the boat, the *S.S. Washington*, on which I had reserved a berth, was just sailing while German *Stukas* bombed the harbor installations and adjacent streets. I still could catch the ship though, I was told, for the *Washington* had not sailed directly to America; it was going to run into port at Le Verdon which lies at the mouth of the Gironde on the Bay of Biscay. But how to get to Le Verdon? No bus or train was running in that direction. I strung my suitcase to my back like a packsack and walked as far as Rennes, where I caught a train at last. The journey took six days. From Bordeaux I traveled by streetcar to Le Verdon.

In the cabin on board I found M. Stéphane Lauzanne, the editor of the Parisian newspaper, *Le Matin*. M. Lauzanne was going to Britain. When we sailed for Southampton after a further delay of a week, M. Lauzanne told me that his bones had turned to water. "There is no hope, no hope at all for France," he said.

"What are you talking about?" I asked. "Poland may be crushed. The French army is intact. Except for some skirmishes in the Saarland, not a shot has been fired."

"The French army has no equipment!"

"No equipment? What do you mean?"

"The equipment is there, but it isn't where it should be. . . . The tanks have been distributed over the whole country. There are tanks in every city: Marseilles, Lyons, Bordeaux, Toulon, Nice, Tours, everywhere. The air force is on the Riviera and in North Africa. . . ."

"Why? Does the high command expect an attack by Mussolini?"

"No, Weygand has persuaded the government that there may be a communist uprising."

"A communist uprising? But Churchill himself says that the communists are joining their units like all other Frenchmen. . . ."

"I am going to Britain," said M. Lauzanne, "to talk with members of the British government. . . . I am going to tell them that the French republic is betrayed. . . . Even now the country is being handed over to Hitler. . . ."

At Southampton M. Lauzanne and many members of the Canadian consular staffs stationed in France went ashore. Their places on the ship were taken by a mass of passengers led by Lord Beaverbrook, the owner of the *London Express*, Helena Rubinstein, the well-known beauty expert, and Arturo and Signora Toscanini. In the course of the first night at sea, I noticed that Signor and Signora Toscanini sat in the library; they had no cabin. Some cots were placed on the top deck for their convenience, but they were driven downstairs by a cold wind and rain. I told the purser that the Toscaninis could have my cabin. I would take a cot on the top deck.

Thus it was arranged. My cot stood between those occupied by Shlomo Grodzensky, the editor of *Der Yiddischer Kempfer*, a socialist-Zionist paper in New York, and Professor Solomon Fineman of Temple University in Philadelphia. Because of the American flag and the presence on board of Lord Beaverbrook, many of my fellow passengers felt quite safe from a German submarine attack. I suspected the opposite: had the German high command been aware of Beaverbrook's presence, they might well have made an attempt to send us all to the bottom. Lord Beaverbrook, and the mission on which he was bound to America, represented a greater danger to the Nazis than an army with banners.

When I landed in New York I could scarcely walk. I had lumbago, sciatica, and a host of similar ailments, abetted by sleeping in the cold wind on a sheet of canvas spread between four stilts.

It took nearly a year to put me back on my feet. While lying down I wrote a small book and gave it the title *The Time Is Now* taken from a minute-by-minute electric time signal flashing from across the Hudson River in full view of the bed where I lay in the apartment house at 90 Riverside Drive.

In *The Time Is Now* I sought to show that Hitler would not be content with conquering the European continent. In accordance with the grand strategy, elaborated by Dr. Karl Haushofer of the Geopolitical Bureau, the Fuehrer would, I thought, make Africa the next objective of his world campaign. True, the British navy in the Mediterranean still barred the German army from setting foot on Africa's shores, but this obstacle, I predicted, would be overcome by the Nazis *walking around* the Old World sea.

The Italian air force was already bombing all British and allied *points d'appui* in the Mediterranean: Malta, Gibraltar, Greece, Crete and Cyprus. From Sicily the Nazi troops and Mussolini's *arditi* would most likely attempt the crossing while swarms of German submarines sought to block the Mediterranean to British ships. From wherever they landed— Tunisia, Algeria or Cyrenaica—the German march of conquest would move inevitably in the direction of the Suez Canal. Egypt and its King Farouk would in all probability, like the Dutch, the Danes and the Norwegians, be made happy with a promise of "liberation" from British domination while the capture of the Canal would bring about, not only a juncture of the Italian and Japanese navies, but cut Britain off from her Far Eastern possessions and military resources.

The immediate objective in the Near East appeared quite clear: after their conquest of Russia, the Nazis would continue their march through the Caucasus, Turkey and Iran, while the German-Italian forces moving east in North Africa would in a gigantic pincer movement seize Sinai, Syria and Iraq, and thus force the British in Palestine and Egypt and elsewhere on "the thin red line" of empire to surrender or else withdraw in the direction of Afghanistan and India, leaving their artillery and other heavy equipment behind.

This was all speculation on my part for the Germans still hadn't reached Stalingrad, nor were they as yet across the Mediterranean. Many of the critics thought the book worse than speculation. They doubted my sanity and dubbed me an armchair strategist, a sensationalist and warmonger who had risen "to new heights of ignorant, irresponsible, malicious jingoism." One novelist wrote that my aim was to create a war hysteria with the object of bringing America into the war against Germany.

I hadn't said a word about the desirability of bringing America into the war. When I entitled the book *The Time Is Now*, I meant that the time had come to reflect, to take stock and ponder the possible consequences for all mankind of the downfall of British world power.

After Hitler's attack on Russia in 1941, I was, in the estimation of American Firsters and Bundists, merely an agent of Stalin. I wanted America to save Russia. I had given myself away, it was said, by supporting the Ribbentrop-Molotov pact. There was no use pointing out that in *The Time Is Now* I had referred to the Nazi-Communist pact as "the work of the two greatest scoundrels of world history, Hitler and Stalin," the lie had been launched on its career and it was hard to overtake it.

The radio program which I, as "a dollar a year man," conducted for the Department of the Treasury in support of United States Savings Bonds was the first victim of the slander campaign. The Secretary of the Treasury, Henry Morgenthau, showed me some letters in which the charge was made that I brought only communists to the program for the purpose of spouting Stalin's propaganda. Not only did I *not* select the persons interviewed—this was the work of Judge Ferdinand Pecora—but a careful examination failed to turn up one single communist in the list of prominent persons who had appeared on the program: Major Alexander de Seversky; Countess Alexandra Tolstoy; Thomas Mann; Heinrich Mann; Klaus Mann; Jarmila Novotna of the Metropolitan Opera; Henri Bernstein, the French playwright; Henri Torrès, member of the Chamber of Deputies; one of the leaders of the Free French in New York, Maurice Maeterlinck; Edna Ferber; Professors Tillich, Borgese and Salvemini; Count Sforza; William Ziff; Dr. Chaim Weizmann; Max Ascoli; Eve Curie; Henri de Kerillis, a (rightist) deputy to the French Chamber; Hendrik Willem van Loon; Dr. Stephen S. Wise; Senator Wagner; and José Iturbi. . . .

With Hendrik van Loon, Hans Kindler, the director of the Washington Symphony Orchestra, and my kinsman, Dr. Joseph R. Sizoo, minister of the Collegiate Church of St. Nicholas on Fifth Avenue in New York, I went around in the Reformed churches raising money for the relief of thousands of destitute sailors and travelers who were left stranded in various American ports on the Atlantic and Pacific.

I spoke all over the country in meetings in support of the Free French; once to 25,000 people in Madison Square Garden together with Jan Masaryk, Dr. Albert Simard and Jacques Soustelle, who was then De Gaulle's chief lieutenant in the western hemisphere. The only belligerent gesture I indulged in, if belligerent it may be called, was to invite the audiences I addressed to rise for a moment in tribute to the men of the Royal Air Force who were bearing the brunt of the Teutonic furor in the Blitz. It was in reality a testing of the audience: if they rose they were friendly. If they refused to rise, as happened more than once in Chicago and other midwestern cities, I knew the audience was hostile and conducted myself accordingly.

In the fall of 1941 I had a visit of two young Palestinians, Peter Bergson and Samuel Merlin, who asked me if I didn't think the time had come for the Jews to raise an army of their own to fight on Britain's side. Bergson and Merlin were accompanied by my old friend, Colonel John Henry Patterson, D.S.O., who commanded the Royal Fusiliers in Allenby's army, the so-called Jewish Legion. Many old people in Palestine, said Bergson, were walking around with capsules of potassium cyanide in their pockets in fear of a Nazi victory at Suez and a wholesale massacre of the Jewish population of Eretz Israel.

"Hitler is killing the Jews as Jews. . . . Let them fight back as Jews, in a Jewish army, in Jewish uniforms and under the Jewish banner," I said in answer to the question.

"Will you," Patterson asked in turn, "repeat what you now say in the presence of the military attachés stationed in Washington? . . . I must warn you that we have consulted the British ambassador Lord Halifax in Washington, and that he is drastically opposed to the idea of a Jewish army. He claims that a Jewish force, either independent or incorporated in the British Near Eastern armies, would place Britain in an embarrassing position *vis-à-vis* the Arabs."

"Is there one single Arab state or Arab mandated territory in the Near East friendly to the British cause?"

"Not a single one," said Patterson. "As a matter of fact a large British force is pinned down in Egypt, unable to join the fighting in the desert because of a possible Egyptian uprising. The Egyptian army officers are pro-German without exception. They have established contact with General Rommel and assured him that they are preparing a royal welcome for him when he reaches Cairo. An apartment is held in readiness at Shepheard's Hotel for the German commander.... The chief of staff of the Egyptian army was arrested as he prepared to fly over to Rommel with the British campaign plans in his pocket."

"The more reason to strengthen the British forces in the Near East by the addition of a Jewish brigade," I said.

When the question was again put to me by Colonel Patterson in a gathering of some 40 or 50 military attachés and other foreign diplomatic representatives in Washington's Mayflower Hotel, I expressed the conviction that Jewish military participation in the struggle would, in the event of victory, greatly enhance the chances of an independent Jewish State emerging from the existing mandatory regime....

Ludwig Lore, a columnist of the *New York Post*, rose to propose my election by acclamation to the position of national chairman of a Committee for a Jewish Army, and elected I was. But I don't know by whom, though the military representatives of half a dozen governments in exile, and as many colonels and generals in uniform representing Latin American republics, raised their hands in my favor.

Back in New York I called at the St. Regis Hotel where Dr. Chaim Weizmann, president of the World Zionist Organization, resided at the time. He expressed his pleasure that I had been elected chairman. His secretary, Meyer W. Weisgal, drew up an agreement under the terms of which the different roles of the Committee for a Jewish Army and the Zionist Organization were clearly delineated. We, for instance, were not to engage in any political activity, nor were we to try and negotiate with the British government or any of its diplomatic agents in America, such as Lord Halifax and Sir John Dill, the top military adviser at the embassy.

The work got under way at once. In a month's time we had branches of the Committee for a Jewish Army in a dozen major cities. The newspapers took notice of us; some like the *New York Post*, the *Washington Post*, the *Los Angeles Times* and the *San Francisco Chronicle* went out of their way to show their support and friendliness.

I wrote a number of open letters to Winston Churchill, President Roosevelt and certain senators and representatives which were published as full-page ads in *The New York Times*, the *Philadelphia Inquirer*, the *Chicago Daily News* and two or three other papers of national prominence. The gist of the letters was a plea for recognition of the right of Palestinian and stateless Jews to go and fight, and if needs be die, for democracy under the walls of Jerusalem. . .

All was going well, we were enlisting thousands of supporters, both Jews and Gentiles, when David Ben Gurion, the leader of the labor party in Palestine, appeared on the scene. The future prime minister of Israel was in a tempestuous mood. He barged into my apartment and without a word of greeting called on me to resign forthwith from the chairmanship of the Committee for a Jewish Army.

"I don't want a Jewish army," he fairly shouted. "I won't have it! I won't stand for it! I will have nothing to do with the gang which propagates the idea of setting up a Jewish army. They are Fascists and terrorists. . . . "

"Is Colonel Patterson a Fascist? You yourself and your friend Itzhak Ben Zvi (the later President of Israel) enlisted in Patterson's Fusiliers in World War I. . . . I consider the colonel a gallant officer and a steadfast supporter of a Jewish Palestine. . . . Besides, Dr. Weizmann doesn't object to the formation of a Jewish army. . . . Nor does Jan Christiaan Smuts! The Field Marshal's name appears at the top of a list of 14,000 signatures by South Africans, Boers and Britons alike, which I have just received."

"I don't care! *I* object! There must be no Jewish army!"

"Why not?"

"You are operating under false auspices!" said Ben Gurion.

"What do the auspices matter so long as we get a Jewish army on its feet? You are a Palestinian! You know the danger better than anyone else. If Britain is defeated in the Near East, all hope of a Jewish Palestine will go up in thin smoke. Why don't you rather join in the effort to stop Rommel? . . . Why don't you take the lead?"

"Palestine is not an independent country. Not till Britain gives the word will Palestinian Jews enter the fray. . . . Lipsky," went on Ben Gurion, addressing himself to Louis Lipsky, the American Zionist leader who was present in my apartment, "it's your duty to see to it that this man stops his agitation for a Jewish army. . . . " Mr. Ben Gurion grew so excited that he clenched his fist under my nose.

Thus I became involved in a quarrel which was certainly not of my making, nor at all to my liking. Denunciations and anathemas from official Zionist sources rained on my head. One Yiddish newspaper in New York changed its habitual reference to me as *der bewusste Freind von Yidden* to *ein Sakono far dem Yiddishen Folk,* "a menace to the Jewish people." A leader of Hadassah, the Women's Zionist Organization, called me a "traitor," though I do not recall what or whom she accused me of betraying. Others, editors of periodicals and spokesmen of Jewish political parties and societies, charged me with having broken Zionist discipline, forgetting that I was never a member of the Zionist Organization and hence not subject to its discipline.

I went straight on with the work of enlisting support for a Jewish army. I never replied to attacks. The raising of an auxiliary force, any auxiliary force, to fight the Nazis appeared too urgent to me to waste time in futile and meaningless controversy. Only in one instance was I forced to take action. This happened when two distinguished rabbis, Dr. Solomon Goldman of Chicago and Dr. Joshua Loth Liebman of Boston preached almost identical sermons one Friday evening. They attacked the Committee for a Jewish Army from their pulpits. I was so used to this that I did not pay the slightest attention. But when word reached me that both doctors had informed their congregations that the Committee was my "private racket" which had netted me "the tidy sum of $50,000 in a few short months' time," I thought they passed the bounds of civilized behavior and instructed Aaron Fishman, an attorney, to investigate, and, if reports were found true, institute proceedings for libel and defamation of character. I took this course because I never received the slightest financial remuneration or compensation as chairman of the Committee, though my successor, Senator Guy M. Gillette of Iowa, received a salary immediately upon assuming office. I believed it reward enough if we should succeed in setting a Jewish army on its feet and thus establish the premises from which, as fruit of the common victory, a wider measure of autonomy or dominion status for the land of Israel might reasonably be expected to follow after the war. . . .*

With our agitation for a Jewish army went a strenuous effort to bring the plight of the Jews in Germany and German-occupied territories to the attention of the American people. Night after night I spoke in churches, temples, synagogues, high schools, universities and public forums all over

*When faced with legal action both rabbis profusely apologized.

the country urging diplomatic intervention and even military action in order to put Hitler on notice that the civilized world would not allow the mass murder of Jews to go unpunished.

If European Jews could not be evacuated to Palestine, I proposed to throw the doors of America open to these refugees. It was all to no avail. The American government did indeed call a conference on refugees in Bermuda in 1942 to which 52 nations sent delegates, but not one of the 52 countries represented in Bermuda or at a second conference on refugees held in Evian-les-Bains volunteered to take in a single refugee. After hesitating a long time, the United States allowed one thousand (1,000) "displaced persons" to enter the country, but when they arrived locked them up in a camp at Oswego. A thousand saved out of millions was but a drop in the bucket. Still, even that small figure was far too high in the opinion of America Firsters and other Fascists. Roosevelt was accused of trying to swamp America with communists.

I wrote to William Temple, the Archbishop of Canterbury, asking him to explain the difference between a Germany that was killing Jews and a Britain barring their road of escape and, when they did manage to escape by sheer superhuman efforts, imprison them behind barbed wire in camps on the island of Cyprus. Though Dr. Temple read my letter in the House of Lords—and commented favorably on it—the consequences of this letter were most disagreeable for me. Winston Churchill did indeed seek to excuse me by saying that as a British subject (which I still was at the time), I had "the full right once a week to tell the British government to go to hell," but this was not good enough for certain "grand moguls" in American Judaism who, in seeking to hide their own inner sense of insecurity, pretended to be *plus royaliste que le roi*. It was I, they charged, who obstructed the American war effort by placing obstacles in the way of our British ally's military campaign in North Africa. One learned professor at a Jewish theological school in Philadelphia declared in a classroom full of rabbinical students that he had good reason to suspect me of being a secret anti-Semite.

In retrospect it is sadly ironical to see certain great American journals, secular and denominational alike, join in commemorating the uprising of the Warsaw ghetto, whereas at the time of its occurrence I stood virtually alone on the platform lauding the heroism of the Jewish boys and girls who refused to be led to the slaughter like dumb animals.

I resigned from the chairmanship of the Army Committee when I could no longer ignore the fact that the Palestinian members of our executive who were all members of the Irgun Zwi Leumi, an underground movement of nihilistic tendencies in Palestine, worked fundamentally at cross purposes with me yet keeping me up in front as a sort of façade of democratic legality. For a time I put the Irgunists down as disinterested young patriots, perhaps a little more vociferous or outspoken than other groups, but without any ulterior motive other than to see their country free to take its place in the ranks of the nations resisting Hitler's drive for world power. In truth the Irgunists were concerned only with building up the prestige of their own political party in Palestine which assumed the name *Herut* (Freedom) after the war and still sits in the *Knesset* as the second largest group. Back in the forties the Irgunists aimed at gaining a reputation in America as the most resolute, daring and devoted Palestinian patriots, by running down David Ben Gurion and Moshe Sharett, the leaders of the labor party and the Trade Union Council, as weaklings, hirelings of the British and little better than Quislings.

Retroactively the claim has been advanced that the Irgun-Herut liberated Palestine by driving the British out. Without batting an eyelash the spokesmen of Herut till this day claim to have brought in the bulk of the illegal immigrants and in general having been the determining factor in achieving independence for the State of Israel. These allegations are too absurd to require refutation. The Irgunists' sole merit lay in their initial endeavors which made a certain impact on public opinion in America and brought many Jews, who stood aside till then, into the general movement of Zion Restored. They forfeited all claims to glory when they, or their partisans, launched into terroristic activities in Palestine, kidnaping and murdering British soldiers and officials and destroying British military installations.

I was all for raising a Jewish army, but not for the purpose of fighting the British.

In the end it was the British government which deprived the Committee of its *raison d'être* by raising a brigade of Jewish volunteers in Palestine and incorporating these in Montgomery's Eighth Army.

It was this brigade whose tanks turned Rommel's right flank at El Alamein and Mareth and, together with the Free French under General Pierre Koenig, achieved the almost incredible victory of Bir Hakkim. The

Jewish suicide commandos were the first in Bardia and Tobruk and they destroyed the Vichy government's harbor installations in Beirut and the airdrome near Bagdad where Nazi troop planes were landing in anticipation of an Iraqi uprising against Britain.

When I saw that the British high command could not bring itself to acknowledge by a single word the invaluable contribution made by the Palestinian Jews to the common war effort, and that not a single British or American newspaper deigned to take notice of Jewish heroism, I wrote a book, *The Forgotten Ally*, setting forth the story of Jewish military participation and the role Palestine played, mainly through its industries and laboratories, as a base and supply depot for the entire British Eighth Army. The book sold a quarter million copies and was translated into eleven foreign languages, including German. It was banned from British Empire territories, but both Ireland and South Africa brought out a clandestine edition while members of the British Intelligence Service in Egypt smuggled a hundred photostatic copies into Palestine itself. The man who photographed the book's pages one by one was Dr. Eliahu Elath, then a major in the British army, later Israeli ambassador to Washington and to London, today president of the Hebrew University in Jerusalem.

The Jewish Brigade also formed the nucleus and backbone of the Army of Liberation which David Ben Gurion called to arms in 1948 when, upon the proclamation of Israel's independence, five Arab countries with a twenty times stronger military potential attacked the new republic only to be hurled back in shame and humiliation. . . .

Our views of the world are perpetually changing. On one point, however, I have never varied: I always took the Jewish people seriously. Though prone to renounce all distinctions of race, nationality and religion from my youth onward—the result, I dare say, of having been brought up in a small country where a certain measure of cosmopolitanism comes almost naturally—I nevertheless identified myself voluntarily and steadily with the Jewish people's national cause to an extent not seen, as far as I know, in the case of any other contemporary Gentile either in America or anywhere else. I do not claim any merit in this matter. My deeper acquaintance with Judaism and the Jewish people proved a greater blessing to me in a quite personal sense than any honors, recognition or reward could have furnished. Without it, on the other hand, I am sure, the course of my intellectual development would have been sensibly different.

Israel, the Jewish people, remain to me of central significance in the history of Western civilization. And this not because of any chosen people concept or special divine revelation, but because the Jews, in spite of the enmity of demonic forces and a thousand deaths, furnish mankind with the key that fits the door through which civilizations enter and leave history; I mean their Messianism, their undying vision and inextinguishable hope of the future.

CHAPTER XI

Still Stir the Ashes of Klaas

On his journey through the inferno, Dante could still hear the branches on the trees sigh their doleful whisper: *no light . . . no hope . . . God has forsaken us. . . .* Our trees on the Western front neither whispered nor sighed. They were all dead. When you looked towards the ridge beyond Arras and Bapaume, you saw that the forest had all but disappeared. What remained was a boundless desolation: heaps of blackened rubble, charred and broken stumps, here and there the bombed and burnt out ruin of a human habitation. The whole valley of the Somme lay under a blanket of snow that winter. The trenches were covered with sleet and ice. Inside the dugouts dirty yellow icicles hung from the ceiling. The frost-covered pit props gleamed like pillars of filthy glass by the candles' feeble light. . . .

That night—it was Christmas eve, 1917—about ten or twelve of us stood or sat or lay in a big dugout, probably twenty feet square. Down the steps of frozen mud rushed a cold wind mixed with the putrid odor of filth and corruption from the latrine buckets standing at the top. Most of us wore our balaclavas under our tin hats, brown woolen masks, leaving only the eyes, nose and mouth exposed. Men were constantly coming down and going up the steps, returning from or moving out to the listening posts, the firing bays, the wiring parties and reconnaissance patrols.

After nightfall our chaplain, Cyril Jones, went from dugout to dugout. Whenever the men raised no objection he read the Christmas story about a great light shining in the darkness and multitudes of the heavenly host announcing the tidings of great joy which shall be to all people.

"Wasn't that all a bloody hoax, sir, just to fool the troops, that song about peace on earth?" one man asked Cyril. "Shouldn't the world be

387

filled with peace by now instead of the stench of corpses?" Cyril put his cap back on but didn't say a word in reply.

At ten thirty sharp on that evening of December 24th, 1917, the German artillery suddenly stopped firing.

"That's a sign they're going to attack at dawn," said Arnot.

"Maybe they ran out of shells," suggested Perryn.

"Oh, hell, we've been hearing that story for three years now. No more shells, no more munitions, no more food, no more nothing. But still they keep on coming. . . . More likely Fritz'll send over a dose of poison gas for breakfast. . . ."

Men began to run to and fro, taking up their positions in the firing bays, in the support and communication trenches. All you heard was the clatter of their hobnailed boots on the duckboards. There were calls for silence. Words of command flew back and forth in the stygian darkness. Then suddenly our artillery stopped firing too, just as abruptly.

A man came through the trench. He wore high boots and carried a flashlight.

"Put that light out, you damn fool!" shouted Arnot.

"Look my man, if you can't talk better language, I may be obliged to put your damn light out."

The flashlight man stopped to light his pipe. He was a staff officer; red tabs on his lapels.

"Sir," I accosted him, "no smoking in the front line! That goes for everybody. . . ."

"The German high command has proposed a twenty-four-hour truce," he came back.

"What for?" asked Coots. "To bury the dead?"

"A twenty-four-hour truce in honor of Christmas!"

Ten minutes before midnight our bugles sounded the cease-fire. Nobody knew at first what the signal meant, for nobody had ever heard it before. But it put all doubt to rest. It wasn't a trick or trap after all. News of the truce was official on both sides.

By the glare of the Very lights we saw them coming over the top. First the coal-scuttle helmets appeared above the parapets. And then their wearers, the men in field gray. For once they carried no guns, no flame throwers, no hand grenades and no cylinders of poison gas. They were unarmed, defenseless.

They stood on the very edge of their trenches with their backs to their own parapets. On our side, too, men were climbing over the top. A descending greenish Very light was caught in the blinding beam of one of our searchlights so that the sky was lit up to noonday brightness.

All at once the Germans began to sing: "*Stille Nacht, heilige Nacht...*" We could see them uncover their heads. They stood with their helmets in their hands.

"Silent night, holy night! ..." I couldn't believe my own ears. All my life Christmas had been a feast of unusual joy and intimacy to me, a time when the worries and sorrows of everyday life vanished and all tensions were relaxed. At the approach of Christmas I had a holiday feeling, an anticipation of a time of carefree human, perhaps all too human, joy. I hadn't felt it that night. But now it came back to me all of a sudden and in a measure overwhelming, and I may well say devastating, as if a miraculous state of grace descended on the world and filled every human heart. Holy night, indeed! All at once they and we were the shepherds in Bethlehem's fields. From all directions came the sound of singing.

Can it ever be forgotten, that moment?

Their engineers, and ours too, clipped holes in the barbed wire for passageways. Soon the troops were building bonfires of yule logs from the debris on the battlefield, the loose stakes and pit props, everything went into the fire. No man's land was no longer no man's land. It was every man's land. As far as the eye could reach the fires were burning. The dark silhouettes of human figures moved about the flames in pairs, in groups, in circles, in multitudes. The men were eating, drinking, laughing, trying on each other's hats, showing each other snapshots of parents, sweethearts and babies.

All along that firing line which wasn't a firing line any longer, those mortal enemies of a few hours earlier forgot all the official slogans of hate and suspicion. In a simple, unostentatious gesture, they celebrated the Lord's supper, reaffirming the "blessed tie that binds" men across all barriers, hurdles and frontiers into one brotherhood.

And then, as it is written in the golden legend, the men gave each other presents like those Magi who followed the star from the East till it stood above the manger and offered their gifts, "gold, myrrh and frankincense," to the holy Mother and Child. They, the Germans, had brought sausages, cigars and beer. Our men handed out cigarettes, bully beef and cartons of jam....

It was to have been a twenty-four-hour truce. At noon on Christmas day when it started to snow again, our artillery laid down a barrage. The truce had been called off. The excuse was given that the Germans hadn't played fair. They had spied out the lay of the land when they came into the open. In ten minutes' time the German artillery replied. In a flash everything was again as it should be: shrapnel and Jack Johnsons screamed through the air and exploded in their appointed places, machine guns rattled, snipers sniped, the Guides went back to their interrupted task of digging a tunnel under the enemy's lines to blow up as many as possible of the friends of a few hours before.

Nearly half a centurry has gone by since that Christmas episode on the Western front. Every detail of that night stands out as vivid in my memory as if it happened last evening. I still hear the voices of the men arguing back and forth. I still see their faces. But what, in the light of later events, did it amount to after all? A handful of soldiers in a blue funk talking so as not to be terrorized by their own thoughts of the last great enemy standing by their side. What is the First World War in retrospect but a skirmish? So much blood has flown since; innocent blood, the blood of forty or fifty millions, not only soldiers, but unarmed civilians, men, women and children.

Since our moment of peace on the Western front we've had a Second World War, the horror of Korea, the torment of Dienbienphu, the beastliness of Algeria where tens of thousands of women and children prisoners perished as they were sent out in the morning to explore the roads for booby traps and land mines before getting something to eat for breakfast. Who shall measure the woe in the earth? Who shall tell us how many children die of hunger each day? Who shall count the tears in South Africa where the Dutch, with the approval of their Church, have turned their country into a slave state! How many natives are choked to death in the Angolan bush under an avalanche of napalm bombs invented and manufactured in America? How many Spanish exiles are to be turned over to Francisco Franco to be locked up in those abominable prisons where thousands were done to death since the end of the civil war for defending their country against a sanguinary monster? . . .

The other day someone drove me in his car from New York to Bronxville. By the side of the road I saw a sign: *This road will be closed in the event of enemy attack*! I couldn't help laughing.

Do the authorities really expect the enemy to come and fight it out on that road by invitation? And if that road is closed, will other roads be open in the event of enemy attack? And to whom will they be open? To children whose eyes have melted in their sockets? To women who have their insides seared with a carbolic detergent? A girl from Hiroshima told me that when the American atom bomb fell, thousands tried to run for the river. But the river water steamed and boiled and they were cooked to death. There must be someone around who remembers the days when the *Stuka* dive bombers came down on the civil population of France. Some roads were closed then too! French soldiers machine-gunned panic-stricken trespassers without the slightest compunction...on orders from higher up....

The main question today is: What can be done, what must be done to prevent the outbreak of the Third World War?

Is this a Christian question? There are not a few, in every country, who aver that this is not a religious, but a political question. They say that it is a question that concerns only the politicians. The Church is occupied with totally different and far more subtle questions.

When the world creaks and cracks like a doomed ship in the midst of a tempest, when the sails and masts are ripped to shreds and some have already broken off and gone overboard, the Church holds ecumenical conferences, world-wide ecclesiastical parliaments in Rome, in New Delhi and elsewhere. According to the correspondent of *Express*, a Parisian newspaper, the gathering of November, 1962, in Rome of nearly 3,000 bishops and prelates, all in their most gorgeous robes and vestments, was "the most stupendously magnificent spectacle ever presented to human eyes."

There are others who, looking upon that solemn ecclesiastical demonstration, ask the question: Can the church still afford to tilt with windmills while the general staffs play with hydrogen bombs?

Of what value are all conclaves and conciliabules, when they scrupulously—no, fearfully—avoid mention of the question that stares us all in the face like a furious tiger: the question of the to be or not to be of the human race. "Where there is love, fear is cast out." The Churches are so fearful these days that they grow shrilly hysterical about the menace of atheism and communism. What we see before our eyes is one of the saddest, most humiliating episodes in the history of Christianity. The prelates have discovered an enemy and they make him as black as the devil. That this "enemy" in the long run would most probably associate himself quite logically with the Christian doctrine of peace and aversion to war and violence, they cannot and dare not even envisage. For they have their dogmas, their eternally unchangeable prescriptions of what God wills and wills not, what to believe and what not to believe, dogmas, frozen cakes of ice in which the human spirit is trapped like a cockroach in Pleistocene lava.

Paul Claudel, of the Académie Française, wrote that "the most contemptible thing" he saw during his ambassadorship in Washington was the list of sermon topics advertised weekly in the American press. He ought to have heard that Luthern *Pfarrer* in Duesseldorf orate on a Sunday in October last year. A heavily gowned brother on whose breast dangled a silver cross, whom I watched going through the motions, chided his congregation for being afraid of nuclear warfare: "Haven't you always known that you must die some day? What does a day sooner or later matter? What difference does it make what sort of death you die?"

And then he declared with a smile on his face what James A. Pike, a bishop of the Episcopal Church in our midst declared within sight and hearing of millions of television viewers: "We are not afraid of the atom bomb, for we have eternal life!" That a half-literate exhorter in the hillbilly country where they are taught that heaven is a sort of Tom Tiddler's Lubberland consoles his congregation with this kind of poisonous pap is understandable. In some quarters it's still considered quite essential for the pigs to learn to die without squealing.

The "symbol" of "eternal life," according to Paul Tillich, is "popular Christian superstition made so with the help of a misunderstood Plato." If Jesus and the evangelists used the phrase, as the New Testament intimates, it is a misrendering of the Hebrew *helek l'olam habba*, which is not time without beginning or end, or an occult experience in some afterlife, but participation here and now in the building of the better world of tomorrow. That is the meaning of acquiring "a share, a portion, in the world to come," for which the Greek expression "eternal life" is a misleading substitution.

In a time of world crisis, such as ours, the Christian Church must draw the people's attention to the significance of events transpiring in the present. If there is no change soon in the course we follow our military political situation will inevitably plunge us into war. We seek peace and security in an arms race. But an arms race has never brought about more than a postponement of war. There are men of the highest intelligence and expert knowledge who warn us that the ultimate catastrophe is not likely to be postponed beyond the year 1975.

Les Eglises Trahissent! "The churches betray God and lead mankind astray." This shocking and terrifying indictment does not come from some center of atheistic or materialistic propaganda or philosophy. It is a cry of pain and sorrow wrung from the heart of the Church of Geneva and its minister, Robert Junod.

The Churches betray God, though they pray for peace and preach sermons without end on brotherhood and good will. They hide their faces from the horror of modern war, but they accept its possibility. They support the military budgets and approve of the present armament race and in many cases commend it, and refuse to act or speak out unequivocally.

Prayers for peace without action for peace are the most idiotic eyewash under the sun. They signify nothing more or less than trying to unload on God's shoulders the work the Churches are called to perform themselves. It's the ecclesiastical equivalent of the vulgar *jemenfoutism* of letting George do it. How otherwise qualify such prayers for peace and the simultaneous manufacture of the most gruesome weapons of war as mockery and derision of the Most High?

Communism and atheism are not the enemy. The enemy is the atom bomb and the hydrogen bomb which both, East and West, are piling up in such quantities that both sides boast that they are fully capable and ready to wipe out the opponent ten times, a hundred times over. Do you see, does anyone in the whole wide world see how an atomic war can be prevented when the armament race is in full swing and made to masquerade as a guarantee of peace and security?

American civil defense speaks of *Megabod*, the British of *Megacorps*. Both expressions signify as much as *a million corpses!* These abstract terms are needed to figure out how many deaths would be caused by the firing of a given number of atom bombs in a certain area, how many may possibly remain alive, how many would be permanently attainted by diseases stemming from radiation. Robert McNamara has told us that *ten million* American dead is the "absolute minimum" in one atomic attack. Persons occupied with such and suchlike calculations and preparations, officers, soldiers, technicians, scientists, men and women workers in the armament industries, are forced to close their hearts to all human sentiment. How else can they bring themselves to do their work?

In his time, the Dean of St. Paul's, William Ralph Inge, used to refer to "the bottomless insincerity" of the British and American press. There never was a more sordid tale of journalistic exaggeration, distortion and sheer invention than that told by the American press in furthering the remilitarization and rearmament of Germany to a point where the Federal Republic again stands at the top with the selfsame leaders in command who plunged the world into unspeakable horror under Hitler.

On Adenauer's 86th birthday, January 5, 1962, I saw the parade of the new German army—ex-soldier organizations; Hitler men, old and new; dreamers of revenge and all the other un-denazified patriots—take six hours to goose-step past the old Chancellor, his cabinet and his generals standing in front of Schaumburg Palace in Bonn.

A local Bonn newspaper went so far that day in its adulation as to remark that Adenauer's "genius" had placed the Chancellor "beyond the petty exigencies of everyday policy" and made him "the virtual brains of the Western alliance. . . ." "The chief inspiration of the remilitarized Federal Republic," added the paper, is "the dynamic directive: the conquest of the East as far as the Ural mountains. . . ."

There you have it: conquest! As a people the Germans have never come to terms with the outcome of the two world wars. They have never expressed regret or shown the least sign of remorse over the commission of the greatest crimes against humanity. Nor is it likely that they will make any *amende honorable* so long as our government and press make of Germany's lack of contrition and repentance our most powerful ally against the East. With our complicity and approval the future of German freedom and democracy has been placed in the hands of the same men who not only instituted nonfreedom in Germany, but sought to spread it by force all over the world.

What tragedy and irony! German unity lasted for about a hundred years and for a hundred years German unity was the world's nightmare. As often as the Germans succeeded in making their national business the center of world interest, the navel of world politics, so often did their country become the hearth of explosion!

Today everything in the world again turns around the German question, around German wishes and aspirations and interests. German claims,

German pretensions, German rearmament and German honor are amongst the principal themes of discussion. But as always, the Germans pay not the least attention to the interests, the honor and the anxiety of others. The President might tell Aleksei Adzhubei, the editor of *Izvestia*, that he has Adenauer's pledge not to equip the new German army with nuclear arms, but General Lauris Norstad* promised the Germans that they can have atomic weapons as soon as they want them, and Franz Josef Strauss,** the head of the Bavarian Christian Social Union, when he was defense minister, stated outright: "We Germans *must* have atomic weapons so that we by ourselves alone can fight the Russians without waiting for the Americans to make up their minds."

In the *Periodical for German and International Politics*, Dr. Albert J. Rasker, a Dutch university professor, writes:

"The most disquieting aspect of the situation is that the guilt for the division of Germany into two parts is always charged to the Russians. . . . Where is the German with enough moral courage to say: 'We West Germans are guilty ourselves, we did it in the full knowledge that it would lead to disaster?' "

The Germans say now that they are for the freedom of the West, for the ideology and image of the free man against those in the East who menace that image. . . .

What do they know about it? They do not even want to remember what attitude they took with regard to human freedom on the day of their bloody glory. They looked upon freedom and human life itself with infinite contempt and did their utmost to destroy both.

In *Die Soldaten Zeitung*, the Soldiers' Newspaper, published in Munich, appear editorials from time to time demanding an act of expiation on the part of America, Britain, France, Russia and other countries which fought the Nazi murder machine in the Second World War. "How long will we tolerate it," asks the Soldiers' paper, "that we are accused of the vilest atrocities in that war when, as we all know, the German people is absolutely without guilt and has *never done the least harm to any other people*. . . ."

As long as such unrepentant self-righteousness prevails in Germany there isn't the slightest chance of international reconciliation. The German militarists have learned nothing and have in fact forgotten everything!

Nobody in the West seems to have the slightest conception of what went

---

*Norstad is quoted from *Deutsche Zeitung*, June 19, 1959.
**Franz Josef Strauss is quoted from *Bonner General Anzeiger*, Dec. 15, 1959.

on in Russia during the years of the Nazi occupation, when Hitler actually gave orders to *depopulate* the Ukraine; that is, *exterminate* its 30 million inhabitants, in order to open up that vast area of good earth for settlement by Germans. The Germans came very near pulling off that fantastic crime of genocide. And this is the horror which stands at the back of all American-Russian divergencies: Russia is afraid of Germany, not of the present Germany, but of the Germany in the making under American aegis.

Talk about threats! In June, 1963, Germany obtained the right to have a voice in selecting atomic targets in Russia. Is it reasonable to expect the Russians to stand by and wait? Aren't they just being provoked and baited to strike the first blow?

In the summer of 1961 America ordered a swift reinforcement of its military potential in Germany on the pretense that Russia threatened a military attack on West Germany. Millions of newspaper readers till this day believe that Khrushchev threatened to seize Berlin that year.

The President's acceleration of war preparations, the dispatch of an additional 250,000 men and the increase by six billion dollars in military expenditures, the whipped-up propagandistic arrival of Vice President Johnson in Berlin accompanied by 1500 American soldiers, and the appointment of General Lucius Clay as the President's personal representative "to give the nation a greater immediate striking power," all these precautionary measures and "defense maneuvers" were undertaken for the purpose of preventing a purely hypothetical Soviet attack on West Berlin.

I was in Germany and watched the mounting anxiety among the common people. Would it be war? Would General Lucius Clay be able to stem the pent-up avalanche of a hundred odd divisions Russia has parked in East Germany and environs? Would the Russian armored juggernaut, which since 1945 is said to stand poised to strike at the North Sea shores and ports, at last start off on its predicted conquest of West Europe? It was curious to notice the absolute silence of Konrad Adenauer and Franz Josef Strauss, the defense minister, in what the American press made look like a major catastrophe standing before the door.

I learned from Professor Renate Riemeck, leader of the Peace Party in the Reichstag, who campaigned in the election under the slogan *Im Geiste Albert Schweitzer's,* "In the Spirit of Albert Schweitzer" (Reverence for Life), that Khrushchev at no time had threatened to advance ... on Hamburg, Kiel, Copenhagen, Rotterdam, Antwerp or Paris. "The only threat

Khrushchev has made so far as I can remember," said Dr. Riemeck, "is the threat to sign a peace treaty with East Germany if negotiations with the West over Berlin do not succeed. That's not a threat of war."

The publisher of *Die Andere Zeitung* of Hamburg, Heinrich Kraschutzki, who was standing by as I talked with Professor Riemeck, remarked: "I will gladly pay 4,000 marks, a thousand dollars, to anyone who can show me one single Soviet war threat in the course of the last three years."

"But we in America hear and read of Soviet war threats virtually every day," I ventured.

"You mean about Krushchev going to bury the West?" queried the journalist.

"No," I replied, "that expression, I know, does not relate to war. . . . Only a few months ago one of two German-born doctors in New York who were giving me a physical examination said to his colleague as they looked at a set of X-ray photographs of my intestinal tract: *'Dieser Mann wird uns beide begraben!'* (This man will bury us both.) They meant that according to what they saw on the photographs, I would, in their own opinion, most likely survive both physicians."

"Those rumors of Soviet war threats," resumed Herr Kraschutzki, "are part of an artificial psychosis created by the manipulators of the armament industries who are deadly afraid of disarmament. Those rumors are spread daily, almost hourly, in order to keep the peoples in a permanent state of fright so that they will readily agree to everything the warmakers propose to keep the tensions alive. . . . "

To this must be added that Adenauer, since his "conversion" to the view that Russia can be dealt with only from so-called "positions of strength," has systematically torpedoed each and every possibility of reunion of East and West by refusing to negotiate with Russia on the conditions of reunion.

Why did the Russians in August, 1961, order Walter Ulbricht to put up a wall between East and West Berlin?

The answer is this: the Russians got wind of the preparations for "Operation Kettle." Under Operation Kettle, a highly mobile section of the Bundeswehr, about five armored divisions, was to take the East German army by surprise, pounce on East Germany's frontiers and make a gap about 50 kilometers wide. The gap was to be kept open for 48 hours to give the East German population an opportunity to stampede into West Germany, while the troops, of course, created all the havoc they could possibly make in blowing up railway stations, harbor installations, warehouses, governmental buildings and so forth.

When the Soviet intelligence learned of the planned coup, a few thousand tanks moved up from the Polish borders and took up a position in and near East Berlin. The West Germans fully counted on such a Soviet intervention and for that reason intended to withdraw after 48 hours or as soon as the Red forces came into view. The Germans were not out to start a war. They hadn't even notified the American command of their little maneuver to sow panic amongst the population of the German Democratic Republic. They were like the man who, half-absentmindedly, throws a banana peel in the path of his approaching enemy in the hope that it might do most good where most needed.

The West German newspapers which published the merest hint about Operation Kettle were quickly suppressed and forbidden to reappear. One of the banned newspapers in its final edition printed this remark: "We published the story of 'Operation Kettle' in the hope and with the wish that it may open thousands of sleeping eyes before German military and political adventurism once again plunges the world into unspeakable disaster...."

When I saw and learned that the "emergency" wasn't an emergency at all, but an attempt to lead public opinion astray on the resumption of atomic testing, and above all just another enterprise to stimulate the sagging economy, I shook the dust of Germany off my feet and sat for a while looking at the North Sea from a veranda of one of the hotels at Scheveningen in Holland.

The next day I stood by the side of an old fisherman on the sea wall peering through his telescope at some scarcely distinguishable dots far out at sea. "On one of those ships is my youngest son," said the old fisher. The man had just told me that his father and two brothers were lost during the First World War when their boat was torpedoed. "In the Second World War one of my boys was deported to Germany as a slave laborer and never again heard of. My other son served in the underground, but was betrayed and shot with eight others in those dunes over there...."

Just as we were speaking three military jets roared by at a very low altitude and in a few instants disappeared from view in a northerly direction.

"That's to reassure and protect us and the thousands of bathers on the beach below," I said, referring to the jet patrol. "They are flying up and down to scare away the Russians."

"How old are you?" asked the fisherman. "Old enough, I'm sure, judging by the color of your hair, to know that those jets are no protection at all, neither for the bathers on the beach, nor anyone else."

"They are part of the deterrent policy!"

"They are part of the magnetic policy," he corrected me. "It's these things which, like a magnet, draw hell nearer every hour."

I was off a few days later on a train which took me from The Hague to the city of Arras once the center of the fighting on the Somme in the First World War. My wife wanted me to put some flowers on the graves of Cyril Jones and Ross MacDonald and some other friends of whom I spoke often to her. In Arras I hired a car driven by a French Fleming who had only one arm which he used more to gesticulate than to chauffeur while proceeding at the speed of 100 kilometers an hour.

"There," he motioned, "is St. Quentin. . . . That cathedral on the hill was ruined in the First War."

"I saw it every night," I said, "for months on end like an immense brazier while the Germans poured in their incendiary bombs."

"Big bonfire, *hein*? . . . You want to see the trenches and dugouts where the Australians and Canadians died?" he asked.

"Show me Loretto Heights, Vimy Ridge and the positions between Bapaume, Péronne and Albert."

"There are only cemeteries now," he said, "and they are almost forgotten. The stone crosses are falling to pieces. . . . Ha, ha! We'll soon be needing new graveyards, won't we?"

"We won't need graveyards in the next war," I countered. "There'll be no corpses, not even a spot of grease where we fall. . . . "

"There won't be anyone left to bury the dead anyway," he said. "It'll all be done by machines next time. Nice, neat, clean job! . . . *Vive l'automation*! . . . Here you have the cemetery of Loretto. Forty thousand Frenchmen lie buried here. Forty thousand poor boys who once thought they were doing something for humanity. . . . And here lie the Canadians who took Vimy Ridge. The roles have been reversed as you may see. Vimy took them in the end. . . . Boom, boom! All that ridge, they tell me, went up in the air one fine morning. The sappers blew it up and tens of thousands of Germans with it! . . . "

"Where are the Germans buried?"

"They? They were buried in pits, in mass graves."

"Two terrible wars passed over this area!" I commented.

"Two only? This here ground has seen a dozen wars go to and fro.... If you care to we'll stop and look into the old trenches and dugouts. Some have been kept intact for tourists to look at. You can still see some skulls and bones lying about.... Do you want to pick up a skull perhaps?"

"No, thanks, I have one...."

Back in Arras I let the driver put me down in front of the restored church. Across the façade ran an inscription drawn up, I was told, by the mayor of Arras.

Ye who come as pilgrims to their graves, climbing the mountain of their death and its bloodstained pathways: Hear the terrible cry of these hecatombs: Peoples, unite! Man, become human! ...

And so across France by train to Cologne on the line to Basel in Switzerland. At the railway station of Coblenz, a man, his wife and two sons entered the compartment. Judging by their clothing and luggage, of which there was a good deal, they were middle-class people, possibly upper middle-class. The two boys, perhaps sixteen and seventeen years of age, stood in the corridor looking at the never-wearying spectacle of the Rhine.

"I've never seen the Rhine so full of traffic," I remarked to the father when he joined us in the corridor. "What's the cargo of all those long tows of barges?"

"*Eisenerz*," he said. "Iron ore. It goes to the steel mills."

"It seems German business is going ahead full speed again."

"Yes," he agreed, "and that's why I am getting out!"

"To Switzerland?"

"No, we, my family and I, are on our way to Marseilles.... We sail for Australia the day after tomorrow...."

"You are emigrating?"

"Yes, we are four of the fifty thousand West Germans emigrating this year."

"Fifty thousand, isn't that an enormous figure?"

"Since the Federal government introduced compulsory military service in '52, the average number of emigrants per year is fifty thousand."

"You mean you are going abroad to escape military service?"

"I am personally not liable to be called, I am too old. But these two boys of mine must join the colors sooner or later. I am getting them out while there is yet time.... My grandfather fell in the battle of Gravelotte in 1870. My father was lost at Verdun in 1916. My youngest brother died in the Russian campaign of 1942. These two boys are not going to die on any battlefield. . . . I really don't like to go abroad. No German likes to separate himself permanently from his native country. . . . But enough is enough. . . . "

"Are all fifty thousand leaving for the same reason?"

"It's the chief reason. We don't have to go abroad because of any scarcity of work or business here in Germany. There is so much work that we have to import workers from Italy and Spain and even from Finland. . . . In fact, there is too much work, too much work of the wrong kind. . . . "

"I am surprised they let you go!" I said.

"So am I," he came back. "I won't feel safe till we cross the Swiss border."

"We shudder to think," said a Swiss newspaper which I bought on arrival at Basel, "what would happen if Germany should get nuclear weapons and throw a bomb on Russian territory."

I shudder still more when I think that the German adventurers might throw a bomb on New York, Washington or Detroit. . . . Would there be time to investigate where the bomb originated? Wouldn't the counter-blow be on its way to Russia within minutes?

Is this a foolish supposition? It is not foolish at all when you stop to think in what school of treachery and villainy the present gang of German generals was brought up!

It is not the differences of opinion in the question of control and inspection which represent the greatest obstacle to general disarmament. *It's the will to disarm that's lacking.* The peoples in East and West are subject to mass suggestion manufactured and steered by giants. The peoples must be made aware of dangers and filled with fears and apprehensions. For without the fears and anxieties of the masses the minority of the giants could not keep its mastery intact. But the giants are also themselves afraid and want to avoid nuclear war.

A Third World War becomes possible only when the giants make an error. The surest way to prevent such an error is total disarmament with all-around universal control.

However, this remedy would damage the interests of the giants both in East and West. In the event of total disarmament the Western financial giant would have to give up his most profitable business and the Eastern giant his striking power. Both disarmed countries would, moreover, lose their power to threaten! . . .

Cutting through the mist of words and spurious patriotism, what we should say in the present harrowing circumstances is this: We, the Churches—God's witnesses and the disseminators of His spirit—condemn war in all its forms. If we have sinned in the past by not doing our duty, today, on the eve of what looks to be the final fall of Christianity, we vow to apply all our strength, all our influence and all our resources in making peace amongst the nations. If madmen insist on closing the eyes of their intellect and heart, and express themselves ready to engage in the most sacrilegious anti-God enterprise imaginable—i.e., to wipe out God's creation—we, from our side, condemn and absolutely reject the use and manufacture of all weapons of war. . . .

We intend to act in the name of the God of peace. No worldly interest will be our inspiration or motive. We reject the immorality of having the goal justify the means. The means must be just as righteous and pure as the objective. We will unmask the lies of bourgeois and communist society: deterrent and terror policies do not deter, but lead all mankind nearer the precipice every hour. When millions of so-called atheists unite to talk and act for disarmament and peace, other millions—Catholics, Protestants, Jews, Mohammedans, Hindus and Buddhists—will also unite. They will become the fire that purifies by making of themselves, their bodies and minds, a wholly acceptable sacrifice. . . .

Instead of shouting "Rather dead than Red," would it not be more Christian to say quietly, "Rather dead than a murderer?"

In Paul Tillich's *Interpretation of History*, written during the aftermath of World War I, occurs the phrase: "In every power there is an element of renunciation of power, and the power lives on this element." How can renunciation of power be achieved? "It cannot be done," says Tillich, "with the aid of state power, but only if a people or the nations as a whole are seized by a transcendental idea and for its sake renounce power. . . . Such an event would be one of the great turning points of history, it would perhaps *create* mankind. . . ."

Renunciation of power, who shall initiate it? Who shall set in motion a great *courant de foi* whereby with mystical energy a single idea is suddenly carried in the minds of millions of individuals, whereby a country, an epoch, a generation becomes kindled like a firebrand and sheds light over the environing darkness?

If a mental state of this nature is to fashion anything enduring, it must be boldly conceived in truly heroic forms. Such an idea would be worthy of America and make this country truly great as a pioneer of the future, great in the things of the spirit, great in justice, great in mutual co-operation, great in love. What matters is *to be great*, not merely to seem great!

If we can attune our minds to the idea's magnitude and simplicity, we may already feel its vital warmth radiating into our mortal world. The idea will grow in the process of fashioning, though it must go through purgatory and hell. Men and women will have to suffer to impress their contemporaries that nothing is more precious, more glorious and beautiful than life. All true creation grows out of the dark humus of rejected utopias. In extraordinary circumstances such as we experience, the utopian, the extraordinary, the seemingly impossible may be the only sensible way.

Even so, it should not be expected that the peace movement will suddenly grow so strong as to sweep the earth clean of the abomination of war and militarism. As ever, only a small minority will stand up for righteousness and common sense. And that minority will be denounced and vilified and hated to an extent that it will be virtually outlawed and given over to the execration of the mob.

"What I see in the offing at not too great a distance," recently wrote Helmut Gollwitzer* to Martin Niemoeller, "is an era of persecution and martyrdom. Rather than follow the peacemakers, the different national states, whether Christian or not, will seek to crush and obliterate them. . . ."

The time to act therefore is now; now, while there is still time to say without fear what we think just and decent. No man has the right to give us the order to die. No American citizen is under any patriotic, moral, social or any other obligation to die for any social-economic system whatsoever.

If we want it so, the world of the future can be happy, wondrously beautiful and free. On the other hand, to leave the disposition of the future to chance or to those whose mentality is warped by their avowed or unavowed lust for power and wealth means death for all of us.

*Professor of theology, Berlin.

Résistez! Résistez toujours! These words: "Resist! Always resist!" which may still be seen in the dungeons of Nîmes scratched on the walls by the manacled hands of the imprisoned Huguenots should be brought back into the open.

For only resistance will give us the right to hope for survival!

And resistance in the present circumstances means: rebellion, refusal to be brainwashed any longer, cease being "a nation of sheep," throw off the death urge with which the present power structure seeks to put us to sleep, and stop accusing everybody who wants somebody else's foot removed from his neck of being an enemy to freedom.

What we need first of all in order to safeguard both the treasures of the past and the rights of the future are two things: a great act of repentance and a great act of faith. Repentance for all our infidelities, our idolatries, our worship of the false gods, our criminal narrow-mindedness, our anathemas against those who are not of our opinion, our crusading spirit by which we identify the relative values of our civilization with the absolute. And last but not least, our inveterate habit of ascribing to God what in essence is but the conceit of the masters of the world's game of guile and blood!

While it is true that we cannot count on the surprises of history, this much we can and do say: No tyranny was ever so systematic, nor no oppression so barbaric, but that there were men and women, small groups, religious conventicles, secret fighters for freedom, willing and able to confound the ignominy that tramples the majority and fight for the truth against the monomaniacs of power and privilege.

A small flame can set an immense heap of wood on fire and the most worth-while things in life and in history have always come from exceedingly small minorities. . . .

Peace to all men of good will. . . *and also to the others!* . . .
Farewell!

Picture Acknowledgments